D0850370

Plato on Pleasure and the Good Life

Plato on Pleasure and the Good Life

DANIEL C. RUSSELL

CLARENDON PRESS · OXFORD

OXFORD
UNIVERSITY PRESS

Great Clarendon Street, Oxford ox2 6dp

Oxford University Press is a department of the University of Oxford.
It furthers the University's objective of excellence in research, scholarship,
and education by publishing worldwide in

Oxford New York

Auckland Cape Town Dar es Salaam Hong Kong Karachi
Kuala Lumpur Madrid Melbourne Mexico City Nairobi
New Delhi Shanghai Taipei Toronto

MIL

With offices in

Argentina Austria Brazil Chile Czech Republic France Greece
Guatemala Hungary Italy Japan Poland Portugal Singapore
South Korea Switzerland Thailand Turkey Ukraine Vietnam

Oxford is a registered trade mark of Oxford University Press
in the UK and in certain other countries

Published in the United States
by Oxford University Press Inc., New York

© Daniel C. Russell 2005

The moral rights of the author have been asserted
Database right Oxford University Press (maker)

First published 2005

British Library Cataloguing in Publication Data

Data available

Library of Congress Cataloging in Publication Data

Data available

Typeset by Newgen Imaging Systems (P) Ltd., Chennai, India
Printed in Great Britain
on acid-free paper by
Biddles Ltd., King's Lynn, Norfolk

ISBN 0–19–928284–6   978–0–19–928284–5

1 3 5 7 9 10 8 6 4 2

This is for Gina,
Jocelyn, Grace,
and Julia,
who made it worth doing

I propose that we now examine the core of philosophy, namely the question of the supreme good.

Cicero, *de Finibus Bonorum et Malorum* IV, 14, trans. Woolf.

ACKNOWLEDGMENTS

Generous support for research came from summer research stipends from Wichita State University (WSU) and from the Fairmount College of Liberal Arts and Sciences, WSU, both in 2001. For continued support of my research at WSU I am indebted to Deans David Glenn-Lewin and Bill Bischoff of the Fairmount College, and to my excellent colleagues in Philosophy, especially David Soles and Debby Soles.

This project took many years to complete, and I have received invaluable help from many wonderful people in that time. Most notable among these are John Armstrong, Hugh Benson, Dan Farnham, Avery Kolers, Scott LaBarge, Mark McPherran, George Rudebusch, David Schmidtz, Nicholas Smith, Rhonda Smith, Bill Stephens, and Tom Worthen. My deepest gratitude goes to Julia Annas and Mark LeBar. In Julia I have a wonderful advisor and a dear friend. In Mark I have constant encouragement, and conversations that usually lead to the ideas I like best. The present work is among the many things I would not have been able to do without them. But of course all of its shortcomings are mine alone.

The initial work for this book began during my time at the University of Arizona. For their immeasurable contributions to my training and development I am forever indebted to the faculty at Arizona, especially Julia Annas, Tom Christiano, Jean Hampton, Chris Maloney, David Schmidtz, and Tom Worthen, as well as to George Rudebusch of Northern Arizona University. These are some of the best people I have ever known.

My greatest debt of all, of course, is to my family, and especially my wife, Gina, as well as Dan and Eileen Russell and Roger and Joyce Butz. None of them could have given more, and I thank them for the love and support that makes my efforts both possible and rewarding.

Portions of this book, in various stages of development, have been presented in various places over the past few years. I am greatly indebted to audiences at the University of Arizona, the Arizona Colloquium in Ancient Philosophy, Northern Arizona University, Creighton University, Wichita State University, the University of Oklahoma, the Society for the Contemporary Assessment of Platonism, and the Society for Ancient Greek Philosophy. Some portions of this book have also appeared in print, and I wish to thank the referees and editors of these journals, which have extended their generous permission to use the following material:

For Chapter 3: 'Pleasure as a Conditional Good in Plato's *Phaedo*', *Archiv für Geschichte der Philosophie*, forthcoming. For Chapter 5: 'Virtue as "Likeness to God" in Plato and Seneca', *The Journal of the History of Philosophy*, 42 (2004), 241–60. For the Epilogue: 'Protagoras and Socrates on Courage and Pleasure: *Protagoras* 349d *ad finem*', Ancient Philosophy, 20 (2000), 311–38.

D.C.R.

Wichita, Kansas
October 2004

CONTENTS

INTRODUCTION: PLEASURE AND THE GOOD LIFE

A good life includes pleasure. Surely if there is consensus on anything about living well, it would be on that. We reflect on our lives and plan for our futures, and none of us is indifferent to either the joys we have known—they make our memories sweet—or the joys we want our plans and projects to make room for. But while such observations can begin reflection on pleasure and the good life, still they are only a beginning, and here begins the real work of figuring out just what sort of place pleasure should have in the good life. And it is at precisely this point that Plato has a lot to tell us. There is, I believe, a plausible and compelling account of pleasure and the good life that emerges from a close reading of several of Plato's dialogues, an account whose distinctive and important features may well be missed on a steady diet of many of the 'standard' modern approaches to pleasure in moral philosophy. So while Plato's view is of obvious scholarly interest, it also proves to be of interest to those interested in a philosophical understanding of pleasure and its value, more generally.

For that reason, I shall begin the present work first by exploring the nature of pleasure at a common-sense level, and then, once we have seen what sorts of questions we need a more theoretically complete and rigorous account of pleasure to answer, by giving a brief overview of how Plato addresses them. In this way I hope to make clear at the outset the sort of interpretation, at a general level, that I shall defend in the rest of the book, to point up what kinds of argumentative burdens one assumes in seeking to motivate and articulate that sort of view, and to suggest what Plato has to offer us as we try to make up our own minds about what kind of thing pleasure is and what kind of place it should have in a good life.

0.1 Why Pleasure Matters

I said at the outset that a good life includes pleasure. To some this will sound like an understatement, and to most it will seem obvious. After all, everyone likes to laugh, everyone enjoys a treat from time to time, everyone has a fancy that he or she[1] will indulge on occasion. But pleasure is important not only, and I think

---

[1] Since English has no gender-neutral pronouns that can be applied to persons, and since it is cumbersome to use expressions like 'he or she', and since not all persons are masculine (as suggested by the old custom of always using 'he'), and since not all persons are feminine (as suggested by the

not even primarily, because we like to 'feel good'. Pleasure is actually an important part of how we live. For one thing, pleasure helps us do things, and do them well. If I am trying to learn to ski, for instance, then it will help if I find it enjoyable, or am confident that I shall soon enough—how else could I commit to learning despite my aching tail-bone? If I enjoy teaching, I shall probably work harder at it, despite all the other demands on my time. And so on. We might say that pleasure has a power to 'glue' us to the things that we find pleasant: in general, I devote more of my attention to things that I enjoy, and that can keep me immersed in them, as I need to be if I am to do them properly. Sometimes it is the pleasure that motivates us, but one need not be motivated by the pleasure of an activity in order for its pleasure to maintain one's attention in it. In fact, enjoying an activity may even *be* the way in which our attention is maintained in it.[2]

For this reason pleasure also tells us very important things about people. When we meet new people, often we want to know what sorts of things they like and enjoy. By learning what someone takes pleasure in, we can tell what sorts of things interest her, and that can tell us a lot about what sort of person she is. In this way pleasures are important because they reflect the sorts of interests and values we have, and are thus an important part of who we are as unique persons. With good reason we may think, with Aristotle, that a crucial basis of the relationship between friends is their sharing of pleasures;[3] as Aristotle points out, childhood friendships often do not last, because the different characters that the friends develop as they mature often value and enjoy different sorts of things. This pleasure that is so important to the friendship is not simply having fun together, although that is important, but is the sharing of interests and preferences, attitudes and values.

Thus we can also see something important about pleasure by noting how our pleasures can change as we change in our interests and values. Perhaps, for instance, I enjoy playing baseball as a way of beating other people in competition. But suppose that over time I begin to see that beating other people is not nearly so interesting as the way that playing baseball makes me a better athlete, or better at contributing to a joint effort, or what have you. Having seen that, I shall still enjoy playing baseball, but I shall enjoy something quite different about it. And indeed the enjoyment itself will be different: enjoying beating someone at baseball is not the same as enjoying developing my skills as an athlete or being part of a team, for these enjoyments consist in being impressed by very different aspects of the game. Part of my changing, then, is coming to have different things occupy my attention, that is, to take pleasure in different

---

new custom of always using 'she', which can even become anachronistic in discussing Greek philosophers, who often take their audience to consist mainly of men), in the rest of this book I shall simply alternate between masculine and feminine pronouns haphazardly.

[2] Aristotle, *Nicomachean Ethics* X.5, seems to agree.

[3] See esp. *Nicomachean Ethics* IX.3, 1165b23–31. Note that making the sharing of pleasures a crucial part of friendship is not thereby to *base* the friendship on pleasure.

things. This shows us how difficult it is to pry our pleasures apart from our values. Pleasures 'reflect' our values not simply because they provide information about what we value, but indeed because taking pleasure in something is often part of the very *act* of valuing it and finding it important.

This fact about pleasure also explains why our perception of the pleasure with (or without) which a person acts colors our assessment of what he does, and of what sort of person he is. We're disappointed if our friends give us gifts but find it a nuisance to do so, however much we may enjoy the gift itself, and even if we appreciate their willingness to endure what they found a nuisance (we have all known some who observe gift-giving occasions only when the fancy strikes them to do so); we still wonder why our friend didn't take any pleasure in doing something nice for a friend—is he really a friend, after all? Is he really the generous person we thought he was? Pleasure tells us a lot about a relationship—and about virtues of character: it makes sense, I think, to say that to practice a virtue is not simply to do certain things, but to do them with certain attitudes and placing certain values upon doing them. A charitable or generous person, for instance, is not just someone who gives, but someone who also 'resonates' with the giving, and this involves taking pleasure in giving. This is more than having a fleeting inclination to give, but to be a person with a firm and stable character that takes pleasure in acts of giving, because one's pleasures have so matured and developed as to endorse what reason finds best.[4] We do find it a real shortcoming in a person to be cold, insensitive, cheerless, or boorish.[5]

These are only some of the reasons that pleasure is important to us, and although I have tried to flesh them out, they still give a rather bare picture of how pleasure works in our lives. None the less, they do make it quite likely that pleasure will be an important part of any good life, at least in so far as living a good life will involve having deep commitments and values. And this brings us round to asking what sort of good pleasure might be. But that question is difficult to answer, due in no small part to the fact that we often speak of very different kinds of phenomena when we speak of 'pleasure'.[6] On the one hand, we often speak of pleasure as a kind of *sensation*, such as the feeling I have when someone rubs my sore, tired shoulders. Pleasure of this sort is a kind of feeling, a qualitative or phenomenal state (as philosophers of mind often call it), of which a 'tickle', a 'rush', or an 'ahh' feeling would be a standard example. So we

---

[4] Hursthouse (1999), chs. 5 and 6 brings out this point nicely. It is important to note that not even Kant disagrees, although he is often misunderstood on this point. What Kant claims (in *Grounding for the Metaphysics of Morals*, orig. 398) is that among cases of doing the right thing (a) for some ulterior motive, (b) because one feels like doing something that happens to coincide with what one ought to do, and (c) because doing so is the right thing to do, even if one does not feel like doing it, moral worth emerges only in case (c). This seems true enough, but of course that is not to deny that an even better case would be one of doing the right thing because it is right, *and with* a cheerful heart because it is right. See also Sherman (1997: 125 f.).

[5] See, e.g., Aristotle, *Nicomachean Ethics* II.3, 1104a22–5, II.7, 1108a23–30; as well as the Stoics, at Diogenes Laertius, *Lives* VII.117.

[6] Here I have benefited greatly from Rudebusch (1999), although my distinction between types of pleasure will depart from his in some important ways.

might say that to enjoy something or take pleasure in it is to feel a certain way, to have a feeling that is occasioned by some thing or activity. On the other hand, we also speak of pleasure as a kind of *emotion*, an affective attitude that one takes toward things, such as the joy one has at the birth of one's child, or the satisfaction one finds in one's work. We might even go so far as to classify our various emotions—gratitude, reluctance, pride, envy, and so on—as different forms of pleasure and pain.[7]

Pleasures that are sensations are importantly different from pleasures that are emotions. Perhaps the most important difference is that an emotion is a kind of attitude, while sensations do not seem to be attitudes. The tingling sensation in my rubbed shoulders, for instance, does not have a content. It is caused or occasioned by something, but it is not *about* anything. A pleasure that is an emotion, on the other hand, is about something, and is the pleasure *that* such-and-such is the case. When my child is born, for instance, I am pleased because there is a certain importance that I attach to this event, and thus I am pleased that this event is taking place. Pleasures such as these seem to be intentional states (again to use the language of philosophers of mind), rather than qualitative ones.

Sensational and emotional pleasures also differ with respect to commensurability. The pleasure I feel in the relief of sore shoulder muscles does not seem to be a different *kind* of thing from the pleasure I feel in the relief of sore leg muscles. By contrast, the pleasure I take in reflecting on a great personal achievement is not the same kind of thing as the pleasure I take in reflecting on a friend's great personal achievement—I could not get the first kind of pleasure from the second kind of source, or vice versa. In these sorts of cases, 'pleasure' is a generic description for different kinds of emotions—here, pride and admiration—and not only are these different from each other, but the same kinds of pleasant emotions are also importantly different depending on their objects, as the pride I take in my own achievements is something I can take *only* in my own achievements. Perhaps I may take pride in a friend's achievements, but this is not to say that in both cases there is just one thing, pride, that I am getting from two different sources. So whereas sensations are *caused* by their objects, emotions are *about* their objects, and consequently sensations can often be compared to each other with an indifference to their respective objects in a way that emotions cannot.

In that case, moreover, it seems that pleasures understood as emotions tell us much more about a person's character and personality than pleasures as sensations do. One of the reasons that pleasure is so important to us is the fact, as we have seen, that our pleasures are very intimately connected to the sorts of values and attitudes that we have. That is why we want to know what sorts of things new or potential friends take pleasure in, why changes in what friends take pleasure in can change and even end friendships, why we take pleasure in

---

[7] And doing so, moreover, would put us in a very ancient tradition; see, e.g., Plato, *Philebus* 47e ff.; Aristotle, *Rhetoric* II.1; Diogenes Laertius, *Lives* VII.111–14; Stobaeus, *Anthology* II.10b.

different things as we develop in our attitudes and priorities, and why it matters to us whether someone who gives does so reluctantly or with pleasure. In these kinds of cases our interest must be in pleasures as emotions, since it is very hard to see how a feeling or qualitative state, with its relatively loose connection to the things that occasion it, could play *this* sort of role in our inner lives and our relationships with other people. If I tell you, 'When I go skiing, I get a certain kind of feeling', what do I really tell you about *myself*? Not very much, and so usually what someone means, and what other people understand, when he says 'I take pleasure in skiing' is that skiing is the sort of thing that he finds worth spending his time on, that he is slow to become bored with skiing, that he finds that he can easily become immersed in skiing, that he would take success at skiing as a reason for pride, and so on, perhaps because he thinks it worth while to be in the outdoors, to get physical exercise, to engage in competition, or what have you. It makes sense, then, for us to ask as a follow-up question, 'What is it about skiing that pleases you so much?' Pleasures that are emotions, then, tell us far more about a person than pleasures that are sensations do.

Such pleasures tell us a lot about a person, we should notice, both for better *and* for worse. This reveals a further difference between these kinds of pleasures: pleasant sensations may be dangerous and, in some cases, perilous, but pleasant emotions can also be mistaken or even confused. The pleasures of fattening foods, for example, may be dangerous if they entice one to forget about one's health; the pleasures of sexual acts may be dangerous if they tempt one to indulge (or develop) perverse desires; but pleasures such as pride, quite apart from any such dangers, can also be *mistaken* or *unfounded*, as when one takes pride in something that is not worth being proud of. When we find that someone is proud of his crimes, for instance, we are even further disturbed that his criminal behavior is paired with so deep a corruption of his emotions. We do not think that his pleasure is itself morally neutral and that only its source is bad, but that his pleasure is *itself* a deep and morally significant mistake, a mistake of placing value where value does not belong. We do not want pride, or joy, or satisfaction, or calm full stop, *whatever* we say about their objects; we want to have those pleasures in the right kinds of ways, about the right sorts of things. Reflection shows us that we need to have *reasons* for the emotions we have, and thus for our pleasures.

Notice also that if it is important to be proud in the right ways and about the right things, it is no less important to be ashamed or regretful in the right ways and about the right things. And so while no one would suppose that painful sensations have any value for their own sake, we do think that painful emotions can have such value. Our lives would be poorer if we were unable to take pleasure in our accomplishments, and they would be poorer if we were unable to find our failures painful.[8] We would be better off without toothache, but we

---

[8] Indeed, as Strawson (1974: 6–25) has famously argued, we cherish even painful emotions, not because they are painful, but because it is in our very nature to have such emotional reactions to certain kinds of things.

would be worse off without a sense of shame, or regret, or indignation, or loss. This also means that when other things are equal there are some pleasures, understood as emotions, that we would be better off without, and some pains that are worth having for their own sake. In this way emotions are unlike sensations; since there is nothing for sensations to be right or wrong about, when other things are equal we simply prefer pleasant sensations for their own sake and avoid painful sensations for their own sake. These two sorts of pleasure, then, stand in importantly different relations to their contrary pains. And they have very different roles to play in our lives.

This fact about pleasures has an important consequence: we cannot maintain that pleasures and pains are intrinsically good or bad, full stop.[9] Pleasure, understood as an emotion, is a kind of attitude that one takes toward other things, and such an attitude will be good or bad depending on whether it is the right kind of attitude to take, on whether it is an attitude we have good reasons to take. And exactly the same will be true of pain, considered as an emotion. Notice, then, that it makes little sense to think of pleasure in this sense as an object of pursuit to be maximized. We do not simply want to have the most and the greatest of such pleasures that we can, but we want to have the right ones, at the right times, about the right things.

That is, we shall want that if we think of ourselves as continuing beings whose existence will be meaningful depending on the kind of things we do and the kind of person we are. Consequently, if we think about what has value *for a being of that kind*, our focus will naturally rest on pleasures understood as emotions, rather than sensations, since as we have seen pleasures of the former kind are a deep part of one's character and personality, and since the project of putting together a future as a being with the right kinds of attitudes, priorities, and values is sure to be far more fruitful than putting together a future as a being who feels as much of a certain kind of sensation as possible. The former holds the hope of living a *life*; the latter only of moving through episodes.

There are, then, more than one sort of phenomenon we describe as pleasure, and these are importantly different both in their own nature, as well as in their roles in a person's character and thus in her life as a whole. It is therefore dangerous to reduce them to the same thing, although philosophers—and the folk psychology they have helped over time to shape—do so on occasion. We find such a reduction, to take one example, in Jeremy Bentham's famous assertion that the pleasure one person gets from an evening of bowling and the pleasure another person gets from an evening of listening to poetry are both, in some sense, the same sort of thing, differing merely in what causes them, and perhaps also in various qualitative differences, levels of intensity, or what have you, so that we can ask what quantity of the one will trade against what quantity of the other.[10] This

---

[9] I shall explore the (often misunderstood) notion of intrinsic goodness in the first chapter.

[10] Bentham famously argued that the pleasures of 'push-pin' are every bit as good as those of music and poetry (*Rationale of Reward*, bk. III, ch. 1), his point being that distinctions in value between

treatment of such pleasures as the same thing found in different sources reduces the emotional engagement one may have in bowling or poetry to something like a sensation, exhibiting only quantitative differences. And even if we think that not all pleasures are the same but fall into different classes—perhaps the pleasures of bowling and the pleasures of poetry belong to different classes, such as 'lower' and 'higher' pleasures, and no comparison can be made *across* those classes[11]—we may still think that pleasures remain commensurable *within* their classes, so that the pleasure of poetry is the same sort of thing as one might have gotten from chess or opera, even if one of them gives a person 'more' of that thing than the others do. This too does not do justice to the fact that such pleasures are not just sensations, but part of one's emotional life.[12]

Of course, the view that pleasures are qualitative states distinct from their causes and which can be compared, at least to some extent, as qualitative states has been a historically influential one, because it has held the promise of a method of evaluating things, choices, activities, and institutions in terms of some good that persons desire as much of as possible and which these things cause. And that method is, after all, ingenious: to evaluate a choice, locate something that we know is desired by the persons affected by the choice, and determine how this choice would fare in the promotion of that desired thing in relation to the alternatives. None the less, upon reflection on pleasure as an emotion, as part of one's character, and as something with an important role to play in one's life as a whole, such a method seems simply inadequate to capture the ways in which pleasure actually seems to matter to reflective, deliberating agents the most. Such an approach requires the goods and evils in question to be quantifiable and commensurable, so that they can be measured and compared, and pleasures understood as the workings of one's emotional life cannot be made to fit that mold, without compromising our understanding of them and obscuring their real importance.

Taking a sensation or feeling, then, as the place to begin trying to understand what pleasure is, leaves us in a very poor position to make sense of the roles that pleasure actually seems to play for us. Although the relation between one's pleasures and one's values is as yet far from clear, it does seem clear that some pleasures—and surely the ones with the most importance in the context of reflecting on our lives as wholes—have far more to do with the sorts of values we have, and thus the sorts of persons we are, than they do with just feelings. When a person stops to think about what she should do with her life, what she wants to know is just how all the various parts of her life might fit together to make a

kinds of pleasures are moot. For a purely quantitative analysis of pleasure, the *locus classicus* is Bentham, *An Introduction to the Principles of Morals and Legislation*, ch. 4.

[11] For incommensurable classes of pleasures, see esp. John Stuart Mill, *Utilitarianism*, ch. 2.

[12] Notice that quite generally the view that an attraction to pleasure and a repulsion from pain are the fundamental reasons for all of our choices, actions, and preferences, does not sit comfortably with an analysis of pleasure and pain as emotions. For we recognize that we need reasons for having the emotional responses we have, beyond the mere fact that we just do have them.

happy life—a life in which she might flourish, and succeed as a human being. Ancient philosophers have never been surpassed for the acuteness with which they perceive the importance of this question; it was because he recognized how vital this question is that Socrates, for instance, engaged in conversation so tenaciously with other people who sincerely believed they had the answer.[13] It is the need to answer questions about what to make of our lives that brings us to the notion of some direction and order for our lives. This is the notion of the final end, or some purpose or meaning in life—what the classical Greek philosophers call a τέλος or 'final end'—and so we can see the kind of reflection I have sketched above as part of a search for a final end. However, it is unclear how a person would construct a good whole life out of something so localized and episodic as a certain kind of feeling. More generally, if it is from the perspective of my life as a whole that I begin to think about what things are good, it is not at all obvious that a certain kind of feeling could play the sort of role in my life—a role we shall need to explore at length—that would lead me to count it a good, belonging to those things that make my life a good life. If pleasure is to have any relevance to how we plan our lives, considered as wholes—and it seems it must—we need a more sophisticated account of what place pleasure has in a good life, and thus also a more sophisticated account of what sort of thing pleasure is.[14]

What we need, then, is an alternative account of what pleasure is that is subtle and sophisticated enough to explain why a person's pleasures tell so much about her, in the ways that we have been discussing. I do not pretend that an alternative conception of pleasure is yet clear, and much of what follows in this book is aimed at arriving at a clearer alternative. However, if we can imagine pleasure—the pleasure of skiing, or teaching, or bringing one's child into the world, say—not as a feeling occasioned by its object but rather as an intentional state by which we attach a certain significance to its object, we shall come to have less confidence in the idea that pleasure so understood is always and obviously good just for what it is. That idea is easier to have about a feeling, because in a feeling there is nothing really 'at stake'. The same is not true, of course, of our attaching significance to something—that just *is* to take a stake in it, and there are clearly good and bad, correct and mistaken, ways of taking stakes. And this feature of pleasure makes it all the more important to understand, since it seems that one can take such a stake in the goodness and meaningfulness in the direction that one's life as a whole is taking, and at that level the mistakes we might make are not merely unfortunate, but potentially tragic. To the extent that

[13] As he says to Callicles (*Gorgias* 492d3–5), 'Please, I beg you, do all you can to sustain the momentum [of our conversation], until there's really no chance of our mistaking the right way to live.'

[14] Perhaps it is no accident that Bentham, who treated pleasures as rather psychologically thin experiences to be quantified and compared merely in terms of intensity, duration, etc., was also very pessimistic about the usefulness of the idea of a person's character as a whole, or indeed of her life considered as a whole. Here I have benefited from the work of Mark Kanaga.

it is worth while thinking philosophically about living well, about the sort of person that one is becoming, and about our values and indeed the nature of our minds, it is worth while thinking philosophically about pleasure. And the place to begin is in thinking about pleasure in the context of the happiness of one's life as a whole, which is exactly where Plato begins.

0.2 What Plato Has to Offer: A Brief Overview

It should be clear that much of the work of constructing an adequate account of pleasure and its relevance within ethical reflection will be the work of constructing a sophisticated moral psychology of pleasure. But much of that work will also consist in developing a conception of goodness and value that will allow us to explain what kind of role pleasure should play, and what kind of good pleasure may be, within a good human life. And it is on both of these fronts, I think, that Plato has much to offer that we cannot afford to overlook.

To put things most succinctly, I argue in this book that Plato regards pleasure as a *conditional good*, the goodness of which depends on, and is given by, the role that pleasure takes on in a virtuous character under the leadership of practical intelligence. This is not to say that Plato has a developed theory of conditional and other kinds of goods; on the contrary, it would be going too far to say that Plato has any developed value *theory* at all. But approaching Plato in these terms will cast the most light on what he does have to say about pleasure and its value, and makes the best sense of the observations about value in general that he does in fact make. In short, I think that in Plato we shall find these ideas, if not the words.

I shall begin in Chapter 1 by defining and clarifying the notions of conditional and unconditional goodness by exploring an important passage in Plato's *Euthydemus* in which we see these notions emerging as Plato discusses the radical difference between virtues of character and all other sorts of goods. Simply put, *conditional goods* are those goods whose goodness depends on their being given a good direction within one's life that they cannot give themselves, while *unconditional goods* are good by their nature and are the source of direction that brings about goodness in other things. Related to this distinction between kinds of goods is a distinction between conceptions of happiness: on what I shall call the *additive* conception of happiness, happiness depends on (is determined by) the various good things in one's life—health and wealth, say, or pleasure, or desire satisfaction, or some recipe of such things[15]—while on the *directive* conception of happiness, happiness depends on (is determined by) the

---

[15] For a defense of hedonism as an account of happiness in Plato, see, e.g., Gosling and Taylor (1982: 71–7); for a discussion of this view see also Berman (1991*b*: 130–9), and Rudebusch (1989: 28 ff.). For desire satisfaction, see Irwin (1992: 205 ff.), (1995: 117 ff.); cf. (1979: 194, 223); cp. Tenkku (1956: 73), who attributes to Socrates the view that 'he who has least desires may be satisfied and consequently happy'.

intelligent direction that all the areas of one's life take together as a whole, as directed by practical reason and intelligent agency. These two distinctions are related in so far as the additive conception makes happiness depend on various conditional goods, whereas the directive conception makes happiness depend on the unconditional good that is intelligent agency. In the *Euthydemus*, I argue, Plato means to distinguish conditional from unconditional goods, and espouses the directive conception of happiness and rejects the additive, making happiness depend on the unconditionally good, which he identifies as wisdom. I then make a number of remarks about the significance of treating pleasure as a conditional good, and of the rather special relation that might be possible between practical intelligence and pleasure on this way of understanding pleasure. I also suggest some shortcomings of the account in the *Euthydemus* of the directive conception, which I address in subsequent chapters.

In Chapter 2, I argue that in the *Gorgias* we find a fuller discussion and defense of the idea that happiness depends on the unconditional good that is intelligent agency, and thus of the directive conception of happiness. This is especially important for understanding Plato's analysis of pleasure. As we shall see, the additive conception posits a gap between intelligent agency and happiness to be filled by something else—pleasure, say, or desire-satisfaction—that intelligent agency brings and which is what determines happiness,[16] while the directive conception maintains that there is no such gap to be filled. Consequently, the directive conception both explains why Socrates argues in the *Gorgias* that virtue 'brings fulfillment and happiness' (507c), and reveals that hedonism is, in its very theoretical structure, in tension with Plato's conception of the nature of happiness and of value in the *Gorgias* at the most fundamental level. Consequently, the directive conception of happiness which best explains Plato's defense of virtue's power to make one happy, also explains his rejection of the idea that pleasure determines happiness.

It is very difficult, therefore, to avoid the conclusion that debates in recent years over the consistency of the refutation of a rather specific form of hedonism in the *Gorgias* with the hedonism that Socrates discusses in the *Protagoras*, have not arrived at the heart of the matter, which is that in the *Gorgias* the search for what makes a person happy is a search for what is unconditionally good. Since pleasure is an conditional good, hedonism is a form of the additive conception of happiness, which Plato rejects in the *Gorgias* and elsewhere. I thus postpone

---

[16] Notice, then, that on one version of the additive conception a hedonist might hold that while all virtuous persons are happy, still virtue has no value of its own, but is valuable only for producing as trouble-free a life as possible, allowing the agent to live in the great pleasures of a mind as untroubled as possible. In fact, this is the view of Epicurus; see esp. *Letter to Menoeceus* 132; *Principle Doctrines* V, XXV; Cicero, *de Finibus* II.42 ff.; Athenaeus, *Deipnosophists* 12, 547a (512 U). Perhaps more subtly, on another version a hedonist might hold that pleasure is best understood as identical to a certain form of activity—and indeed to virtuous activity, so that the life of virtue is happy because that life is identical to the life of greatest pleasure. Rudebusch (1991: 37–40), (1994: 165–9), (1999) attributes this view to Plato, at least in the 'Socratic' (or 'early') dialogues. We shall explore Rudebusch's view in Ch. 2 (see also, Russell 2000*b*).

discussion of the *Protagoras* until the epilogue. There I argue, on the one hand, that proponents of the view that Plato espouses the hedonism discussed in the *Protagoras* have not appreciated how fundamental a shift in conception of happiness and value this view would require Plato to have made. And I argue, on the other, that the *Protagoras* does not depend for its argumentative success on Plato's endorsement of hedonism anyway.[17]

In Chapter 3 I explore further the analysis of pleasure as a conditional good, arguing that it is only by understanding pleasure as a conditional good that we can make complete sense of all that Plato says about pleasure in the *Phaedo*. As many commentators have noticed, in the *Phaedo* Plato seems to denigrate any sort of power with respect to happiness that we might take pleasure to have, and at the same time celebrates the philosopher's life—brought into sharp relief on the day of Socrates' death—as satisfying and joyful. Consequently, some of Plato's commentators have concluded confidently that he is an ascetic, and others with equal confidence that he is a hedonist. I argue instead that Plato makes pleasure a conditional good, that is, a good with no goodness of its own, but depending on the goodness with which intelligent agency gives pleasure the right kind of place within one's life. In its own right, then, pleasure is neither good nor bad; what is good or bad is the way in which one incorporates pleasure into one's life and concerns, so that pleasure is at once a part of the life lived well, and itself powerless to make one happy, since it does not determine its own place in one's life, and even potentially dangerous, should one fail to give it the right place. In the *Phaedo*, I argue, pleasure is neither a good nor an evil, full stop, but is a conditional good, becoming either good or evil depending on the role it plays in one's life.

In Chapter 4 I explore further just what it means to give pleasure a role to play in one's life. The distinction between the additive and directive conceptions of happiness, we should observe, is also a distinction between conceptions of happiness that make happiness depend on one's flourishing in some aspect or other of one's life, on the one hand, and those that make happiness depend on the flourishing in all aspects of one's life, under the direction of intelligent agency. On the directive conception, then, happiness is *holistic*, consisting in the flourishing of all of those dimensions of a person that make her a human being—complete with passions, emotions, desires, pleasures, and pains. Here I focus on the *Republic*, especially books IV and IX, arguing that on Plato's view pleasure is part of the good life not as a supplement to intelligent agency, but as a part of our nature that intelligent agency transforms and causes to flourish. This reconstruction of Plato's view, I argue, makes the best sense of the importance Plato assigns to pleasure in demonstrating the happiness of the virtuous life: the virtuous are happy because they live the life of integrated and flourishing human beings, which are among other things *affective* beings; virtue, then, is the psychic health of a human being as a *whole* human being.

---

[17] None the less, readers who would prefer to begin an investigation of pleasure in Plato with the *Protagoras* should feel free to read the epilogue first.

The transformation and integration of pleasure within a healthy, flourishing human psyche I shall refer to as the 'rational incorporation' of pleasure by practical intelligence. It is, moreover, a central theme of Plato's *Philebus*, which I discuss in Chapters 5 and 6. In Chapter 5 I explore Plato's identification of the good life with 'likeness to God', which has often been interpreted as threatening Plato's ability to sustain a suitable conception of *human* happiness. If that threat is real, then perhaps in Plato's account of the good life we should find not the rational incorporation of our affective by our rational nature, but the rejection of our affective nature as not part of who we really are, or should aspire to become. By contrast, I argue that the work of likeness to God within Plato's ethics is to show not that part of our nature belongs to us and another part does not, but that part of our nature brings direction, order, and harmony to other parts of our nature that have no such direction of their own. This fresh look at likeness to God approaches it from the perspective of the *Philebus*, as well as from the Stoic perspective, especially as we find it in Seneca. So far from rejecting the rational incorporation of pleasure, I argue, likeness to God turns out on this approach to be a kind of *account* of rational incorporation, treating pleasure as among the inchoate materials of the self out of which intelligent agency constructs a complete and flourishing existence.

Notice also that on this account of rational incorporation, it will make sense for Plato to make pleasure necessary for happiness: pleasure is part of human nature, and so the question is not whether the good life will be pleasant or not, but only what sort of role pleasure must play in the good life. Consequently, as I argue in Chapter 6, in the *Philebus* Plato recognizes that pleasure is necessary for happiness—not because he denies that virtue is enough to make one happy, but because on his view virtue is the rational incorporation of all aspects of the self, including the pleasures with which we attribute value and importance to other things in our lives. Pleasure, in other words, is necessary for happiness precisely *because* virtue is the right kind of whole to be enough for happiness. Notice that rational incorporation allows us to explain the consistency of the necessity of pleasure for happiness with the sufficiency of virtue for happiness, as impressive a sign of its explanatory power as there ever could be. Such a view affords a new approach to thinking about pleasure in the good life, which makes pleasure a part of happiness by making it a part of virtue.

Notice that such a view of the role of pleasure in the good life rests upon a psychological account of pleasure as a kind of attitude that can be renewed and transformed under the leadership of intelligent agency. In particular, it requires what I shall call the *agreement model* of psychic conformity, which is the view that our affective nature is sufficiently subtle to grasp and adopt the direction that our rational nature gives it, so that these natures can work together in cooperation.[18] Unfortunately, it is at this point that Plato begins to run into

---

[18] For a discussion of processes of cultivating emotions in an Aristotelian context, see Sherman (1997: 83–93).

trouble. Although Plato does speak of the relation between these natures in terms of the agreement model, he also speaks of them in terms of the *control model*, the view that our affective nature lacks such subtlety and thus will conform to reason only by being restrained and curbed, but not internally transformed. I discuss these two models as they appear in various forms in Plato's *Republic*, *Laws*, and *Timaeus*, in Chapter 7, exploring the tension between these models, as well as Plato's motivation for speaking in the terms of both. The problem, however, is that Plato does not seem to have chosen one over the other as an account of psychic conformity, nor to have found a theory that unifies the perspectives on our psychology that each represents. And without a unified psychological account of the harmony that rational incorporation posits between pleasure and intelligent agency, Plato's ethical analysis of pleasure lacks a supporting psychological analysis of pleasure. Now I shall argue that the control model, which is in tension with Plato's account of rational incorporation, is also more independently problematic than the agreement model which supports his account of rational incorporation. None the less, in the end Plato still falls short of the unified psychological account he needs, in ways that are both interesting and instructive for us now. Plato, it seems, has much to offer us that is new, both for understanding fresh possibilities for thinking of pleasure as part of the good life, and for appreciating the implications that these possibilities have for—and the demands they place on—other areas of moral philosophy and psychology.

0.3   Plato on Pleasure: The Current Debate

At the most general level, this book presents Plato as having an essentially unified conception of the relation of pleasure to virtue and happiness, which never involves hedonism. This much should be clear from the preceding overview. To say that that view is unified, however, is not to say that its defense rests specifically on any assumptions about the unity of doctrines in the Platonic dialogues generally, and so the debates over 'developmentalist' and 'unitarian' approaches to the dialogues will turn out to have mercifully little bearing on what follows. Surely the unavoidable controversy over whether Plato, at any point in his career, was a hedonist, will more than suffice to occupy us at present.

However, the fact that there is so much diversity of opinion among readers of Plato where both hedonism and developmentalism are concerned, makes it a bit surprising that for all the attention that the topic of pleasure in Plato's ethics has drawn, particularly in the last two or three decades, including a number of excellent books offering quite different views of Plato on pleasure, still no full-length treatment of the topic has appeared in which Plato is treated as having a unified, non-hedonist view of the value of pleasure. Terence Irwin, who discusses pleasure at length in his *Plato's Ethics* (Oxford, 1995), believes both that

Plato was, at one time, a hedonist, and that he later threw this position over for another. For different reasons, J. C. B. Gosling and C. C. W. Taylor (*The Greeks on Pleasure*, Oxford, 1982) argue that Plato moves from one view of the good to another, and at least at some point his view is a hedonist one.[19] George Rudebusch's more recent *Socrates, Pleasure, and Value* (Oxford, 1999) presents a unified account of Plato's view, at least in the so-called Socratic dialogues, but argues that that account is a hedonist one.[20] And while Julia Annas argues in *Platonic Ethics, Old and New* (Oxford, 1999) that Plato's view is largely unified and non-hedonist, none the less it falls outside the scope of that work to offer a full-length discussion of the matter.[21]

There is, then, a rather startling lacuna in the literature on this very important area of Plato's ethics. It is this lacuna that I shall try to fill with this book. More than that, however, I have also tried to situate the issue of pleasure within the broader context of Plato's thought about value in general, and his treatment of non-moral goods in particular, and thus also within the conception of virtue and happiness that I think Plato both needs and strives to articulate. Deep sensitivity to such larger issues is not wholly absent in the current literature on pleasure in Plato's ethics (Irwin is especially sensitive to these issues, I think), but is still less common than one might reasonably expect, and so I shall try to fill that part of the lacuna as well.

0.4   Texts Used

For the Greek texts of Plato's dialogues I have used John Burnet's edition of the Oxford Classical Texts (1900–7), although for the *Phaedo* I have used the new Oxford edition (edited by E. A. Duke *et al.*, 1995), and I have also consulted E. R. Dodds's Oxford edition (1959) of the *Gorgias*. For English translations of Plato's dialogues I have relied primarily on those in John Cooper's recent edition of *The Complete Works of Plato* (Hackett, 1997), except for the *Phaedo* for which I have used David Gallop's Oxford translation (1993), and except for the *Gorgias* and the *Republic* for which I have used Robin Waterfield's Oxford translations (1994 and 1993, respectively). I have also found helpful Reginald Hackforth's English edition of the *Philebus* (*Plato's Examination of Pleasure*, Cambridge, 1945), as well as Robin Waterfield's translation (Penguin, 1982). For translations

---

[19] According to Irwin, Plato shifts from the view that the good is pleasure, to the view that the good is desire satisfaction. Gosling and Taylor also depict a shift in Plato away from the view that the good is pleasure; however, it is not entirely clear to me precisely what Plato shifts toward, on their view.

[20] It must be noted, however, that the hedonism of Rudebusch's account is strikingly subtle and sophisticated, and represents in my opinion a significant advance over all previous hedonist accounts of so-called Socratic philosophy.

[21] The same unavoidable scope limitations apply also to Irwin (1995). There is also the pioneering work of Jussi Tenkku (1956) to consider. However, it is rarely possible to situate Tenkku's view in this debate, which of course post-dates him, and so throughout I shall refer only to particular observations of his as they seem salient.

of texts pertaining to Hellenistic philosophers I have relied mainly on Brad Inwood and Lloyd Gerson's *Hellenistic Philosophy*, 2nd edn. (Hackett, 1997), except where indicated. For Aristotle's *Nicomachean Ethics* I have relied on David Ross's translation as revised by Ackrill and Urmson (Oxford, 1980). Other translations of various texts have been used in a few places, and I note them as they arise.

1

Goodness and the Good Life:
The *Euthydemus*

Plato makes it clear that thinking about the value that something—pleasure, or anything else—should have in your life begins naturally with reflection on what it makes sense for a person to want to get out of life in the first place. This is, at any rate, where Plato's reflections on the nature of value begin, most notably in the *Euthydemus*. It is important to see that Plato's reflections begin where they do because that, Plato holds, is where reflective people usually begin when they think about what really matters to them in life. Everyone, he notes, wants to be happy, or fare well (εὖ πράττειν), and no one disagrees about whether a good life is what he wants to live (278e3–279a1). But that is only where reflection about value *begins*, and it is quite another matter to determine just what a good life amounts to (279a1 ff.). Philosophical theorizing, then, is not supposed to replace ordinary reflection, but to extend it and give it a focus that we may fail to recognize without more rigorous thought. In fact, it may even turn out that many of our pre-theoretical notions must actually be given up.

For that reason, I shall begin our reflections on the nature of value with Plato in the *Euthydemus*. Doing so, I believe, will afford insight into the different sorts of roles that different goods play in our life, and thus with a crucial choice between ways of thinking about what happiness is, a choice we may not have realized we had: in particular, a choice between the idea that happiness depends on the things in our life in regard to which we act and choose (our health, our wealth, our projects, and so on) and the idea that happiness depends on the wisdom with which we act and choose in regard to those things. As we shall see in the first section of this chapter, Plato defends the latter idea in the *Euthydemus*, as he argues that happiness depends on how we give each part of our life the right sort of place in our life considered as a whole. The idea of giving things the right place in our life I shall call, in the second section, the 'rational incorporation' of them, and I shall explore what it could mean for pleasure, in particular, to be rationally incorporated into a person's life on this model of practical rationality.

1.1 Some Distinctions in Goodness: The *Euthydemus*

What makes a life happy? Obviously, answers differ. As Aristotle observed, people tend to give different answers depending on what they prize in their own lives, and even depending on what is going on in their lives at the moment.[1] But beneath these different answers lies a more fundamental difference between *kinds* of answers. Some answers make happiness depend on the good *things* in a person's life, or on such good things at least in so far as they have been given direction in one's life as a whole.[2] After all, money, for instance, cannot make you happy if it sits idle, or if you become miserly or prodigal in your use of it, say, but perhaps on this sort of view money can make you happy (or happier) if you are also virtuous in your use of it. Other answers, however, make happiness depend on the *intelligent agency* with which a person leads her life. On this view, the *money* itself has no power to make you happy at all, even if you use it virtuously; rather, what makes a difference with respect to happiness is the practical intelligence, or wisdom, with which you formulate attitudes and priorities with respect to money—the wisdom, that is, with which you give it a place in your life. In other words, on this view to say that money is good in the hands of a virtuous person is really to say that a virtuous person is good where money is concerned, and it is the goodness of that person, and not really the money at all, that goes toward making her happy. The view that happiness depends on the 'ingredients' added into one's life I shall call the *additive* conception of happiness; and the view that happiness depends on the intelligent agency that gives one's life the direction it needs to be healthy and flourishing, I shall call the *directive* conception of happiness.[3]

At stake between these conceptions of happiness is whether happiness is determined[4] by what is the source of all proper direction in one's whole life, or

---

[1] *Nicomachean Ethics* I.4, 1095a20–6, I.5, 1095b14–6.

[2] It seems clear that every account of happiness that takes seriously the idea of one's life as a whole requires that the ingredients of one's life be given direction; notice that even Callicles, despite the crudeness of his hedonist conception of happiness, is committed to the idea that the pleasures one should want are those characteristic of the kind of person Callicles thinks is best (*Gorgias* 497d–499b). Consequently, the view that goods can make us happy even when they are totally directionless is the first view that Plato attacks in the *Euthydemus*.

[3] This distinction (although not the terminology) is also found in the Stoics' claim that while we choose and pursue certain goods, our success depends not on our achieving them, but on our choosing and pursuing them in a rational way; famously, the Stoics say that our goal is like that of an archer, who has a target that he means to hit, but whose goal is not that an arrow should be in the target, but that he should aim and shoot well with respect to the target. However, this sort of distinction is seldom brought to bear on Plato. For the archery analogy see Cicero, *de Finibus* III.22–5, V.20–1; see also Cicero's report (*de Finibus* V.16–22) of Carneades' division of six views on the ultimate good into two basic camps, which correspond to what we have called the additive and directive conceptions of happiness.

[4] I shall speak throughout of what 'determines' happiness, rather than of what 'suffices for' happiness; whether or not virtue is sufficient for happiness is, of course, a controversial issue, which I do not wish to bias in advance. A further advantage of looking for what determines happiness is that it focuses, as Plato does, on what is causally responsible for making a good life a good life, without

whether it is determined by some or other of the things that must be given a direction they do not give themselves. Clearly, this difference will make all the difference for understanding what happiness comes to. The additive conception will be quite familiar from the idea that happiness consists in pleasure, say, or desire-satisfaction, or even engaging in certain projects (including doing 'good deeds'), since all of those goods require the right sort of direction to be good, but none the less are often said to determine happiness. But, despite the great familiarity of the additive conception, further thought about the nature of value shows more problems for it than we might see at first. Or so Plato tells us in the *Euthydemus.*

In a notorious passage of the *Euthydemus* (278e–282d) Plato considers these two conceptions of happiness and argues in favor of the directive conception.[5] Plato has Socrates start by noting two truisms: that we all want to be happy and do well; and that happiness depends on the good in our lives (278e). The difficult task is to determine what happiness and goodness are, and at this point Socrates considers two fundamental alternatives. First is the view that happiness comes about from *good things*, like wealth, good looks, fame, and good fortune:

'[Since] we all wish to fare well (εὖ πράττειν), in what way would we fare well? Would we fare well if we had many good things?'...

[Cleinias] agreed.

'Well then, what sorts of things are there that happen to be good for us? It doesn't seem very difficult, and doesn't take a very grandiose man to produce a ready answer—everyone would tell us that being wealthy is a good thing, right?'

'Yes, quite,' he said.

'And so also being in good health and being beautiful, and being nicely outfitted with other bodily goods?'

He concurred.

'But surely an influential family, and power, and prestige in one's own circles are, clearly, good things.'

He said they were.   (279a1–b3)[6]

Moreover, as Socrates notes we do not simply want to have these things, but to *do* things with them; so this list can be extended to include *projects* and *undertakings* as well:

'So would it do us any good if we should only *have* these things, but were not to *use* them? For instance, if we had plenty to eat but didn't eat it, or plenty to drink but didn't drink it, would that do us any good?'

'Certainly not,' he said. . . .

assuming either that that cause 'achieves' happiness as a distinct goal or that that cause is itself constitutive of happiness (although I shall argue for the latter). Of course, I do not pretend that the locution 'determines' is at this point pellucid, but the discussion that follows can be seen as an attempt to cash it out much more precisely.

[5] On the radical nature of Plato's shift in notions of happiness, cf. Annas (1999: 39 f.); see also Chance (1992: 69).   [6] Translations of *Euthydemus* are my own.

'So, Cleinias, this would be enough to make someone happy: both to possess good things *and* to put them to use?'
'That's how it seems to me.'   (280b8–c3, d7–e3)

The idea here is straightforward enough: things like these, the ways that they increase our opportunities for undertaking projects, the projects they make possible, and even the projects themselves have their own sort of power with respect to happiness. On this view, what makes me happy is the fact that I have *these* things, that I am *accomplishing* things of *this* sort, and so on. This, of course, is the view I earlier called the additive conception of happiness, and here Plato recognizes its immediate attractiveness.

But Socrates does not stop there. He notes that when we think about these ingredients, we see that their *direction* matters. Socrates had also listed wisdom as a good,[7] and it now turns out to be a very special good. This is because even *using* good things might do us no more good than simply having them but leaving them alone does (280b7–8). Rather, it depends on what we make of them:

'So, Cleinias, would this be enough to make someone happy: both to possess good things and to put them to use?'
'That's how it seems to me.'
'In what way?' I said. 'If someone should put them to *good* use, or even if he didn't?'
'If he puts them to good use.'
'Well said!' I said. 'I think it will be more the opposite [of happiness] if someone were to put something to bad use, than if he were to leave it alone; the former is bad, while the latter is neither good nor bad. Or isn't this what we say?'
He agreed.   (280d7–281a1)

However, Socrates notes that this thought tends to shift the responsibility for our happiness away from ingredients in one's life, and onto the intelligent *agency* that gives them direction in one's life—that is, onto what Socrates calls knowledge, a form of practical wisdom:[8]

'So,' I said, 'when it comes to using the things we said earlier were the good things—wealth, health, beauty—the correct use of all these sorts of things is knowledge, which leads and directs our behavior; or is it something else?'
'It's knowledge,' he said.
'So knowledge, it seems, provides for people not only good fortune but also good action, in all their possessing and doing.'
He agreed.
'My God!' I said. 'Then do *any* of our other possessions do us any good without intelligence and wisdom ($\phi\rho\acute{o}\nu\eta\sigma\iota\varsigma$ $\kappa\alpha\grave{\iota}$ $\sigma o\phi\acute{\iota}\alpha$)? ... The upshot of all this, Cleinias,' I said, 'is presumably that *all* of the things we said at first were goods—well, the account of them is

---

[7] See 279c1–280b6; we shall return to this passage below. It is also important to note that in what follows I shall take 'wisdom' and 'virtue' to be more or less interchangeable, as it is generally acknowledged among scholars that Plato intends no real distinction between them in this passage.
[8] Annas (1993: 59) notes that Socrates' gloss of 'knowledge' in this passage—so foundational in Socratic ethics—as practical wisdom poses a serious challenge to the traditional view that Socrates is an 'intellectualist', reducing moral virtue to a knowledge that consists in the ability to give definitions, etc.

not about how they themselves, in their own right, are good by their very nature (αὐτά γε καθ᾽ αὑτὰ πέφυκεν ἀγαθά), but rather it seems to be this: if ignorance should lead them, they're greater evils than their opposites, to whatever degree they are able to encourage the bad person who is leading them; but when intelligence and wisdom lead them, they are greater goods—although neither of them *themselves*, considered in *their own* right, are of any value at all (αὐτὰ δὲ καθ᾽ αὑτὰ οὐδέτερα αὐτῶν οὐδενὸς ἄξια εἶναι).'
'Apparently,' he said, 'and as seems plausible, it is just as you say.' (281a6–b6, d2–e2)

This is a most interesting development: things and projects that we initially take the good life to consist in turn out not to have any value of their own after all, because none of them brings the *direction* that makes for a happy life. The value of these things, then, depends entirely on the direction that a wise agent gives them. So Plato contrasts things besides wisdom that need direction, with the wisdom which *is* the source of direction that our lives need. That is why Socrates says wisdom is good without qualification, and is what determines happiness:

'So what follows from what we've said? Isn't it this, that of the other things none is either good or bad, and that of these two, wisdom is good, and ignorance bad?'
He agreed.
'Well, then let's have a look at what's left,' I said. 'Since all of us desire to be happy, and since we evidently become so on account of our *use*—that is, our *good* use—of other things, and since knowledge is what provides this goodness of use and also good fortune,[9] every man must, as seems plausible, prepare himself by every means for this: to be as wise as possible. Right?'
'Yes,' he said. (281e2–282a7)

Here Plato makes it clear that the key to happiness is found not in the goods or even the projects that form the 'ingredients' of a person's life, but in the *agency* of the person herself that gives her whole life direction and focus, and which therefore determines her happiness.

Notice that Socrates says in one breath that things besides wisdom are greater goods if wisdom directs them (281d6–8), and in the next breath that nothing is good except wisdom (281e3–5). This raises two very serious questions. The first, of course, is why we should think that nothing is good except wisdom. Although we shall see that the argument in the *Euthydemus* for this claim is importantly incomplete, none the less some of Plato's reasons for holding this view will emerge as we proceed more carefully through the passage, as will the value theory it appears to embody. And so for now I wish to draw our attention to the second question, which is how something can be a greater good than something else if it is not a good in the first place.[10] Clearly, Plato's point is to distinguish a strict or proper sense of 'good' from a qualified or secondary sense, and to say that only wisdom is good in the strict sense, since only wisdom is good 'by its very nature' (see 281d8–e1). Consequently, Plato takes wisdom to have a radically different kind of value than anything else has: wisdom has not only a superior

---

[9] The claim that knowledge provides good fortune is controversial, as Plato seems to recognize. I shall return to this issue below.
[10] For comment, see Irwin (1992: 202–4); see also (1995: 74 f., 117–20); and Annas (1999: 44).

value but also a unique value that is built into its very fabric—it alone is good itself, by its very nature, and considered in its own right. But what exactly does that mean, and what exactly is this difference in goodness?

1.1.1   Some distinctions in goodness

We can get a better grip on this question by distinguishing certain basic value-theoretical categories within which such a question must be answered.[11] We can see these categories if we begin by distinguishing three queries we can make about anything of value:

1. *For what purpose is it valuable—for its own sake, or for the sake of something else?*
2. *Is it valuable in its own right, or must value be brought about in it?*
3. *Does it bring about value in other things, or does something else bring about value in it?*

The first issue concerns our *reasons* for valuing something: if we value something as a means to something else, then we say it has *instrumental* value, whereas if we value it for its own sake as an end, then it has *final* value.[12] Being healthy, for instance, is a final good,[13] since we want it for its own sake, while taking medicine is a means to health, and thus an instrumental good;[14] likewise, enjoying oneself is valued as an end, whereas money-making is valued as a means.

The second issue concerns the *source* or *location*, so to speak, of a thing's value: some things are good by their very nature; whereas other things depend on something else for their goodness.[15] Things that are good by their nature are *intrinsic* goods—their goodness is self-contained, as it were, and does not rely on another source; things in which goodness must be brought about, on the other hand, are *extrinsic* goods. To capture this contrast, we can say that extrinsic goods are *undifferentiated*: they are neither good nor bad, until goodness or badness is brought about in them by the agents involved with them. A career, for instance, can occupy either the right or wrong part of one's life, and so goodness

---

[11] For the definitions of and distinctions between these categories, I am greatly indebted to Christine Korsgaard's seminal paper, 'Two Distinctions in Goodness' (1983). This is an important paper which ancient scholars have not sufficiently appreciated; e.g., as far as I can see the only other critic to bring Korsgaard's paper to bear on the *Euthydemus* is Lesses (2000: 351).

[12] See Korsgaard (1983: 170).

[13] It goes without saying that something can be a final good without being a final end, in the eudemonist's sense.

[14] Cf. *Gorgias* 467c ff. for Platonic examples of what we are calling instrumental and final goods. Cp. also Plato's claim at *Republic* II, 357b–d that things like pleasure are pursued for their own sake, which makes them final rather than instrumental goods. Plato also distinguishes there a class of goods that are valued in both ways (see also Korsgaard 1983: 185); I shall take it as given that there are such goods, but shall not need to discuss them here.

It is sometimes thought that the classification of final and instrumental goods, which Socrates introduces in his discussion with Polus in the *Gorgias*, ought to be aligned with the classification of goods in the *Euthydemus* (e.g. Vlastos 1991: 228–30). However, as we shall see the *Euthydemus* passage concerns quite a different distinction between goods (cf. Annas 1993: 56 f.; Brickhouse and Smith 1994: 110 f.).   [15] See Korsgaard (1983: 170).

must be *brought about* in one's career, and therefore careers are extrinsic goods. Of course, to give *your* career the right place in *your* life is to differentiate it as a good, and in this sense we can say that such an extrinsic good has become differentiated;[16] still, an extrinsic good is never differentiated in its own right, since something else must differentiate it. In this way extrinsic goods are unlike intrinsic goods, which are not merely differentiated, but *differentiated in their own right*, by their very nature.[17]

The distinction between intrinsic and extrinsic goods can be made even clearer if we distinguish them from final and instrumental goods, with which they are often conflated.[18] In particular, *extrinsic goods can be final goods*:[19] Many things that need something else to make them good can still be valued for their own sake once they have been made good. So while a career that has been given the right place in one's life is an extrinsic good, this is *not* to say that it can be only an instrumental good, rather than an end or final good, as careers sometimes are.[20] Something is extrinsically good because of *where its goodness comes from*, and it is an end because of *how we value it* as having the goodness that it does, wherever that goodness comes from. Clearly, very many extrinsic goods will be final goods; moreover, since some extrinsic goods are final goods, not all final goods are intrinsic goods. Therefore, the distinction between intrinsic and extrinsic goods, and that between final and instrumental goods, are importantly different distinctions.[21]

One reason why people are often apt to conflate these distinctions, I think, is the mistaken assumption that when something depends on something else for its goodness (is extrinsically good), the thing it depends on must *always* be some

---

[16] As Korsgaard (1983: 179) says, conditional goods whose conditions are met must be understood as 'real particulars: this woman's knowledge, this man's happiness [i.e. in Kant's sense of 'happiness'], and so on'.

[17] Notice that intrinsic goods will all be final goods. More precisely, we should say that intrinsic goods will be final rather than instrumental goods, *in the first instance*. There is nothing to prevent an intrinsic good, such as virtue itself, from being valuable both finally and instrumentally (cf. *Republic* II, 357c–358a); still, intrinsic goods are to be valued primarily as final goods, and never as instrumental goods only (this is also, of course, the force of Kant's claim that persons are to be regarded as ends, and not as means only, *Grounding* 428 ff.). However, as we shall see, although all intrinsic goods are final goods, not all final goods are intrinsic goods. This is an important point, since these distinctions are very often run together.

[18] Of course, one *might* identify intrinsic with final goods and extrinsic with instrumental goods on the basis of some theory about their equivalence, but in most cases this is due to mere carelessness; see Korsgaard (1983: 169–73).

[19] See Korsgaard (1983: 172 ff., 180); see also Lesses (2000: 351). This is an important point to recognize, as readers sometimes mistakenly assume that since Plato (*Republic* II, 357b–d) says that pleasure is a *final* good (that we do not pursue it for the sake of something else), he must therefore think that it is an *intrinsic* good (that it must be good by its very nature).

[20] The relations between these categories of goods are complex and interesting. For example, although choosing a career is an instrumental good—we need to make the choice not for its own sake, but for the sake of surviving, etc.—it does not follow that the career we choose must therefore be an instrumental good; see Schmidtz (1994).

[21] What would be a case of an intrinsic good? Interestingly, fewer examples of intrinsic goods— properly understood—present themselves than in the case of extrinsic goods. In fact, this is perhaps the most interesting fact about intrinsic goods; as I shall argue below, there is really only one thing that is intrinsically good, or could be, and that is wisdom.

further end that makes it valuable as a means.[22] But there is more than one way of construing the dependence of one thing on another for its goodness. A meal, for instance, may be said to depend for its goodness on the skillful chef who made it, or it may be said to depend for its goodness on my hunger which it will satisfy. If one thing's dependence on another for its goodness were *always* of the latter sort, then all extrinsic goods would be instrumental goods, since the dependence relation must be understood *solely* in terms of means and ends. But that cannot be quite right: surely the fact that it takes good people to make careers good, and good chefs to make meals good, does not mean that good careers, or good meals, must be only instrumental goods; by keeping these distinctions separate, we can avoid that awkward conclusion, and avoid the mistaken conclusion that good careers or meals must therefore be intrinsic goods, when what we mean is that they are (or can be) final goods. So there must also be forms of dependence other than those that concern means and ends, and finding some other form of dependence would shed more light on the precise nature of intrinsic goods and their difference from extrinsic goods. And our discussion of the third issue will reveal exactly that further form of dependence.[23]

The third question asks about a thing's *active or passive role* in the production of value: some things have the power to bring about goodness in other things; while some things must have goodness brought about in them by something else. A career, to continue our example, must have goodness brought about in it, whereas the practical intelligence of the one pursuing it brings about its goodness, as she gives it the right place in her life. We can capture this difference by saying that practical intelligence is *differentiating*: it is what brings about the goodness in other things, like careers, which are not differentiating, since they do not direct themselves. Goods of the former type are *unconditional* goods: their goodness is not conditioned by something else's bringing goodness about in them, but they are responsible for bringing about goodness in other things. Goods of the latter type are *conditional* goods, which have goodness brought about in them by unconditional goods.[24] Conditional goods are good depending entirely on how one behaves in relation to them, and unconditional goods are those by which one behaves well in relation to other things.

This distinction is clearly connected to the distinction between intrinsic and extrinsic goods.[25] But before discussing that connection, notice that the distinction between conditional and unconditional goods is apparent in Plato's distinction between wisdom and all other goods, which he construes as the difference between what directs well and what must be directed. Accordingly, some scholars have cast the distinction between wisdom and all other goods in

---

[22] See also Korsgaard (1983: 171 f.).   [23] Ibid., (182 f.).
[24] This distinction is familiar from Kant's claim (*Grounding*, 393 f.) that only the 'good will' is unconditionally good, because its goodness is not conditioned on anything else, while the goodness of everything else is conditioned on it, as the good will is what brings about goodness in everything else. Here we find the idea that it is one's rational agency that is the source of goodness in all things, since it is what gives other things good or bad direction.
[25] In fact, they are coextensive; see Korsgaard (1983: 178 f.).

the *Euthydemus* as a distinction between conditional and unconditional goods.[26] However, those scholars have *not* construed that distinction as I have done here. In particular, we must note three points about the distinction between conditional and unconditional goods that are often overlooked.

One is that unconditional goods, as we have seen, are so in virtue of their active role with respect to goodness.[27] It is sometimes said that a good that is always good—good on all occasions—is therefore an unconditional good.[28] But although an unconditional good is good all the time, the point of this distinction is not the *frequency* with which a good thing is good. For instance, something that is always instrumentally valuable would be a most remarkable instrumental good, but it would not therefore be an unconditional good,[29] since it is not a good that makes other things good.[30] An unconditional good is what *conditions* the goodness of other things. Moreover, treating the distinction as a distinction in frequency of goodness threatens to collapse the distinction altogether. A conditional good, after all, has been made good by an unconditional good, and thus has become differentiated; but once a conditional good has become differentiated as a good, there is no reason it should not always be good, and thus no reason why it should not be an unconditional good, after all. But even when a conditional good has become differentiated, there remains the difference in *role* between what brings goodness about and what has goodness brought about in it. An unconditional

---

[26] See esp. Vlastos (1991: 230 f.); Annas (1993: 57); and Lesses (2000), who suggests (352) that the unconditional goodness of wisdom may be the point of Socrates' saying that wisdom is good in itself at 281e1. See also Reshotko (2001).

[27] Kant makes a similar point in the opening lines of the *Grounding* (orig. 393): 'Intelligence, wit, judgment, and whatever talents of the mind one might want to name are doubtless in many respects good and desirable, as are such qualities of temperament as courage, resolution, perseverance. But they can also become extremely bad and harmful if the will, which is to make use of these gifts of nature and which in its special constitution is called character, is not good. The same holds with gifts of fortune; power, riches, honor, even health, and that complete well-being and contentment with one's condition which is called happiness make for pride and often hereby even arrogance, unless there is a good will to correct their influence on the mind and herewith also to rectify the whole principle of action and make it universally conformable to its end.' (*Grounding*, trans. Ellington 1993.) Although Kant's understanding of such things as 'courage' and 'happiness' in this passage raises familiar complications, especially in the context of ancient eudaimonism and virtue theory, we can easily note the root idea of a vast difference between the sorts of things that need to receive direction in order to be goods on the one hand and what gives those things their direction on the other.

[28] See Lesses (2000); Reshotko (2001).

[29] See Reshotko (2001), who claims that virtue is an instrumental good which is unique in *always* being instrumental with respect to our ultimate goal, and therefore an 'unconditional' good. On the surface, it may appear that Reshotko is claiming that some things can be both unconditionally good, *and* extrinsically and instrumentally good; but her usage of 'unconditional' is heterodox, and what she is in fact claiming is that there is never any circumstance in which virtue will fail to be instrumentally good. That instrumental goods should differ in this sort of way is, of course, most interesting, but we should note that it is *not* a point about unconditional goods, *strictly speaking*.

[30] See Korsgaard (1983: 193), who considers and rejects the view that conditional goods can become unconditional goods by being good in all contexts; the problem with this view, she says, is that it obscures the important differences in 'internal relations' between conditional and unconditional goods within the agent. Rather, a conditional good whose conditions are met is still a conditional good, because its goodness consists in 'its having been decently pursued'.

good is so not because of the ubiquity or frequency of its goodness, but because of its *active role* in the *production* of goodness in other things.[31]

This is why unconditional goods are differentiating. We may be able to speak of various 'conditions' under which all kinds of things may (fail to) be good, but when we speak of goodness full stop the fundamental distinction is that between what flows from the source of all goodness, on the one hand, and what is that source on the other.[32] This is especially clear in the context of eudaimonism, where we must distinguish between the good things that one incorporates into one's life in a rational way, and what it is that so incorporates them. At present we are speaking of conditional goods not in just any context, but in the special context of determining what makes something good as part of a person's happy life. In this context, the conditions on something's goodness are of a specific kind: since no thing or even project could ever make itself the right part of your life, just by itself, the condition on the goodness of things in your life is your

---

[31] Lesses (2000: 356), for instance, says that 'ideal friendship'—friendship between virtuous persons—is an unconditional good, since there is nothing to keep such a friendship from always being a good. However, even such friendship is still a conditional good, since it must become differentiated by the virtue of the friends, who make the friendship good. In fact, notice that such a friendship will also be an extrinsic good, since friendships require direction in order to be good; this does not, of course, keep such a friendship from being a final good, or end. This is an important mistake to avoid; indeed, on this line of reasoning Lesses argues that many goods besides wisdom are unconditional goods, and therefore that the 'goods' that Socrates concludes are not really good at all, must be only those goods he had specifically mentioned earlier in the passage, in order to leave room for other goods (such as ideal friendship) that are goods in the way that wisdom is (see Lesses 2000: 352). This reading lacks textual support, however, and flies in the face of Plato's manifest intent in this passage to show that wisdom is a *unique* kind of good.

[32] As Korsgaard (1983: 181) puts it, the unconditional good (for Kant, the 'good will') acts as 'the source and condition of all goodness in the world; goodness, as it were, flows into the world from the good will, and there would be none without it'. This 'flow', she argues, transpires as the rationality with which one chooses with respect to a thing 'confers' value up on it, 'as the object of a rational and fully justified choice. Value in this case does not travel from an end to a means but from a fully rational choice to its object. Value is, as I have put it, "conferred" by choice.' (Korsgaard 1983: 182 f.) The unconditional good, then, is strictly speaking defined in terms of its role as an active, productive force in bringing goodness about in other things that have no goodness of their own (cf. Korsgaard 1983: 179 f., 183 f.).

Two caveats are in order. For one, it should be clear that appealing to this distinction between conditional and unconditional goods in the context of Platonic ethics does *not* commit one to the view that Platonic 'wisdom' is identical to Kantian 'good will'. I shall claim only that they occupy broadly the same conceptual space in a specific context, namely that of the producer of goodness in other things through the rationality with which one acts. (For Kant, good will is, we might say, the flourishing of the rational self, whereas Platonic wisdom or virtue is the flourishing of the whole self, including what Kant calls the 'empirical' human nature. See also Sherman 1997: 15–20.) And, for another, although Korsgaard sometimes speaks of conditional goods (e.g. paintings) as things that are good only if certain conditions are met (e.g. only if the paintings can be viewed; see 186 f.), and unconditional goods as good in all circumstances (see, e.g., 178), this is not definitive of the basic distinction, but an application of it to extended sorts of test-cases (see 184). On the contrary, when she speaks of things as having value *as part of one's life*, the condition that makes them good is their having been chosen, desired, and pursued in rational ways, the latter being unconditionally good. In such cases, the condition under which a conditional good is good, is in fact the unconditional good—choice and pursuit in accordance with right reason—that gives them their value in the first place (e.g. 180, 182 f., 190). This is a feature of the distinction that eudaimonists should certainly take advantage of.

giving them the right place in your life, that is, your desiring, choosing, and pursuing them in a rational way. In this context, then, the most fundamental distinction between unconditional and conditional goods is that between the wisdom of the agent who acts, and the things in regard to which the agent acts wisely—just as Plato says it is. This is because happiness is both a matter of what you *do* with your life, and a matter of what *you* do with your life.[33]

Second, a proper understanding of conditional and unconditional goods further explains how extrinsic goods can be final goods. Some extrinsic goods will depend for their value on ends that they serve as means, but not all will. A wisely pursued career is an *extrinsic* good, since it depends on something else to make it good, but it can still be an end, since its goodness need not depend (or depend entirely) on some further end that it serves; it can depend instead on the wisdom with which it is pursued as an end. Conditional goods are extrinsic goods, and they can be ends, rather than means. In fact, the vast *majority* of ends in a person's life will be conditional, extrinsic goods; after all, *everything* in a person's life needs to be given direction by wisdom, and the dependence of these things on wisdom for their goodness does nothing to keep them from being valued for their own sake.[34]

And third, conditional goods have no power with respect to happiness. This is in fact the point of making such things conditional goods, properly understood: they do not have any power with respect to happiness to be unleashed, by virtue or by anything else. Understanding goodness as a function of something's role with respect to one's life and character, as opposed to a quality that something can simply *have*, just like that, shows that it is a mistake to think that conditional goods, however worth while they may be, somehow make one happy by virtue of what they are. Moreover, this fact also reveals the significance—and indeed the *necessity*—of making *virtue* the unconditional good: virtue is the intelligent agency that rationally incorporates all the dimensions of a life into a harmonious and integrated whole. Virtue is the unconditional good because it is the only thing that *could* be—it is *agency*, active and directive, and it directs in accordance with *right reason*; *that* is why virtue can play the appropriate *productive* role that unconditional goodness requires, and why it is on *virtue* that everything else depends for its goodness. It is not the case that virtue is part of a happy life only if it is made the right kind of part of one's life, since there is no way to make being the right kind of person the wrong part of your life.[35] A moment's thought shows why virtue—understood as the proper working of one's soul as

---

[33] Notice, then, that in the context of eudaimonism it is not enough to say merely that virtue is the condition on which other things can be good, but why virtue should be that condition—why, that is, virtue plays the special role that that condition plays. This point is very often overlooked, because, I suspect, the special nature of the conditional/unconditional distinction within the context of eudaimonism is insufficiently appreciated.

[34] It is therefore important to note that I do not share Vlastos's view that the only things valuable for their own sake are those that make a contribution of their own to happiness (Vlastos 1991: 207 f., 224 f.; cf., e.g. Brickhouse and Smith 1994: 103); I shall return to this below.

[35] As Aristotle puts the point, there is no need to bring a virtue into a mean, as it just *is* the mean (*Nicomachean Ethics* II.6, 1107a22–7). Notice, however, that we cannot say the same for 'virtuous projects', such as feeding the hungry; I shall return to this below.

a whole—must be this kind of good: virtue is not one thing among many to be incorporated into one's life, well or badly, but the thing that does the job of incorporating other things into one's life well.

These observations about conditional and unconditional goods have some important consequences. One is that conditional goods are coextensive with extrinsic goods. They are in fact two sides of one coin: extrinsic goods rely on something else to bring about goodness in them, and thus are conditional goods; and conditional goods are not differentiated in their own right, and thus are extrinsic goods, requiring differentiation from some other source. Another is that unconditional goods are coextensive with intrinsic goods. With respect to happiness, no thing, state of affairs, or project is good by its own nature, except for one's wise behavior in relation to all other things. Consequently, the only thing that could be good in its own right is the agency that directs our behavior according to right reason. Likewise, as we have seen such agency is the only thing that *could* be unconditionally good: agency is active and directive, and so is the only thing that could bring about the right kind of direction in all areas of a person's life, the only thing that could play the active, differentiating *role* of an unconditional good.[36]

We can now understand the difference between the directive and the additive conceptions of happiness as follows. On the directive conception of happiness, the unconditionally good is what determines happiness: happiness depends on the wise agency with which one directs all the aspects of one's life, since it is on this agency that goodness in one's life ultimately depends. On the additive conception, however, conditional goods are what determine happiness: it may take wisdom in order for one's pleasures, desires, or projects to be good, but once they are good, they assume or reveal—somehow—their own power to make a person's life a happy one.[37] Moreover, we can also see how wisdom, on the directive conception, makes other things good: it does so by changing our attitudes, priorities, and actions so that we give other goods the right place in our life, in accordance with right reason.

---

[36] This, of course, is why Kant says that only the 'good will' is unconditionally good (*Grounding* 393 f.); and the details of Kant's thesis aside, we can surely appreciate the motivation behind the idea that the unconditionally good must be the *kind* of thing that the good will is, namely a form of wise agency.

[37] In a recent article, Dimas (2002) evidently tries to have it both ways: on the one hand, goods besides wisdom 'boost' happiness when directed by wisdom (the additive conception; see esp. 3 f.), and, on the other, success is internal to the very exercise of wisdom, which is constitutive of happiness rather than productive of some other benefit (the directive conception; 13 f.). Consequently, he is committed to the view that, somehow, both wisdom and other goods are involved in producing value, *and* that those other goods have no value themselves (10 f.); he reconciles this by claiming that, whilst wise behavior constitutes happiness, other goods do not merely provide opportunities, but opportunities that their recipients *certainly will* take—opportunities that those goods will 'induce' their recipients to take (16 ff.). This rather convoluted view is the result of trying both to make wisdom constitutive of happiness, and to give other goods some power of their own with respect to happiness. By contrast, Chance (1992: 69) notices and calls attention to the important shift in the *Euthydemus* from happiness as depending on *things*, to happiness as depending on the *wise use* of things. We cannot have it both ways.

1.1.2   The directive conception of happiness in the Euthydemus

Now that the distinction between the additive and directive conceptions of happiness is clearer, as are the fundamental value-theoretical categories underlying that distinction, we should focus on three features of Plato's discussion of happiness and goodness in the *Euthydemus* that make it clear he is arguing for the directive conception and rejecting the additive conception. First, although Plato lacks the technical terminology to distinguish intrinsic from extrinsic goods, he does grasp the distinction itself. Recall the following passage:

'... [A]ll of the things we said at first were goods—well, the account of them is not about how they *themselves*, in *their own right*, are good by their very *nature* (αὐτά γε καθ᾽ αὑτὰ πέφυκεν ἀγαθά) ... but when intelligence and wisdom lead them, they are greater goods—although neither of them *themselves*, considered in *their own right*, are of any value at all (αὐτὰ δὲ καθ᾽ αὑτὰ οὐδέτερα αὐτῶν οὐδενὸς ἄξια εἶναι).'   (281d2–5, d8–e1)

Here Plato clearly distinguishes between different *sources* of value: things besides wisdom may be good, but they are never good in themselves, by their very nature. Since this is precisely the point of contrast for Plato between such goods and wisdom, which alone he says is good without adding any qualification (281e4–5), wisdom must be good by its very nature and in its own right—it must be *intrinsically* good—while all other goods are *extrinsically* good. By drawing our attention to this contrast, Plato is arguing that what determines happiness is the wisdom that has its own goodness and its own power to make other things good—that is, he is arguing for the directive conception of happiness.

Second, Plato focuses on wisdom as the key to happiness because of its *active, productive role* in bringing about goodness in all the areas of a person's life. This is why Plato tells us that wisdom plays a special role among goods, because all other goods depend on being 'used' properly in order to be good, while wisdom determines the goodness of all other things by 'using' them properly; only wisdom is *differentiating* of other things, and thus *unconditionally good*. Plato focuses on the directive conception of happiness, by drawing our attention away from the ingredients of one's life as the key to happiness, and onto the wise agency that gives one's life direction.[38]

Here we also see how wisdom makes other things good. Although Plato compares wisdom to skills like carpentry, he also draws some important contrasts. For one thing, while other skills literally use things as tools or supplies, wisdom 'uses' things in quite a different sense. For while Plato speaks of how ordinary skills 'use' other goods, and use them well,[39] when he turns to knowledge and wisdom he glosses 'using' (χρῆσθαι) as 'leading' (ἡγεῖσθαι): 'the correct use of all these sorts of things', Socrates says, 'is knowledge, which leads

---

[38] This rules out, then, the view that wisdom makes other things good by using them as instrumental goods toward some purpose that is a final good, such as virtuous activity or even happiness itself. For the former view, see Brickhouse and Smith (1994), (2000a), (2000b); for the latter, see Reshotko (2001), and Irwin (1992), (1995), who identifies happiness with desire-satisfaction.

[39] See 280c1, 5, 280d3, 6, 280e2, 3, 5, 281a2, 3, 8.

and directs (ἡγουμένη καὶ κατορθοῦσα) our behavior' (281a8–b1), and Plato continues to speak of 'leading' when he describes the difference between wisdom and ignorance in handling the things in our life (281d6–e1). Plato gives this gloss on 'use' because wisdom 'leads and directs' not other goods themselves, but our *behavior* or *activity* (τὴν πρᾶξιν) with respect to them (281b1). Unlike carpentry, which literally uses tools and materials, wisdom is a skill that directs *us* as we go about our lives; the 'materials' of this skill are not in the *first* instance money, health, or beauty, but *how we behave* with respect to money, health, and beauty.[40] Wisdom makes money good for its possessor, not by bringing about any change in the *money*, or even by pursuing or accomplishing some particular project with the money, but by bringing about a change in the *agent* where money is concerned. Wisdom is not one skill among many, but a skill of living, which puts every part of one's life together in a rational way.[41]

Wisdom makes other things good, then, by giving them the right place in one's life, a place that they cannot give themselves. For example, if Jack is especially good looking, his good looks may turn out good or bad for him; if he becomes vain, or manipulative, gets by with fewer talents, exploits sexual partners, and so on, he will be worse off than if he had been plain but sensible, honest, talented, and loving. So when Jack incorporates his looks into his vicious way of life, his looks are part of the wrong direction of his life. Now, we cannot say that Jack's good *looks* have made him worse off; rather, *Jack* has made *himself* worse off by giving his appearance the wrong place in his life.[42] Consequently, the value of things like good looks, Plato says, is fluid (281b–d): value is not in the ingredients of one's life, but in how one puts together one's life as a whole; and so Plato says of such goods, 'if ignorance should lead them, they're greater evils than their opposites, to whatever degree they are able to encourage the bad person who is leading them' (281d6–7). Conversely, wisdom makes such things good by rationally incorporating them into one's life. My career, friends, and family do not determine or augment my happiness, if I am wise; *I* determine my happiness, by giving my career, my friends, and my family the right place in my life, so that my life becomes well lived where these things are concerned. That is why Plato says of such things 'when intelligence and wisdom lead them, they are greater goods' (281d8). Wisdom makes other things good, then, by making our behavior rational with respect to them. The right use of other goods, Plato says, is the rational control of ourselves.

[40] It is, of course, simpler (if less precise) to make this point by saying that wisdom directs a person's wealth, etc., as Plato does at 281d.

[41] Cf. F. White (1990: 126). *Con.* Brickhouse and Smith (1994: 109), (2000a: 143), (2000b: 84–7), who argue that wisdom deals with other goods by using them as instrumental goods for the pursuit of virtuous projects (e.g. feeding the hungry), and by arranging one's circumstances so that such instrumental goods will be available. The wise person will surely make such uses of other goods, but this cannot be the whole story, as by itself it does not account for the fact that wisdom is in the first instance a skill that directs one's *self* with respect to other goods.

[42] And notice that a person can make that sort of mistake with anything: possessions, a career, even friends and family, and *even* 'good deeds' like feeding the hungry or sheltering the homeless—one can give *any* of these things the wrong place in her life.

Finally, notice that on this understanding of wisdom as a skill, the goodness of one's life consists in the *exercise* of that skill in one's life—one's living one's life in a rational way—rather than in what wisdom secures or accomplishes. Consequently, the directive conception motivates Plato's claim that success consists in the very exercise of wisdom. According to Plato, the success of wise activity is completely *internal* to the activity; or, as Socrates says:

'Wisdom,' I said, 'surely *is* good luck (Ἡ σοφία δήπου, ἦν δ' ἐγώ, εὐτυχία ἐστίν)—even a child would know *that!*'
He was surprised; after all, he is still so young and naïve. Recognizing that he was surprised, I said, 'Don't you know, Cleinias, that *aulos*-players have the very best of luck when it comes to playing a song for the *aulos* well?'
He agreed.
'And so,' I said, 'for masters of letters, when it comes to reading and writing?'
'Certainly.'
'Well, do you think that anyone has better luck with the perils of sea than those who are wise about seamanship, on the whole?'
'Certainly not.'
... 'So,' I said, 'do you think that you'd have the very best luck by acting with a wise person, rather than an ignorant one?'
He agreed.
'Therefore, it is wisdom that makes people have good luck, in every case. I mean, surely wisdom wouldn't ever go astray in any way, but must always act correctly and have good luck—otherwise, it wouldn't be wisdom.'
We ended up agreeing (I don't know how) that, in summary, the matter is this: when there is wisdom, the one who has it has no further need of good luck.   (279d6–e6, 280a4–b3)

According to Plato, if you have wisdom, you do not need to tack on any goods of fortune in order to be successful, because wisdom *is* good fortune (σοφία... εὐτυχία ἐστίν, 279d6).[43] Plato's claim that a wise captain succeeds at sailing[44] cannot be that a wise captain would never let himself be exposed to peril or could always overcome it; wisdom is neither omniscience nor omnipotence. But the wise captain, even in perilous conditions, can still succeed at *sailing well*, as an intelligent, skillful, and prudent captain would sail. Moreover, Plato says that that sort of success is all the success one ever needs, since with such success there is 'no further need of good luck' (281b2–3).[45] On Plato's

---

[43] *Con.* Irwin, (1992: 205 ff., 211 ff., 214 f.), (1995: 67 ff., 76 f., 117 ff.), cf. (1979: 141, 194, 223), who argues that on Plato's view wisdom is sufficient, but not necessary, as an instrument for success.

[44] Actually, Plato says that the wise captain succeeds 'on the whole' (ὡς ἐπὶ πᾶν, 279e6). With this premise so qualified, we would need a further premise to conclude that the wise captain sails successfully, just in virtue of sailing skillfully. This, I think, is the reason for Socrates' remark that he does not know how he and Cleinias arrived at that conclusion (280b1); thus, while Plato is *offering* this view of success here, I do not think he is fully *articulating* it here. I shall return to this below.

[45] *Con.* Brickhouse and Smith (2000*b*: 80), who claim that good luck in this passage is twofold, including both those good things that one cannot control, and those good things that one can; all that Socrates means, they say, is that there is no need to add the *latter* kind of good luck to wisdom. However, there is surely no textual support for this idea in the *Euthydemus*, and in fact Socrates seems to reject such a view, as he says that when wisdom is present, *no* added good luck is needed (οὕτω τοῦτο ἔχειν, σοφίας παρούσης, ᾧ ἂν παρῇ, μηδὲν προσδεῖσθαι εὐτυχίας, 280b2–3). If Plato's view in the

view, success is determined not by the completion of some action, but by how one *engages* in all action with wisdom and intelligence. Success, then, is not so much a 'what' as it is a 'how'—it depends on how one does whatever one does, because success at acting wisely must always be available to a wise person, who has no need of further good luck.

This view of success is possible only on the directive conception of happiness. If our success in life is always available, so long as we act wisely, then happiness must depend not on the things that we secure and accomplish, but on the wisdom with which we behave where they are concerned.[46] And it is for this reason that for Plato there is only *one* unconditional good: intelligent agency, or what Plato calls wisdom. Wisdom is the only thing differentiated as good just in its own right, and the only thing differentiating with respect to other things. Plato's argument, then, is that wisdom is the only unconditionally good thing, because only wisdom could have the power of intelligently directing one's life as a whole, so that wisdom alone has the power to determine happiness.

It seems clear, then, that in the *Euthydemus* Plato is defending the directive conception of happiness against the additive conception, since he makes happiness depend on what is good in its own right and productive of all other goodness, which he says is wisdom, or intelligent agency. The directive conception of happiness explains why Plato says in the *Euthydemus* that only wisdom is good by its nature, and not made good by something else. It explains why wisdom is a skill, since wisdom brings about goodness in other things. It explains why things besides wisdom are not good in their own right, since they are conditional goods relying on wisdom to bring goodness about in them. It explains why things besides wisdom, even when they have been made good, are none the less powerless with respect to happiness, since they are conditional goods that have no such power. It explains how wisdom directs, in the first instance, not the circumstances of our lives, but our behavior and our attitudes in response to those circumstances. And it explains why wisdom is successful in its very exercise, since happiness depends on the rationality with which one acts.[47]

Euthydemus is that there is a form of good luck that wisdom itself lacks, he certainly is doing all that he can to conceal it, as he says merely that with wisdom there is no further need of good luck, *simpliciter*.

[46] Recently, however, Brickhouse and Smith (2000*b*: 85–7) have argued that success is always available to the wise, *and* that success consists in accomplishment rather than mere exercise, by arguing that wisdom judges what accomplishments are possible given the resources at hand. Fair enough, but the more we take this line seriously, the more we are pushed toward seeing the key to happiness as the rationality with which one acts, rather than in accomplishing specific types of action, such as exhorting one's neighbors to righteousness, or giving to the needy (what they call, in general, 'beneficent activity', (1994: 109), cf. (2000*a*: 143), (2000*b*: 86). I discuss this view in the next section.

[47] At *Laws* I, 631b–d Plato again seems to suggest an account of goods similar to that in the *Euthydemus* when he distinguishes 'human' benefits like health, beauty, physical strength, and wealth from 'divine' benefits like good judgment, rational self-control, justice, and courage. For he claims that the former depend on and look toward the latter, and that the latter include and thus ensure the former. This suggests the view, as in the *Euthydemus*, that human 'benefits' are not good in themselves, but serve as 'matter' for proper use, where it is that use itself that is good. We see this again at *Laws* II, 661a–d, in the Athenian's argument that conventional goods (health, beauty, wealth, etc.) are not good *simpliciter*,

1.1.3 *The additive conception of happiness: some alternatives*

The fact that the directive conception of happiness makes sense of Plato's claim that wisdom is success is especially telling. Alternative accounts of how wisdom makes other things good tend to suppose that it does so by using those things to bring about other things, which are the things that happiness really consists in. Notice first that such alternatives are versions of the additive conception, since they make happiness consist (in whole or in part) in conditional goods that wisdom has put to use and which then acquire their own power with respect to happiness. And second, none of them—*because* they are versions of the additive conception—can take Plato's thesis about wisdom entirely seriously, since on the additive conception success *cannot* be the exercise of practical wisdom alone, but must consist in something that wisdom secures or accomplishes. I shall consider here three alternative accounts of how wisdom is related to happiness in the *Euthydemus*: first, the view that happiness consists in noble pursuits that wisdom makes possible; second, the view that happiness consists in the satisfaction of desires that wisdom makes it possible to satisfy; and third, the view that wisdom determines happiness, but conditional goods none the less make further contributions of their own to happiness.

Some scholars explain how wisdom makes other things good by focusing on the notion of 'use' in skills that use materials and tools, arguing that wisdom uses things like wealth as instruments to achieve other goals. Thomas Brickhouse and Nicholas Smith offer one such view, on which goods besides virtue are instrumental for virtuous activity. On their view, money, for instance, is a good for the virtuous person, who uses it as a means to what they call 'beneficent activity', such as exhorting one's neighbors to righteousness, as in Socrates' case, or giving to the needy.[48] So as a hammer has value in so far as it facilitates a carpenter's activity, things besides virtue have value when they facilitate virtuous activity. Virtuous activity and everything else, on this view, differ as final and instrumental goods, respectively.[49]

---

but are valuable to just and pious people, and a curse to unjust people. However, he also claims there that conventional evils *are evil* for just people, and conventional goods *are good* for just people. But we need not suppose this to mean that conventional goods and evil are good and evil in their own right (see also Annas 1999: 42), but only that things like health and strength are helpful for the just, but not for the unjust (and likewise, *mutatis mutandis*, for things like sickness and weakness). For things like sickness hold back the just in a way that they do not hold back the unjust, since being held back is a hindrance to be avoided only if one is held back from good action. Nor is this to maintain that things like health are necessary for happiness, since what is necessary for happiness are not such goods themselves, but the place one gives them (or their opposites) in one's life. *Con.* Bobonich (1995: 138), who suggests that health may be part of what contributes to the happiness of the wise and part of what contributes to the unhappiness of the unwise (say, by facilitating more unwise behavior).

[48] Brickhouse and Smith (1994: 109), (2000*b*: 86), cf. (2000*a*: 143). Irwin (1992: 205–13), (1995: 117 f.) also makes goods besides virtue (and even virtue itself) instrumental goods, but says that they are instrumentally valuable inasmuch as they are useful for desire-satisfaction, which on his view constitutes happiness. We shall turn to Irwin's view below.

[49] Actually, Brickhouse and Smith capture this value-theoretical distinction as a distinction between what they call 'dependent goods' and 'independent goods' (see esp. 1994: 103 *et passim*).

Note that this view would explain both why virtue has a different kind of value from other things, and what it means for virtue to 'make' other things good by 'using' them. And surely there is no denying that many goods besides wisdom will be good because of their instrumental value for virtuous purposes; money is a ready example. But why should we think that this is *the* difference— or even the main difference—between wisdom and other goods? After all, it is difficult to see how things like pleasure might be *instrumentally* valuable at all, and it is extremely difficult to see how things like health, friends, and family are to be *only* instrumental goods that one uses to further virtuous projects (would it be virtuous in the first place to treat them as such?).[50] Glossing the difference between virtue and other goods as the difference between final and instrumental goods cannot capture all the ways that a skill of living constructs a good life.

But, aside from this problem, this view also presses the notion of 'use' too far, effectively ignoring Plato's gloss on 'use' in the case of wisdom as 'leading and directing our behavior' (ἡγουμένη καὶ κατορθοῦσα τὴν πρᾶξιν, 281b1). Plato's point is that whereas a carpenter's tool is a hammer, say, the wise person's 'tool'—what he 'uses' or directs—is actually *himself.* In that case, the things that the wise person acts in regard to can be either instrumental *or* final goods. The central issue is not how he uses them to accomplish some other goal, but how he puts his life together with respect to them.

Finally, and perhaps most importantly, notice that this view conflates the thesis that virtue consists in virtuous *activity* with the thesis that virtue consists in virtuous *projects.* As Brickhouse and Smith correctly note, Plato holds that one is to be called happy because of what he does, and not merely because of some inert but admirable state of his soul.[51] In this sense, 'virtuous activity' is used synonymously with 'virtue', the addition of 'activity' serving only to clarify that by virtue we understand a specific psychic constitution which is essentially

However, it is not entirely clear exactly what the latter distinction is, since it often seems to straddle both the extrinsic/intrinsic distinction and the instrumental/final distinction. Consider their definition of an independent good as 'a good in virtue of nothing other than itself', and of a dependent good as 'a good in virtue of its contribution to or employment by some good other than itself' (1994: 103). Consider also such statements as 'anything other than wisdom that is good has its goodness dependent on the agent's wisdom' (2000*a*: 138); this may be saying that such things are good for the sake of wisdom, or that they have their goodness instilled in them by wisdom (and their treatment of the dependence relation seems to go both ways). This ambiguity is especially unfortunate since extrinsic goods can be final goods; note also that 'intrinsic' is treated as the opposite of 'instrumental', at (1994: 104). Their distinction between 'dependent' and 'independent' goods, then, is not adequately sensitive to the value-theoretical categories that we need to distinguish. However, their comment (2000*b*: 84 f.) that on their view things like good looks, when not required for virtuous action, have no value at all strongly suggests that their concern is the distinction between instrumental and final goods.

[50] See also *Republic* II, 357b–c, *Gorgias* 467c. See also Bobonich (1995: 112–16) for criticism of such a narrow conception of use.

[51] Brickhouse and Smith (1994: 114), citing *Gorgias* 507b5–c5. See also Aristotle, *Nicomachean Ethics* I.5, 1095b30–1096a4, who also rejects a 'static' conception of virtue as an account of happiness.

practical and active.[52] However, from this observation about virtue they conclude that

Socrates drives home his point, not by arguing merely that the soul of the good person is more orderly than that of the intemperate person, but by showing that the good person always *does well*. What qualifies the good person as being 'blessed and happy' is the fact that he or she succeeds in his or her actions.[53]

But from the fact that happiness is active rather than static, it does not follow that happiness must consist in specific types of projects—'beneficent activity'— that must come off successfully in order for one to be happy.[54] So although the wisdom that Plato has in mind in the *Euthydemus* is clearly a form of *practical* wisdom—it is not a state which might act, but a *skill* with which we *do* act— none the less Plato nowhere suggests in the *Euthydemus* that that activity must be some special type of project to be completed, as opposed to the activity at a more general level of living one's life in a rational way. Plato seems to think of 'doing well' not as completing some noble project but as behaving in a rational way, whatever one is doing, and however uncooperative external circumstances may turn out to be.

In fact, in order to take seriously Plato's account in the *Euthydemus* of wisdom and success, we have to think of wisdom in terms of how one *behaves* in acting, rather than in terms of what one *accomplishes* in acting.[55] Recall Socrates' claim that wisdom itself is not only a form of success (279d6), but is also all the success one could ever need: 'when there is wisdom, the one who has it has *no further need of good luck*' (μηδὲν προσδεῖσθαι εὐτυχίας, 280b2–3, emphasis added). But of course the outcome of every project depends on external circumstances,[56]

---

[52] It is also important to note that it is in this sense that I shall intend the phrase 'virtuous activity' when it appears in this book. It is especially important to keep in mind that I do not intend by this phrase to speak of the activity characteristically associated with a virtue (e.g. as running into a burning building is often associated with courage), as if one could engage in 'virtuous activity' by doing what a virtuous person does, but not on the basis of the kind of internal states from which the virtuous person does it (see also Aristotle, *Nicomachean Ethics* II.4). To engage in virtuous activity, then, is to act from a virtuous character.   [53] Brickhouse and Smith (1994: 114), emphasis in original.

[54] Again, Carneades' distinction between views placing the greatest good in the right kind of *aiming*, and views placing the greatest good in the right kind of *outcome*, is instructive here; Cicero, *de Finibus* V.16–22.

[55] It is worth noting that these two ways of construing virtue as activity correspond to two readings of a notorious passage of the *Apology* (30a7–b4), as saying either that virtue makes good things like wealth, or that virtue makes things like wealth good. Brickhouse and Smith (2000b) defend the former reading, which is in line with their view that virtue needs to produce such goods in order to carry out its characteristic projects. Plato's account of wisdom as identical to success in the *Euthydemus*, however, clearly seems to favor the view that virtue makes things good, since the account of wisdom and success requires that success be a matter of how one acts, rather than what one accomplishes with the cooperation of circumstances beyond one's control. (On the latter reading of the *Apology* passage, see Annas (1999: 49 and n. 58).)

[56] Brickhouse and Smith (1994: 114–17) consider and reject the idea that virtue may be a skill of adapting to the circumstances at hand, on the grounds of *Republic* I, 335b2–e6, which says that virtue must always benefit and never harm others, and on the grounds of *Apology* 38a1–8, which depicts Socrates' divine commission to improve his neighbors. However, the point of the *Republic* passage is not that the virtue consists in constant beneficent projects; the point is rather a modal one, that virtue

even in the case of a wise person who exercises what control he has in arranging for those circumstances that make his projects possible, and even if he undertakes only those projects that seem possible given his present circumstances.[57]

It is important to remember at this point that *all projects—even beneficent projects—are conditional goods*, since all projects can take the wrong place in one's life. I do not do well to feed the hungry, or exhort my neighbors to righteousness, if in doing so I deprive my own children of the time, attention, and guidance they need from me as a parent, say, and which I am obliged as a parent to give them.[58] Projects require direction from a holistic skill of living that grasps all of one's priorities and values and puts them together in the right sort of way. Projects, then, are undifferentiated; and while they *become* differentiated as good when one engages in them in the right way, they are still conditional goods. Conditional goods never become unconditional goods, even when they have been differentiated, for to be a conditional good is to be dependent for goodness on an unconditional good. Wisdom, on the other hand, is unconditionally good, because it is a holistic skill that puts projects together *so that* they can be virtuous projects. And this is why it is so important to distinguish the projects we engage in wisely from the wisdom with which we engage in them: the directive conception of happiness makes happiness depend on the wisdom with which we engage in projects, while this version of the additive conception makes happiness depend on the projects themselves—and for that reason cannot take seriously what Plato says about wisdom and success.

Neither can the view that virtue is instrumentally valuable for, but distinct from, happiness. Terence Irwin defends one such view: since our common-sense[59] conception of happiness requires that one have no frustrated desires, but since one

---

is such as to benefit, and never such as to harm (cp. the analogous Stoic claim at Diogenes Laertius, *Lives* VII.103; Stobaeus, *Anthology* II.5d). Moreover, from the fact that Socrates (or anyone) has a special commission, and even ought to take great trouble to make sure that he can fulfill it, it does not follow that he cannot be happy if circumstances prevent him from carrying it out; nor do Brickhouse and Smith demonstrate that it does. This is to say that Socrates has something to aim at, not that his happiness requires a certain outcome from his aiming.

[57] See Brickhouse and Smith (2000*b*: 83 f.). Brickhouse and Smith claim, for instance, that 'even when it is an exotic disease that must be diagnosed and treated, virtue results in health' (2000*b*: 84); and also, 'if one is in a position to get the best use possible from the resources one has, one will also be in a good position to use one's resources in such a way as to produce other resources one needs' (2000*b*: 86 f.). But, of course, this raises many questions: What if there is no doctor available for the virtuous person to bring in for diagnosis and treatment? What if the disease is too rare to be diagnosed? What if no treatment exists? And so on. Accordingly, they qualify their thesis that virtue guarantees a high level of control over one's circumstances with the caveat that 'what action constitutes noble action is crucially dependent upon the circumstances the agent finds herself in, which are, in turn, dependent upon the agent's assessment of what can be put in the service of noble action' (2000*b*: 85 f.). They try to retain the success of wisdom, then, by arguing that if one makes the best use of available resources, then one will be able to use them to get the resources one needs for success (2000*b*: 86 f.). Even so, they surely cannot maintain that wisdom is a guarantee of success in their sense (see 2000*b*: 87), as man is yet to discover how to *make* circumstances cooperate with his endeavors, however modest those endeavors may be.

[58] Nor do I see how even a divine commission to do so would change this fact.

[59] For the special emphasis that Irwin places on such considerations, see Irwin (1992: 208 f., esp. 213); see also (1995: 68, 106).

cannot always control the circumstances necessary to satisfy the desires one may happen to have, Socrates must base his belief that wisdom suffices for success on the thesis that the wise person adapts her desires to the circumstances at hand, so that she is always guaranteed of having only those desires that she actually can satisfy.[60] On Irwin's view, wisdom is a special kind of good because only wisdom can *guarantee* satisfaction of desires; all other goods are good only in so far as they are generally useful, but not strictly necessary, for desire-satisfaction.[61]

On this view, wisdom is instrumentally valuable for desire-satisfaction,[62] just as all other goods are, but is of greater instrumental value than any other good. Of course, the view that all goods besides happiness (or desire-satisfaction) are only instrumentally valuable will inherit all of the difficulties that plague the view that all goods besides wisdom are only instrumentally valuable, which we discussed above. It also faces a number of special problems. For one thing, on this view wisdom has the same *kind* of value—instrumental value—as all other goods, and this thesis is most pallid in comparison to the clearly *radical* difference that Plato says holds between wisdom and all other goods.

More important, this view also fails to take seriously Plato's point about wisdom and success. As Irwin concedes, while this view enables Socrates to defend the sufficiency of wisdom for success, a serious complication arises on this view for the claim that wisdom is *necessary* for success, since there could in principle be a vicious set of desires that it is feasible enough to satisfy. Accordingly, Irwin concludes that Socrates must have overlooked this fact about his thesis.[63] He must have overlooked it indeed, as in the *Euthydemus* he claims not only that wisdom is both sufficient and necessary for success but also that wisdom *is* success, and all the success one needs. In fact, on Irwin's view, Socrates' claim that wisdom is success must be not merely over-ambitious but patently false, since *desire-satisfaction* is success, while wisdom is distinct from and (at best) sufficient for desire-satisfaction.

Irwin's view illustrates how the additive conception places a gap between a person's wisdom and a person's success, which must be filled by some *further* good that wisdom secures, such as noble accomplishments or, as in this case, desire-satisfaction. But Plato perceives no such gap in the *Euthydemus*. Now Plato clearly realizes that he needs to say more about how wisdom could be the same thing as success—he does, after all, go out of his way to have Socrates concede that he does not know exactly how he arrived at that conclusion

---

[60] See Irwin (1992: 205 ff.), (1995: 117 ff.), cf. (1979: 194, 223). Cp. Tenkku (1956: 73), who attributes to Socrates the view that 'he who has least desires may be satisfied and consequently happy'.

[61] Irwin (1992: 205–13), (1995: 117 f.).

[62] See Irwin (1992: 211 f.), (1995: 67 ff.). Irwin (e.g. 1995: 67, cf. 1979: 141) often bases the instrumentality of virtue on the fact that Socrates believes both that we do all for the sake of happiness (*Euthydemus* 279a ff.), and that if we choose something for the sake of something else, then we do not choose it for its own sake (*Lysis* 220a–b). However, as Lesses (1985: 172) rightly notes, the latter claim in the *Lysis* covers only *distinct* objects of pursuit, and thus implies nothing about objects which are pursued for the sake of objects which they *constitute*. Nor, of course, does *Euthydemus* 279a ff. give any support to the idea that happiness is the only final good.

[63] Irwin (1992: 214 f.), (1995: 76 f.). See also Gosling and Taylor (1982: 74 f.).

(280b1)—but what is clear is that he *does* believe *that wisdom is success*, and we should be able to take that thesis seriously, even if we find that it stands in need of further articulation and defense. However, the additive conception of happiness is *formally incapable* of taking such a claim seriously, since it makes happiness depend on something besides wisdom itself that wisdom brings about. If Plato holds any version of the additive conception, then his silence about the gap between wisdom and success is not merely odd, but simply inexcusable and indeed disingenuous, since it is his declared aim in the *Euthydemus* to investigate what happiness really consists in.

But perhaps this is too hasty. Perhaps there is a way to take Plato's claim about success seriously while maintaining the additive conception after all. Gregory Vlastos argues that wisdom makes other things good because, if one is a wise (virtuous) person, then one will be happy, although goods besides wisdom can increase the wise person's happiness. On this view, virtue may be able to bring about happiness, but such happiness will still admit of further increases when other sorts of goods are added in. Virtue, then, unleashes the power of other goods to make you happier, if only in small ways, so that with them one might achieve not merely happiness, but *complete* happiness.[64]

On Vlastos's view, conditional goods are like salt in one's soup: both have to be added in the right sort of way, but once they're added in properly one improves your soup and the other your life, entirely by its own power and nature (after all, I don't make my soup saltier, the *salt* does), and they fail to do so only if one makes some positive *mistake* about them. Thus wealth, or physical beauty, or prestige, we might say, has a life-improving power of its own, although its power is unleashed only when certain other conditions are met. On this view, a virtuous person's life becomes happier as wealth, or beauty, or prestige is added; they themselves improve one's life, even if some people bungle things so badly that these goods are no longer able to do for them what it is otherwise in their natural power to do.[65] In a word, on this view the meeting of the conditions on a conditional good do not

---

[64] It is therefore important to note that while Vlastos sometimes speaks of virtue as the 'condition' under which other goods are good, he does *not* mean that virtue is an unconditional good in the strict sense. Rather, he means that other goods have just the sort of life-improving value that conventional thought takes them to have, but only if one is a virtuous person. For a discussion of this aspect of Vlastos's view, see Annas (1999: 44), who argues persuasively that Plato's aim in the *Euthydemus* is to deny of such goods precisely this sort of conventional value: 'if conventional goods add to the happiness of the virtuous person in a conventional way—add to her happiness in their own right— then Plato would be switching around between radically different ways in which conventional goods and evils can play a role in virtuous and vicious lives.'

[65] It might be possible to read Aristotle as defending this account of conditional goods—which, in J. Solomon's translation (1984), he calls 'natural goods'—at *Eudemian Ethics* VII.15: 'A good man, then, is one for whom the natural goods are good. For the goods men fight for and think the greatest—honour, wealth, bodily excellences, good fortune, and power—are naturally good, but may be to some hurtful because of their dispositions.' This might suggest that natural goods are good in their own right, in a completely conventional sense, if only something (such as vice) does not obstruct them; in that case, they would not need to be given any special, positive direction in order for them to be goods, although certain kinds of direction may be able to thwart their goodness. I am not persuaded that this *is* in fact Aristotle's view, but I raise the possibility of such a reading only to clarify the sort of view in question. I thank Mark LeBar for bringing this passage to my attention.

make the agent good where that thing is concerned, but *unleash* the goodness that that thing naturally has, its natural power to add to one's happiness.

One advantage of this view, it seems, is that it makes the difference between wisdom and other things a radical one, since only wisdom can determine happiness. Happiness has many ingredients, and among them is wisdom, but wisdom still is not one ingredient among many. Another is that it explains how one might make choices among things, none of which can determine happiness: although health, for instance, cannot make one happy itself, it can make a wise person happier than if he were wise but ill, and thus is worth choosing. And this view also seems to have the great merit of positing no gap between wisdom and happiness, which preserves the spirit of Plato's claim about the identity of wisdom and success. On Vlastos's view, wisdom suffices for happiness, although other goods may be able to increase that happiness.

However, on closer inspection Vlastos's view turns out to have none of these advantages. For one thing, on Vlastos's view it turns out that all good things—not only wisdom—have some power of their own with respect to happiness. But in the *Euthydemus* Plato goes to great length to show that the value of things conventionally called 'good' is actually fluid—they can actually be *bad* things for a vicious person to have—and that they do not have the power with respect to happiness that conventional thought attributes to them. By contrast, on Vlastos's view, while conventional thought about value is mistaken in the case of vicious people, it must have been right all along when it comes to the virtuous; consequently, goods besides wisdom have no power with respect to happiness for vicious people, and yet have a straightforward power with respect to happiness for virtuous people— the power to increase their happiness.[66] This view seems convoluted in the extreme: somehow, things Plato says have no power with respect to happiness turn out to have some such power after all, since it is there for wisdom to unleash.

Interestingly, Vlastos does not say *how* wisdom unleashes that power. He does not see the difference between conditional and unconditional goods as a difference in how goodness is brought about. Rather, on his view, if the possession of wisdom is a materially necessary condition for the goodness of health, say, while there are no such necessary conditions on the goodness of wisdom, then health is a conditional good, and wisdom an unconditional one. The difference, then, is simply a difference in *when* wisdom and health are good, and not in *why* wisdom and health are good in different ways. But, in that case, it is not clear *why* wisdom should have a special role with respect to happiness, nor *why* it should be necessary for the goodness of other things. Those other things turn out to have conventional value, after all; why then should they not make some improvement to the unhappy lot of vicious, foolish people? And if we do not account for wisdom's power with respect to happiness in terms of its active role in producing goodness, why should *wisdom* be the determining condition for other goods, and why should *it* be unconditionally good itself? Yet as soon as we understand the

[66] See Annas (1999: 44).

distinction between conditional and unconditional goods as one of active role, and thus come to have the much-needed answers to these sorts of questions, it is no longer clear how a conditional good could have its own power with respect to happiness to be unleashed in the first place.[67] Vlastos's view, then, cannot make out the difference between wisdom and other goods after all. Here the directive conception does better: virtue is the unconditional good because it is the only thing that can play the reasonable, active role of the unconditionally good.[68]

Moreover, Vlastos's view is neither plausible nor necessary as an account of how we choose among things that do not determine happiness. Vlastos argues that Plato must allow things besides wisdom to have some power with respect to happiness, in order to explain why, in Vlastos's colorful example, a wise person would have a reason to choose a clean bed over a filthy one.[69] But notice how odd it is to think that the reason one would choose to spend the night in a clean bed rather than a filthy one is that the cleanliness of one's bed will make a difference with respect to the happiness *of one's life as a whole.* Many things may hang on sleeping in one bed versus another, but presumably the tenor of one's very existence is not one of them. Of course, Vlastos recognizes that such low-level cases may strain our intuitions about happiness, and so he focuses on more monumental goods, such as freedom from a gulag. But this does not change the fact that Vlastos's claim applies across the board to all goods besides virtue, including less-than-monumental goods of the very sort that Socrates himself focuses on. And why shouldn't the reason for preferring a clean bed to a filthy one, and freedom to a gulag, be exactly what it seems to be—that filthy beds are nasty, and gulags are awful places? On the directive conception, this is just what we can say. The difference between wisdom and other goods is a difference in unconditional and conditional goods, and thus a difference in what does and what does not determine happiness. But of course even conditional goods, such as physical comfort, hygiene, and freedom, can be valued and even prized entirely for their own sake, since the distinction between conditional and unconditional goods is simply different from the distinction between instrumental and final goods. There is no puzzle about how we should choose between other things, even if wisdom is all that determines happiness.

---

[67] See also Annas (1999: 42): '[Conventional goods] can, presumably, encourage and sustain virtuous activity by facilitating virtuous action, but they do not add to the happiness of the life of the virtuous in their own right. . . . They can't produce or remove happiness in their own right; only virtue and vice can do that.'

[68] It is not enough, then, merely to point out that virtue has a unique role with respect to happiness; we must also show what it is about virtue that gives it this special role. This point is frequently overlooked: scholars recognize that virtue has a special role with respect to happiness, but very few offer an account of why it should be *virtue,* rather than something else, that should have this special role. Of course, it sounds very edifying to say that virtue has this role, but as Epicurus pointed out we are not entitled to edifying-sounding claims about, merely on the grounds that they sound edifying ('Those who place [the highest good] in virtue alone and do not understand what nature demands—transfixed as they are by the luster of the word ["virtue"]—will be set free from the greatest error if they should consent to listen to Epicurus,' Cicero, *de Finibus* I.42, my translation). We have to argue for such claims, and that means showing exactly *what* kind of power virtue has, and exactly what that power *does.*   [69] Vlastos (1991: 215 f.).

Vlastos's view that a thing's goodness must be explained in terms of its own contribution to happiness is motivated by his belief that eudaimonism entails that all goods are good in virtue of conducing to happiness.[70] Vlastos appeals first to *Symposium* 205a2–3: 'Of one who wants to be happy there is no longer any point in asking, "For what reason does he want to be happy?" This answer is already final.'[71] Vlastos concludes that all things that are desirable for their own sake, that is all final goods, 'must be components of happiness, for this is the only way in which they could be desired both for their own sake (as they are said to be) and for the sake of happiness (as they must be, for [according to *Symposium* 205a2–3] happiness is "the question-stopper"—the final reason why anything is desired . . .)'. Of course, from the fact that there is nothing beyond happiness for the sake of which one could desire happiness, it does not follow that everything we desire for its own sake must be a component of happiness. The missing premise, according to Vlastos, comes at *Gorgias* 499e7–8: 'The good [= happiness] is the final end (τέλος) of all our actions; everything must be done for its sake.'[72] And so Vlastos argues that if (1) happiness is the only end beyond which nothing can be desired—the only thing that is *all* that we want—and if (2) everything else we desire we desire for the sake of that end, then (3) everything besides happiness that we desire must make some contribution to our happiness. But Plato is not committed to premise (2); all that he says in *Gorgias* 499e7–8 is that our actions with respect to instrumental goods must in the end be explained in terms of *some* final good we intend to achieve by them, in other words, that the instrumental value of one thing entails the final value of some other thing.

Here again the directive conception of happiness does better: money, say, and physical comfort cannot do anything to make a person happy, under any conditions, but one's *attitude* toward money and physical comfort can make a tremendous difference in one's happiness. And, on this account, there is nothing to keep a person with the right sort of attitude toward money and physical comfort from preferring plenty to poverty, or a clean bed to a filthy one, for its own sake. Eudaimonism requires that our particular ends be unified by our final end of living a happy life. It does not prevent those particular ends from being ends in the first place.[73]

---

[70] See Vlastos (1991: 207 f., 224 f.). See also, e.g. Brickhouse and Smith (1994: 103).
[71] Trans. Vlastos (1991: 203).   [72] Ibid., 224 f. The insertion of '[= happiness]' is Vlastos's.
[73] Indeed, consider the view of Seneca: ' "Well, then," says the opposition, "if virtue is not impeded by good health and repose and freedom from pain, will you not seek these things?" Of course I shall, not, however, because they are goods but because they are in accordance with nature and because I shall avail myself of them judiciously. And what good will they involve? Simply this: proper choice. When I put on clothing that is appropriate, when I walk as I should, when I dine as becomes me, it is not the dinner or the walk or the clothing that are good but my own program of observing in every act a measure which conforms to reason. I must add that choice of becoming clothing is a desideratum, for man is by nature a tidy and well-groomed animal. Becoming clothing is therefore not a good per se, but the choice of becoming clothing is; the good lies not in the thing but in the quality of selection. Our modes of action, not the things we do, are honorable' (*Letter to Lucilius* 92.11–12, trans. Hadas 1958). On Seneca's view, it makes sense to prefer presentable clothing to shabby clothing (*ceteris paribus*) not because presentable clothing has any value of its own, but because it is better for beings like us

Perhaps the greatest problem for Vlastos's view, however, lies in his assumption that happiness can be incomplete, and can be improved and increased by degrees, if only small ones. But happiness is what we predicate of a life when it is a success, and when nothing is missing;[74] indeed, that is the point of Plato's making it a truism that happiness is always the final answer to questions about what we want: happiness is the final thing we want, because there is nothing beyond it that we *could* want—that is what happiness stands for. If beyond happiness there is something further—'complete' happiness, say— then happiness cannot be the 'question-stopper' that Plato says it is, after all. Consequently, by specifying that by 'happiness' he means that beyond which nothing more could be wanted, Plato has misled us, just as Socrates has misled Cleinias by holding out virtue as the key to our complete and final end of happiness.[75] As Cicero said, happiness is by its nature complete: 'What can be less commendable', he asks, 'than [the view] that someone should be *happy*, but not happy *enough*? Whatever is added to something that is enough, is too much; but no one is *too* happy, so no one is happier than happy.'[76]

---

to choose things that suit our dignity; it makes sense, then, to prefer presentable clothes to shabby clothes, even though the clothes have no value of their own, because the *choice* of the presentable clothes is good, and is in accordance with right reason. See Russell (2004: 250 ff.); *con.* N. White (1990), who, in my opinion, is not sufficiently sensitive to this line of thought in Stoicism. We shall return to this line of thought in Ch. 5; for further discussion of the idea that happiness as the final end is consistent with pursuing other final goods that do not conduce to happiness, see Russell (2003).

[74] See also Aristotle, *Nicomachean Ethics* I.7, 1097a24–b24.

[75] Likewise, Reshotko (2001: 333 and n. 19) claims that, for Socrates, virtue suffices not for happiness, but for the greatest degree of happiness possible given one's circumstances, or what she calls 'maxhap'. This view replaces talk of happiness as potentially incomplete with talk of happiness-like states that do not, in fact, qualify as happiness on account of their incompleteness. But this is no solution of the problem; again, Socrates claims that wisdom is *success*, and not something success-like, but not in fact success, which on this view turns out to require the cooperation of external circumstances after all—precisely the thesis Socrates is at such pains to reject in the *Euthydemus*. Reshotko's view, we should notice, seems to be motivated by the assumption that happiness is a goal to be reached by virtuous action in much the same way that a finish line is a goal to be reached by running; in both cases, the goal is something that one may be said to approach by degrees. But it is not at all clear to me how happiness could be an independent goal that one might achieve by means of a certain kind of living, as opposed to a goal that consists in a certain kind of living.

[76] My translation; see Cicero, *de Finibus* V.81–3. Cicero is responding to Antiochus' defense of the view that while virtue is sufficient for happiness, it is not sufficient for *complete* happiness, which requires other goods in addition. Likewise, Vlastos (1991: 216 n. 64) argues that since one unhappy person can be unhappier than another (citing *Gorgias* 479d, *Euthydemus* 281c2), it must follow that happiness can admit of degrees as well. But, while Vlastos is aware of the similarity of his view to the one Antiochus discusses (n. 63), he shows utterly no concern over Cicero's objection. Modern critics have been no more convinced than Cicero was; see Annas (1999: 43 f.); Bobonich (1995: 108–11); and Irwin (1979: 248 f.).

This fact explains, I think, why Brickhouse and Smith go to so much trouble to make all goods besides virtue instrumental goods. As we have seen, they hold the additive conception of happiness inasmuch as they make happiness dependent on wise activity rather than on the practical wisdom with which one acts, and on the additive conception goods are to be understood as good in virtue of their contribution to happiness; but since they also hold that happiness is complete, the only contributions to happiness that goods besides wisdom could make would have to be instrumental, and not constitutive.

Consequently, notice that on Vlastos's view the gap between wisdom and success resurfaces. At first sight, Vlastos appears to avoid that gap, since he allows wisdom to determine happiness. But the gap has merely been moved: instead of a gap between wisdom and happiness, we now have a gap between wisdom and *complete* happiness, to be filled by various 'mini-goods' and their curious power to make happiness complete. And so Vlastos's version of the additive conception inherits the same fatal problem as all the others: it requires a gap between wisdom and success that Plato insists is not there.

Thus our choice between an additive and a directive conception of happiness comes down to a choice between happiness as depending on what wise agency secures through activity—the ability to engage in certain kinds of activity, or the ability to satisfy desire, or the availability of goods besides virtue, or indeed pleasure—and happiness as depending on the wise agency with which we engage in activity. Plato's view that wisdom is success clearly declares for the latter, and only the directive conception of happiness can tell us exactly why that should be so: wisdom is success because happiness depends on the practical intelligence that puts one's life together.

1.1.4 Success in the Euthydemus

We should also notice, however, that Plato's presentation of the idea that wisdom is the same as success in the *Euthydemus* is seriously incomplete in some important ways. First, as we have seen, Plato makes a point of showing Socrates concede that he does not know exactly how he arrived at that conclusion about wisdom and success (280b1). And Plato has good reason to be reserved in his confidence in this conclusion, since it is one thing to say that the wise are lucky as a rule (ὡς ἐπὶ πᾶν, 279e6), and luckier than the unwise, and quite another to say that with wisdom, there is no further good luck *at all* that one could need for success (μηδὲν προσδεῖσθαι εὐτυχίας, 280b2–3). We need more of an argument to the effect that the very exercise of wisdom is its own success than Plato offers in the *Euthydemus*—and, I think, Plato knows it.[77]

Furthermore, it is clear, to be sure, that Plato thinks that success lies in the very exercise of wisdom, and not in some other state of affairs that wisdom (generally) accomplishes. However, it also seems that his skill analogy works against him here, since skills like carpentry are valuable in virtue of what they produce; and so it is not clear how the idea that wisdom is constitutive of happiness could be made from within the analogy of wisdom to a productive skill. Plato is aware of this problem as well, as he draws attention to it in the second protreptic in the *Euthydemus* (288d–293a; see especially 291d–293a) without resolving it.[78]

Finally, without further explication of the notion of 'wisdom' Plato may be in danger of collapsing the directive conception of happiness into the additive

---

[77] It is for a reason, after all, that Brickhouse and Smith (2000*b*: 80) distinguish luck that concerns what one *can* control, from luck that concerns what one *cannot* control.

[78] For further discussion of this problem, see Annas (1993).

conception. Wisdom, we may worry, is too narrow—too 'intellectualist'—to take us all the way to an account of happiness in a human life as a whole.[79] We are, of course, rational beings, but we are also affective beings, and our emotions, our desires, our passions, our pleasures, and our pains are parts of our lives as well. To leave them out of account is to give an account of happiness that may be too pallid to be recognizable *as* happiness. And it is also to account for happiness by appealing to one dimension of one's life, as the additive conception does, rather than to the integration and harmony of the whole of it. The directive conception, by contrast, focuses on wisdom as the determinant of happiness because only wisdom is capable of integrating and harmonizing the whole of one's life. But in the end the directive conception will be no more holistic than the additive, unless it can be shown that wisdom is not something local and narrow—merely one dimension of one's life among many—but rather subsumes the whole of one's self. And that is no easy matter.

I wish to explore these issues in the following chapters. I shall argue in the next chapter that Plato does manage to articulate and defend his identification of wisdom with success after all, in the *Gorgias*, although I do not believe that he will be able to capture this point from within the skill analogy. Moreover, in the next chapter and those that follow, I shall look more closely at the relationship between wisdom, or virtue, and pleasure, arguing that Plato does understand wisdom as holistic in the right way for happiness, subsuming pleasure and the other aspects of the agent's humanity within itself.[80] In order to understand the holism of Plato's conception of wisdom and virtue, we must look more closely at how virtue 'incorporates' parts of one's life, and one's pleasures in particular, into one's life as an integrated, harmonious whole.

1.2   Virtue, Pleasure, and the Good Life: 'Rational Incorporation'

As we have seen, practical intelligence makes one happy by making one whole: in every area of her life, the wise person has the outlook, attitudes, and priorities that it makes sense and is healthy for a fulfilled, reasonable human being to have. Practical intelligence, in other words, rationally incorporates all the dimensions of one's life into a healthy and integrated whole. We have already seen quite a bit that is important about rational incorporation, and given a number examples of it in relation to things like wealth, careers, physical beauty, family relationships, and so on. But although we have spoken of certain 'external' goods (e.g. wealth) as well as 'bodily' goods (e.g. good looks), there is an important class of goods missing: what we can call 'psychic' goods, such as cleverness, wit, and good memory, as well as

---

[79] I thank Bill Artz for pressing this point in an earlier version of this chapter.

[80] However, in the final chapter I shall discuss Plato's failure at developing a unified philosophical psychology to account for the holism of wisdom that his account of the good life requires.

such affective states as emotions, desires, pains, and pleasures. These are important, since they turn out to have a rather special relationship to virtue.

For our purposes, there is a most notable difference between psychic goods and other kinds of goods: whereas rational incorporation—what Plato calls 'good use', or 'leading and directing'—of external and bodily goods is giving our behavior the direction it needs with respect to those goods, psychic goods will often be constituents of our behavior itself. Directing my behavior with respect to wealth, for instance, will be a matter of how I act and prioritize with respect to wealth, as well as how I formulate desires for wealth, how my emotions change with gains or losses in wealth, ways in which I enjoy gains in wealth and am pained at losses, and so on. Bodily and external goods, then, are the kinds of things that you can direct in this way or that, but your pleasures and your emotions are always parts of the *you* who does the directing.[81]

It is therefore important to understand *how* psychic goods such as pleasure are rationally incorporated into a good life—especially because such goods are conditional goods, and thus depend for their goodness on the direction they take in one's life. Many philosophers have said that although we reject certain pleasures, we never reject them as the pleasures that they are, but only on account of the consequences that might follow them.[82] But this cannot be quite right, because pleasures require a direction, and without the right kind of direction certain pleasures can become evils. Our estimation of a shoplifter or her actions, for example, surely does not improve if we learn that the shoplifter takes enormous pleasure in her shoplifting, is proud of it, finds other people's losses amusing, or what have you; on the contrary, such pleasures only make the shoplifter worse. This is because, as we saw in the introduction to this book, a person's pleasures tell us a great deal about what type of person she is—for better *or* worse. If pleasure were always good, and forgone only when it would prove a bad bargain, we should be *less* troubled by the pleased shoplifter than by an indifferent one, and much less than by a regretful one: if pleasure were intrinsically good, then the world should be a better place, if only by a little, for the pleasure that the shoplifter experiences in shoplifting, even if the world would be better off, all things considered, if she stopped shoplifting altogether. But of course just the opposite is true: the fact that she enjoys shoplifting as worthwhile makes her behavior only that much worse.[83] Here, pleasure understood as an affective capacity for finding value in things around us has

---

[81] We would also need to distinguish from these goods the goods of having people that we love in our lives; for such people, it seems, also become 'part' of us in a way that wealth cannot—however much I come to love money, it can never become a 'second self' for me (see Aristotle, *Nicomachean Ethics* IX.4, 1166a31–2)—but then again they are not literally the sorts of 'parts' of us that the parts or dimensions of our psyche are. And there are yet more distinctions between conditional goods that a complete account would need to draw. But I am unable to pursue the point here.

[82] A *locus classicus* of this view is Bentham's discussion of the 'four sanctions' in the first chapter of *An Introduction to the Principles of Morals and Legislation*.

[83] Cp. Aristotle's remarks on the 'self-indulgent' person, who does what she sees is wrong, but does so by choice and without regret, and is therefore worse and less corrigible than the incontinent person (*Nicomachean Ethics* VII.4, 1148a13–7, VII.7, 1150a16–32, VII.8).

been incorporated into a person's life in the wrong way, since this person is finding value in the wrong sorts of things, and that is a serious strike against the quality of her life considered as a whole. The oft-heard refrain that no pleasure is rejected for its own sake seems plausible only as long as we restrict our thinking to pleasures as sensations (does it always seem plausible, even then?), but of course that restricted way of thinking does not take us very far in thinking about pleasure in our life as a whole.[84] But if we think of pleasure as a kind of affective attitude that ascribes value to the object of the pleasure—an attitude that has real ethical significance—then it seems quite clear that we do reject certain pleasures *as* the pleasures that they are, and even praise some pains as the pains that they are.[85]

Notice also that the direction that pleasures need is a direction that must be brought to them by something else. They do not direct themselves. For this reason, it is also particularly implausible to think of psychic conditional goods as having their own life-improving power, even if only in certain kinds of lives; for saying so suggests that there is some direction that they take on their own. But although our pleasures and our emotions always go in some direction or other, they do not take any particular direction under their *own* power. They do so only as part of the character of which they have become part. Since it is the direction within one's character that determines whether such goods actually do us any good or not, we cannot say that they do us either any bad *or good* under their own power. It takes vice to make them bad, *and* it takes virtue to make them good;[86] there is no such direction that they have by default. Such pleasures, then, will be good or evil depending on the direction the agent gives them in her life. Consequently, such pleasures are conditional goods, and require rational incorporation—and rational incorporation of a rather special type, since such pleasures are themselves kinds of attitudes and behaviors, rather than merely things in relation to which we behave and form attitudes.

How, then, does virtue give good direction to a psychic good? If rationally incorporating something like wealth means directing my behavior with respect to wealth, how do I rationally incorporate my pleasures, which are *part* of my behavior? Virtue directs a psychic good, I suggest, by making that good a part of virtue itself. While a person has a virtue with respect to wealth when wealth is

---

Of course, we might defend the view that pleasures can be 'bad' only in the sense of having painful consequences by claiming that our repulsion by the shoplifter's pleasure is due to the fact that such behaviors *tend* to lead to more painful consequences later on. And, as far as I am concerned, anyone who is satisfied with such a just-so story is welcome to it.

[84] We shall further explore the inadequacy of this conception of pleasure for eudaimonism in Ch. 2, as we examine Socrates' refutations of Callicles' hedonism in the *Gorgias*.

[85] e.g. consider Aristotle's claim that a feeling of shame or remorse is an admirable thing in a young person who has erred; *Nicomachean Ethics* IV.9.

[86] And I think that a good case can be made for reading Aristotle in this way too, even in the passage of the *Eudemian Ethics* I mentioned above: we identify things that are good by nature for human beings by determining what things are part of the life of a person whose nature has been fulfilled and actualized, for only in such a person do these goods take on the right sort of direction in a human life.

given the right sort of place in his or her life, wealth itself cannot become part of his or virtue itself—it is not part of the psyche at all, and thus not part of the good order of one's psyche. But, as we have seen, other dimensions of our lives are not like that. When pity or fear is given the right sort of place in a person's life, not only does that person have a virtue *with respect to* pity or fear, but she also has a virtue *of* pity, or a virtue *of* fear. In other words, to give your emotion of pity the right place in your life is not to develop the right attitude toward something distinct from the 'you' that deliberates about such things, but rather to develop a sense of pity that is itself virtuous, pitying the right people, for the right reasons. This is, moreover, why we say that wisdom is neither static, nor a matter of accomplishing noble projects. Wisdom is active, but its function in the first instance is to unite all the dimensions of one's life by rationally incorporating them; this is why the 'good use' of these things is wisdom 'leading and directing our behavior'. Some dimensions of our life wisdom incorporates by transforming our attitudes with respect to them, and others it incorporates, I argue, in so far as they are the very attitudes that it transforms.

This is, I think, an especially plausible model for understanding how wisdom rationally incorporates pleasure into a good life. Pleasure is a good within the self, and when transformed by reason, it becomes not merely directed by virtue, but a part of one's virtue. My capacity for finding enjoyment and fulfillment in the things that I do needs to be given direction by right reason if I am to live well, and reason directs this dimension of myself when I take pleasure in the sorts of things that it is good that I take pleasure in. In that case, my pleasure becomes one of the ways in which I find value in things, people, and activities around me, taking joy in the value and importance that it is reasonable for me to place in them. So understood, we can see that pleasure is always a part of a person's character, for better or worse; and this seems plausible, since, as we have seen, few things tell us more about people's characters and who they are than the sorts of things that they find rewarding and enjoyable. In a virtuous person, pleasure is part of good character. Good character is one that is directed by reason, but here the 'directing' is a matter of reason's suffusing all the practical dimensions of the self—emotions, desires, pleasures, pains, attitudes, priorities, and so on—with intelligence and harmony, so that they are not so much 'controlled' by reason, as they are harmonized, transformed, and indeed 'informed' by reason.

The details of this account of pleasure and the good life are still far from clear, but it is this account that I shall develop and articulate in the following chapters, as we find it unfolding in a number of Plato's dialogues. For that reason, I turn now to the *Gorgias*, where Plato develops the directive conception of happiness in just those respects in which the *Euthydemus* is incomplete. In the *Gorgias* Plato shows, for one thing, how virtue can be both productive and valued for its own sake, by showing how virtue can be its own product, and, for another, how virtue, so understood, can be the same as success, or happiness. This is an especially important result, as it seems to settle recent debates over whether Plato in the *Gorgias* allows for happiness to consist in the pleasure that virtue brings. For to affirm that he does is to assume a gap between virtue and happiness to be filled by pleasure, and, as we shall see, this is precisely the sort of gap that Plato in the *Gorgias* argues is not there. After the *Gorgias* I shall turn to Plato's *Phaedo*, where I argue that the idea of a conditional good does real work. In particular, it is only by understanding pleasure as a conditional good that we can make complete sense of all that Plato says about pleasure in the *Phaedo*. And in the chapters that follow (Chapters 4–7), we shall look more closely at the rational incorporation of pleasure, the relation of pleasure and virtue to each other and to happiness, and the shape of the psychological model that Plato needs in order to sustain his account of pleasure and its place in the good life.

2

Pleasure, Virtue, and Happiness in the *Gorgias*

Plato believes that wisdom, or virtue, is successful in its very exercise. We see this in the *Euthydemus*:

'Wisdom,' I said, 'surely *is* good luck (Ἡ σοφία δήπου, ἦν δ' ἐγώ, εὐτυχία ἐστίν)—even a child would know *that*!' . . . We ended up agreeing (I don't know how) that, in summary, the matter is this: when there is wisdom, the one who has it has no further need of good luck.   (279d6–7, 280b1–3)

Wisdom is good luck, and it is all the good luck one could ever need for success. Successful exercise of the skill that wisdom is, then, must be completely internal to the exercise of it. Plato explains this idea by pointing out that whereas other skills use tools and materials, wisdom 'uses' other things by directing the agent's *behavior* with respect to them: 'the correct use of all these sorts of things is knowledge, which leads and directs our behavior' (281a8–b1). The correct use of other things is the rational incorporation of them into one's life, which is, in fact, the transformation of one's attitudes, values, priorities, and choices with respect to them—it is a matter, that is, of what sort of place one gives such things in one's life. Consequently, such things have no goodness of their own; where they are concerned, goodness or badness comes into being as such things are given either a good or bad part of one's life, rationally or irrationally incorporated into one's whole life. And to incorporate all of the dimensions of one's life into a rational, integrated whole is to live a successful, flourishing, happy life, which is, after all, what we all want. Agents become good in relation to things, and in doing so flourish as agents.

   This position rests on a number of theses, none of which is beyond question. For one thing, Plato supposes that we can speak of one's life as a whole and the quality of it, and that people can, and do, and should think about their character in terms of their life as a whole. He also supposes that a life so considered has a goal—a *single* goal—which should be characterized as the happiness of one's life as a whole. Of course, these ideas are commonplace in ancient virtue ethics, and their articulation and defense in ancient virtue ethics has received considerable attention.[1] But certain other controversial ideas within Plato's position demand our more immediate attention here. Consider Plato's treatment of wisdom as a productive skill, an idea that was to prove extremely controversial in the ancient world. In the *Euthydemus* Plato construes wisdom as a skill that yields an *outcome*, as navigation is for producing safe arrivals, military skill is for producing victorious campaigns, and medicine is for producing cured bodies (see 279e–280a). But, as critics have noted, this notion of a skill is in tension with Plato's idea that a skill can be successful just in virtue of how one engages in it. How could it be the case both that wisdom produces something—it is, after all, a form of *practical* intelligence—and that its success none the less consists in its exercise, rather than in its producing a distinct outcome?

This is a deep problem. Recall Plato's thesis that success, or flourishing, or happiness, consists in the rational incorporation of all the dimensions of one's life—that is, in the wisdom with which one lives one's life. I have argued that this is the thesis that emerges when we take seriously the nature of conditional and unconditional goodness with respect to happiness. But even if we are convinced that the unconditionally good—wisdom, or intelligent agency—makes for a good life, why should we think that it is *all* that a complete and fully successful life should require? Isn't this a disturbingly thin conception of human flourishing? In particular, while this view shows that wisdom is the *efficient cause* of happiness—what brings a happy life into being as a happy life—why should we think that wisdom is also what *constitutes* the happiness that it creates? This question is clearly related to the question about skill: if wisdom is what produces, how can it also constitute what it produces? And, even if we accept this point about wisdom, it is still another matter to say that the *skill analogy* could ever support it. In fact, Plato himself draws attention to this very problem for the idea that wisdom is a skill in the *Euthydemus*, only to leave Socrates in *aporia*.[2] And so in the *Euthydemus* it is left as a puzzle how wisdom could be a skill, *and* could be valuable entirely for its own sake, rather than for its distinct product.

Unfortunately, there is no reason to think that Plato ever came to see clearly how wisdom can be successful in its very exercise from *within* the skill analogy, in the *Euthydemus* or anywhere else. Moreover, even leaving questions of skill aside, we have seen in the previous chapter that Plato explicitly draws attention to a lacuna in his very argument (280b1) for the claim that wisdom is successful

---

[1] For a good recent discussion see Annas (1994a), esp. ch. 1. It is also worth pointing out that there is considerable controversy at present about whether and how character traits have any bearing on action and explanations of action; but I shall not take that question up here.

[2] See 288d–293a, esp. 291d–293a. On this problem, see esp. Annas (1993: 63–6), and also (1994a: 397 ff.), who recognizes that this is in principle a surmountable problem, and one which the Stoics in particular did later surmount. The product of wisdom, on the Stoic view, is a life lived according to reason, and that product is no more distinct from wisdom than the products of such skills as dancing and acting are from the exercise of those skills; see Cicero, *de Finibus* III.23–5. Moreover, the Stoics were able to make sense of wisdom as successful in its very exercise from within their conception of skills generally, which consist primarily in the agent's grasp of the intellectual structure of the skill, rather than in the achieving (or the attempt at achieving) some distinct outcome.

purely in its exercise. What we do have, then, is an idea that Plato takes very seriously, and shapes his view of the relation of wisdom to happiness. What we do not have yet is an articulation and defense of that idea with which Plato himself is fully satisfied. So what we need is an argument for this conception of happiness and success that is grounded in our nature as rational human agents.

The *Euthydemus* offers no such argument. But it is here that the *Gorgias* becomes particularly important, for two basic reasons. One, there Plato shows that since our happiness consists in flourishing according to our distinctive nature as human beings, and since our nature as human beings consists in our intelligent agency, our happiness consists entirely in the excellence of that agency. In that case, doing all things well—being active as intelligent agents—would be the same thing as happiness, since to live in such a way is the same as flourishing and being fulfilled as the kind of complete being that a human is by nature (506d–507a, c). And two, in the *Gorgias* Plato holds that the 'product' of wisdom is, in fact, the same thing as the exercise of wisdom, since both the product and the exercise consist in behaving and living well. A person who has the virtues, Socrates says, 'is bound to do whatever he does well', and this means that he will act well with respect to the gods and to other people, with respect to what he chooses to seek and to avoid, and with respect to what he turns away from and what he endures (507a–c)—in short, he will act well in every area of his life. What virtue, or wisdom, 'produces' in such a person, then, is a life in which all of one's various concerns and dimensions are integrated into a rational whole. Wisdom produces a wise way of living, and, of course, this way of living is no different from the very practice of wisdom itself. This way of understanding the 'product' of wisdom also allows us to see that Plato identifies wisdom and success not by making the notion of success thin and narrow, but by making the notion of wisdom rich and full.

In the *Gorgias*, then, we find a more complete articulation of the idea that happiness depends on the unconditionally good, which is the intelligent agency that makes all of the dimensions of one's life take on a goodness that none of them has in its own right. This articulation comes by way of a more detailed look at the practice of wisdom and its relation to the life that it produces, and a more detailed look at the nature of success for human beings as the kinds of beings that they are by nature. And that is to say that in the *Gorgias* Plato offers a more articulated statement and defense of the directive conception of happiness.

However, not only does the *Gorgias* shed light on Plato's defense of the directive conception of happiness, but that conception also sheds light on Plato's discussion of pleasure and hedonism in the *Gorgias*. This is especially significant, as many discussions of the *Gorgias* in recent decades have focused on Socrates' refutation of Callicles' hedonism in that dialogue, asking whether Socrates' refutation is broad enough to count as a refutation of hedonism full stop, or is narrow enough to be compatible with some form of hedonism that Plato himself endorses after all, and very many have argued that the latter is the case.[3]

---

[3] The *locus classicus* for this view is Gosling and Taylor (1982: 69–77, esp. 76). See also Rudebusch (1989), (1992: 70), (1994), (1999: ch. 5); N. White (1985: 146, 150 f.); Irwin (1979: 135, 196 f., 199);

Unfortunately, in the midst of this controversy it has been not so much stated as assumed that Plato is working with what we have called the additive conception of happiness, and so the question simply has not arisen whether the conditional goodness of pleasure (or perhaps of desire-satisfaction) should on Plato's view count against its being what determines happiness. But, as we shall see, all that changes as soon as we recognize that there *is* an alternative to the additive conception, and appreciate the reasons for thinking that Plato preferred that alternative in the *Gorgias*. The question whether or not the arguments in the *Gorgias* are consistent with hedonism, therefore, strikes deep to the very core of Plato's conception of value and the nature of happiness.

I argue in the first section of this chapter that Plato's reliance on the directive conception of happiness explains the general course that Socrates' discussion takes with his companions in the *Gorgias*. More specifically, I argue that his discussion follows the pattern of the *Euthydemus* passage: Socrates and his companion seek to determine what goods happiness consists in; the goods with which they begin turn out to need direction in order to be part of a good life; they conclude that those goods therefore cannot be what happiness consists in, after all; and Socrates concludes that happiness consists in wisdom and intelligence, since these account for the direction and harmony of the whole of one's life. This structure is repeated in each of Socrates' exchanges on the key to happiness in the *Gorgias*—and especially in his refutation of Callicles' hedonism—as each of Socrates' interlocutors abandons his candidate for the good as soon as it is shown that it must be differentiated by something else in order to be good. In that case, in the *Gorgias* Plato must understand the determinant of happiness to be the unconditional good.

In the second section, I take a closer look at Socrates' own argument that virtue determines happiness. Not only does Socrates' argument articulate the nature of virtue as a skill, and the nature of success and flourishing for human beings, but it also removes the gap between virtue and happiness which hedonism—and all forms of the additive conception of happiness—takes to be there, requiring, as it does, that the pleasure of a virtuous life, rather than virtue *per se*, must be what accounts for the happiness of that life. I conclude by discussing some alternative accounts of goodness in the *Gorgias*, focusing especially on the possibility that hedonism need require no such gap between virtue and happiness after all, on the grounds that virtuous activity and the greatest pleasure are identical. Exploring this alternative will, I think, serve to bring the difference between the directive and additive conceptions into sharper relief, and will point in a rather interesting direction for understanding the rational incorporation of pleasure.

C. C. W. Taylor (1976: 170); and the more tentative Tarrant (1994: 116–18). Irwin (1995: 111–14), cf. (1979: 204), argues none the less that the *Gorgias* does reflect Plato's misgivings about, and retraction of, hedonism subsequent to the *Protagoras*, on the grounds that the argument about pleased cowards (497d ff.) presents a serious challenge to any form of quantitative hedonism, and that Socrates denies the priority of pleasure over the good (500a2–4).

2.1　Happiness and the Good in the *Gorgias*

The *Gorgias* represents a joint search among four people for what determines happiness, and can be broken roughly into four corresponding parts—Socrates' discussion with the rhetorician Gorgias (449c–461a); his discussions with Gorgias' students Polus (461b–481b) and Callicles (481b–505c); and Socrates' own account of goodness (505c to the end). In each of these parts we find a different account of what determines happiness, as Socrates' interlocutors each begin with a conception of what the happy life is like, and explain what sort of thing within that life they take to be responsible for its happiness. Since at present we are mainly interested in Socrates' discussion of hedonism with Callicles and his own account of goodness, I shall look at his discussions with Gorgias and Polus only so far as is adequate to display how each discussion is ultimately underwritten by the directive conception of happiness.

2.1.1　Gorgias and Polus on the unconditional good

Gorgias argues that the life of an educated, refined, and articulate person with political power and influence is the happy life (452d). Moreover, the education and the power are connected, since the sort of expertise Gorgias takes this person to have is expertise in matters of justice, that is, in matters of right and wrong (454a–b, 459c ff.), and special skill in these areas brings political prominence and influence. And what is responsible for this person's happiness is, of course, just what Gorgias teaches—rhetoric (449a), or the art of directing public affairs on matters of justice by means of persuasion (454b–455a). Consequently, Gorgias says that this expertise is concerned with 'the most important and valuable aspect of human life' (451d7–8) and the best thing of all (452d5–6), and Socrates takes him to mean that rhetoric is 'the greatest of human blessings' ($\tau\grave{o}$ $\mu\acute{\epsilon}\gamma\iota\sigma\tau o\nu$ $\mathring{a}\gamma a\theta\grave{o}\nu$ $\tau o\hat{\iota}s$ $\mathring{a}\nu\theta\rho\acute{\omega}\pi o\iota s$, 452a5; see also 452b3, c1–2, c6–8, d3–4).

Socrates' reaction to Gorgias' position (460a–461b) is instructive: he responds by arguing that, in essence, rhetoric is the greatest good *only* if it constitutes a moral expertise on the part of the rhetorician, by which he has become a just and morally good person. In fact, Socrates argues that Gorgias himself is committed to this view: if one is a true expert, and a true expert in morality and justice, then how could such a person fail to be moral and just himself? How, that is, could an expert in morality and justice aim at immoral and unjust purposes, while exercising that very expertise? This is an uncomfortable question for Gorgias, who seeks to distance himself from any of the misdeeds of the rhetoricians he trains, just as the boxing instructor is distanced from any abusive behavior that his pupils may commit (456c–457c). But, as Socrates points out, the rhetorician's expertise is in the area of right and wrong, which just *is* the expertise of morally appropriate conduct (460a–461b),[4] and such an expertise as that is very special. Whereas an expertise like boxing can be used in a morally appropriate or

---

[4] Cf. Irwin (1979: 127).

inappropriate way, depending on the moral character of the boxer, an expertise in morality and justice *is* what determines the moral character of the expert. Such a skill, then, is uniquely holistic: other skills can be used in this way or that, depending on one's character, but the skill of justice and morality is what gives all other skills and activities in one's life the right direction. It is no good to say that a student might give the skill he learns from Gorgias the wrong place in his life, as a boxer might do with his skill at boxing; for the skill that Gorgias teaches appears to be a skill of giving all other things the right place in one's life. And there is no wrong place for that skill to occupy in one's life.

Therefore, if rhetoric is the greatest good, then it must be the same as moral virtue in one's character as a whole. But if that is not really what Gorgias takes rhetoric to be, then not only is Gorgias' own account of rhetoric as an expertise of right and wrong highly suspect,[5] but also that expertise will be consistent with living an unjust life, which Gorgias is apparently unwilling to allow to be a happy one—and, in that case, Gorgias must allow that rhetoric is at best a conditional good, depending for its value on something else to give it the right sort of direction in one's life, a direction it cannot supply on its own. Notice, then, that Socrates assesses Gorgias' conception of what determines happiness by questioning whether such a thing could be an *unconditional* good. And as soon as Gorgias' candidate proves to be only conditionally good, in Gorgias' own opinion, Plato brings Gorgias' interchange with Socrates to a close.

Likewise, Polus offers his own view of what a happy life is like, and he even gives an example of the very life he has in mind—the tyrant Archelaus, who had usurped a throne, disposed of all rival claimants, and gone on to live in impunity (471a–d). Unlike Gorgias, Polus is willing to consider happy even those lives that are conventionally regarded as wicked. All that happiness depends on, in Polus' view, is power and personal freedom (461b–481b), since happiness consists in a life of power in which one does whatever one feels like doing in the community (466b–e, 468e).

Here again Socrates responds by questioning whether the alleged good—in this case, the 'power' of doing whatever one feels like doing—could, in fact, be

---

[5] And that would be embarrassing to Gorgias as a professional, especially as a professional who advertises. See Kahn (1983: 80–4), who claims that Socrates is relying on the professional pressure upon Gorgias in constructing this *ad hominem* argument—i.e. an argument designed to show tensions between his interlocutors' manifest beliefs and commitments. (I shall argue in the epilogue that Socrates uses a similar strategy against Protagoras.)

The *ad hominem* nature of Socrates' argument is important to recognize. While it is not, of course, our purpose at present to analyze the merits of Socrates' argument, but only its structure, still I should point out that most objections (like Polus', 461b–c) to Socrates' argument claim that this argument depends on Gorgias' agreement to certain claims—that anyone who knows right and wrong must be a moral person (460b–c), that he will make a student moral (460a), and so on—which Gorgias need not, and perhaps even does not, really accept; see, e.g., Irwin (1979: 126–9). But it seems clear to me that Gorgias will be challenged *even if* these objections hold, and so they are not entirely relevant in the end. For it may be possible for someone to extricate himself from the problems that Socrates poses for Gorgias, but it may not be possible *for Gorgias himself*, given the conception of the good life on which his position and indeed his career are founded.

what determines happiness. The problem that Socrates points out, simply put, is that when we do what we feel like doing, normally we still do so for a *reason*—there is something we take to be good that we want to bring about by doing what we do (467c–468c).[6] However, that means that if someone does what he feels like doing, but it turns out not to be in his interests to have done so, then, strictly speaking, he has not done what he really wanted to do (468d–e).[7] But, in that case, the sort of power that Polus has in mind, and thus the rhetorical ability that gives a person that power (462b–466a), cannot by their own devices give the right sort of direction to one's life and projects (467a, 468c–e).[8] Rather, it would need direction from some other source. In his discussions with Gorgias and Polus, then, Socrates has shown that if rhetoric is conceived as an expertise that gives direction to one's life as a whole, then it is difficult to separate it from moral wisdom, and if rhetoric is anything less than such an expertise, then it is only conditionally good, and thus not the determinant of happiness.

Moreover, when Polus tries to avoid this conclusion by modifying his conception of power to include not only doing what one feels like doing but also doing so with impunity (469c–470a, 471a–d), Socrates points out that Polus is still unable to make power an unconditional good. For Polus agrees that committing injustice is, after all, a contemptible thing (474c7–8), and is therefore[9] a bad thing (475c–d).[10] And here Polus faces a dilemma: if he does believe that committing injustice is contemptible, then he needs to rethink his commitment to a life which can be good independent of justice and morality; and if

---

[6] It is a matter of controversy whether this argument deals with apparent goods, i.e. with what agents take to be good, or whether it deals with the objective good, which is not agent-relative. I suggest that it deals with both apparent goods and with the objective good: on Polus' view, power is the good, and objectively good, although power is the power of obtaining apparent goods. My interpretation of the argument differs considerably from that of Penner (1991); see also Penner and Rowe (1994); Brickhouse and Smith (1994: 87 f.). On Penner's view, the Socratic account of desiring, wanting, and wishing holds that all desiring is *really* for the good, and not merely for what agents take to be good. Likewise, my own view is that Socrates believes that (1) doing what seems best can fail to achieve the goal one aimed at in doing what seemed best; that (2) it is also an open question whether actually achieving that goal is consistent with living well, that is with one's final end of happiness; and that (3) since everyone really wants to be happy, and only the real good will make one happy, everyone really wants the real good. (Of course, the sense in which everyone really wants that needs to be specified; see Brickhouse and Smith (1994: 88–91); cf. Rudebusch (1999: 45 f.).) However, I also believe that *in Socrates' argument with Polus* his focus is limited to (1), which is all that he needs in order to show that one does not live well by doing what seems best to one.

[7] For an excellent discussion of this argument see Rudebusch (1992: 65 f.); Brickhouse and Smith (1994: 85–7).

[8] *Con.* Weiss (1992: 302–4), who claims that Socrates opts to mock Polus' conception of power rather than set about challenging it soberly, even using technically invalid argument.

[9] This argument is, of course, very much compressed here, as it takes a number of steps (474d–475e) for Socrates and Polus to infer 'bad' from 'contemptible', since Polus denies that they are the same thing (474c8–d2).

[10] It is a much-vexed question whether the evaluative terms employed in the argument are all indexed to the same point of view, namely that of the agent; I agree with Irwin (1995: 100), who argues that the point of view in question throughout the discussion is taken by Polus to be the agent's (this is, in fact, how Socrates raises the issue, 469c1–2; see also e.g. 474b3–7). See also Berman (1991a: 270 ff.; and esp. Johnson (1989: 200–2). For the contrary view, see, e.g., McKim (1988: 46); Vlastos (1967); Kahn (1983: 91 f.); Dodds (1959: 249); Irwin (1979: 157–9).

he does not believe that such a life is contemptible, then he must rethink his reliance on the majority of the Athenians as witnesses to his position—and Polus is quite determined to have popular opinion corroborating on his side.[11] Consequently, if a person takes seriously the idea that committing injustice, even with impunity, is a bad thing—and it seems that Polus *does*, in the end, take this idea seriously—then rhetoric and the power it brings are just as capable of achieving bad things as good things, and thus of making a person even worse off (476a–481b); consequently, rhetoric and power, as Polus understands them, are not unconditionally good. And, as he had done with Gorgias, so here Plato draws to a close the discussion of Polus' claim that such a good could be what determines happiness.

When Socrates asks Gorgias and Polus to specify what makes for a happy life, then, Socrates expects them to tell him what is the *unconditional* good, which *by its very nature* is good for its possessor and is what determines his or her happiness. This is manifest in the way in which Socrates criticizes Gorgias and Polus for having failed to specify what makes for happiness, as he points out the conditional goodness of their candidates, that is, the fact that they are not good at all without the right sort of direction from some other source. Just as in the *Euthydemus*, the search for happiness in good things (here, rhetorical skill and power) comes up short as soon as those things are shown to need a direction that they cannot give themselves. It also becomes increasingly clear that, in Socrates' view, happiness must consist in the wisdom and intelligence that accounts for the direction and harmony of the whole of one's life. For this is the point of showing that things besides wisdom and virtue require the direction of wisdom and virtue in order to be good at all; consequently, virtue, and not those other goods, must have a power all of its own with respect to happiness. Moreover, not only is it clear that Socrates is working with the directive conception of happiness but also the fact that his companions become increasingly perturbed with each refutation suggests that they too understand that the search for what determines happiness is a search for what is unconditionally good. And this search for the unconditional good gives us the framework we need for assessing both Socrates' refutation of Callicles' hedonism, and Socrates' own account of what makes for a happy life.

2.1.2 *Callicles on the unconditional good*

Callicles is only too willing to concede what Polus would not—that conventional ideas about justice are mistaken, and even wickedly so (481b–505c). To justify

---

[11] For Polus' great concern with the backing of popular opinion, see 466a, 470c, 471c–d, 472b, 473e, 474b. Cf. Kahn (1983: 94 f.). I therefore put little stock in Callicles' objection that Polus' defeat was due merely to embarrassment or a sense of shame (482c–483a), understood as reticence to stand behind what he really thinks; Callicles is followed in this assessment of Polus as ashamed, by Johnson (1989: 204–6); see also Kahn (1992: 256 f.); and Dodds (1959: 263, 279), who claims that, unlike Callicles, 'neither Gorgias nor Polus had the courage of his convictions'.

his conception of the good life, he appeals not to popular opinion[12] but to 'nature'. Nature, he says, separates people into two kinds: the naturally superior and dominant, and the naturally inferior, who can gain dominance only by restraining the naturally superior people by means of laws and conventions. Nature smiles upon the man who is able to defend himself against all comers; this man is fit by nature to dominate inferior persons (483c–e), taking what of theirs he desires without payment and with impunity, as Heracles drove off Geryon's cattle (484a–c). This is why conventional ideas about justice are *wickedly* mistaken: the run of common people subvert the natural order and establish laws and norms which would keep superior men from asserting their natural right to dominate (483b–e). This natural order, Callicles says, is *true* justice, not the sham justice of common lawmakers and moralists. Therefore, there is no conflict between justice properly understood and the pleonastic lifestyle of one mighty enough to obtain it.

So Callicles gives us a picture of what the happy life is like, but what exactly is it about this life that accounts for its happiness? Here again Callicles departs in an important way from Polus: whereas Polus had conceded that doing whatever one feels like doing is desirable when it fits into a larger structure of goals in the right sort of way, Callicles instead thinks of doing whatever one feels like doing as *an end itself.* There is not some further goal that doing what one feels like doing is supposed to achieve in life; the whole point just is to live without restraint, satisfying one's every desire—this is what Nature wants for her ideal person (492e ff.). Hence the ideal person must not restrict or curb these desires, for to do so would be to succumb to the inauthentic, unnatural values embraced by common people; rather, he must pursue self-indulgence with impunity, as a dictator (491d–492c). This removes the need for fitting what one sees fit to do to what one 'really' wants. Doing as one sees fit, in Callicles' ideal life, can be done just for the sake of it. The point, then, is indulgence for its own sake.[13]

Socrates is surprised at this suggestion: doesn't constant indulgence also require constant desires to be indulged (493b–494a)? Callicles embraces this result, since he thinks that the intensity and greatness of the desire determines the greatness of the pleasure of indulging it; it is by letting desires expand, he says, and satisfying them that one finds happiness:[14]

[I]s being hungry, and eating when one's hungry, an example of the kind of thing you're thinking of?
Yes.
And being thirsty and drinking when one's thirsty?
Yes, and experiencing desire in all its other forms too, and being able to feel pleasure as a result of satisfying it and so to live happily (τὰς ἄλλας ἐπιθυμίας ἁπάσας ἔχοντα καὶ δυνάμενον πληροῦντα χαίροντα εὐδαιμόνως ζῆν). (494b7–c3)

---

[12] See Irwin (1979: 138 f., cf. 147).
[13] For an excellent discussion of Callicles' conception of the good, see Rudebusch (1992); see also (1989: 33–8).   [14] See Irwin (1995: 105).

Socrates is surprised again: would someone whose desires were great for, say, scratching or indecent sexual acts[15] live a happy life just by satisfying those desires (494c–e)? Callicles finds this kind of talk highly distasteful, but Socrates' strategy here is clear: it seems that there are people who possess what Callicles says determines happiness—constant indulgence of intense desires—but who do *not* seem thereby to live the sort of life which Callicles says is the happy one. Rather than deny that intense enjoyment of indulged appetites determines happiness, however, Callicles bites the bullet and allows even such persons as these to be examples of living well (495a–d). Why would Callicles make such an unfortunate concession as that? Actually, it is not difficult to see why he would do so, *if* he appreciates Socrates' approach: if the pleasure of indulgence makes happy only those who lead a certain kind of life, then such pleasure would require something else to give it the right sort of direction after all, and so would not turn out to be unconditionally good. Consequently, if Callicles says that indulgent pleasures are unconditionally good, then he *must* say that all the indulgent are happy. But, in the end, can Callicles coherently maintain this account of what determines happiness?

There are two related features of Callicles' account that, as Socrates' objections will reveal, make it highly problematic. One is that on Callicles' view the good *life* is composed of good *experiences*, namely experiences of great and intense indulgence. As he says, the good is 'experiencing desire in all its other forms too, and being able to feel pleasure as a result of satisfying it *and so to live happily*'. The advantage of this idea, of course, is that it allows him to avoid questions about the desirable structure of one's life as a whole, within which indulgence may not always fit, as Polus learned. But this comes at the cost of denying the image of the naturally ideal person for whose happiness indulgence was meant to account in the first place. And this points up the second issue: in the end, it really *does* matter to Callicles what type of person one is. Callicles did not, after all, start out with the thesis that pleasure was the good, and conclude that the naturally superior person must therefore be happy. Rather, he first identified that type of person—that sort of life as a whole—as the happy one, and then offered the pleasantness of such a person's life as an explanation of his happiness. Callicles does not, then, really dismiss the relevance for happiness of the structure of one's life as a whole, and that threatens his thesis that indulgence could determine happiness, because indulgence is not structured. Reducing happiness to episodes of indulgence, then, is not only desperate but also futile. Or so Socrates insists in a pair of arguments against Callicles' hedonism.

---

[15] As Kahn (1983: 105–7) points out, Socrates' choice of the sexually indecent man (κίναιδος, the passive adult partner in male homosexual relations) here is especially relevant, since being a κίναιδος entailed loss of citizen status in Athens; the life of the κίναιδος, then, is particularly out of line with the kind of public life to which Callicles is committed as the good life.

2.1.3   The refutation of Callicles' hedonism, part 1: happiness, pleasure, and episodes

In his first argument against Callicles' hedonism, the so-called 'argument from opposites' (*c.*495e–497d), Socrates points out that happiness turns out to be quite episodic on Callicles' conception of the unconditional good. And that, Socrates argues, shows that indulgent pleasures cannot be the unconditional good after all: while episodes of indulgent pleasure come and go, happiness does not, and so neither can the good that determines happiness.

Socrates begins by arguing that pleasure is not the good, since it is not related to its opposite (pain) as the good is to the bad. First of all, good things like health and happiness, and bad things like illness and unhappiness, are jointly exhaustive and mutually exclusive: one must be *either* healthy *or* ill, but not neither, and not both—and the same rule applies to happiness and unhappiness (495e2–496b7). Consequently, this rule must apply to the good and the bad as well, since they determine happiness and unhappiness, respectively. And so if we lose or keep any candidates for the good and the bad together, then they are not, in fact, the good and the bad:

> Whenever we find a person losing and keeping the same things at the same time, then, we'll know that we're not faced with the good and the bad. Do you agree with me about this? Please think carefully before answering.
> Yes, I agree without any reservation at all.   (496c1–5)

In fact, Socrates argues, this is just what we find in the case of pleasure and pain. First, all desire is, by itself and as such, unpleasant, whereas the satisfaction of desire is what is pleasant: it is pleasant to eat when one is hungry, for instance, but the hunger itself is unpleasant, and the same applies to other sorts of desires (496c6–d5).[16] Second, the experiences which Callicles recommends—such as eating when one is extremely hungry, say—have *both* a component of desire and a component of satisfaction; therefore, the experience involves pleasure and pain at the same time:

> Now, your position is that the pleasant component of this situation is due to the drinking, isn't it?
> Absolutely.
> It's pleasant for a thirsty person, anyway.
> Agreed.
> Which is to say, for someone who's feeling distress?
> Yes.
> Do you realize what the consequence is? When you say that a person is drinking, you're saying that someone who's feeling is distress is feeling pleasure at the same time. . . . Am I right or not?
> You are.   (496e2–6, 8–9)

---

[16] See Rudebusch (1999: 40–2), who rightly remarks that even if we enjoy building up certain appetites (see Gosling and Taylor (1982: 73)), none the less our enjoyment of them depends on our believing that we shall be able to satisfy them; otherwise, they are simply uncomfortable.

But this is exactly what Socrates and Callicles had agreed we could *not* say in the case of living well and living badly:

Well now, according to you it's impossible to live well and at the same time to live badly.
Yes.
You've agreed with me, however, that pleasure and distress can coincide.
Yes, I suppose they do. (496e9–497a3)

Consequently, feeling pleasure cannot be living well, and feeling pain cannot be living badly, and so pleasure cannot be the good:

It follows that to feel pleasure (τὸ χαίρειν) is not the same as to live well (εὖπράττειν), and that to feel distress (τὸ ἀνιάσθαι) is not the same as to live badly (κακῶς [sc. πράττειν]) either. And therefore the pleasant and the good are different. (497a3–5)

Does this argument work? The argument may give the appearance of being too swift—of being merely clever rather than significant and probative. Perhaps Callicles is mistaken to think that happiness, as a feature of one's life as a whole, should be composed of pleasant episodes, since on that view such episodes, being both pleasant and painful, should compound into both a happy and an unhappy life as a whole.[17] But that is not Callicles' only alternative: perhaps happiness is not determined by the pleasures of particular episodes that are pleasant-on-balance, yet maximizing such episodes in one's life could yield an indulgent *life* as a whole—the life of an indulgent person—with its own characteristic pleasure.[18] In other words, Callicles might deny that happiness consists in the sum of pleasant episodes, yet maintain that the life spent indulging in such episodes is its own kind of life with its own kind of satisfaction and meaning. In that case, pleasure could still be what makes Callicles' happy person happy.

On the additive conception of happiness, this is precisely the sort of tack that Callicles should take: to be happy one must be a person of a specific sort, and it is the characteristic pleasure of that sort of person that accounts for his happiness. And, more generally, if Callicles means to defend some form of hedonism, he need not limit himself to considering only indulgent, episodic pleasures. It is interesting, however, that Callicles takes no such tack at all, but instead grumbles and complains, accusing Socrates of childish behavior (499b). Hence the obvious question: why *doesn't* Callicles take this sort of tack himself, rather than becoming sullen and sulky, as if he'd actually been forced to give up

---

[17] See Irwin (1979: 198) for the view—correct, in my opinion—that Callicles does think of happiness in this way. I am not persuaded by the view that, for Callicles, happiness is a feature of particular episodes and moments, such that happiness of one's life is nothing more than an accumulation of such episodes; see N. White (1985: 149–51); Berman (1991b: 125). Still, it is worth noting that on the latter view Callicles would still be refuted: if a happy episode is identical to a pleasant episode, then since a pleasant episode is a mixture of pleasure and pain, and thus a mixture of good and bad, a happy episode should also be an unhappy episode. N. White (1985: 151) claims that the upshot of such an argument would not be to deny that there are degrees between being fully badly off and fully well off, but to show that, according to Callicles, there can be no such thing as being fully well off.

[18] Cf. Irwin (1995: 107), (1979: 202); see also Gosling and Taylor (1982: 72–4).

something important? If some form of hedonism exists which is viable as an account of the good, why does it never surface in the *Gorgias*?

One reason, some have suggested, might be that Plato wishes to defend some form of hedonism himself, on which the overall pleasure of being a certain sort of person is what makes such a person happy, and thus leaves this possibility up his sleeve. But this is surely rather far-fetched as a reading of the *Gorgias*, and in any case it entails that we cannot understand the *Gorgias'* lesson about the good and happiness on its own terms, the key kept oddly hidden from our view. This is especially unfortunate, since on this view either Plato refuses to divulge what he takes to be the key to happiness, which is after all his declared aim in writing this dialogue, and indeed appears to offer instead a very different account of the key to happiness, which makes no evident appeal to pleasure at all (see 503d–509c); or Plato refuses to allow Callicles the benefit of a superior form of hedonism to consider, preferring instead to attack a weaker version of an opposing view than he knew to be potentially available. On this view, the key to their entire inquiry into happiness and the good lies in something that Plato refuses to allow Socrates and his companions to discuss.[19]

Fortunately, this view is also unnecessary, as it is motivated only by the assumption that Plato must hold the additive conception of happiness. But on the directive conception, Plato's strategy—and Callicles' consternation—becomes clear. As soon as we start to take seriously the idea that happiness means becoming a certain kind of person, we have to fit the projects of our lives—even projects of pursuing indulgent experiences—into a larger structure of goals, if only the goal of being indulgent with impunity. But Callicles' whole point for introducing indulgence as what determines happiness was to *avoid* just such a demand for a larger structure, since the demand for that sort of structure led to Gorgias' and Polus' downfall. Yet to the extent that Callicles thinks of the happy life as being a whole of a particular kind, he must concede that indulgence would require direction with respect to one's life as a whole in order to make that life a happy one. Since that is a direction that indulgence itself cannot provide, indulgence cannot be unconditionally good. On the directive conception of happiness—and only on that conception—Callicles *must* concede that indulgence cannot be what determines happiness—unless, of course, he can find a way to derail and break off the discussion, which is exactly what he tries to do, and what Gorgias takes him to task for doing (497a6–c2).

Even on Callicles' view, then, happiness requires a structure in order for episodes to compound into a happy life, and that means that such episodes are not unconditionally good. This reveals a deep point on Socrates' part: since happiness

---

[19] It is sometimes said that Plato's hedonism is withheld from Callicles because Callicles is not prepared to receive it without distortion. But the question is not whether we can find a just-so story every time we need one, once we have taken it is as a datum that Plato is a hedonist and commenced work on the *Gorgias* on that basis; on the additive view, we usually can find some such story or other. The question is whether the additive or the directive view makes the best sense of the dialogue as a whole and on its own terms.

requires a structure, whatever determines happiness must be *holistic.* Notice why Socrates says that pleasure cannot be identical to the good. Happiness is like health and unlike intense pleasure in at least one important respect. Certain intense pleasures presuppose the presence of pain in order to exist: in order for me to enjoy the intense pleasure of satisfying some sharp desire, I have to have a sharp desire—the pain of wanting is essential to the pleasure of getting what I want so badly.[20] And so in the case of the indulgent pleasures I am pleased *because* I am also in some respect pained. But health is not like that: we do not say that I am healthy *because* I am also in some respect sick; in fact, if I am sick in any respect, then I am not healthy. And the same point applies to happiness: one's life is happy not because it is also in some respect unhappy. This is so because happiness is not happiness-on-balance—it does not consist in a preponderance of happiness over unhappiness, as if the two were mixed together (much less *necessarily* mixed together in order for happiness to obtain), any more than health is a mixture of health and sickness in which there is a preponderance of health over sickness. Happiness is predicated of one's life *as a whole,* and not in virtue of the happiness of some parts of one's life that 'outweigh' the wretchedness of the rest. What determines happiness, then, must bring goodness to the whole of one's life. Because indulgent pleasure is episodic, it cannot account for this goodness, which must be holistic.[21] Indulgent pleasure, therefore, cannot be uncondition-ally good, and thus, on the directive conception, cannot determine happiness. But as soon as indulgent pleasure is replaced with the pleasure characteristic of some way of life, one must open the door again to the idea of a rational structure for one's life as a whole, which is precisely what Callicles meant to avoid. And that is why Callicles finds the argument so annoying.

This problem for Callicles is a general problem for any attempt to explain the goodness of a whole life, with a particular structure that makes it a good life, in terms of pleasure, which does not generate that structure itself but must fit within it. And so the problem that Socrates points out in his first refutation holds not merely for episodic and indulgent pleasures but for all forms of pleasure and thus all forms of hedonism, *if* we take as primary the idea that what matters is the kind of life one leads. Understood as a debate about the uncon-ditional good, then, Socrates' argument from opposites can be seen to be deep, rather than merely ingenious. And it also forces Callicles to focus his attention where it originally was, and where it should have remained: on a conception of the kind of person it is good to become and the kind of whole life it is good to live. Not surprisingly, this is exactly where Socrates directs his second argument.

[20] See Rudebusch (1999), ch. 5, who argues that Socrates distinguishes the good from this sort of pleasure by showing that the good does not depend on the existence of a requisite desire, whereas this sort of pleasure, e.g. drinking when thirsty, does presuppose a requisite desire (namely, thirst). See also Irwin (1979: 201).

[21] Pleasure also fails to be holistic in another way that Socrates points out: we need not, at any given moment, be experiencing either pleasure or pain, but we cannot say the same about how well or how poorly one lives one's life (497c–d)—one cannot do both, one cannot do neither, and one cannot live one's life well in one moment and then poorly in the next.

2.1.4   The refutation of Callicles' hedonism, part 2: pleasure and the life you lead

Socrates next attacks Callicles' hedonism by arguing that it actually turns out to recommend lives that Callicles clearly thinks are worthless (497d–499b). These are, in particular, the lives of foolish people and cowardly people, who of course are just the antithesis of the shrewd, daring man that Callicles takes to be the happy man.

The argument is straightforward. If someone is a good person, Socrates begins, then there must be some quality about him that is good and in virtue of which we call him good (497d–e). Now Callicles agrees that brave men are good, cowards are not; and that clever men are good, fools are not (497e). This is just what we should expect, since 'bravery' and 'cleverness' are just the sorts of features that Callicles sees in his image of the ideal man (468b ff., 491a–d). But, as Socrates points out, it is difficult to maintain that the quality of Callicles' ideal in virtue of which we call him good is his tremendous enjoyment. After all, Callicles does not regard fools or cowards as good people, and yet we find them enjoying themselves—in fact, they tend to enjoy themselves to no less a degree than intelligent and brave people do (497d–498c). Consequently, Socrates says, if we insist that what marks those who live well is the pleasure that they experience, we must also admit that these experiences seem no less common or intense in them than they do in scores of people who, on Callicles' view, live very badly indeed.

Socrates proceeds to drive home his conclusion at great length and with much repetition: if there is little to tell between good and bad people in terms of pleasure and distress, and if pleasure and distress are goodness and badness, respectively, then there is little to tell between good and bad people in terms of goodness and badness. Since there must be something in virtue of which good people are good, and this must of course be some sort of goodness, pleasure and goodness cannot be the same thing:

Didn't you agree that good people are good because they possess good qualities, and bad people are bad because they possess bad qualities? And aren't you also claiming that there's no difference between good and pleasure, or between bad and distress?
Yes, I am. . . .
So anyone who feels pleasure is good, and anyone who feels distress is bad?
That's right.
And aren't people good and bad to a greater or lesser or roughly equal degree depending on whether they experience these feelings to a greater or less or roughly equal degree?
Yes.
And didn't you say that fools and cowards experience roughly the same intensity of pleasure and distress as clever people and heroes, or even that cowards feel more, in fact?
Yes.
Could you help me work out the consequences of our position? . . . [W]hile there's little to tell between good people and bad people in terms of how much pleasure and distress they experience, bad people might experience more?

Yes.

This means that there's little to tell between good people and bad people in terms of how good and bad they are, doesn't it? And that, if anything, bad people are better than good people? Apart from what we've already said, doesn't the idea that pleasure and good are the same have these additional consequences? I don't see how you can avoid this conclusion, Callicles, do you? (498d2–499b3)

How should Callicles respond to this line of argument? This depends on how he thinks of the relation between goodness and happiness. On the additive conception of happiness, he should feel fairly little distress. Notice that Socrates seems to talk as if pleasure were just one thing, such that we could find it among cowardly and courageous people alike. But surely one cannot have the pleasures of a courageous person without *being* a courageous person, any more than one can have the pleasures of visiting the seashore by visiting the prairie. In that case, Callicles could still maintain the identity of pleasure and goodness by specifying the particular sorts of pleasures he identifies with goodness. And there are a number of ways for Callicles to do so: perhaps he could argue that the courageous are better served in terms of pleasure in their lives as a whole than cowards are, or that the pleasures characteristic of the courageous are incommensurably superior to those .of the cowardly, and so on. In any event, if Callicles could show that pleasure of the proper sort—pleasure that has the right sort of direction in one's life—is good, then there should be nothing in Socrates' argument to stop him from identifying such pleasure with goodness itself, and making it what determines happiness.

But, curiously, this is not the course that Callicles actually takes. Instead, he immediately concedes not only that there are good and bad pleasures, but *also* that what is good and worth seeking in life is something quite different from what is pleasant:

Do you [Socrates] really think that I or anyone else would deny that there are better and worse pleasures?
Oh no! You're behaving terribly, Callicles. First you claim that such-and-such is the case, and then that it isn't the case.... It seems that what you're saying now is that there are better and worse pleasures. Is that right?
Yes.
Well, beneficial pleasures are good and harmful ones are bad, aren't they?
Yes.
And aren't they beneficial if they have a good effect and harmful if they have a bad effect?
Yes, I agree....
Good experiences are the ones we should be going for, shouldn't we, whether they're pleasant or unpleasant? They're what we should be concerned with, aren't they?
Yes.
And hadn't we better avoid bad ones?
Obviously.
Yes, because Polus and I decided, as you may remember, that the good in some form or other should be the reason for doing anything.... It follows that the good in some form

should be the goal of pleasant activities (as much as of any other kind of activity), rather than pleasure being the goal of good activities.
That's right.   (499b6–d3, e3–7, 500a2–4)

Why is Callicles prepared to concede so much, so soon? On the additive conception of happiness, there is no reason for Callicles to back down from the idea that pleasure is the good, unless he is too stubborn or too unimaginative to see that those 'good' pleasures could underwrite some new form of hedonism. Again, perhaps Plato has a hidden agenda and wishes to defend just some such form of hedonism himself, despite the confidence with which Socrates appears to think that he has simply put hedonism to rest.

But, again, there is a more plausible answer: Plato has no such agenda, because he subscribes to the directive conception of happiness. For, on that conception, the very fact that pleasures must be directed and differentiated in order to be good is precisely the problem for *any* form of hedonism: in order for pleasures to be good, our pleasures must be given a direction that they do not give themselves. And that is to say that pleasures are conditional goods, and consequently that the goodness of good pleasures is dependent on that agency that differentiates them from bad pleasures. On the directive conception, the materials that our agency makes good do not determine our happiness. Our intelligent agency does that.

And that is exactly the direction that Socrates' discussion takes, once Callicles concedes that there are good and bad pleasures: if pleasures can be either good or bad (499b–e), then since goodness is always our goal (499e–500a), we need intelligence and skill in order to bring about goodness in this and indeed every area of our lives:

It follows that the good in some form should be the goal of pleasant activities (as much as of any other kind of activity), rather than pleasure being the goal of good activities.
That's right.
Now, is just anyone competent to separate good pleasures from bad ones, or does it always take an expert?
It takes an expert.   (500a2–6)

Socrates then argues that rhetoric is not the sort of expertise that we need (500a–503d), but that virtue is, since virtue is an expertise that brings about the kind of organization and harmony that our lives need (503d–505b, 506c–509c), and therefore determines our happiness in life (507b8–c7; more on this claim below). Socrates, we see, is making a crucial turn in the search for goodness: our focus has been on the ingredients of a life as what makes it good or bad, when, in fact, our focus should be on the intelligent agency we need in order to give our lives the direction we need. He is, in other words, steering us away from an additive conception of happiness and toward a directive one—just as he does in the *Euthydemus*—on which happiness depends on the intelligent agency with which one lives one's life.

Socrates' second argument shows a very basic problem for the additive conception of happiness: as soon as we take seriously the idea that it matters *what kind of person* a person turns out to be, we are committed already to the overriding importance of some feature of a person that brings about the kind of shape in everything else about the person that is needed in order to be a person of the right kind. This is exactly the bind that Callicles finds himself in, since he wants to think of happiness as tied to a certain kind of character, but cannot then make that happiness consist in the pleasures of that life.[22] Even if shrewd and bold pleasures are better than, and different in kind from, idiotic and cowardly pleasures, it is still the case that in order for pleasure to become good it must be given the right sort of shape and direction—and it does not supply this shape and direction for itself. And likewise for every other conditionally good thing in one's life.

This turn in the argument has two very important consequences for Callicles at this point in the dialogue. For one thing, it requires him to drop not only the fairly crude hedonism with which he began, but also hedonism of *any* sort at all, because hedonism is the view that pleasure is what determines happiness, and Callicles now recognizes that happiness requires specific direction that pleasure itself cannot give.[23] For another, it requires him to think about what it means to give oneself appropriate direction, and this line of thought leads quite naturally, as Socrates points out, to thinking about psychic health and the temperance—which Socrates treats here as virtue entire—we need in order to make sense of our lives. This is a deep point: it seems that, as Aristotle would later note,[24] people who think about what happiness means are led to think about the moral virtues not (*pace* Callicles) because of unnatural conventions that co-opt their thinking, but because the fact that happiness requires direction leads us naturally to think about what aspects of a person might give the whole person the right sort of direction.

So there is a pattern that we find in both the *Euthydemus* and Socrates' conversations with each of his companions in the *Gorgias*: wherever we begin in thinking about what makes a happy person happy, we are brought back to the

---

[22] Tenkku (1956: 75), notes that Callicles is primarily committed to his ideal life, but argues that for this reason it was unfair of Socrates to introduce the scratcher and the κίναιδος. This objection seems to miss Socrates' strategy of showing Callicles that his conception of the good life is ill served by his conception of the good.

[23] *Con.* Gosling and Taylor (1982: 74–6), who argue that Socrates refutes only Callicles' crude hedonism, and not a more 'enlightened' hedonist view, such as that discussed in the *Protagoras*, according to which happiness consists not in immediate gratification but in the overall, long-term enjoyment in one's life as a whole. However, as they note (74 f.) there is no particular reason to think that a shrewd, daring life will be more pleasant overall than a foolish, cowardly life (and if Plato thinks there is some such reason, then it is disingenuous of him to keep it out of Callicles' defense). What is more, this is again to bring the discussion back to thinking about being the right sort of a person as a whole, which, as Socrates demonstrates, is very awkward for one who thinks that pleasure determines happiness, since pleasure itself cannot give one's life the kind of shape it needs for happiness. Its goodness, then, would be dependent on what did give this shape, leaving pleasure at most a conditional good, thereby refuting the hedonist thesis that pleasure is an unconditional good. It is also worth noting that, for this reason, the suggestion that Plato himself could take seriously the idea that pleasure is the good, although pleasure requires an 'art' or skill (τέχνη) to give it the appropriate direction (as it does in the *Protagoras*), now looks even more implausible; I shall return to this in the epilogue.   [24] See esp. *Nicomachean Ethics* I.7.

idea that happiness depends on a skill of living; for whenever they learn that a candidate good requires our leading and directing it in order for it to be good, Socrates' companions give up their claim that that candidate is, in fact, what determines happiness, rather than the intelligent agency that does that leading and directing. We see this in Socrates' conversation with Gorgias, who agrees that the happy person lives by skill, but is then brought to see that rhetoric cannot be that skill unless it is a holistic skill of living, rather than one skill among many that can be misused and thus requires the direction of a skill of living. We see this pattern again in Socrates' conversation with Polus, who denies that one needs a skill of living on the grounds that all one needs is to be able to do what one wishes, and rhetoric enables one to do that. Socrates points out to him that when we do what we wish, we still want it to fit within a larger structure of action which will make us happy. But it takes a skill to achieve that larger structure of action, and a skill of living, because that larger structure is one's life as a whole, and again rhetoric is not that skill. And we see this pattern also in Socrates' conversation with Callicles, who argues that one does not need a skill of living on the grounds that doing what one wishes need not be desired within a larger structure of action after all, at least when one is powerful enough to do what one wishes with impunity. Socrates points out that giving up on a larger structure of action is to give up on the idea that what one wants is to be a certain kind of person. It is to adopt an episodic conception of happiness, which is both incoherent in its own right and incapable of characterizing a good life rather than a poor one. For Plato, there is no getting around the point that happiness depends on a skill of living that gives one's life the right sort of direction it needs, since happiness depends on what kind of person one is.

2.2 Socrates on Virtue and Happiness

And giving the right sort of direction, Socrates says, is just what virtue does for a person:

Now, what does it take to be a good human being? What does it take to be a good anything, in fact? It always takes a specific state of goodness, doesn't it? I don't see how we can deny that, Callicles.

And whether we're talking about a good artefact, a good body, a good mind for that matter, or a good creature, what it takes for these states of goodness to occur in an ideal form is not chaos, but organization and perfection and the particular branch of expertise whose province the object in question is. Right? I agree.

In every case, then, a good state is an organized and orderly state, isn't it? I'd say so.

So a thing has to be informed by a particularly orderly structure—the structure appropriate to it—to be good, doesn't it? I think so.

Doesn't it follow that a mind possessed of its proper structure is better than a disordered mind? It's bound to be.

But a 'mind possessed of orderly structure' is an orderly mind, isn't it? Naturally.

And an orderly mind is a self-disciplined mind? Absolutely.

From which it follows that a self-disciplined mind is a good mind.... If a self-disciplined mind is good, then a mind in the opposite state is bad. In other words, an undisciplined and self-indulgent mind is bad. Yes.   (506d2–507a7)

There are two things we must notice about this passage. One is that 'self-discipline' (σωφροσύνη) is a source of direction that produces benefit in one's life, and the other is that living according to this direction is to realize the 'specific state of goodness' that makes a human a good human. Let us examine these points more closely.

The self-disciplined mind (ἡ σώφρων ψυχή, 507a5), Socrates says, is the mind that brings about the right kind of order, structure, and harmony within a person that the happy life needs. And this is virtue: not only is self-discipline itself a virtue but it also accounts for the fact that a self-disciplined person is also just and pious (δίκαιος καὶ ὅσιος, 507b4) and courageous (ἀνδρεῖος, 507b5) as well. These virtues differ, Socrates suggests, in terms of what kinds of things they concern (other persons, the gods and family,[25] choice and avoidance), but at bottom they are all the same sort of thing—appropriate action (507b1–8), which is the result of self-discipline (καὶ μὴν ὅ γε σώφρων [sc. ψυχή] τὰ προσήκοντα πράττοι ἄν, 507a7–8):[26]

Now, a disciplined person must act in an appropriate manner towards both gods and his fellow human beings, because inappropriate behaviour indicates a lack of self-discipline. Yes, that's bound to be so.
Well, 'appropriate' is used of the way we relate to our fellow human beings, it means 'just'; and when it's applied to the way we relate to the gods, it means 'religious'. And, of course, anyone who acts justly and religiously is a just and religious person. True.
He's also bound to have courage, because a disciplined person doesn't choose inappropriate objects to seek out or avoid. No, he turns towards or away from events, people, pleasures, and irritations as and when he should, and steadily endures what he should endure. It follows, Callicles, that because a self-disciplined person is just, brave, and religious, as we've explained, he's a paradigm of goodness. Now a good person is bound to do whatever he does well and successfully, and success brings fulfillment and happiness, whereas a bad man does badly and is therefore unhappy. Unhappiness, then, is the lot of someone who's the opposite of self-disciplined—in other words, the kind of self-indulgent person you were championing.
That's my position, and I believe it to be true. If it really is true, it looks as though anyone who wants to be happy must seek out and practice self-discipline, and beat as hasty a retreat as possible away from self-indulgence.   (507a7–d2)

---

[25] It is important to remember that the Greek notion of 'piety' is broad enough to cover not only religious commitments but also commitments to family, friends, and other kinds of associates.
[26] The similarities between Plato and the Stoics with respect to grouping the virtues as kinds of engaging in appropriate action (in Stoicism, τὰ καθήκοντα), differentiated with respect to the different venues of appropriate action, are unmistakable; see Stobaeus, *Anthology* II.5b2; Plutarch, *On Stoic Self-Contradictions* 1034c–d; cf. Seneca, *Letter to Lucilius* 113.24. See also Schofield (1984); and Annas (1994a), ch. 19. It is also worth noting that Cicero seems to follow Plato's lead in the *Gorgias* in treating 'temperance' as a fundamental virtue that perceives what is worth while, fitting, and appropriate for a rational being in every area of virtue; see esp. *de Officiis* I.93–8 (and note similarities in his treatment of greatness of spirit, I.67–9, 93–4, with II.18), cf. *Tusculan Disputations* III.14–18 (where temperance is glossed, somewhat awkwardly, as 'frugality').

According to Plato, virtue determines happiness, because it is virtue that brings the right kind of shape and direction to all the dimensions of a person's life. Throughout the *Gorgias*, Socrates and his interlocutors keep coming back to the realization that direction is what a life needs to be happy, and that the virtues are what bring that direction—that the virtues, in other words, determine happiness. That is, after all, why Socrates is so confident that our happiness depends on virtue (507c–509c), since his entire argument is that virtue alone is unconditionally good.

It is sometimes argued, however, that here Plato's argument relies on a verbal trick.[27] The trick, the objection goes, is Socrates' inference from the claim that the virtuous person 'does well' ($\epsilon \hat{v} \ \pi \rho \acute{a} \tau \tau \epsilon \iota \nu$, $\kappa \alpha \lambda \hat{\omega} \varsigma \ \pi \rho \acute{a} \tau \tau \epsilon \nu$, 507c3, 4) to the conclusion that that person is happy ($\mu \alpha \kappa \acute{a} \rho \iota o \varsigma$, $\epsilon \mathring{v} \delta \alpha \acute{\iota} \mu \omega \nu$, 507c4), which does not follow. All that follows from the claim that the virtuous person 'does well', the objection goes, is that such a person does a good job of whatever he undertakes to do, or behaves in an appropriate manner. It only *appears* to follow that the virtuous person is also happy, since $\epsilon \hat{v} \ \pi \rho \acute{a} \tau \tau \epsilon \iota \nu$ is ambiguous: in the premise, it has the sense of 'behaving appropriately', but in the conclusion, Socrates exploits its other sense as 'faring well' or 'flourishing', that is, having a happy life. Socrates, then, has told us that virtue does well, but he has not told us what it is about a life of doing well that brings happiness. On the additive conception, the force of this objection is obvious, and we can insist on being shown what it is *about* the life in which one does everything well that makes that life happy. And for this reason, we should also note, the appeal to hedonism looks increasingly attractive as a way of filling the gap between behaving well and happiness that Plato otherwise allegedly fails to fill.[28]

But if we take seriously the idea that in the *Gorgias* the search for what determines happiness is a search for what is unconditionally good, then it will become clear that Socrates' conclusion does follow from his premises, *even if* 'doing well' is used in a different sense in the conclusion than in the premises. Consider Socrates' first premise:

The self-disciplined person ($\acute{o} \ \sigma \acute{\omega} \phi \rho \omega \nu$, 507c1) is completely good, i.e. good in every way ($\mathring{a} \gamma a \theta \grave{o} \varsigma \ \tau \epsilon \lambda \acute{\epsilon} \omega \varsigma$, 507c2–3).

This, Socrates says, follows from the fact that, as we have seen, in all the most fundamental areas of a person's moral life—how one chooses and avoids (507b4–8), how one treats other persons, how one performs one's duties and is part of one's relationships (507a7–b4)—the self-disciplined person does what is good and appropriate, bringing proper direction and order to each part of his life: 'It follows, Callicles, that because a self-disciplined person is just, brave, and

---

[27] See esp. Dodds (1959: 335 f.), whose view has been quite influential.

[28] This sort of move is displayed most clearly by Irwin (1992: 207 ff.), (1995: 106–21), who claims that without appealing to desire-satisfaction in the virtuous life, Socrates cannot defend the idea that virtue makes one happy. See also Tarrant (1994: 117), who argues that pleasure is needed as the ultimate explanation of the value of the good.

religious, as we've explained, he's a paradigm of goodness' (507b8–c3).[29] Although Socrates' discussion of the virtues is highly compressed, he makes it quite clear that his point is that the good person is completely good because he has virtue entire. And so Socrates observes next that 'a good person is bound to do whatever he does well and successfully' (507c3–4); and so his second premise is that:

The good person does well and finely whatever he might do (εὖ τε καὶ καλῶς πράττειν ἃ ἂν πράττῃ).

Notice how important this observation is: if Socrates is correct, then he has identified something that will bring about goodness no matter where it is, and which one cannot incorporate into one's life in a bad way. It does not need direction from without, since it is what gives everything its proper direction. And this is, of course, to say that virtue meets precisely that criterion for being the unconditional good that has defined the search for the good throughout the whole dialog. In this regard, virtue is importantly unlike pleasure, or power, or political influence—only virtue can claim to be what *makes* the good life good. Therefore, Socrates should then conclude, as of course he *does* conclude, that

The person who does well at all these things is blessed and happy.   (507c4–5)

This person is blessed and happy because he has the good that gives his life as a whole the kind of direction that it needs to be a happy life. To show that virtue does well at whatever it does *just is* to show that virtue is the unconditional good. This is, after all, exactly the sort of argument we should expect Plato to give at this point, since it reveals that virtue is exactly the kind of skill that Socrates and his companions in the *Gorgias* have come to see that they need for happiness.

For one thing, it is a holistic skill: it cannot be misused or misdirected, and it brings direction to the whole of one's life. For another, virtue is a skill that aims at a certain mode of living that constitutes the ordered and harmonious existence peculiar to the rational beings that we are. In that case, to show that virtue does well at whatever it does is also to show that virtue is the key to happiness that Socrates and his companions have been looking for. Throughout the *Gorgias* Socrates and his companions return to the point that happiness depends on agency, because happiness requires that one's life, in all its dimensions, take the right sort of direction, and only agency can supply any direction whatsoever to one's life.

Moreover, it is not just any agency that gives the right sort of direction, but virtue in particular. This is because the direction that happiness requires is that of flourishing as the kind of being that humans are, and that, Plato argues, is a *rational* being, one that behaves on the basis of reasons, which exhibit order and

---

[29] Cataloging the areas of a virtuous person's life, and the success he displays in each of them, and likewise the failures of the vicious, became a common (if occasionally tedious) practice in later antiquity; see esp. Stobaeus, *Anthology* II.5b9–13.

appropriateness.[30] In that case, however much one may prize being a dissolute and wanton person, and however much satisfaction one may seem to find in such a lifestyle, what we *cannot* say is that his dissoluteness has made him a *good human being*. This is a point about human nature. We can make the same sort of point even about plants: however much I may prefer, say, a failing, weak cactus as a decoration for my windowsill, and in that sense declare that, given my preferences, such a cactus is a 'good' one, I *cannot* say that such a cactus is a *good cactus*. Questions about what makes a good cactus are not settled by considering such preferences, but by determining what is the natural state of health for a cactus.[31] Likewise, what constitutes flourishing in a human is not to be settled by appeals to tastes, for dissoluteness, or cruelty, or tyranny, or anything else. It is settled by determining what kinds of beings we are, and what the health of such a being, *as* that kind of being, amounts to. And this is why the unconditional good is what determines happiness: the unconditional good must be a form of rational and intelligent agency, and living according to rational, intelligent agency constitutes the health and flourishing of humans as the rational beings that they are by nature. Consequently, on Plato's view, the exercise of the skill that brings direction to one's life and the mode of living that is one's peculiar good as a rational being, are the *same*—and *that* is why doing all things well and being blessed and happy are the same. Plato does not slide from 'doing well' to 'flourishing'. He *argues*, and argues well, that they are the same thing. On Plato's view, virtue is unconditionally good, and the only thing that *could* be. And, of course, this is just what the directive conception of happiness maintains: happiness is determined by the intelligent agency with which we live our lives.

We can now also see how Plato's argument in the *Gorgias* illuminates the conception of wisdom and success that he offers in the *Euthydemus*. According to the *Gorgias*, virtue is a special kind of skill: its aim—the proper mode of existence for a rational being—is the same as the very *performance* of the skill itself. Consequently, the *Gorgias* explains why wisdom guarantees success, and all the success one could ever need, as Plato says it does in the *Euthydemus*, since wisdom aims only at its own performance, which is the same as the good life of a rational agent. In that case, wisdom does not fall short of success so long as one acts wisely; failure comes only when one acts unskillfully, that is, unwisely.[32] Moreover, wisdom can be both a productive skill—it produces a wise mode of living—*and* valuable for its own sake, since a wise mode of living is valuable for

---

[30] Cf. the Stoic view that 'good' is not an inert quality that we come across, but an active form of agency we engage in that produces benefit, and in particular, benefit for the kinds of beings that we are by nature (see Diogenes Laertius, *Lives* VII.94).

[31] For this analogy, the point that 'good' is an 'attribute adjective', and the deeper point about the structure of a virtue-theoretical account of flourishing in general, I am, of course, indebted to Hursthouse (1999), ch. 9, who, in turn, expresses her indebtedness to Philippa Foot.

[32] This is to be contrasted with a 'stochastic' skill, such as medicine or navigation, which aims primarily at a distinct outcome, is valued for the sake of (its tendency to produce) that outcome, and fails when it falls short of that outcome, even though it is possible to have acted skillfully and well despite such failure. For a discussion of this contrast, see Annas (1994*a*), ch. 19. (Notice that since Brickhouse and Smith (1994), ch. 4, (2000*a*), ch. 4, and (2000*b*) make success consist in virtuous

its own sake, being the good life of a rational being. Consequently, although it does not appear that Plato managed to depict this account of wisdom *from within* the skill analogy, none the less Plato has managed to articulate a radical account of the nature of virtue and happiness: virtue determines happiness, because a life lived according to virtue is the same as the good life for a rational being.

2.3   Virtue, Happiness, and Pleasure: An Alternative

I have argued that if we want to understand what Plato thinks happiness consists in, it is of the utmost importance that we first understand the structure of Plato's argument for the connection between virtue and happiness. It has often been said that in merely refuting Callicles' hedonism Plato leaves room for other forms of hedonism to be true, that is, for pleasure to be what happiness consists in after all. But this is seriously misleading. By concentrating on the nature of Callicles' particular and rather narrow conception of hedonism, we overlook the more basic conception of value that underwrites Socrates' critique of it, a conception of value that rejects any attempt whatsoever to construct happiness out of the ingredients of one's life, such as pleasure or anything else. We also overlook the importance of the structure of Plato's own defense of virtue: virtue is not one of the ingredients of one's life, but rather what gives all of those ingredients direction and integrates them into a harmonious whole in a way that they are incapable of doing for themselves. For Plato, this means that virtue determines happiness. In other words, Plato explains the relation between virtue and happiness by showing us what virtue is in its very nature. He refuses to appeal to any good besides virtue, but which virtue secures, to explain how it might be that virtue could make us happy.

This is a point that hedonism cannot accept. As I have spoken of hedonism, a hedonist is committed to the view that if virtue brings happiness, it does so because it also brings pleasure, and it is the *pleasure* that *makes* one happy. This is a most important fact to notice about hedonism, since it is one thing to say that the virtuous are happy, and quite another to say that their virtue is what their happiness consists in,[33] and hedonism is consistent with the former statement, but not the latter. Hedonism is, therefore, a species of the additive conception of

activity considered as virtuous *projects*, as I argued in Chapter 1, they are committed to thinking of virtue as a stochastic skill; hence their insistence that further good luck is needed in order for exercise of the skill to succeed.)

[33]   Brickhouse and Smith (2000a: 128 f.) capture this idea in their distinction between virtue as a 'component or constituent good' and as an 'instrumental good'. See also Epicurus, who insists that the virtuous are happy, but emphatically denies that happiness consists in virtue. Epicurus claims that virtue does lead to happiness—in fact, he goes so far as to claim that virtue is sufficient for happiness (*Letter to Menoeceus* 132)—but vehemently denies that virtue is what makes us happy; rather, it is tranquility (ἀταραξία) that makes us happy, while virtue merely allows us to avoid the unnecessary complications that lead to anxiety and distress (ταραχή). In fact, Epicurus is deliberately shocking in making his point that things like virtue have no value of their own, saying that he spits on the 'noble', and people who praise the noble, when its link to pleasure is severed (Athenaeus, *Deipnosophists* 12,

happiness, according to which happiness depends on goods that need direction that they do not give themselves, that is, on conditional goods. As such, hedonism inherits a general feature of the additive conception that we noted in the previous chapter: it requires that there be a gap between virtue and happiness, to be filled by some conditional good such as pleasure, or desire-satisfaction, or the fruition of some project, or simply a further stock of various other goods.[34]

But perhaps this way of capturing hedonism is too crude: what if the pleasure that virtue brings, and which is what makes us happy, were not some *further* good *distinct* from virtue that virtue secures, but in some way *identical* to virtue itself? After all, Plato argues that virtue brings happiness by showing that virtue is identical to the good mode of living for rational beings; perhaps if that mode of living were also identical to the most pleasant mode of living, then Plato need not choose between the thesis that happiness depends on virtue and the thesis that happiness depends on the greatest pleasure, since these come to the same thing. This argument seems to allow us to embrace hedonism *without* positing a gap between virtue and happiness, and thus without presupposing the additive conception of happiness. In that case, we would not have to choose between hedonism and the directive conception of happiness. We could have it both ways.

The form of hedonism that would make this possible has been skillfully articulated and defended by George Rudebusch in his recent book *Socrates, Pleasure, and Value* (1999), which represents, in my opinion, an especially sophisticated and subtle analysis of pleasure and its relation to virtue and happiness in Socratic philosophy. In particular, Rudebusch rightly reminds us of a common ancient conception of pleasure—what he calls 'modal pleasure'—which is pleasure not of *feeling* but of *activity*. For instance, we can say that for a golfer the activity of playing golf has its own peculiar pleasure, which is neither identical nor reducible to some sort of pleasant sensation that attends the activity. Such activity is characterized, for instance, by the absence of boredom in the agent, by the agent's being 'absorbed' in the activity, by the value the agent attaches to the activity, and so on. Treating pleasure as 'modal' rather than 'sensate' has the benefit of allowing Socrates to avoid treating the good as a kind of experience or episode, as he criticizes Callicles for doing; for modal pleasure is not a feeling but an activity, and lives considered as wholes are constructed out of activities far better than out of feelings. Moreover, Rudebusch argues, since for Socrates virtuous activity is identical to the best form of pleasure, Socrates is a 'modal hedonist': the good, for Socrates, consists in the optimum pleasure that is identical to virtuous activity. On this view, Socrates can hold both virtue and

---

547a; see also *de Finibus* I.42). This is a deliberately extreme position, but it does demonstrate vividly the difference between the idea that virtue *leads to* happiness and the idea that happiness *consists in* virtue.

[34] These species of the additive conception are defended by Gosling and Taylor (1982); Irwin (1992) and (1995), esp. ch. 8; Brickhouse and Smith (1994), ch. 4, (2000*a*), ch. 4, and (2000*b*); and Vlastos (1991), ch. 8 (who places a gap not between virtue and happiness, but between virtue and 'complete' happiness, respectively).

optimum modal pleasure to be the highest good, since he takes them to be the same thing.[35]

I think that Rudebusch is correct both to focus on modal rather than sensate pleasure as a reconstruction of a Socratic or Platonic conception of pleasure, and to argue that optimum modal pleasure is identical to virtuous activity. Where I disagree with Rudebusch is in his claim that Plato's (or Socrates') acceptance of these claims shows that he is a hedonist. My disagreement is based on three considerations: first, my reading of the *Gorgias*, on which Plato's account of the relation between virtue and happiness allows no gap between them;[36] second, the fact that modal hedonism *does* require such a gap after all, despite the identity of virtue and optimum modal pleasure; and third, the fact that modal hedonism proposes to fill that gap with a conditional good. I have already discussed the first consideration at length, so let me now explain the other two.

It is important to observe that Rudebusch's view does not make virtue a means to happiness, but it does posit a gap between virtue and happiness none the less. That gap exists because modal hedonism requires virtue and modal pleasure to play different roles in the *explanation* of the happiness of the happy life.[37] Consider the following two statements:

The life of virtue, because it is the healthy life of a rational being, is happy;

and

The life of virtue, because it is also the life of optimum pleasure, is happy.

Notice an important difference between these two statements. The first tells us that virtue makes one happy because of what virtue is by its nature. It is not merely that *the healthy life of a rational being* is the same thing as *the life of virtue*;

---

[35] See Rudebusch (1991: 37–40), (1994: 165–9), (1999), esp. chs. 6–7, 10, *et passim*; see also Ryle (1949: 107–10), from whom I have borrowed the example of the golfer and the analysis of the golfer's pleasure; and esp. Aristotle, who offers both a 'negative' account of pleasure as the absence of psychic impediment in activity (*Nicomachean Ethics* VII.12), and a more 'positive' account of pleasure as a kind of psychic involvement in activity (*Nicomachean Ethics* X.1–5).

[36] Consider also Plato's characterization of virtue as the health of the soul. The true expert, Socrates says, both in the area of the body and the soul, knows how to bring about the good of the object of his expertise (503d–504b). The doctor, for instance, knows what is good for the body— namely physical health—and can bring it about; it is the health itself which is the good of the body in Socrates' example and which the doctor brings about (504a–b, e–505a). Surely the same must be the case when we consider the health of the soul, which Socrates' example of the doctor is meant to illuminate (505b). There, the true expert of the soul brings about its good by making it orderly and 'healthy' (504b–d, 505b); and whereas physical health is the good *of the body*, the health of the soul is the good *simpliciter*, it is *our* good. It would be very odd, then, if the doctor brings about the good of the body by bringing about physical health, but the expert of the soul by bringing about the health of the soul does not thereby bring about our good, that by possessing which we live well, except incidentally. For if it is not virtue but something else which virtue secures (e.g. pleasure or desire-satisfaction), or if it is not virtue *per se* but virtue *qua* something else, which is our good, then Socrates' example of the doctor is amazingly ill chosen. For that example is meant to show that the result of expertise is the achievement of the particular good of the thing in question. (As F. White (1990: 121 f.), puts the point, the final good of the soul is virtue, as the final good of the body is physical health; see also Tenkku (1956: 91). If this is Socrates' point, and if we are properly identified with the soul, then virtue is our good strictly speaking.)   [37] See Russell (2000*b*).

rather, it is that the former tells us what the latter *is*.[38] By contrast, the second statement says that what makes us happy is not virtue itself, strictly speaking, but pleasure. For although (*ex hypothesi*) *the life of optimum pleasure* is identical to *the life of virtue*, the former does *not* tell us what the latter *is*—any more than it tells us what piety is, say, despite the fact that (again *ex hypothesi*) the life of optimum pleasure is identical to the life of piety. Consequently, while the first statement illuminates the relation of virtue to happiness by revealing the nature of virtue itself, the second does not. In that case, the second attempts to explain how virtue makes one happy by appealing to something distinct from what virtue is *per se*. And that is to put a gap between virtue and happiness, after all: virtue makes us happy not because it is virtue, but because it is optimally pleasant. Nor could it be otherwise, if what one means to defend is any form of *hedonism*. To be a hedonist, one must explain virtue's contribution to happiness on the grounds that the optimal pleasantness of the life of virtue is what accounts for the happiness of that life. Without such an accounting, we are left merely with the view that the life of virtue, which is the happy life, is also the life of optimized modal pleasure—an interesting and important view, to be sure, but *not hedonism*.[39]

To remain a hedonist, then, one must account for the happiness of the virtuous person by appealing to the pleasantness of the virtuous person's life. Not only does this posit a gap between virtue and happiness but it also requires that that gap be filled by a *conditional good*. This might not be obvious when the pleasure we have in mind is the pleasure of a mode of life in accordance with virtue. This is, after all, a rather special pleasure: it is the pleasure of someone who has transformed his affective life into a healthy and flourishing one. Such pleasure has been *differentiated*: it is no longer the case that such pleasure as *that* may be either good or bad, depending on what one makes of it, because one has *already* made something good of such pleasure. Put another way, conditional goods are 'undifferentiated'—are neither good nor bad, but become so depending on what an agent does with them—only when considered in the abstract. In the life of a particular person, however, pleasure has already begun to assume some role or other, and so will be good if that role is good, and bad otherwise; and, of course, the pleasure of virtue is necessarily pleasure that has assumed a *good* role in a person's life. Why, then, should we say that a form of hedonism that makes happiness depend on *that* kind of pleasure is a species of the additive conception of happiness? Why shouldn't we say instead that modal hedonism makes happiness depend on an unconditional good, since the pleasure of virtue could never fail to be a good thing?

The answer, quite simply, is that pleasure—even the pleasure of virtue—is *still* a conditional rather than an unconditional good. To be sure, it has become

---

[38] After all, the President of the United States, for example, is the same individual as the Commander-in-Chief of the U.S. armed forces, but the latter office does not tell us what the former office *is*, or vice versa.

[39] Cf. Weiss (1990*a*), who criticizes Gosling and Taylor (1990) for failing to appreciate this sort of point in another context.

differentiated as a real good, and could not become otherwise differentiated and remain the pleasure that it is. But the distinction between unconditional and conditional goods is a distinction between what brings good direction and what needs good direction that it cannot supply for itself; and wisdom brings to our pleasures a direction that they cannot give to themselves.[40] Therefore, while the pleasure of virtue is by definition pleasure that has become differentiated as a good, it is still a conditional good, because it takes wisdom and good character to effect that differentiation in one's affective life. Consequently, since modal hedonism requires that we explain the happiness of the virtuous in terms of a conditional good, it is a species of the additive conception of happiness, after all.

This difference in formal structure between the additive and the directive conceptions of happiness brings into sharper relief what is perhaps the chief difference between them: the directive conception takes more seriously the idea the *holistic* nature of happiness than the additive conception does. This fact about happiness is crucial to Plato's argument that virtue makes one happy, as he concentrates on showing that virtue makes us happy because it is the one thing that can grasp *all* facets of our life—our choices, our pursuits, our relationships, our fears and emotions (see 506e–507c)—and make them all good; it is the wholeness, completeness, and integration of the entire person that makes for happiness. Plato's argument makes it clear that one's happiness depends on the *whole* of one's self and existence, and not on this or that strand of it. Contrast this with the view that the life of virtue is happy not in the first instance because of its overall rational pattern and structure as a harmonious and integrated life, but because of *some dimension or other* of that life. To say that Plato is a hedonist, for instance, is to say that the life of virtue is a happy life because it is identical to the most pleasant life—because, that is, of *that* particular dimension of that life. But this is inimical to Plato's position at its most fundamental level: for Plato, happiness is a whole, and so happiness cannot be determined by a conditional good, but only by the unconditional good of virtue, since only virtue can bring harmony to one's life *as* a whole.[41]

2.4 Conclusion

Discussions of Plato's treatment of pleasure in the *Gorgias* have centered primarily on whether or not Plato leaves room there for hedonism, and so they have tended to focus on the specific sort of hedonism that Plato criticizes there. But much more instructive is an understanding of the more fundamental conception of value that Plato develops and employs in the *Gorgias*. From this

---

[40] I explore this aspect of the distinction at some length in Ch. 1.

[41] It may be objected that Plato leaves some room between virtue and happiness after all, on the grounds that in the myth at the end of the *Gorgias* (523a–527a) he shows that virtue 'pays' because it holds out the promise of distinct rewards in the hereafter. However, this objection rests on a misunderstanding of that myth, the point of which is that the reward of a life of virtue is a *continued* life of virtue, since only virtue could be the reward for virtue; see Russell (2001).

perspective, the real payoff of understanding Plato's criticisms of hedonism is a deeper appreciation of just how Plato understands the relationship between goodness and happiness. For in the *Gorgias* the search for what makes a person happy is a search for what is unconditionally good. This makes sense of how Socrates and his interlocutors react to discovering that an alleged key to happiness requires something else to give it the right sort of direction in order for it to be a good; for this just is to show that such a thing is at best only conditionally good, and thus not a determinant of happiness. It also makes sense of Plato's observation that the only thing that could be the real key to happiness is something that gives everything good direction, and needs no such direction itself. On this way of reading the *Gorgias*, Plato's inference from the fact that virtue makes us do all things well to the claim that virtue is what makes us happy (507c) is a most natural inference to make. And it explains why Plato should focus as he does on the holistic nature of virtue, as being what integrates and harmonizes all the dimensions of a human life. This is to show that virtue is unconditionally good, and thus what determines our happiness.

Furthermore, on this way of thinking about goods hedonism cannot get off the ground, for a number of reasons. For one thing, pleasure is at best a conditional good—any goodness it could have must be dependent on the direction that virtue gives it—and so cannot be unconditionally good; it cannot, then, be what determines happiness, as hedonism says it does. For another, hedonism requires that we account for the happiness of the good life in terms of pleasure, whereas Plato accounts for happiness exclusively in terms of virtue in its own right. Moreover, Plato accounts for happiness in terms of virtue as a whole—as the total integration of the whole person—and not in terms of one of the aspects or dimensions of the virtuous life; so even if the life of greatest pleasure is in some sense identical to the life of virtue, it is not that the life of virtue is happy because it is the life of greatest pleasure, but that the life of greatest pleasure is happy because it is the life of virtue. The order of explanation makes all the difference, and Plato clearly rejects the order of explanation that hedonism requires. And this fact is most revealing of Plato's fundamental conception of value. For Plato, happiness is a matter not of the ingredients of the good life, but of the whole self living that life in a rational way. Happiness is not made of various good things added in together, even if virtue is among them. It is constituted by the very rationality with which all of those things are incorporated into one's life, and that is what virtue is.

I have shown that, as far as Plato is concerned in the *Gorgias*, pleasure is *at best* a conditional good. Of course, that is not to show that pleasure *is* a conditional good, or indeed to say what kind of good, if any, pleasure might be, and thus what sort of place pleasure may have in the good life. In the next chapter, we shall explore the *Phaedo*, in which it emerges that pleasure is a conditional good after all, and we shall see further in the chapters that follow what sort of role pleasure plays in the good life, and especially what the rational incorporation of pleasure into the good life amounts to.

3

Pleasure as a Conditional Good in the *Phaedo*

Plato's *Phaedo* is about the last day of Socrates' life, and it seeks to explain why Socrates' last day, and especially his confident demeanor on his last day, make a fitting ending to his life, tragic though it may be. But the *Phaedo* is also a *celebration* of that life filled with the love of learning and wisdom, and of the self-sufficiency that such a life brings, leaving one ready to face whatever twists fate should bring. As such, the setting of the *Phaedo* affords Plato the perfect opportunity to reflect on what it is to live a happy, meaningful life, and what sorts of concerns should shape one's life, and one's character, as a whole. So here Plato raises one of the central questions of ancient ethics—and of human existence: what does it take to live well? One of the answers to this question that Plato considers at some length is the common view that to live well is to live pleasantly, and this is no surprise given the attraction that this sort of view has held for philosophers and laypersons alike. The *Phaedo*, therefore, affords a fine starting-point for identifying what role Plato takes pleasure to have in a well-lived life considered as a whole.

What is rather more surprising, however, is the broad diversity of views on this issue that Plato has been said to hold in the *Phaedo*. On the one hand, some modern scholars argue that the treatment of pleasure in the *Phaedo* is compatible with, and even suggestive of, the idea that to live pleasantly is to live well—that is, a form of hedonism.[1] On the other, some scholars, ancient and modern, have argued that the *Phaedo* contains an unmitigated rejection of pleasure as an evil, that is, that Plato in the *Phaedo* is an ascetic.[2] Now we may well suspect that any dialogue that could motivate such diametrically opposed readings must be more complex than either reading could suggest on its own, and for this reason some scholars have sought to find a third way, arguing, for instance, that in the *Phaedo* the good life requires not scorn for but integration

---

[1] Bostock (1986: 31–3) suggests this, although with mild reservation (34). See Gosling and Taylor (1982), ch. 5 for a spirited defense of a hedonist reading of the *Phaedo*.

[2] Two prime examples of this tradition are the Neoplatonists Damascius and Olympiodorus, discussed below. See also, e.g., Hackforth (1955: 49); cf. Gallop (1975: 88); and see Spitzer (1976: 113), who discusses Zeller, Grube, Jowett, Archer-Hind, and A. E. Taylor as proponents of asceticist readings of the *Phaedo* (Spitzer himself disagrees; see esp. 116 f.).

of the body and its pleasures; or that pleasure is not *the* good, but still is *a* good; or that pleasure is not to be removed from the best life, but none the less lacks genuine value.[3] But while a third way may be promising, unfortunately proponents of third ways have had surprisingly little to say about *exactly* what Plato's view is in the *Phaedo*: What does it mean, really, to 'integrate' pleasures into one's life? What sort of a good is pleasure, and why? If pleasure lacks genuine value, what kind of value might it have? Consequently, in the analysis of pleasure the *Phaedo* still remains an under-explored dialog.

One common assumption in this debate, however, is that (certain) pleasures must be either good or bad in their own right, and by working on this assumption we shall probably find Plato's view in the *Phaedo* rather difficult to make out. In contrast, I argue that in the *Phaedo* Plato believes that what makes a pleasure good or bad is the sort of place one gives it in one's life. Instead of asking, say, whether the pleasures of sex, considered as a type, are themselves good or bad, I think that Plato would ask whether or not the pleasure a particular person finds in sex is underwritten by a skewed or a reasonable sense of what is important. For Plato, pleasure is a complex mental state by which we attach some form of importance to its object, such that (roughly speaking) our priorities determine what kinds of things we find pleasurable, and what we find pleasurable about them. So whether pleasure is a good or bad part of someone's life will depend on how well her pleasures track the sorts of priorities and concerns that it is good for a person to have in order to live well. For Plato, I argue, pleasure is a *conditional good*: whether or not pleasure is a good depends on the role it plays in one's life.

Treating pleasures as conditional goods will, I believe, make the best sense of Plato's observations about pleasure and the good life in the *Phaedo*. In the first section of this chapter, I shall discuss the view that Plato defends asceticism in the *Phaedo*, and argue that this view rests on the mistaken assumption that, for Plato, pleasure is bad in its own right, and not in virtue of one's giving it the wrong place in one's life. I argue in the second section that in the *Phaedo* Plato also rejects the hedonist view that pleasure is the good, since taking pleasure to be the good is incompatible with the sorts of priorities one needs in order to make any kind of good out of pleasure in the first place. I conclude by showing how the notion of a conditional good affords a new and richer understanding of Plato's discussion of pleasure and value in the *Phaedo*.

3.1   Why Plato is Not an Ascetic

Asceticism as a thesis about value is not a single view, but includes a range of views, such as that pleasure should hold no more interest for one than, say, whether the number of stars in the night sky is odd or even; or that pleasure is to

---

[3] See, respectively, Spitzer (1976); Tenkku (1956: 102–4, 111, 118); and Weiss (1987).

be avoided; or that it is an outright evil. And it is perhaps no great surprise that some of Plato's readers have thought that he must endorse some form of asceticism or other in the *Phaedo*, since it is after all impossible to read the *Phaedo* without noticing the austerity of the philosophical life that Plato praises there. Certainly the harshest passage is Socrates' so-called 'Defense Speech' (63e–69e), in which he explains his confidence in the face of his imminent death and his refusal to resist suicide, by arguing that death is nothing more than the awaited separation of soul from body (64c). And upon reflection this separation seems to be what philosophers practice for throughout their lives (64a), inasmuch as philosophers cultivate radically different values from those of most people, whose lives are mainly concerned with services to their merely mortal condition (64d–69e).

Consider in particular the following passage from Socrates' Defense Speech:

'Do you think it befits a philosophical man to be keen about the so-called pleasures of, for example, food and drink?'
'Not in the least, Socrates,' said Simmias.
'And what about those of sex?'
'Not at all.'
'And what about the other services to the body? Do you think such a person regards them as of any value? For instance, the possession of smart clothes and shoes, and the other bodily adornments—do you think he values them highly, or does he disdain them, except in so far as he's absolutely compelled to share in them?'
'I think the genuine philosopher disdains them.'
'Do you think in general, then, that such a person's concern is not for the body, but so far as he can stand aside from it, is directed towards the soul?'
'I do.'
'Then is it clear that, first, in such matters as those the philosopher differs from other people in releasing his soul, as far as possible, from its communion with the body?'
'It appears so.'
'And presumably, Simmias, it does seem to most people that someone who finds nothing of that sort pleasant, and takes no part in those things, doesn't deserve to live; rather, one who cares nothing for the pleasures that come by what of the body runs pretty close to being dead.'
'Yes, what you say is quite true.' (64d2–65a8)

Consequently, Socrates says, the genuine philosopher should think of death as a kind of 'purification' (κάθαρσις) of the soul, as it becomes free of the body and its concerns (67b7–d6; cf. 69b8–c7). Moreover, Socrates insists that the difference that this attitude makes between the philosopher and the 'ordinary' person, in terms of their values and priorities, yields radically different conceptions of the virtues:

'[I]f you care to consider the bravery and temperance of other people, you'll find it strange.'
'How so, Socrates?'
'You know, don't you, that all others count death among great evils?'

'Very much so.'

'Is it, then, through being afraid of greater evils that the brave among them abide death, whenever they do so?'

'Very much so.'

'Then, it's through fearing and fear that all except philosophers are brave; and yet it's surely illogical that anyone should be brave through fear and cowardice.'

'It certainly is.'

'And what about those of them who are well-ordered? Aren't they in this same state, temperate through a kind of intemperance? True, we say that's impossible; but still that state of simple-minded temperance does turn out in their case to be like this: it's because they're afraid of being deprived of further pleasures, and desire them, that they abstain from some because they're overcome by others. True, they call it "intemperance" to be ruled by pleasures, but still that's what happens to them: they overcome some pleasures because they're overcome by others. And that is the sort of thing that was just mentioned: after a fashion, they achieve temperance because of intemperance.'

'Yes, so it seems.'

'Yes, Simmias, my good friend; since this may not be the right exchange with a view to goodness, the exchanging of pleasures for pleasures, pains for pains, and fear for fear, greater or lesser ones, like coins; it may be, rather, that this alone is the right coin, for which one should exchange all those things—wisdom; and the buying and selling of all things for that, or rather with that, may be real bravery, temperance, justice, and, in short, true goodness in company with wisdom, whether pleasures and fears and all else of that sort be added or taken away; but as for their being parted from wisdom and exchanged for one another, goodness of that sort may be a kind of illusory façade, and fit for slaves indeed, and may have nothing healthy or true about it; whereas, truth to tell, temperance, justice, and bravery may in fact be a kind of purification of all such things, and wisdom itself a kind of purifying rite.' (68d2–69c3)[4]

And here we must ask, what is this 'purification' that the philosopher seeks? And in seeking it, is the philosopher—and Plato himself—committed to some form of asceticism?

3.1.1   *The Neoplatonist interpretation*

The Neoplatonist Olympiodorus in his commentary on the *Phaedo* answers strongly in the affirmative. According to Olympiodorus, there are three kinds of activities: the natural and necessary (e.g. eating, sleeping), the natural and unnecessary (e.g. sexual intercourse), and the unnatural and unnecessary (e.g. wearing finery).[5] Olympiodorus claims that Plato's philosopher does without, and in fact forcibly resists, the second and third of these (*Commentary on the* Phaedo 3.5), and that his attitude toward the first is like one's attitude toward avoiding a talkative neighbor, someone who is intrusive and bothersome (4.3). Olympiodorus does not say that Plato rejects certain *attitudes* toward these

---

[4] We shall return to the confusing, and controversial, 'exchange' metaphor in the next section.

[5] Olympiodorus, *Commentary on the* Phaedo 3.5.1–13; cp. Damascius, *Lectures on the* Phaedo I.69.6–9, who also includes the necessary and not natural (e.g. shelter).

activities; rather, he treats the activities *themselves* as types, and portrays Plato as an ascetic about all of them. Consequently, the philosopher, says Olympiodorus, is not one who seeks moderation in pleasure and desire, but rather seeks to become completely affectless (ἀπάθεια), and thus to extirpate pleasure and desire altogether.[6]

Likewise, the Neoplatonist Damascius in his lectures on the *Phaedo* claims that whereas one kind of philosophical education involves moderation of passions (which is discussed, he says, in the *Republic* and *Laws*), a higher kind involves the avoidance of the passions, and the highest the complete ignorance of the passions and even of one's very ignorance of them; the latter two kinds of education, he says, are espoused in the *Phaedo* and *Theaetetus*, respectively (*Lectures on the* Phaedo I.75).[7]

Olympiodorus and Damascius clearly interpret the austerity of the *Phaedo* as asceticism. We can see how vigorously they propounded this interpretation if we understand the Stoic notion of the extirpation (ἀπάθεια) of the passions (πάθη) that these philosophers appropriate—and in terms of which they frame their comments on pleasure in the *Phaedo*[8]—and how they reinterpret it to embrace a form of asceticism that the Stoics themselves had eschewed.

The Stoics had held that all passions are irrational—or rather, unreasonable— and unnatural, as they reflect groundless and potentially dangerous ways of viewing the world. The various passions are all species of four basic genera: pleasure, pain, desire, and fear; and in particular pleasure, simply put, is an 'irrational elation' (ἄλογος ἔπαρσις) over something as having a certain importance, when it does not in fact have that importance.[9] And, of course, the Stoics say that the wise person will not be subject to passions, so understood—he will be, in this sense, passionless (ἀπαθής). In a way, then, when Olympiodorus and Damascius say that the goal of the philosopher should be not moderation in pleasure and pain and the other passions but rather their extirpation (ἀπάθεια), in Stoic terms their point is merely that there is no right way to be unreasonable, or no right way to be mastered by one's passions. Since pleasure, understood in this strict sense as a πάθος, is always irrational, of course the virtuous person will not try to partake of such pleasures 'in the right way', since that is impossible, but can treat them correctly only by getting rid of them entirely.

The question remains, however, whether or not there are any *other* mental states that are pleasure-like but which are *not* unreasonable, and of which one may be able to partake in the right way after all. It is here that Damascius and Olympiodorus part ways with the Stoics, in a most revealing way. For, on the Stoic view, pleasures have counterparts (or 'opposites', ἐναντία) that are reasonable

---

[6] Olympiodorus: καὶ τέλος αὐτῶν [sc. φροντιζόντων] ἡ ἀπάθεια (*Commentary* 4.3.16).

[7] Whether or not this is a fair assessment of the relevant passages of the *Theaetetus* is a very controversial matter, to which we shall return in Ch. 5.

[8] Framing Platonic theses in terms of Stoic theses was not uncommon among ancient Platonists; e.g. it is quite common and explicit in the Middle Platonist Alcinous' *Handbook of Platonism*.

[9] See Diogenes Laertius, *Lives* VII.110–16; Stobaeus, *Anthology* II.9–10e; see also Galen, *On the Doctrines of Hippocrates and Plato* 4.2.9–18, 4.4.16–18, 24–5.

affective responses.[10] According to the Stoics, in addition to the various πάθη there are also

> three good states [of the soul] (εὐπάθειαι), joy, caution, and wish. And *joy is opposite to pleasure, being a reasonable elation.* . . . So just as there are certain passions which are forms of the primary ones, so too there are good states subordinate to the primary; . . . [and] forms of joy are enjoyment, good spirits, tranquility.   (Diogenes Laertius, *Lives* VII.116, emphasis added)

Pleasure understood as an unreasonable elation is a constituent of bad character, or vice, being as it is a failure of practical reasoning, and indeed a kind of psychic illness.[11] But pleasure understood as a reasonable elation is 'joy'; joy, in Stoic psychology, is not a πάθος, but an εὐπάθεια, or good affective response.

In fact, the Stoics say that joy is a state of soul that we shall find in the wise person. For although the wise are not disposed to passion, still they are not cold or hard-hearted, but are characterized instead by the εὐπάθειαι:

> [The Stoics] say the wise man is also free of passions (ἀπαθής), because he is not disposed to them. And the base man is 'free of passions' in a different sense, which means the same as hard-hearted and cold. . . . And they say that all virtuous men are austere because they do not consort with pleasure nor do they tolerate hedonistic [actions and attitudes] from others; and there is another kind of austerity, in the same sense that wine is said to be 'austere' [harsh] (which is used medicinally, but not much for drinking).   (Diogenes Laertius, *Lives* VII.117)

And of such joy (which Seneca also calls 'gladness', *laetitia*) Seneca writes,

> Do you think that I am now taking many pleasures from you when I remove things that come by chance, when I insist that hopes, those extremely sweet delights, must be avoided? No, on the contrary: I do not want you ever to lack gladness. I want it to be born in your home; and it is born, if only it is inside of you.   (*Letters to Lucilius* 23.3)[12]

The Stoic distinction between types of pleasure as either reasonable or unreasonable is most instructive for our purposes. Take, for instance, the question whether it is good or bad to find pleasure in sexual intercourse. For a Stoic, this would seem to be the wrong question. We distinguish good and bad pleasures not primarily[13] in terms of what they are the pleasures *of*, such as sex, but in terms of whether one's enjoyment of sex is an unreasonable elation— whether, that is, someone's pleasure in sex takes sex to have an importance that

---

[10] Fear and desire have reasonable counterparts as well (caution and wish, respectively), but, somewhat notoriously, pain does not.

[11] It is worth noting that the Stoics take advantage of the fact that πάθος in Greek connotes disturbance, suffering, and constitutional disorder (cf. English 'pathology' and cognates); cf. Gosling and Taylor (1982: 421). For the Stoics' treatment of passions (πάθη) as 'illnesses' and 'ailments' see Diogenes Laertius, *Lives* VII.115; Stobaeus, *Anthology* II.10e; Galen, *On Hippocrates' and Plato's Doctrines* 4.5.21–5, 5.2.3–7.

[12] Trans. Nussbaum (1994: 399). We shall discuss Seneca's view of joy in greater detail below.

[13] I say 'primarily' because, on the Stoic view, it will, of course, turn out that there are some things that we cannot enjoy in a reasonable way at all (e.g. spiteful glee at someone else's bad luck is one such case, Diogenes Laertius, *Lives* VII.114).

it does not really have.[14] In that case, we should understand the Stoic notion of the extirpation of the passions (ἀπάθεια) not as affectlessness, but a monumental revision of one's priorities and values that entails an equally monumental revision in one's emotional life.[15]

Understanding the Stoic notion of ἀπάθεια allows us to see more clearly what is at stake in the way that Damascius and Olympiodorus appropriate and transform that notion. In contrast to the Stoics, Olympiodorus and Damascius understand the extirpation of the passions (ἀπάθεια) as *complete* affectlessness, rather than extirpation of *unreasonable* passions (πάθη) that leaves room for other sorts of affective states. Their view is not that the pleasures of eating, sex, and luxury are reasonable or unreasonable depending on the *attitudes* toward eating, sex, and luxury that they reflect. Rather, their view is that such pleasures are, by their very nature, unreasonable, full stop. For Olympiodorus, such *things* as sumptuous meals and even sexual intercourse[16] are to be actively avoided as such; such *things* as eating and sleeping, which the philosopher cannot avoid, are to be dealt with only 'briefly and perfunctorily' (3.5), as one might deal with a bothersome neighbor (4.3). According to Olympiodorus, then, it is not possible to enjoy even life's simple pleasures *as* simple pleasures; there is no right way to enjoy eating, sex, or luxurious surroundings at all—about such things Olympiodorus is an extreme ascetic.

Moreover, and quite strikingly, Damascius (*Lectures on the* Phaedo I.164) explicitly considers and rejects a reading of *Phaedo* 69a6–c3 on which the life of virtue is attended by what would appear to be εὐπάθειαι. The passage concerns Socrates' claim at 69b1–5 that 'the buying and selling of all things for [wisdom], or rather with [wisdom], may be real bravery, temperance, justice, and, in short, true goodness in company with wisdom, whether pleasures and fears and all else of that sort be added or taken away...'.[17] According to some of Plato's inter-preters, Damascius says, the 'pleasures and fears' which may attend the truly virtuous life are joy (εὐφροσύνην) at freedom from the body, and the complete avoidance of what is alien (τὴν τελέαν φυγὴν τῶν ἐκτός), respectively. These pleasures and fears, on this interpretation, clearly are not what the Stoics would

---

[14] Likewise, for Epicurus (*Letter to Menoeceus* 127) what makes the desire for, e.g., a sumptuous meal a groundless (or unreasonable) desire is not the fact that the meal is sumptuous, but one's thinking that it is really more important to have a sumptuous meal than a plain one; but if we remove that groundless opinion, then the desire for a sumptuous meal becomes quite innocuous. Cf. *Key Doctrines* XXIX, XXX, *Vatican Sayings* 59. For this feature of Epicurus' distinction between kinds of desires see esp. Annas (1992: 192 ff.); see also Nussbaum (1994: 111–15).

[15] I should point out that I do not share the view (see, e.g., Gosling and Taylor (1982: 421)) that, for the Stoics, the only thing that a virtuous person enjoys is the attainment of virtue itself—as if virtue was somehow distinct from the *life* one lives virtuously and capable of being 'attained' and enjoyed as such. This view, I take it, is closely related to the widely held assumption, which I also reject, that if something is an indifferent—such as one's health, or loved ones?—then it is 'at best peripheral' to one's life (again, see Gosling and Taylor (1982: 415)), and therefore, presumably, little worth enjoying, in *any* way. But I cannot pursue the point here.

[16] Nocturnal emission, he says, will suffice for the philosopher (who is evidently always male, and happy to leave the business of populating the earth to less noble sorts of folks).

[17] We shall examine this controversial passage closely in the next section.

call πάθη, but bear a resemblance to the εὐπάθειαι.[18] However, Damascius explicitly rejects this reading of the passage, preferring the interpretation that the virtuous life which such affections may attend cannot be the *fully* virtuous life, which is completely purified of all such πάθη.[19] So Damascius refuses to treat the 'pleasures and fears' in this passage as εὐπάθειαι, and insists on treating them as πάθη. But, more than that, he treats them as πάθη at the cost of denying that the life of virtue which they attend can be a life of genuine virtue, *despite* Socrates' description of that life as one of 'real (τῷ ὄντι) bravery, temperance, justice, and, in short, true goodness (ἀληθὴς ἀρετή) in company with wisdom' (69b2–4). It seems clear, then, that Damascius' denial of anything like εὐπάθειαι in the life of real virtue is what motivates his interpretation of the text, and not vice versa. Consequently, by extirpation Damascius means eliminating all such pleasures from one's life as far as possible, rather than revising one's attitudes toward, and hence one's enjoyment of, their objects.

It is difficult to tell whether Damascius and Olympiodorus take this attitude toward all pleasures alike or to physical pleasures only, since neither of them discusses Plato's claim (114e3–4) that although the philosopher is not keen on bodily pleasures, he is keen on (ἐσπούδασε) the pleasures of learning (τὰς περὶ τὸ μανθάνειν). However, on their view, what makes a pleasure bad is not the kind of attitude that it is toward an object, but the nature of that object itself. And so even if we were to restrict their asceticism to bodily pleasures, they would still hold the rather extreme view that what makes a sexual pleasure a bad thing is not that it constitutes or reflects a wrong attitude about sex, but that it is a pleasure *of sex* in the first place. This is surely a far more extreme view than Plato seems to take elsewhere, as when he says in the *Euthydemus*, for instance, that there is nothing bad about 'bodily' luxuries such as wealth *per se* (281d–282a), but that goodness or badness where wealth is concerned depends on how we lead and direct our behavior with respect to wealth (281b). It seems unlikely, then, that Plato himself would condemn the enjoyment even of wealth and the physical comfort it brings, full stop, rather than the enjoyment of wealth that results from skewed values where wealth is concerned.

What is clear in any case is that Damascius and Olympiodorus take a very hard line, insisting that the *Phaedo* teaches us to despise pleasure, however understood, as an unwelcome nuisance, if not a downright evil. It would be unfortunate if they should be right in this, since it would leave the *Phaedo* with very little to tell us about how to live a good human life—for if they are correct, then a good *human* life is just the sort that we should not be seeking to live in the

---

[18] Recall that the Stoics say that fear (φόβος), which is an unreasonable expectation of something bad, is replaced in the virtuous person by 'caution' (εὐλάβεια), which is a 'reasonable avoidance' (εὔλογος ἔκκλησις); see Diogenes Laertius, *Lives* VII.110–13, 116.

[19] We should note that Damascius does make brief mention of εὐφροσύνη, his word for joy, as part of the philosopher's experience at *Lectures on the* Phaedo I.33, 49, 292. Presumably, this refers to the second-rate philosopher, given his claim of complete affectlessness for the first-rate philosopher, who displays 'genuine' virtue (see also I.75 for the distinction between the second-rate philosopher of the *Phaedo* and the first-rate philosopher of the *Theaetetus*).

first place. Their picture of a good life is a life in which the agent is actively fighting against his humanity and mortality, unable to be whole as he is, and thus eagerly awaiting death's final purification. But that is not a happy life, and it is not happy even if death really is a final purification. Their prescription is not to live well as human beings, but to get by with the rubbish we're stuck with until we can leave our humanity behind.

3.1.2 *Socrates joyful*

Can this way of reading the *Phaedo* be sustained? Before answering that question, we should note how great a burden of proof rests on the asceticist reading of the *Phaedo*.[20] After all, asceticism as a philosophical position is hardly the default view that one is left with upon denying that pleasure is an unconditional good.[21] Asceticism, even about bodily pleasures, is a strange and startling view, and a person has to go out of his way to hold it. And the asceticist reading of the *Phaedo*, I argue, has two very serious strikes against it.

The simplest and perhaps the greatest strike against such an interpretation of Plato in general, and the *Phaedo* in particular, is how starkly it conflicts with Plato's depiction of Socrates' own life, in the *Phaedo* and elsewhere, a life that Plato does not merely describe, but indeed celebrates.[22] Socrates appears to us in the *Phaedo*, as so often, genuinely enjoying himself, and in the *Phaedo* we see most vividly in Socrates a man with a deep capacity for enjoying life, and time spent in company and conversation with good friends. In fact, Socrates' good spirits in the *Phaedo* are rarely surpassed in other dialogs, and the fact that he is so depicted on the very day of his death is surely no accident—on the contrary, the good spirits with which Socrates faces his death while everyone around him is distraught is precisely where the dramatic development of the *Phaedo* begins. For it is Socrates' good spirits that prompt his companions to ask just how a philosopher ought to face death, and this question sets in motion all the arguments that follow (see 61c ff.).

In fact, the depiction of Socrates in the *Phaedo* captures what Seneca would later call 'joy' (*gaudium*), which is not giddiness or sensuality, but a strong sense of inner peace—a reasonable elation:

Real joy (*verum gaudium*), believe me, is a stern matter. Can one, do you think, despise death with a care-free countenance, or with a 'blithe and gay' expression . . . ? Or can one

---

[20] I do not think that that burden can be met simply by insisting, as Damascius does, that the philosopher in the *Phaedo* must be a second-rate one, since, as we have seen, this flies in the face of Socrates' explicit description of this philosopher and his virtues as 'genuine' (69b2–4). We can arrive at that conclusion only if we have already decided that a good Platonist must be an ascetic.

[21] This point can be easy to miss; e. g. Passmore (1970: 40 f.) suggests both that Plato's view is simply that 'the philosopher is not "much concerned" with eating and drinking, or sexual relations, or personal adornment', *and* that this amounts to 'some measure of asceticism'.

[22] Hackforth (1955: 49) suggests that it is Plato, but not Socrates, who is the ascetic. But this is a rather odd thing to say, given the enthusiasm with which Plato himself celebrates Socrates' joyful life in the *Phaedo*.

thus open his door to poverty, or hold the curb on his pleasures, or contemplate the endurance of pain? He who ponders these things in his heart is indeed full of joy; but it is not a cheerful joy. It is just this joy, however, of which I would have you become the owner; for it will never fail you when once you have found its source. The yield of poor mines is on the surface; those are really rich whose veins lurk deep, and they will make more bountiful returns to him who delves unceasingly. So too those baubles which delight the common crowd afford but a thin pleasure, laid on as a coating, and every joy that is only plated lacks a real basis. But the joy of which I speak, that to which I am endeavoring to lead you, is something solid, disclosing itself the more fully as you penetrate into it.   (Seneca, *Letters* 23.4–5, trans. Gummere (1996))

The ascetic interprets Socrates' confidence in the face of death as an outgrowth of a sort of pain, the pain of an annoying confinement to the world of crude matter. But confidence in the face of death can also be an outgrowth of a sort of *pleasure*, namely the joy of someone confident, contented, and at peace, who realizes that his happiness is entirely within his own power and is the sort of thing that no one can take away from him, whatever else they may take away. That is the joy that Seneca has in mind, and it is just this joy that we find in Socrates. It is a deep joy that endures—and indeed best shows its worth—even when lightness and cheer have gone.[23]

One can see the joyful Socrates in the *Phaedo* in many ways. For instance, consider how we find Socrates in the *Phaedo* delighting in the company of his friends. He jokes with his friend Phaedo (89b), and laughs at Cebes' charmingly hard-headed way (62e8–63a3): 'When Socrates heard [Cebes' objection] he seemed to me pleased at Cebes' persistence, and looking at us he said: "There goes Cebes, always hunting down arguments, and not at all willing to accept at once what anyone may say." ' The latter is especially interesting, as it suggests that the kind of enjoyment that Socrates finds with his friends is based on what he has always found likeable in them. That he finds them likeable on his last day alive suggests that Socrates is the same in his joy on that day as on any other day. Most of all, we see Socrates joyful as, unlike his friends, he is not upset even by the approach of his hour of death; even as he drinks the hemlock, he does so 'with good humour and without the least distaste' (117c4–5), and responds to his friends' subsequent sobbing by encouraging them: ' "What a way to behave, my strange friends! . . . Come now, calm yourselves and have strength." ' (117d7–e2; cp. 60a) And it is, after all, for this joy—this calm in the face of death, even suicide—that Socrates' friends call him to account, and which is the impetus for the whole dialogue that follows.

To invoke Seneca's analogy, Socrates is indeed a mine whose riches run surprisingly deep: the more pressure he faces, the more character we find he has with which to carry on in equanimity. What we see in the Socrates of the *Phaedo* is a man of deep joy—a man who is the same in feast or famine, facing long life

---

[23] Moreover, Plato's depiction of a joyful Socrates in the *Phaedo* can, in turn, illuminate just what Seneca's conception of joy comes to; at any rate, it offers an alternative to the much darker picture of Stoic joy envisioned by Nussbaum (1994: 398–401).

or imminent death. He is surely not the picture of a surly curmudgeon who is indifferent to the mortal world around him, and just as glad to be quit of it. Socrates' virtue is clearly not the 'purificatory' virtue that Olympiodorus and Damascius recommend. On the contrary, no philosopher has ever been portrayed as more fully a part of his world and the lives of the neighbors he finds in it.[24] But how can we reconcile this image of a joyful Socrates with the undeniable austerity of the *Phaedo*?

3.1.3 Socrates' Defense Speech revisited

This brings us to the second strike against the asceticist reading of the *Phaedo*: Socrates' discussion of pleasure in his Defense Speech does not support it after all. Let us turn again to those harsh passages in the Defense Speech, for even in the harshest passages Plato is not committed to asceticism, even about 'bodily' pleasures.

As we have seen in our discussion of the Neoplatonist interpretation, a key to understanding the place of pleasure in the good life lies in our choice between treating pleasures as either good or bad things in their own right, on the one hand, and treating pleasures as becoming either good or bad depending on what sort of place one gives them in one's life, and what sorts of attitudes and character traits one develops toward them, on the other. What kind of 'purification', then, does true virtue bring to one's pleasures? And just what is the philosopher's attitude toward pleasure?

Recall Socrates' discussion at 64d2–65a8 of the true philosopher's attitude toward the pleasures of food, drink, sex, or service to the body.[25] In particular, we can identify there the following five claims.

1. The philosopher is not keen on (ἐσπουδακέναι) the pleasures of food, drink, or sex (64d2–7).
2. The philosopher does not regard fine services to the body as of any value (ἐντίμους), but wishes to be finished with service to the body altogether (64d8–65a3).
3. The philosopher does not find any of the things just mentioned pleasant (65a4–5).
4. The philosopher does not partake in (μετέχει) any of them (65a5).
5. The philosopher cares nothing (μηδὲν φροντίζων) for any of them (65a6–7).

Now (1) presents no particular impetus to asceticism: there is a difference between enjoying food, drink, or sex in the right way, and being the sort of person who makes a serious pursuit of the pleasures of food, drink, or sex—after all, not every gourmet is a gourmand—and the latter sort of attitude is the sense of 'being

---

[24] Indeed, on a 'purificatory' reading of Socratic virtue, the *Apology* and the charges against a 'meddlesome' Socrates in it become simply unintelligible.

[25] We shall return to the controversial passage at 68d2–69c3 in the next section.

keen on' (ἐσπουδακέναι) such things. And I think that we can say the same thing about claim (5), which denies that such things are what a philosopher devotes mental energy to (φροντίζων). On their own, neither of these claims necessarily motivates asceticism.

But perhaps the other claims might. For one thing, (2) may suggest the modestly ascetic view that pleasures—at least those of bodily finery—are of utterly no interest, like the oddness or evenness of the stars. For Socrates says not merely that the philosopher refuses to place them on a pedestal, but indeed that the philosopher would just as soon be done with the body altogether. And, for another, (3) and (4) may suggest an even bolder form of asceticism, that the philosopher wholly shuns such pleasures—that he has nothing to do with them at all. Indeed, these refrains in the Defense Speech are echoed in other parts of the dialogue as well, where Socrates says that 'true philosophers abstain from all bodily desires, and stand firm without surrendering to them' (82c2–5), and again that 'the soul of the true philosopher abstains from pleasures and desires and pains, so far as it can' (83b5–7). However, on closer inspection we shall find that these sorts of claims express the same sort of point we find in (1) and (5) after all, namely that what the philosopher avoids and disdains is not *pleasure*—not even bodily pleasure—full stop, but only *unhealthy ways* of partaking of pleasure.

Let us look first at claims (3) and (4). Notice how striking a claim they seem at first to make: not only does philosophy change the philosopher's attitude toward pleasure, but it also changes his very *capacity* for pleasure, as he is described as 'someone who [3] finds nothing of that sort pleasant, and [4] takes no part in those things' (65a). This is much stronger than the claim that philosophy changes one's attitudes toward pleasure; rather, this suggests that philosophy actually removes even the simplest forms of bodily pleasure altogether. But how on earth could philosophizing change the fact that, say, quenching one's thirst is pleasant, as (3) might seem to suggest it does? Does philosophy also remove pain, or indeed the sources of pain, such that no pleasant cessation of pain is ever brought about, as (4) may suggest it does? Such a wholesale change not only in our values but also in our very physiology surely calls for discussion and defense, but Plato's text offers none. So what sort of detachment from pleasure is recommended in (3) and (4)?

It is surely important here to note how Socrates introduces (3) and (4), namely, in the mouths of people who do not share, or much understand, the philosopher's values: 'And presumably, Simmias, *it does seem to most men that* someone who finds nothing of that sort pleasant, and takes no part in those things, doesn't deserve to live' (65a4–6, emphasis added). Now Socrates makes it clear in the *Phaedo* that he thinks that ordinary people are motivated above all by pleasure and pain (e.g. 68c–69a). The philosopher, on the other hand, has very different values, priorities, and motivations; for he has noticed that the mortal nature conveys very striking and convincing reports about what is allegedly real and important through the vocal messengers of pleasure and pain, and learned that those objects are neither real nor ultimately important. Philosophers, then, 'do not walk on the same paths as those who, in their view, don't know where they are going' (82d3–4). Consequently, his experience of pleasure and pain will be revised: someone who is able to achieve such detachment and objectivity with respect to the objects of physical pleasure and pain will not interpret those experiences in the same way, as messengers with urgent and true messages, and thus will not make those experiences a priority. The philosopher's life with respect to physical pleasures and pains is just not like that of others, and that is why that life seems so bizarre to those others.

And it is from here that we are in sight of the answer to our question about the proper attitude to pleasure. For pleasure is not a mere sensation, but a way of registering the value we attach to the objects of our pleasure, and it is from the attaching of the wrong sorts of values to things that the philosopher becomes 'purified'. We can see this in Socrates' later discussion of the psychology of pleasure:

'Lovers of knowledge recognize that when philosophy takes their soul in hand, it has been veritably bound and glued to the body, and is forced to view things as if through a prison, rather than alone by itself; and that it is wallowing in utter ignorance. Now philosophy discerns the cunning of the prison, sees how it is effected through desire, so that the captive himself may co-operate most of all in his imprisonment.'   (82d9–83e7)

Consequently, Socrates says:

'the soul of the true philosopher abstains from pleasures and desires and pains, so far as it can, reckoning that when one feels intense pleasure or fear, pain, or desire, one incurs harm from them not merely to the extent that might be supposed—by being ill, for example, or spending money to satisfy one's desires—but one incurs the greatest and most extreme of evils, and does not take it into account.'   (83b5–c3)

The pleasures that Socrates has in mind are not merely the sensations our bodies feel when we are gratified. Rather, they represent kinds of attitudes—they represent what a person has made into a driving concern and a target for his energies. Socrates' focus is on pleasures that come to dominate a person. More precisely, he focuses on the pleasures to which one comes to sell oneself as a willing captive; for Socrates describes such a person as ὁ δεδεμένος συλλήπτωρ τοῦ δεδέσθαι, or a person in bonds who is an accomplice in his own binding (82e7).[26] What exactly is this 'imprisonment'? This is Cebes' question, and to it Socrates replies:

'It's that the soul of every human being, when intensely pleased or pained at something, is forced at the same time to suppose that whatever most affects it in this way is most clear and most real, when it is not so; and such objects especially are things seen, aren't they?' 'Certainly.'

---

[26] Notice also Socrates' description of the sensation he produces by rubbing his sore leg as 'this state *that people call* "pleasant"' (60b4, emphasis added), and the pleasures of food and drink as '*so-called* pleasures' (64d3, emphasis added). Perhaps he means to draw our attention to the difference between simple experiences that we may naïvely think are all that there is to pleasure, and the philosophically richer conception of pleasure that he wishes to discuss. But this is to speculate.

'Well, isn't it in this experience that soul is most thoroughly bound fast by body?'
'How so?'
'Because each pleasure and pain fastens it to the body with a sort of rivet, pins it there, and makes it corporeal, so that it takes for real whatever the body declares to be so. Since by sharing opinions and pleasures with the body, it is, I believe, forced to become of like character and nurture to it, and to be incapable of entering Hades in purity; but it must . . . have no part in communion with the divine and pure and uniform. . . . It's for those reasons, then, Cebes, that those who deserve to be called "lovers of knowledge" are orderly and brave; it's not for the reasons that count with most people . . .'   (83c5–e6)

Notice what Socrates thinks makes pleasure especially powerful as a psychic phenomenon, and thus potentially especially dangerous: pleasure and pain have a curious power, especially when intense, to convince the agent of the clarity, reality, and importance of their objects. As a result, one can eventually come to identify the concerns of such pleasures and pains as the things that really matter, and thus to adopt the concerns of the 'body'[27] as one's true concerns. And this is why so many people have a mistaken conception of the virtues: the virtues, they think, are skills of handling the 'body's' concerns (68d2–69c3). But those skills handle the body's concerns as governing concerns of the agent, and thus keep the agent from the true virtues of the philosopher. Those virtues are 'purificatory' only in the sense that they involve a revision of priorities and a proper reassessment of the agent's governing concerns.

What matters about pleasure, then, are the sorts of priorities in the agent that it represents. Once we understand that Socrates' target is the mistaken priority that all too many people give to pleasure, we find it far less surprising that he should claim that 'true philosophers abstain from (ἀπέχονται) all bodily desires, and stand firm (κατεροῦσι) without surrendering to them (καὶ οὐ παραδιδόασιν αὐταῖς ἑαυτούς)' (82c2–5), or that 'the soul of the true philosopher abstains from (ἀπέχεται) pleasures and desires and pains, so far as it can' (83b5–7). All that the context of these passages requires is that the philosopher not take such desires as his motivation for virtuous behavior—as his reason for being the sort of person he is—but rather cultivate a love for knowledge. The philosopher abstains from such desires and refuses to yield himself to them in the sense that his motivations, priorities, and values are simply elsewhere, and it is these different values that govern his actions and attitudes. For what he condemns are not pleasures *simpliciter*, but pleasures which reflect mistaken evaluative attitudes and priorities.

Socrates' point, then, seems to be that there is no value-neutral perspective on pleasure. Rather, pleasure is inextricably bound up with the kinds of pursuits—including the attitudes and values one has in those pursuits—of which they are the pleasures. And this implies that pleasure cannot be treated as an unconditional good, since pleasure is one way that a person attributes value to the things around her—a value that pleasure can attribute in a mistaken way.[28]

---

[27] As I argue in the next section, Plato in these passages means by 'body' not merely the physical body, an entire set of concerns that are bound to our nature as mortal, corporeal beings.

[28] We shall return to this point in later chapters, and particularly in Ch. 4 on the *Republic*.

This fact about the psychological nature of pleasure can also help us to make sense of Socrates' rather harsh discussion of pleasure in the Defense Speech, and in particular his claims (3) that the philosopher does not find pleasant the pleasures of food, drink, sex, or bodily elegance, and (4) that the philosopher does not partake of such pleasures. Surely Socrates does not deny that philosophers experience physical pleasures; Socrates himself experiences them in the dialogue (e.g. 60b–c). Rather, Socrates' point is that the philosopher does not experience them *as* reporting to him what things are worth treating as important in their own right. Perhaps many people experience pleasures just as if they displayed their goodness like a flag.[29] But what Plato tells us is that pleasures do not display that flag all by themselves, but only in so far as we choose to see them as displaying it. It is just that most people make that choice by default, because such pleasures are after all very cunning, all by themselves.

Given these radical differences, what must ordinary people think when they come upon the philosopher? Presumably, they would be surprised to find someone who does not live and prioritize and enjoy the same things in the same way that they do. Indeed, they may be so surprised that they suppose that this person simply does not understand pleasure, and does not appreciate why pleasant things give life its value. Rather, they will think that this person has failed to perceive the importance and reality of pleasant things, so much so that he seems not to take pleasure in them or give them any notice; the poor soul, they will think, has missed out on what life is really about, and thus has so wasted life that he 'doesn't deserve to live' and 'runs pretty close to being dead' (65a5–6). The philosopher's attitude toward pleasure is so different from the ordinary person's that the philosopher seems to him not to enjoy pleasure at all—not as he understands it, anyway. And, of course, the ordinary person would be right; his mistake comes in thinking that his own pleasures reflect what is real and important.

Moreover, this reading also makes sense of the claim that (2) the philosopher does not regard fine services to the body as of any value (ἐντίμους; 64d8–9); for what Plato takes to be the most interesting fact about pleasure is the way that it reflects and reinforces attitudes about the object of a pleasure. The philosopher does not enjoy pleasure as the non-philosopher does, since the latter values pleasure as such and for him this gives a distorted appearance of value and importance to its object; the philosopher, on the other hand, has escaped this trap, and understands what real value is, and this determines what he enjoys and how he enjoys it.

It seems clear, then, that Plato's harshness about pleasure in the *Phaedo* is not suggestive of asceticism after all. Plato's point seems to be that ordinary people do not see the philosopher's life as pleasant, because the philosopher does not engage in pleasures as they do, owing to her privileged perspective on the nature of the objects of pleasures. Unlike his Neoplatonist commentators, Plato in the

---

[29] Cf. the Epicurean thesis that all pleasure is self-evidently good, and indeed the sole criterion of goodness; see Cicero, *de Finibus* I.30.

Phaedo condemns not certain types of pleasures as such, but pleasures that reflect the wrong kinds of attitudes and priorities. In other words, Plato treats as evils not the pleasures themselves, but the irrational ways in which people all too often incorporate certain kinds of pleasures into their lives.

Socrates is confident in the face of death, then, not because he is surly about the mortal world, but because he has avoided developing the wrong kinds of priorities, priorities that would have him think that his happiness depends more on his ability to rearrange the world so that it meets his desires than on the strength with which he faces what cannot be changed. And that is to say that Socrates, in the *Phaedo*, is joyful—a good thing, too, since such a life as that is a far better candidate for a happy, flourishing life than would be a life spent in chronic discontentment with the human condition. A depiction of Socrates joyful, therefore, is a depiction of a life in which pleasure has taken the right direction. If this is the sort of depiction of Socrates that Plato offers in the *Phaedo*, as I have argued that it is, then in the *Phaedo* Plato actually comes out *against* asceticism.

Pleasure, therefore, would seem to be a *conditional good*: whether or not our affective life is a good one depends on whether it is guided by reason and thus reflects the right sorts of priorities. But perhaps in that case some will suppose that hedonism could turn out to be true, for it may be that although pleasure depends on the leadership of reason for its goodness, none the less the goodness it comes to have could be what makes a happy life happy. The question, then, is whether some form of pleasure might be the highest good to which all other goods—such as the virtues and other goods of the soul—are to be referred, or in terms of which their goodness is to be explained. As I shall explain now, Plato's view in the *Phaedo* is that it is not.

3.2 Why Plato is not a Hedonist

Hedonism is no more a single theory than asceticism is. Philosophical hedonists differ over what they understand pleasure to be (e.g. whether pleasure is a feeling; whether pleasure can be maximized; whether pleasures are commensurable, etc.), how they believe good things are connected to pleasure (e.g. whether things are good which maximize pleasure, in this way or that, etc.), how they think people deliberate and act with respect to pleasure (e.g. whether all deliberation either is or only ought to be hedonistic, etc.), and so on. But all forms of philosophical hedonism are committed to a thesis about value and the explanation of value, namely that pleasure is the central locus of value, all other values being understood as dependent, in some way or other, on the value of pleasure.[30] Hedonism is (or entails) the view that everything that is good is good

---

[30] See also Aristotle, *Nicomachean Ethics* X.3, 1174a1–12 for the idea that pleasure's being the good is incompatible with something other than pleasure being valuable for reasons that cannot be referred to pleasure.

because it either is properly connected to pleasure, or is pleasure.[31] In saying this, I mean to describe hedonism at the highest level of generality, and my claim is that no theory counts as hedonism that does not subscribe at least to this thesis about the role of pleasure in the explanation of value.

One benefit of this way of understanding hedonism is the great breadth and diversity of hedonist theories that it encompasses. Could it encompass Plato's view as well? Perhaps it could, however much the philosopher's values are revised and differ from those of ordinary people. For, although one's pleasure or enjoyment changes in important ways, it could nevertheless be said that the good still is that (new) pleasure. It is still possible, then, that what makes anything valuable in the end is the particular kind of pleasure it gives (or in some sense is), and perhaps we can say the same about the philosophical life and its pleasure.

This is a serious contender as a way of taking Plato's view of pleasure in the good life—in fact, certain texts in the *Phaedo* have been taken in the scholarly literature to suggest some such form of hedonism. For instance, we have already noted Plato's claim that the philosopher is keen on (ἐσπούδασε) the pleasures of learning (τὰς [ἡδονὰς] περὶ τὸ μανθάνειν; 114e3–4), and it seems clear that these are not the same sorts of pleasures as those he criticizes in Socrates' Defense Speech (63e–69e, especially 64d3–e1, 65a6–7). And, while Plato warns against being mastered by one's desires (68e–69d), perhaps the difference between the philosopher and baser persons is not that only the latter are 'bent on maximizing pleasure' while the former is not, but rather that the hedonism of the former is 'very much better thought out'.[32] Perhaps, then, the philosophical life contains wholly new pleasures in virtue of which it is the most pleasant life—and perhaps it is *this very fact* that makes the philosophical life so worth while.

Whatever the merits of such a view on its own, this cannot be Plato's view in the *Phaedo*, for Plato cannot espouse hedonism of any sort in the *Phaedo*. On this question I think that the most probative text is the so-called 'Affinity Argument', in which Socrates' discussion of the affinity of the soul to the divine shows that referring the goods of the 'divine' aspects of our nature to the goods of our 'mortal' aspects is unnatural for us. This argument is typically overlooked in this context. But, as I shall argue, in the Affinity Argument we can see that identifying with the 'divine' side of one's nature is the goal (τέλος) of human life,[33] and it entails that pleasure cannot be regarded as worth pursuing for its own sake in a life that fulfills that τέλος. Understanding our τέλος, then, shows us that pleasure cannot be the good. But first, we must return to an important passage from the Defense Speech in the *Phaedo* around which much of the

---

[31] This formulation is deliberately open-ended, to allow for a variety of interpretations of 'connected to pleasure' and 'is pleasure'. I discuss a few such interpretations in Russell (2000*b*) and (2003).

[32] See Bostock (1986: 31 f.); *con.* Gallop (1975: 103), who rejects this reading.

[33] This is a version of the thesis, found in several of Plato's dialogues, that our goal is 'likeness to God' (ὁμοίωσις θεῷ); see esp. *Phaedrus* 246d, 248a, 249c; *Timaeus* 47c, cf. 89e–90d; *Laws* IV, 716b–d; *Republic* X, 613a–b; *Theaetetus* 176a–c; *Philebus* 28c–30e. I discuss this thesis at length in Ch. 5; see also Annas (1999), ch. 3; and Sedley (1997).

discussion of pleasure in the *Phaedo* has centered in recent years, and which some commentators have taken to imply a form of hedonism. Does it?

3.2.1   Phaedo 69a6–c3 and the 'exchange metaphor'

As we have seen, Socrates raises a rather interesting point about people who develop forms of 'temperance' which have as their point securing a predominance of pleasure over pain: such people, he says, are 'temperate through a kind of intemperance', because their interest in being clever about pleasures is due to their being ruled by pleasure as a driving concern—'they overcome some pleasures because they're overcome by others' (68e2–69a4). He then makes the following observation, which is at the heart of our present controversy over hedonism:

'... [T]his may not be the right exchange with a view to goodness, the exchanging of pleasures for pleasures, pains for pains, and fear for fear, greater or lesser ones, like coins; it may be, rather, that this alone is the right coin, for which one should exchange all those things—wisdom; and the buying and selling of all things for that, or rather with that, may be real bravery, temperance, justice, and, in short, true goodness in company with wisdom, whether pleasures and fears and all else of that sort be added or taken away; but as for their being parted from wisdom and exchanged for one another, goodness of that sort may be a kind of illusory façade, and fit for slaves indeed, and may have nothing healthy or true about it; whereas, truth to tell, temperance, justice, and bravery may in fact be a kind of purification of all such things, and wisdom itself a kind of purifying rite.'   (69a6–c3)

The interpretation, and indeed the translation of this strange passage are very controversial. The controversy stems from Socrates' comparison of wisdom to a coin: '... it may be, rather, that this alone is the right coin, for which one should exchange all these things [πάντα ταῦτα]—wisdom; and the buying and selling of all things [πάντα] for that, or rather with that, may be... true goodness in company with wisdom' (69a9–b3). As Gosling and Taylor note, a coin (considered purely as a medium of exchange) is valuable not for its own sake but only for what one is able to get for it in an exchange. So when Socrates talks of an exchange between pleasure, on the one hand, and the 'coin' of wisdom, on the other, they argue, he must mean that wisdom, like a coin, is only instrumentally valuable, presumably for the intelligent acquisition of pleasure.[34] Socrates, it would seem, must be a hedonist, since he holds that goods of the soul are valuable only for the sake of securing certain pleasures.

What is the right conclusion to draw from Socrates' comparison of wisdom to a coin? Since metaphors do not, unfortunately, interpret themselves, and since Socrates is a bit sketchy about exactly which aspects of the metaphor are relevant to his point about wisdom and which not, it is not entirely obvious what conclusions we are to draw. But some conclusions would be clearly unwarranted.

---

[34] Gosling and Taylor (1982: 92 f.); they make a similar argument about the instrumental value of wisdom as a 'purificatory rite' (καθαρμός) at 69c3 (93 f.).

For example, the most annoying thing about money is that once you have spent it, you no longer have it to spend; but surely in saying that wisdom can be 'exchanged' for other things, and that other things can be 'bought' with it, like a coin, Socrates does not mean to say that by exercising my wisdom I shall come to have less wisdom to exercise.[35] And, surely, Socrates does not mean that the best thing a person can do with her wisdom is to get rid of it in favor of other things she likes better. As with all metaphors, it is possible, and perilous, to press this 'exchange' metaphor too far.[36]

It seems clear to me that the hedonist reading of the passage also presses this metaphor too far. One thing that we know Socrates means to establish in this passage is the foolishness of thinking that goods of the soul, like temperance, are to be referred to pleasure—it is, after all, his denial of that very point that *motivates* his metaphor. It would be most extraordinary if Socrates were to counter the thesis that the goods of the soul are only instrumentally valuable for the sake of pleasure with the thesis that the goods of the soul are, indeed, only instrumentally valuable for the sake of pleasure. Moreover, on this reading it seems that Socrates' disagreement with popular misconceptions about the value of pleasure relative to the virtues would be simply that most people are not clever enough in how they avoid some pleasures for the sake of others.[37] But clearly his disagreement is much deeper than that—it concerns whether any such cleverness as that could be a coherent conception of a virtue in the first place. Indeed, Socrates claims that the philosopher exchanges all pleasures and pains for wisdom, and thus possesses genuine virtue—and all of this, he says, is *irrespective* of the presence or absence of pleasure and pain in her life (καὶ προσγιγνομένων καὶ ἀπογιγνομένων καὶ ἡδονῶν καὶ φόβων καὶ τῶν ἄλλων πάντων τῶν τοιούτων, 69b4–5).

Perhaps, however, Socrates could have a deeper sort of disagreement with the 'popular' conception of virtue, but which would still not rule out Socrates' defense of some form of hedonism: perhaps what Socrates objects to is not the act of referring the virtues to pleasure *per se*, but of referring them to *bodily* pleasures—in which case he could still hold that certain intellectual pleasures were the highest good. After all, Socrates does say that one should be keen on the pleasures of philosophy (114e3–4), and Phaedo remarks that among the group assembled on Socrates' last day it was customary to take pleasure in philosophical conversation (59a3–5), as one would expect among a group who claim to be desirers and lovers (ἐρασταί) of wisdom (66e2–3). Moreover, the most reasonable assumption is that the 'pleasures' Socrates discusses in the exchange passage are to be understood as the same sorts of pleasures that motivate the

---

[35] Cf. Bluck (1955: 155); Gooch (1974: 154 f.).

[36] It is surely wise counsel, as Bluck (1955: 155) advises, not to press these metaphors, since Socrates' point seems to concern not the method of exchange but the ends or goals of exchange; cf. Hackforth (1955: 193).

[37] See Bostock (1986: 32), who claims that the philosopher's hedonism is 'very much better thought out' because it 'takes the longer view'.

faux-temperate person, not more elevated philosophical pleasures. But, even so, we still cannot say that the passage *motivates* hedonism. All we would be warranted in saying is that it is possible that, for all Socrates says here, the philosophical life is the most pleasant. But, of course, that would not entail that Socrates subscribes to hedonism,[38] much less that hedonism is a correct theory of value.

Moreover, even if we take Socrates' metaphor to be demonstrating that we are to exchange one thing for something we value more, the hedonist reading of the passage still would not go through, since that reading requires us to reverse the order of exchange that Socrates himself presents. What Socrates says is to be given in exchange ($\delta\epsilon\hat{\iota} \ldots \kappa\alpha\tau\alpha\lambda\lambda\acute{\alpha}\tau\epsilon\sigma\theta\alpha\iota$) is not wisdom, but 'all these things' ($\pi\acute{\alpha}\nu\tau\alpha \ \tau\alpha\hat{\upsilon}\tau\alpha$, 69a10)—that is, the pleasures, pains, and desires that he had just mentioned (69a7–8); and what they are exchanged *for* ($\dot{\alpha}\nu\tau\iota \ o\hat{\upsilon}$, 69a10) is wisdom.[39] The 'exchange...for...' relation is asymmetric: I can exchange ($\kappa\alpha\tau\alpha\lambda\lambda\acute{\alpha}\tau\epsilon\sigma\theta\alpha\iota$) my nickel for ($\dot{\alpha}\nu\tau\iota$) your piece of candy, but, of course, I cannot exchange your candy for my nickel. The exchange Socrates has in mind is not one of using wisdom to secure other things, but of trading those other things for wisdom—that is, I take it, managing one's dealings with other things so as to become a wiser person.[40] At the end of the exchange one is to have *acquired* the coin (wisdom), not spent it.[41] And this seems clearly in keeping with the

---

[38] To their credit, Gosling and Taylor acknowledge this fact in (1990: 115 f.); see also Bostock (1986: 34); Weiss (1990a: 117). Their main point is simply that the critique of pleasure in the *Phaedo* is not inconsistent with the hedonism discussed in the *Protagoras*, an issue I shall simply leave aside at present; but see Russell (2000a) and the epilogue to this book.

[39] Cf. Weiss (1987: 58), who suggests rendering 69a9–10 as '... but that sole right coin, for the sake of which all these things [pleasures, pains, and fears] ought to be exchanged [with each other] is *phronēsis*...'; see also Gooch (1974: 154 f.). (Notice that Weiss takes 'all these things' to be exchanged not for wisdom but with each other; I prefer the former interpretation, but for our purposes I see no reason to argue for one over the other here.)

[40] Notice that Gallop's translation of 69b1 ($\kappa\alpha\grave{\iota} \ \tau o\acute{\upsilon}\tau o\upsilon \ \mu\grave{\epsilon}\nu \ \pi\acute{\alpha}\nu\tau\alpha \ \kappa\alpha\grave{\iota} \ \mu\epsilon\tau\grave{\alpha} \ \tau o\acute{\upsilon}\tau o\upsilon$), which is friendlier to the reading of 'exchange' that I am opposing, has Socrates make an unfortunate shift in mid-sentence from buying and selling other things 'for' wisdom to buying and selling them 'with' wisdom, which suggests a shift from wisdom as the *yield* of exchange to wisdom as the *medium* of exchange. This would be a most extraordinary shift (which seems to be unintentional on Gallop's part; see (1975), note ad loc.), not only because 'or rather' is a very cooperative rendering of a simple $\kappa\alpha\acute{\iota}$ but also because it makes Socrates' metaphor seem not merely cryptic, but openly confused. Much better, I think, is a rendering like Hackforth's, 'if all our buying and selling is done for intelligence and with its aid' (1955: 55). (Grube (1997: 60), we should note, appears to leave $\kappa\alpha\grave{\iota} \ \mu\epsilon\tau\grave{\alpha} \ \tau o\acute{\upsilon}\tau o\upsilon$ untranslated, apparently treating it as an unnecessary restatement of the main idea of the clause.)

[41] I also think that the 'buying and selling' metaphor is no more than another—although admittedly less felicitous—way of restating the point of the 'exchange of coin' metaphor. Thus I would replace Gallop's rendering of 69b1–2 with 'buying and selling all things both for this and with this [i.e. wisdom]' and treat this phrase as equivalent in purpose to 'exchanging all these things for wisdom' as in 69a10. Moreover, I agree with Gallop (1975), ad loc., that 'with wisdom [$\mu\epsilon\tau\grave{\alpha}$ $\phi\rho o\nu\acute{\eta}\sigma\epsilon\omega\varsigma$]' at 69b3 modifies 'true goodness [$\dot{\alpha}\lambda\eta\theta\grave{\eta}\varsigma$ $\dot{\alpha}\rho\epsilon\tau\acute{\eta}$]' (cp. the similar modification of 'just' ($\delta\acute{\iota}\kappa\alpha\iota o\nu$) and 'pious' ($\ddot{o}\sigma\iota o\nu$) by 'with wisdom' ($\mu\epsilon\tau\grave{\alpha}$ $\phi\rho o\nu\acute{\eta}\sigma\epsilon\omega\varsigma$) at *Theaetetus* 176b2–3), as opposed to being the means by which—that 'with' which—other things are bought and sold; see also Weiss (1987: 59). Likewise, it seems natural that wisdom and virtue or goodness are identified, and that 'true goodness in company with wisdom' distinguishes the virtue that is wisdom from the spurious, popular sense of 'virtue' he is criticizing. Hence I also take the $\pi\acute{\alpha}\nu\tau\alpha$ at 69b1 to refer to the pleasures,

intended message of the entire discussion in this part of the *Phaedo*, which is that if you think of the goods of soul as having value for the sake of something else, then you have missed the point about why they really matter in the first place. And beyond that, I think, the metaphor simply does not go.

The 'exchange' passage is the greatest hope of the hedonist interpretation of the *Phaedo*, but this hope quickly fades on the reading that makes the best sense of the exchange metaphors, the best sense of the syntax of the passage, and the plainest philosophical meaning of the passage in its context. But, more than that, one of the very central passages of the *Phaedo*—the so-called 'Affinity Argument'—rules out a hedonist interpretation of the *Phaedo* altogether, to my mind, and to that passage we turn now.

3.2.2   The Affinity Argument

In the Affinity Argument (78b–84d), Socrates argues that humans have two natures, one of which he calls 'body' and the other 'soul', and argues for the immortality of the soul on the basis of its affinity or likeness to the divine, which is immortal. This is a long and complicated argument, and a full analysis of it would take us well beyond our scope. But there is much to learn from this argument that can be made fairly clear.

Socrates' aim is to show that in addition to the mortality of human nature, human nature is also in part divine, and he establishes this thesis through a rather long chain of arguments. His argument is that, first, composite things are those that are given to dispersion and destruction, and this class maps onto the class of things that vary and are inconstant,[42] while non-composite things, by contrast, are free from dispersion, and are marked by their constancy and unvarying nature (78c–e). Second, Socrates says that body is akin to sensible and unintelligible things, which are inconstant and thus composite and subject to dispersion (78d–e), whereas soul is akin to insensible and intelligible things, which are constant and non-composite (78c–d, 79a–b, e). This affinity of the soul to non-composite things, Socrates says, can be seen both because the things that intellect grasps are, like the soul itself, not visible or sensible things (79a–b) and because wisdom is an understanding of things that are pure and unvarying, such that the soul must be of like nature in order to enter their company (79c–e). Finally, these two classes—the inconstant and destructible, and the constant and indestructible—map onto the two disjoint and exhaustive classes of all things, the mortal and the divine[43] (respectively). Owing to the soul's capacity to direct

---

etc. of 69a7–8, that is as equivalent to πάντα ταῦτα in 69a10; I do not think, in particular, that πάντα at 69b1 is meant to include virtue (see Weiss (1987: 60) for criticism of this view), or that wisdom is the means for virtue, as some have suggested (e.g. Gooch (1974: 154–8); and the subtle view of Weiss (1987: 60–2)).

[42] Gallop (1975: 138) discusses the logical relation between 'the incomposite' and 'the unvarying' in greater detail.

[43] Socrates speaks of the divine realm interchangeably as the realm of abstract entities and the realm of God; cf. Gallop (1975: 143).

and govern the body, the soul most resembles the divine, and the body most resembles the mortal (79e–80b).

This bifurcation of human nature is important to Socrates' discussion of death in the *Phaedo* because it shows, first, that if the body is relatively durable, then the soul must be that much more so (80c–d); and second, that the soul that has identified with its 'divine' aspect through the proper pursuit of philosophy will go upon death 'into the presence of the good and wise God' (80d7):

> 'If it is in that state, then, does it not depart to the invisible which is similar to it, the divine and immortal and wise; and on arrival there, isn't its lot to be happy, released from its wandering and folly, its fears and wild lusts, and other ills of the human condition, and as is said of the initiated, does it not pass the rest of time in very truth with gods? Are we to say that, Cebes, or something else?'
> 'That, most certainly!' said Cebes.   (81a4–11)

For, Socrates says,

> 'the company of the gods may not rightly be joined by one who has not practised philosophy and departed in absolute purity, by any but the lover of knowledge. ... [B]y following reasoning and being ever within it, and by beholding what is true and divine and not the object of opinion, and being nurtured by it, [the soul] believes that it must live thus for as long as it lives, and that when it has died, it will enter that which is akin and of like nature to itself, and be rid of human ills.'   (82b10–c1, 84a8–b3).

So a human being is composed of two natures, body and soul (79b), and thus is a compound of the two universal natures, the mortal and the divine (80a–b). The question, then, is given that one cannot identify with both of these natures, with which ought one to identify? That is, since these two natures draw one's attention in different ways and call upon one to ascribe value, importance, and reality to different things, to which ought one to pay greater heed?

This question is especially pressing for Plato, given the way in which he draws the distinction between 'soul' and 'body'. For Plato is not, I think, merely making the claim that we are part physical and part mental. Rather, his distinction is meant to capture a distinction between two major sets of concerns that humans have and may choose to identify with. Humans are part 'body', for Plato, inasmuch as humans are characterized by instability: like all things in the physical world, humans change, vary, and fluctuate; hence they have needs and desires to be filled up with what they lack. But humans are also part 'soul' inasmuch as they have a certain stability: the soul, being stable, is capable of contemplating the fundamental and eternal truths of reality, which are themselves always stable and never admit of change or fluctuation. Given this diversity of concerns that we have, how are we to find concerns that bring the right kind of unity to our lives? Both sorts of concerns are real, but with which are we to identify?

Plato makes it clear that the philosopher is to identify with the soul,[44] the divine nature, and not with the mortal. That is why the philosopher is able to

---

[44] Cf. Gallop (1975: 88).

take his place in the company of the gods after death, since his soul has been disencumbered from his mortal nature, thus allowing the pure to know the pure (80d–81a, 82b–c, 84b; 67a–b).[45] But in what does our mortal nature consist? We must naturally assume that it includes our physical body; but it also seems to include the activities of the soul that the soul has inasmuch as it is associated with mortal nature:

'…if [the soul] is separated from the body when it has been polluted and made impure, because it has always been with the body, has served and loved it, and been so bewitched by it, by its passions and its pleasures, that it thinks nothing else real save what is corporeal—what can be touched and seen, drunk and eaten, or used for sexual enjoyment—yet it has been accustomed to hate and shun and tremble before what is obscure to the eyes and invisible, but intelligible and grasped by philosophy; do you think a soul in that condition will separate unsullied, and alone by itself?'
'By no means.'
'Rather, I imagine, it will have been interspersed with a corporeal element, ingrained in it by the body's company and intercourse, through constant association and much training?'
'Certainly.'
'And one must suppose, my friend, that this element is ponderous…'   (81b1–c9)

Socrates' account is self-consciously mysterious and occult (he goes on to explain that such souls as these become phantoms and wraiths that haunt tombs and graves), and it is not clear what we should make of these occult images. But what is clear is that the 'corporeal element' that weighs such souls down is the result of the kinds of pursuits and interests that have occupied it in life. Identifying with the 'corporeal' aspect of one's nature, then, amounts to taking certain concerns as central and defining of one's priorities: eating, drinking, strong feelings and sensations, having sex. This is not to say that those concerns are themselves corrupt by their nature, only that their being made *central* in one's life is corrupting. The difference between the natures that make up every human, then, is ultimately a difference in concerns: for the pleasures to be got from acting, and for the wisdom and intelligence that guides our acting.[46]

This suggests that 'body' in this argument is taken to refer not merely to the literal body but also to the mortal and human activities of the soul, as opposed to its proper activity of soul, strictly conceived. Clearly, then, the category of 'body' will include bodily pleasures, which are, strictly speaking, experienced in the soul.[47] But will it include all pleasures generally? I think that it will. For

---

[45] Cf. Gallop (1975: 140), who claims that 79c2–e7 includes a tacit assumption of Empedocles' principle that 'like knows like' (DK 31.A.86, B.109).

[46] It certainly seems to press Socrates' haunting image too far to treat the soul as some quasi-material substance that becomes literally impregnated with some heavy matter; Gallop (1975: 143 f.) expresses some such concern; cf. Hackforth (1955: 93, note on 82d).

[47] See 65a6–7, where bodily pleasures are said to be those which come through the body (διὰ σώματος), presumably to the soul; see also Bostock (1986: 26–8). Bostock also discusses issues that arise from this view, such as whether the philosopher's soul—devoid of its uniquely 'human' functions—can retain personal identity after death; space and scope prevent us from exploring that question here.

emotions, feelings, desires, and pleasures are mental phenomena for Plato, yet they are part of our varying nature and not our stable nature, so they would fall on the 'body' side of Plato's distinction. None the less, it is difficult to know where to place pleasures of philosophic activity, say, on this distinction, understood in terms of variability and stability.

However, this distinction must also be understood in terms of the very different roles that different parts of our nature play in relation to each other. The import of the distinction between the divine and the mortal, Plato makes clear, is that it distinguishes what can bring rational direction, and what stands in need of such direction. This is apparent in Socrates' claim that it is the ordinance of nature that the divine rule the mortal:

> 'Now look at it this way too: when soul and body are present in the same thing, nature ordains that the one shall serve and be ruled, whereas the other shall rule and be master; here again, which do you think is similar to the divine and which to the mortal? Don't you think the divine is naturally adapted for ruling and domination, whereas the mortal is adapted for being ruled and for service?'
> 'I do.'
> 'Which kind, then, does the soul resemble?'
> 'Obviously, Socrates, the soul resembles the divine, and the body the mortal.'   (79e9–80a9)

These two aspects of our nature that Socrates calls 'soul' and 'body', it seems, have not only an important metaphysical difference but also an *ethical* one: one of them is able to bring direction to the whole organism by directing the other, and it is unnatural that the order of direction should be reversed. In other words, Socrates' distinction between 'soul' and 'body'—the 'divine' and the 'mortal'—is meant to be coextensive with the ethical distinction between that aspect of us that is fit to give direction and shape to our lives, and that aspect of us that must be given that direction and shape.[48] So, to speak very simply, my ability to think about what it makes sense for a rational being to do—my practical reason—ought to be giving shape and direction to my impulses to get angry at other people, say, and not vice versa. This is how Nature has designed

---

[48] His assumption that they *are* coextensive, however, seems to me problematic. Socrates does seem to understand pleasure as transformed by virtue to be part of the good character of the philosopher (more on this below). In that case, pleasure is 'fit to serve'—its goodness is dependent on the goodness of the virtue that transforms it, and is, therefore, a conditional good. However, the assumption that such conditional goods are coextensive with our 'bodily' nature seems unwarranted, since some of the things that virtue transforms, and thus are conditional goods, can be peculiar to our 'stable' nature. Indeed, Plato says in the *Phaedrus* (247d1–5) that the mind of a god finds a kind of pleasure (εὐπαθεῖ, d4) when it beholds the forms. (It is instructive to note that, as we have seen, the Stoics would later appropriate εὐπαθεῖν in order to describe the reasonable affective disposition of the sage to all things, which constitutes a lack of passion (πάθη) but not a form of coldness or sterility.) And at *Phaedo* 114d8–115a3 he contrasts the pleasures of learning to 'alien' (ἀλλοτρίους, e2, cf. e5) pleasures, suggesting that such pleasures are not alien but proper to the soul—even classifying it, evidently, alongside the virtues. In a word, the distinction between what leads and what serves seems to me highly instructive, but it is unhelpful of Plato to explicate it in terms of a distinction between 'mind' and 'body'. Unfortunately, Plato's double-mindedness on this issue—that transformed pleasure is part of good character, and that pleasure is 'merely mortal'—will last his entire philosophical career without a satisfactory resolution; but I shall not pursue the point here.

us to function, by pairing our 'mortal' nature with a 'divine' nature to guide it. For Socrates, we are to say the same about the relation between reason and pleasure. This is so because the first is able to grasp and bring about a certain kind of order in one's life that the second is incapable of grasping or bringing about on its own.[49] And this is as true of the pleasure of philosophic activity as it is of any other: in order for pleasure to be a good thing in one's life, it must take on a form within one's life that it does not take on by itself, but only under the direction of reason. The distinction between what is more or less stable turns out, I think, to be somewhat incidental. More to the point is the distinction between what, like the divine, is such as to lead and direct and what, like the mortal, is such as to be led and directed.

This development in Plato's distinction between the divine and the mortal has an important ethical consequence: since we are not to subordinate the guiding part of our nature to the guided part, and since pleasure belongs to the guided part, it is unnatural for us to take pleasure of any kind to be the good for the sake of which we live, or to which we refer all of our actions and choices—and it is certainly unnatural to refer our development of the goods of the self to pleasure. That would be to identify with the sorts of concerns that are not capable of bringing about the right kind of order to one's life. In short, since all pleasure is part of our 'guided' nature, every form of hedonism would therefore subordinate our guiding ('divine') nature to our guided ('mortal') nature—just what it is a central point of the *Phaedo* to reject.

3.2.3 *Pleasure as a conditional good*

Consequently, this difference between our 'divine' and our 'mortal' nature is also a difference between what in us is unconditionally good and what is conditionally good. The ethical difference between our divine and mortal natures, that is, is a difference in their active role in bringing direction to one's life, integrating it into an orderly and harmonious whole. The key to happiness, then—and the center of the philosophical life—lies in the rationality and intelligence with which we live, bringing a direction to all the parts of our life that they do not bring to themselves.

Plato is not a hedonist, then, because pleasure is conditionally good, depending on what place one gives it in one's life, and happiness depends on the unconditionally good—wisdom and intelligence—that brings the direction that a good human life requires. Nor is he an ascetic, since he clearly does believe that pleasure can be given the right sort of place in one's life; and so there must be a form of pleasure that is reasonable, since the pleasures of a distorted sense of priorities can never take the right place in one's life. And this, of course, is the joy that we see particularly in the Socrates of the *Phaedo*: he is joyful in the face

---

[49] This, I take it, is also the sense of Socrates' calling the body an evil (κακοῦ) at 66b5–6, since his focus there is also on the body's power to distract the soul from the truth. As Hackforth (1955: 49 f.) points out, this point is made also in the account of human creation at *Timaeus* 43b–c.

of death because he recognizes that the goodness of his life consists in the goodness of his soul, which no one can take away. His joy, his contentment, his gladness—these are not the source of the goodness of his life, but rather his appreciation in his affective nature of that goodness. Joyfulness is not so much the reward of being the right sort of person, or what the goodness of such a person's life consists in, as it is the way that beings like us recognize the goodness of our lives and our selves. Hedonism, in referring all other goods to the supreme good of pleasure, gets this point exactly backwards, on Plato's view.

Pleasure as a conditional good also shows us something about how pleasure can be rationally incorporated into one's life. As we have seen, what Plato thinks is most significant about pleasure and pain is the fact that they both reflect and reinforce a person's attitude toward the reality and importance of the objects of pleasure and pain. It is this fact about pleasure that explains the mistake that so many people make, who are so stricken by the intensity of certain pleasures that they think 'nothing else real save what is corporeal—what can be touched and seen, drunk and eaten, or used for sexual enjoyment' (81b4–6); and this also explains why the philosopher is suspicious of intense pleasures and pains, which have this enticing power (82d ff.). So pleasures and pains can reinforce one's attitudes toward their objects. We have also seen how they reflect such attitudes, since it is the philosopher's change in his attitudes about such objects that radically revises his attitudes toward the pleasures of those objects.

However, if pleasures reinforce and reflect one's attitudes toward their objects, and if pleasures are bad when they attribute the wrong sorts of value to their objects, then pleasures should not be bad, but on the contrary quite reasonable, when their objects really do have the sort of value that one enjoys them as having. And this result is borne out in the *Phaedo*. For one thing, it makes a perfect fit to Plato's depiction of a joyful Socrates that is the centerpiece of the *Phaedo*. It would also explain why the philosopher, despite his condemnation of the pleasures that most people occupy themselves with, is none the less keen on pleasures of his own: the pleasures of learning (114e) come about only for one who correctly values the objects of learning, and thus these pleasures reflect and are an outgrowth of her attitude, which just is the *correct* attitude to have. And it explains why, as Socrates so vividly demonstrates, philosophers have such different attitudes toward pleasures than other people do: in many people, their attachment to pleasure has come to dominate their perspective on their life; in the philosopher, pleasure has instead been harmonized with a rational perspective on life as a whole, having received the guidance and direction of reason. It is little wonder, then, that Plato should celebrate as he does the joyfulness of the philosophical life.

Pleasure of the sort that has been our focus in the *Phaedo* is a good within the self, and, when transformed by reason, it becomes not merely directed by virtue, but a part of one's virtue. My capacity for finding enjoyment and fulfillment in the things that I do needs to be given direction by right reason if I am to live well, and reason directs this dimension of myself when I take pleasure in the sorts of things that it is good that I take pleasure in. In that case, my pleasure becomes one of the ways in which I find value in things, people, and activities around me, taking joy in the value and importance that they really do have. So understood, we can see that pleasure is always a part of a person's character, for better or worse, and this seems plausible, since few things tell us more about a person's character and who they are than the sorts of things that they find rewarding and enjoyable. In a virtuous person, pleasure is not merely something that we have good character with respect to. It is transformed and becomes part of good character itself.

The joy of the philosophical life is pleasure, understood as an affective and evaluative attitude, transformed into part of the virtuous outlook itself. In fact, it is consistent with the *Phaedo* to tell a similar story concerning even the more ordinary pleasures, such as those of eating, drinking, and sex. On the view I am attributing to Plato, to take pleasure in something is a matter of enjoying it *as* having a certain value for the one enjoying it. If the pleasures of eating, drinking, and sex are the sorts of things that one can partake of in innocuous and rational ways, one is then able to enjoy them in the right way, that is as having the kind of value they do have. It is not only the gourmand who can enjoy the pleasures of eating—in fact, someone who is able to enjoy them for what they are, and no more, may indeed enjoy them most.[50] If one can enjoy life's pleasures for what they are, rather than as reports insisting that our concerns as needy beings ought to be our masters, then the same sorts of activities and sensations go from being compulsions and excesses to being the sorts of pleasures they really should be. In a word, in engaging in life's simple pleasures I need to understand that doing so is not what my life is about at the end of the day. When I understand that, I can engage in them *as* simple pleasures, even as Socrates himself is seen to do.

It would, I think, be going too far to put this account of gustatory and sexual pleasures into Plato's mouth in the *Phaedo*. The most that we can say is that, given what Plato does say in the *Phaedo*, it would be quite possible, even most natural, to take 'bodily' pleasures to be conditional goods. More than that, the best explanation of the complexity of Plato's attitude toward pleasure in the *Phaedo* is that pleasures are conditional goods. And this is already a subtler, richer, and more nuanced account of pleasure in the *Phaedo* than we may have thought possible.

Perhaps this is why the view that pleasure is good or bad depending on whether its object really has the sort of value that one enjoys it as having— depending on whether the pleasure reflects the right kinds of priorities and concerns—is also the view that the Middle Platonist Alcinous attributes to Plato. Alcinous claims that an emotion (πάθος) is 'an irrational motion of the soul' (*Handbook of Platonism* 32.1), of which the basic forms are pleasure and pain (32.2).[51] There are several outstanding features of Alcinous' account of the πάθη

---

[50] Such, in fact, is the view of Epicurus; see esp. Diogenes Laertius, *Lives* X.130–2.
[51] Trans. Dillon (1993).

that are especially worth noting here. One is his treatment of pleasure primarily as a response to value in its object:

We say [that the emotions (πάθη) come about] 'in response either to something bad or something good', because the presentation of a thing of indifferent value does not provoke an emotion; all emotions arise as a result of the presentation of either something good or something bad. For if we suppose that something good is present to us, we feel pleasure; in the imminence of such a thing, desire; while if we suppose that something bad is present, we feel distress, and if imminent, fear.   (32.1)

For this reason, Alcinous allows that some pleasures are natural, necessary, and proper:

Of emotions, some are 'wild', others 'tame'.[52] 'Tame' are such as belong naturally to man, being necessary and proper to him. They remain in this state as long as they preserve moderation; if they come to exhibit lack of moderation, they become bad. Such are pleasure, distress, anger, pity, shame. *It is proper, after all, to feel pleasure when things are in accordance with nature,* and to feel distress at the opposite situation.   (32.4, emphasis added)

Pleasure, then, is appropriate when it is 'moderate'. Interestingly, Alcinous glosses a 'moderate emotion' as an emotion which reflects a *correct* evaluative attitude: a 'moderate' pleasure is a pleasure taken in a way that it is natural and appropriate for a human being. By contrast, then, pleasures which 'exhibit lack of moderation' must be contrary to nature—they reflect an unrealistic estimation of the importance of their objects in the life of beings such as us.[53]

Hence it is Alcinous' concentration on the psychology of pleasure as an evaluative response that allows him to avoid the distortions of Olympiodorus and Damascius, and instead distinguish a class of affective states that constitute realistic and appropriate responses to presentations. So, despite the fact that pleasures as such are neither good nor bad (32.7), nevertheless certain forms of pleasure are rational and appropriate (32.4), depending on their relation to one's priorities. In our terms, this is to say that pleasure is a conditional good, and it is this understanding of pleasure in Plato's ethics that emerges from a close reading of Plato, and especially the *Phaedo*.

But we are still short of a full account of pleasure and the good life in some important ways. In the *Gorgias*, it is clear that happiness depends on unconditional

---

[52] Alcinous is clearly referring to *Republic* IX, 589a–b and Plato's depiction of the irrational part of the soul as a hydra-like beast with many heads, some of which are tame and some wild. It is interesting to note, however, that for Plato the beast's heads had represented desires and appetites in particular, and not 'passions' more generally, as in Alcinous' reference; see Dillon's note ad loc. (1993: 196). Alcinous' indifference to strict lines of division between these 'parts' of the soul is characteristic of many ancient thinkers in Plato's tradition (e.g. cp. Galen's assimilation of anger to the disobedient horse of the *Phaedrus* (*On the Doctrines of Hippocrates and Plato* 3.3.13–24), which for Plato had represented appetite and not emotion; see also Aristotle, *Nicomachean Ethics* I.13, 1102a26–32). We shall return to this passage of the *Republic* in Ch. 7.

[53] Moreover, Alcinous' understanding of 'moderation' makes it clear that moderate emotions are not a species of the incorrect ones. Thus the moderate emotions, in Stoic terms, are εὐπάθεαι— affective responses that are reasonable and natural.

rather than conditional goods, and in the *Phaedo* that pleasure is a conditional good. That means, of course, that happiness does not depend on pleasure; but it also means that pleasure *is a good* of some sort, and what is less clear thus far is exactly what kind of *role* pleasure plays in the good life, and why it matters that pleasure should play it. It is important for us to get clear about this. For one thing, it will cast more light on the notion of 'rational incorporation' that I raised in the first chapter as a way of understanding how the unconditional good makes other things good. But it will also cast more light on what it might be like to live the sort of life that Plato tells us is best. It is one thing to have a 'blueprint' for the good life that gives a plain sketch of it, and another to have a 'model' of the good life that we can turn over in our hands and inspect from all sides. And here Plato's *Republic* is a great help.

4

Pleasure and Moral Psychology in *Republic* IV and IX

We have seen that Plato believes that practical wisdom, or virtue as a whole, is an unconditional good—the only unconditional good, in fact—and that the unconditional good is what determines happiness. This is what I have called the directive conception of happiness, and it says that happiness consists in the wisdom with which one lives. But unless we say more about this account of happiness, we seem to face a dilemma: how can we show that the life of wisdom is attractive, without making the happiness of that life depend on some dimension of that life or other, instead of on its rational structure as a whole?

One benefit of the additive conception of happiness, of course, is that it does well at showing that a certain mode of living is attractive, and thus a reasonable candidate for happiness—because it is so pleasant, or satisfying of desires, or productive of successful projects, or nicely equipped with life's amenities. Unfortunately, it does so at the cost of making happiness 'dimensional' rather than holistic: a happy life is so because of that dimension of it that is its pleasantness, say. A happy life is a unity, and is happy on account of the kind of unity that it is. This is not to say that the additive conception renders the good life a disordered ragbag; the pursuit of desire-satisfaction or successful projects may well give one a final end around which to organize all of one's actions and choices.[1] But it *is* to say that the happiness of that life is not in that organization as a whole, but rather in some aspect (or aspects) of it. It is for this reason that Plato rejects the additive conception of happiness, as he focuses instead on the intelligence with which one lives one's life and brings order and harmony to every area of it.

Here, of course, the directive conception does much better, as it focuses precisely on the intelligence or wisdom that makes one's whole life good and is manifest in every dimension of one's life. But it seems, at first anyway, to have much less to say about why the life of wisdom is attractive. Even worse, the directive conception may leave us with a candidate for happiness that seems

---

[1] And, of course, Epicurus, e.g., argues that 'tranquility' ($\dot{\alpha}\tau\alpha\rho\alpha\xi\dot{\iota}\alpha$), or 'katastematic pleasure', is exactly that kind of final end (see also Russell (2003)).

altogether too thin and sterile to be recognizable as real happiness at all. Perhaps if I were wise, my life would be orderly; but what I want is a *happy* life, and not merely a 'tidy' one, which sounds altogether too drab. This is not to say that this or any candidate for happiness must appeal to all people alike. Perspectives on the good life can become damaged, warped, and distorted, and no candidate for happiness should be held hostage to perspectives of those types. But the problem remains that a life's being 'orderly' is not necessarily the first thing that even reasonable, mature persons would cite as making the happy life happy. And this problem, I think, accounts for the appeal of the additive conception, both in its own right and as a framework for interpreting Plato. Perhaps we are better off allowing that wisdom is the efficient cause of a good life, but is not its goodness.

This problem for the directive conception is made better by the fact that 'good', as I indicated in Chapter 2, is an attributive adjective. We can call a failing cactus 'good', if we like that sort of thing in a cactus, but we cannot call it a 'good *cactus*'. Moreover, even if we can call the life of a failing cactus a 'good life' ('the kind of life I happen to want for my cactus'), we cannot call it a 'good *life of a cactus*'. What will count as a good existence for a cactus depends on the kind of thing that a cactus is and what counts as health and flourishing for that kind of thing.[2] Likewise, anything we call a 'good *life of a human being*' must take account of the fact that we are rational beings who need justifying reasons for acting and choosing as we do.[3] Whatever our flourishing is, it must be the flourishing of *that* kind of being. And, as I argued in Chapter 2, it is for this reason that Plato says that the wise do well and are happy (*Gorgias* 506d–507c).

However, to say that a human is a rational being is not necessarily to say that a rational being is *all* that a human is.[4] We are also passionate, emotional, desirous, affective beings; and, as I argued in Chapter 3, although pleasure cannot be an unconditional good, there is still good reason to think that pleasure should be a conditional good, and thus *some* kind of good. Perhaps the affective parts of our nature cannot give themselves their proper direction, much less unify and direct our whole nature, but no account of our nature—and thus of our flourishing—can leave them out. In fact, to leave out these parts of our nature is *also* to make happiness dimensional rather than holistic. Happiness consists in something that is holistic, both in concern and compass, *and* in substance. If our happiness depends on our practical rationality, then our practical rationality must not only look after all areas of our life but also bring all areas together within itself so as to yield an integrated whole.

Here we return to the notion of wisdom as 'rational incorporation' that I sketched in the first chapter. My concern for wealth, for instance, is one area of my life and my self. It is also an area in which I need wisdom, or practical

---

[2] See Hursthouse (1999), ch. 9.

[3] For a good discussion of this idea (and its application within Stoic ethics), see Engberg-Pedersen (1986: 168–77).

[4] See Sherman (1997), ch. 1 for an intriguing discussion of this issue and its very different treatments by Aristotle, the Stoics, and Kant.

intelligence, if I am to use wealth well in my life. But recall that, on Plato's account, the proper use of wealth on my part is actually my intelligent directing of my behavior ($\pi\rho\hat{a}\xi\iota\varsigma$) with respect to wealth (see *Euthydemus* 281a8–b1). Notice, then, that as I develop in wisdom, my attitudes and priorities with respect to wealth become transformed by wisdom, and this suggests that they become part of the actual, concrete form that my wisdom takes in my life. This transformation is what I mean by saying that wisdom rationally incorporates this area of my life into an orderly, organic whole, and it is even more pronounced in the case of my desires and pleasures, which are themselves among those very mental attitudes that wisdom transforms as it rationally incorporates each area of my life. On this account of wisdom as rational incorporation, wisdom does not merely direct each part of my self, but fuses every part of myself into an organic whole which is then what my wisdom, my practical rationality, *is*. Wisdom, in that case, is holistic in *exactly* the right way for happiness. On this account of rational incorporation, it is a mistake to think of wisdom's leadership in directing our affective nature as one thing acting on something distinct from it. Rather, rational incorporation is to capture the different relations internal to something that is, and functions as, a whole.[5] Our practical rationality, that is, is not one part of our nature that directs the rest, but rather our whole nature, in so far as the whole exhibits an order and harmony that is in accordance with right reason. It includes every dimension of our nature, but not every dimension plays the same sort of role within that whole.

In this chapter, I argue that it is this conception of wisdom, and its relationship to pleasure in particular, that Plato seeks to defend in the *Republic*. Pleasure, on Plato's view, is a crucial element of the good life, not because wisdom is inadequate for happiness without it, but because pleasure is a part of our nature that wisdom transforms and causes to flourish. Transformed, rationally incorporated pleasure is not the 'payoff' of the life of wisdom, but one of the forms that wisdom takes in one's life. That life is happy not just as the life of a rational being, but also as the life of a fully *human* being.

But here we must exercise great care. We must not slide from the claim that the life of wisdom counts as happiness because of the way that wisdom transforms our affections, to the claim that our affections so transformed are themselves responsible for our happiness. The former says that the unconditional good determines happiness because it is appropriately holistic, whereas the latter says that conditional goods can (wholly are partially) determine happiness themselves, once their conditions are met. And that, of course, is the crucial difference between the directive and additive conceptions of happiness.

Therefore, when Plato argues in *Republic* IX that the supreme pleasantness of the virtuous life is a particularly great consideration in demonstrating that the virtuous life is happy, we must ask whether this argument espouses the additive

---

[5] We shall explore this idea at greater length in Ch. 6, as we examine Plato's own account of the complex internal relations of all sorts of wholes in the *Philebus*.

or the directive conception of happiness. On the additive conception, the argument is straightforward: the virtuous life is happy because the virtuous life is also the life of supreme pleasure, and the life of supreme pleasure is happy. On the directive conception, the argument is much more subtle: the virtuous life is happy because the virtuous life is the life of a fully integrated, healthy, and flourishing psyche, as demonstrated by (among other things) the transformation of the affective dimensions of the virtuous person's psyche, and such a life is the happy life. On this view, the demonstration of that flourishing in the affective aspects of the psyche is a demonstration of what psychic health is for a human being, and how virtue *is* that health. It demonstrates how virtue rationally incorporates all the areas of our life into a flourishing unity.

In the first part of this chapter, I shall set out this need for interpretive care in more detail, by looking at its connection to a more general problem for understanding how Plato thinks virtue benefits its possessor in the *Republic*, to which any adequate reconstruction of the 'pleasure arguments' in book IX must respond. In the second and third sections I shall offer a new approach to these arguments, arguing that Plato's strategy is to demonstrate that virtue benefits its possessor on the grounds that the virtuous person, and only the virtuous person, possesses a healthy and harmonious psyche. Plato's conception of pleasure in book IX, I argue, is a form of apprehending one's life as satisfying and worth living, and his argument is that having the true form of such pleasure means that one's life is, in fact, satisfying and worth living, and that one's psyche is healthy and harmonious. And such pleasure is to be found only in the virtuous person.

This way of understanding Plato's analysis of pleasure in the *Republic* not only preserves the allegiance to the directive conception of happiness that Plato has shown in the *Euthydemus, Gorgias*, and *Phaedo* but also motivates it by further articulating the holistic nature of virtue or wisdom as the determinant of happiness. Furthermore, it is my hope that this way of understanding Plato's analysis of pleasure will afford modern readers a fresh avenue for thinking about the nature of pleasure and its relation to happiness, and what it means to determine the quality of a life on the basis of its pleasantness.

4.1   Virtue, Pleasure, and Happiness in the *Republic*: Some Problems

Both the additive and the directive conceptions of happiness can account for the importance of pleasure in the happy life, but only the former will make pleasure a determinant of happiness. It is clear that Plato makes virtue the determinant of happiness in *Republic* IV (441c–445e), where he argues that the virtuous person lives with her soul in its perfect, healthy, and harmonious condition, and his point clearly is that there is no question whether a life so lived is the happy one. And whatever makes its possessor's life a happy ($\epsilon\upsilon\delta\alpha\iota\mu\omega\nu$) one, is what truly benefits its possessor:[6]

'Goodness, then, is apparently a state of mental health, bloom, and vitality; badness is a state of mental sickness, deformity, and infirmity.'
'That's right.'
'Isn't it the case, therefore, that goodness is a consequence of good conduct, badness of bad conduct?'
'Necessarily.'
'Now we come to what is, I suppose, the final topic. We have to consider whether moral conduct, fine behaviour, and being moral (whether or not the person is known to be moral) are rewarding, or whether it is wrongdoing and being immoral (provided that the immoral person doesn't have to pay for his crimes and doesn't become a better person as a result of being punished).'
'It seems to me that it would be absurd to consider that topic now, Socrates,' [Glaucon] said. 'Life isn't thought to be worth living when the natural constitution of the body is ruined, even if one has all the food and drink and wealth and power in the world. So how could it be worth living when the natural constitution of the very life-force within us is disrupted and ruined?'   (IV, 444d13–445b1)

We shall take a much closer look at this argument in a moment. For now, notice that on this argument what explains the fact that virtue makes one happy is the very nature of virtue itself. But things become more complicated in *Republic* IX, when Plato offers a pair of arguments purporting to show that the virtuous life is the life of greatest pleasure (580c–588a). The first of the 'pleasure arguments' (580c–583a) is that although different lives seem most pleasant of all to those who advocate them, only the philosopher—the epitome of a virtuous person—has the knowledge and experience needed in order to make a true judgment about which life is most pleasant. Since the person with the most privileged perspective identifies the virtuous life as most pleasant, that life must be the most pleasant. In the second pleasure argument (583b–588a), Socrates claims that some pleasures are more real and genuine than others, and that only the philosopher experiences these real pleasures. For while most so-called pleasures are merely a matter of escaping from pain, the philosopher scales the true heights of pleasure, by satisfying the greatest part of the soul with the understanding of reality. Moreover, when the whole soul accepts the leadership of reason—as it does in the virtuous person—each of the parts of the soul enjoys its own greatest pleasures (586e–587a).

We shall examine these arguments in greater detail below as well, but already they seem to differ in strategy from Plato's defense of virtue as its own reward in book IV. How are we to square this defense of virtue in book IX with the defense in book IV? If Plato is arguing in book IX that virtue's pleasantness makes virtue a benefit to its possessor, then it is not clear how this fits with his claim in book IV that virtue is a benefit to its possessor because of what it itself is; yet it is not easy to see what other role the pleasure arguments of book IX might be playing

---

[6] Cf. Reeve (1988: 28); Sachs (1963: 145–7); Kirwan (1965: 171, 172 f.); Irwin (1995: 190).

in the dialog. How are we to take the claim that virtue is rewarding because it is most pleasant, when this claim is put alongside the claim that virtue is its own reward? Does *virtue* make its possessor happy in its own right, or is the idea rather that virtue is supremely pleasant, and *pleasure* makes one happy?

What, then, makes the virtuous person happy, virtue or the pleasure of virtue? At stake here is what sort of benefit Plato takes virtue to be, and how he thinks that virtue makes its possessor live well. What conception of value and benefit does Plato have in the *Republic*?[7] We can put into sharper relief the precise philosophical issue that is at stake here, by seeing why certain approaches to this issue that we might take will not do.

Perhaps the easiest approach is to say that virtue makes its possessor happy *both* in its own right, *and* because of the pleasure it brings its possessor. Perhaps, that is, we should conclude simply that Plato is presenting two distinct ways in which virtue makes its possessor happy, one in book IV on the grounds of what virtue is in its own right, and another in book IX on the grounds of the pleasures associated with virtue.[8] The fact that virtue is pleasant, on this view, is one of the facts about virtue that explains virtue's power to make its possessor happy, and the nature of virtue is another.

However, it does not seem that this can be the sort of argument that Plato is giving, for three reasons. One, this interpretation of the *Republic* would make the value theory of the *Republic* extremely complicated—much more so than Plato ever lets on in the *Republic*. If the nature of virtue and the pleasure of virtue *each* explain why the virtuous are happy, then both virtue and pleasure are our good, or parts of it, but nothing in the dialogue prepares us for the thesis that each of *two* things is (part of) our highest good. Much less does anything in the *Republic* prepare us for the value-theoretical complications that such a thesis would raise,[9] which would be far greater than Plato seems to recognize in the *Republic*.[10] How are these twin goods of virtue and pleasure related to each other? How is each related to happiness? How do they figure in one's motivation? How are they unified into a single good life? Not only does the *Republic* offer no answers, it does not even raise the questions. If this interpretation were correct, we should

---

[7] There are also two more basic problems that the pleasure arguments raise: one, what it means to say that a virtuous life is 'more' pleasant than a vicious life, since their pleasures are incommensurable; and two, how there can be any rational adjudication between parties, each of whom takes his own life to be the most pleasant. I shall address these problems as they emerge in our analysis of the pleasure arguments, below.

[8] This may be the intent of the rather startling claim of Kirwan (1965: 171) that we find 'the *equation* of happiness and pleasure in Book IX' (italics added).

[9] Cf. Irwin (1995: 235), who notes one important difference between these facts: 'People who value what they regard as justice in the belief that it is a non-instrumental good, but who value it for a feature it does not have or for a non-essential feature it has, are not just people.' It is important to note, however, that my point here is about how these facts about virtue differ not in terms of agents' motivations (as important as that issue is), but in terms of the proper explanation of virtue's producing happiness. None the less, we can see with Irwin that if Plato is defending virtue from the standpoint of a virtuous person, praising virtue for its pleasantness may well seem out of place.

[10] I have benefited here from conversation with William Stephens.

wonder whether Plato recognized the complexity of the value theory he had constructed for himself, but failed to mention it, or was simply nodding.[11] Either way, the central moral position of the *Republic* becomes quite a mess if Plato is offering these two distinct defenses of virtue in books IV and IX.[12]

Two, notice that on this interpretation Plato's account of the happy human life renders it dimensional rather than holistic. On this view, Plato did not think it enough to point out the nature of the virtuous life, but thought it necessary to point out its pleasantness as well, in examining the happiness of that life. In that case, virtue must be incomplete without pleasure, and thus not the kind of all-encompassing good that happiness requires. But this means that the virtue with which one lives is but one dimension of one's life, as, presumably, is the pleasure of so living; and so on this view happiness belongs not to the whole of one's life, but to a pair of its dimensions that are individually incomplete. So this view cannot take seriously the holism of happiness, and it would therefore be unfortunate if Plato held it.

And three, if virtue is unconditionally good while pleasure is conditionally good—as, I have argued, Plato thinks it is—then on this interpretation happiness is determined both by the unconditionally good and by a conditional good. But, of course, the whole point of that distinction within eudaimonism is to pick out the different roles that different types of goods play with respect to happiness, a difference that this interpretation cannot take seriously.

A more common approach to the problem is to say that while Plato argues in book IV that virtue makes its possessor happy, in book IX he moves to very

---

[11] See N. White (1984: 415 f.), who speculates that Plato had not worked out the issues surrounding the relation of pleasure and happiness here. Reeve (1988: 151–4) argues that while pleasure is the content of the peculiar goods of the psychic parts, and that 'the content of the best and happiest life is the pleasure of knowing the truth,' still 'neither knowledge nor pleasure is the good . . .'. On this view, however, it remains unclear to me precisely how pleasure is to fit into the argument whereby Socrates shows that virtue (including knowing the truth) is our good on the grounds that it makes us happy. The problem also comes in addition to the fact that Socrates offers no argument whatever for the view that pleasure is a good; on the contrary, Socrates deals very brusquely with the idea that pleasure is a sort of goodness earlier in the *Republic* (505b–c, 509a, see also 580c–581e; cf. Gosling and Taylor (1982: 101–3), and N. White (1979: 226)).

[12] It has also been suggested to me by Richard Geenen that the defenses of virtue in book IX may be intended to show a thesis not addressed in book IV, namely that the virtuous person is happy even on the rack. But I shall not adopt this reading of the *Republic*, for (at least) two reasons. First, this reading goes against the clear purport of book IV, on my reading of it. The thesis in question concerns the question of virtue's 'profitability', and we should notice that when Socrates suggests returning to the question of virtue's profitability, Glaucon answers that they have already settled that question (445a–b)—that is just the upshot of the health analogy. Indeed, Socrates' whole goal in the health analogy was to show that the denial of virtue's profitability was predicated on a false theory of value, and that once we see what virtue and vice are, we see that happiness depends on virtue. Pleasure and pain are not able to override this fact. That is why Glaucon recognizes how ridiculous it is to think that vice can make one happier than virtue can (445a–b). And Socrates fully agrees; his only worry is that the argument has not been sufficiently articulated (445b). As I argue below, if there is any discontinuity between books IV and IX on this point, I am not sure what Plato could have done differently if he had explicitly intended to hide it from view (cf. Gosling and Taylor (1982: 99)). Second, on this reading of the *Republic* it still remains the case that pleasure explains why the virtuous are happy (in particular, why they are happy on the rack), again leaving us with a dubious value theory in the *Republic*.

different considerations about virtue, which are meant only to 'praise' virtue in some less specific way, by adding a welcome postscript about how pleasant a virtuous life is, say. As John Mabbott and Richard Kraut argue, Plato appeals to the pleasure of virtue simply to show that a life of virtue need not be *devoid* of pleasure.[13] Alternatively, Terence Irwin suggests that the focus of the arguments is on reason's ability to make us good judges of things like pleasures.[14] And Julia Annas and Nicholas White have each suggested that Plato is here considering some of the 'natural consequences' of virtue, perhaps an appeal to the sorts of considerations that would get the attention of certain of the dialog's inter-locutors or readers.[15]

Unfortunately, approaches of this sort are difficult to reconcile with the fact that the two pleasure arguments of book IX are purported proofs of the *happiness* of the virtuous life, and not mere 'praise' for the virtuous life. This is quite clear from the text. For one thing, the pleasure arguments follow on the heels of a first argument the conclusion of which is that the virtuous are happy, and they are immediately introduced as 'second' and 'third' proofs. What else are we to infer but that they are meant to be proofs of the same conclusion?[16] And, in fact, Socrates implies exactly that when he introduces his first pleasure argument:

'Shall we hire a town crier, then, or shall I be the one to proclaim ... *the happiest person to be the best and most virtuous person*—that is, the person who possesses the highest degree of regal qualities and who rules as king over himself?...'
'You can make the announcement.'
'All right, then. *That's the first proof,* but I wonder how *the second one* strikes you.... [namely, that] of the three kinds of pleasure, the most enjoyable ... is that which belongs to the intellectual part of the mind; one's life becomes most enjoyable when this part of the mind is one's motivating force.'
'Of course. I mean, when a thoughtful person recommends his own way of life, he ought to be taken seriously...' (IX, 580b8–d1, 583a1–5, emphasis added)

We may well conclude, 'If Plato intended to separate his proofs of the greater pleasantness of the philosophic life from the proof of the greater *eudaimonia* of the just life, then he has certainly done his best to conceal that intention by his manner of introducing the second proof'.[17] I think we can say the same of the third proof as well, which Socrates introduces as follows:

'*That makes it two,* then, one after another: immorality has twice been defeated by morality. In Olympic fashion, *here's the third round*...I wonder whether you'll agree

---

[13] See Mabbott (1937: 472–4); and Kraut (1992: 313 f.). Cf. also Plato, trans. Waterfield (1993: 439), note on 580d; and Rowe (1984: 106). Mabbot goes so far as to claim that the arguments in book IX about happiness and pleasure are entirely dispensable for the project of the *Republic*; see Kirwan, (1965: 171); and Foster (1938: 230) for well-placed criticisms of this view.

[14] See Irwin (1995: 294). However, the actual role of pleasure in Plato's defense of virtue is somewhat unclear to me on Irwin's view, and Irwin does not raise the question how pleasure is related to happiness in *Republic* IX. C. C. W. Taylor (1998: 68) is also difficult to classify.

[15] See Annas (1981: 294, 314, cf. 168, 316, 326 f.); N. White (1979: 79, 233 f.).

[16] Cf. Gosling and Taylor (1982: 99–102); Reeve (1988: 153 f.).

[17] Gosling and Taylor (1982: 99).

that only the philosopher's pleasure is true and pure, while the others are illusory...'
(583b1–5, emphasis added)

Clearly, Plato sees the considerations about pleasure as *part* of the argument that virtue makes its possessor happy.

Moreover, there is no reason to say that Plato shifts from a discussion of virtue as beneficial for its own sake in book IV, to a discussion of virtue's 'consequences,' such as its natural pleasantness, in book IX.[18] There is no independent reason to separate the purport of books IV and IX in this way,[19] and in fact Plato introduces the arguments of books VIII and IX as *completing* the argument begun in book IV. After discussing the analogy between a good state and a good soul in book IV, Socrates begins book V as follows:

'So that's the kind of community and political system—and the kind of person—I'm calling good and right. Given the rightness of this community, I'm describing all the others as bad and flawed: not only are their political systems wrong, but they also influence individuals' characters incorrectly. And I see them as falling into four categories.'
'What four categories?' [Glaucon] asked.
I was on the point of listing them and explaining how, in my opinion, each in turn evolved out of the preceding one, when Polemarchus [interrupted me].   (449a1–b1)

Socrates starts this comparison of lives for the explicit purpose of completing the argument of book IV that virtue benefits and vice harms its possessor (see 444e–445e). And at the beginning of book VIII, which moves seamlessly into book IX, Socrates makes it clear that he is taking up the unfinished business of the end of book IV and the beginning of book V:

'But now that we've finished with all that [i.e. the material of books V–VII], let's try to resume our journey by recalling where we were when we took the side-turning that led us here'.
'That's no problem,' [Glaucon] said. 'You were talking, much as you are now, as if your discussion of our community were complete. You were saying that you'd call good the kind of community you'd described at that point, and its human counterpart . . . Anyway, you claimed that, given the rightness of our community, all the rest were flawed, and you said, if my memory serves me well, that of these remaining political systems, four types would be worth mentioning, and that we ought to see where they and their human counterparts go wrong, so that we can decide whether or not the best person is also the happiest person, and the worst the unhappiest, which we can only do once we've seen all these types of human being and reached agreement as to which is best and which is worst.

---

[18] Socrates says at 358a that he does intend to speak later of virtue's consequences. I agree with White that we should understand these to be the 'natural' consequences of virtue, i.e. those that virtue secures all on its own, as opposed to virtue's 'artificial' consequences, which virtue secures only given certain conventions and institutions (N. White (1979: 29, 79)). But I do not agree with Annas and White that Socrates is *here* speaking of these consequences. It should be noted, however, that Annas takes the two pleasure arguments as purported proofs of the virtuous person's happiness, but thinks that they do not, in fact, serve as such, that is, that Plato 'is actually starting again . . . despite the talk of "three proofs" ' (Annas (1981: 306)).

[19] See N. White (1984: 400–3 and nn. 18–19). Strangely, Guthrie (1975: 475, 537) seems to be of two minds about this.

I had just asked which four political systems you had in mind, when Polemarchus and Adeimantus interrupted. . . . Why don't you resume your stance, then . . . ?'   (543c4–544b2, 5)

Now the discussion of the four bad types of person occupies all of book VIII and the first portion of IX. In book IX Socrates considers the 'dictatorial' type of person, and it is in comparing this type of person with the virtuous person that Socrates' pleasure arguments emerge. In Socrates' opinion, his defense of virtue in book IV was left unfinished, as the prelude to book V makes clear, and he declares his intent to finish it in VIII and IX. Plato has not changed tack.[20]

What is more, Glaucon makes it absolutely clear that they are going through the arguments surrounding the comparison of good and bad lives 'so that we can decide whether or not the best person is also the happiest [εὐδαιμονέστατος] person, and the worst the unhappiest' (544a).[21] And immediately after the final pleasure argument, Socrates takes Glaucon back to the question they raised in book II (358e–367e) and first began to answer in book IV (444e–445b):

'All right,' I said. 'At this point in the argument, let's remind ourselves of the original assertion which started us off on our journey here. Wasn't it someone saying that immorality was rewarding if you were a consummate criminal who gave an impression of morality? Wasn't that the assertion?'
'Yes, it was.'
'Well, now that we've decided what effect moral and immoral conduct have,' I said, 'we can engage him in conversation.'   (588b1–8)

Socrates then introduces his famous image of the soul as an amalgam of a man, a lion, and a monster, and using this image Socrates argues that only one hierarchical structure of the parts of the soul is worth having (588b–592a), concluding that

'in so far as the mind is a more valuable asset than the body, it's more important for the mind to acquire self-discipline, morality, and intelligence than it is for the body to become fit, attractive and healthy.'
'You're absolutely right,' [Glaucon] said.
'Then anyone with any sense will put all his energies, throughout his life, into achieving this goal.'   (591b3–c2)

The 'effect [that] moral and immoral conduct have' must be taken to include the results of the pleasure arguments, for it is at their conclusion that Socrates says they are now ready to return to their original question. Socrates' discussion of pleasure in *Republic* IX is so framed on both sides by an explicit return to the

---

[20] See Gosling and Taylor (1982: 99 f.).
[21] The view of Gosling and Taylor (1982: 103 f.) is difficult to classify. They claim that, while Socrates denies that pleasure is the good, none the less in the absence of an account of the good Socrates argues for the superiority of virtue on the basis of other, set criteria, including pleasure. However, this still leaves it unclear to me just how Socrates understands pleasure to be related to happiness. For Socrates is not arguing for the superiority of virtue in any old way, but by showing that virtue makes its possessor *happy*.

project of book IV, that it is clear that the pleasure arguments themselves must be a crucial part of that very project.[22] Therefore, if Plato was arguing that virtue is beneficial for its own sake in book IV, then he means to argue for the same thesis in books VIII–IX.

So the view that the pleasure arguments are to be disconnected somehow from the project of book IV clearly differs from Plato's own assessment of how these arguments fit into the rest of the dialog. Nor, therefore, does it do any good to suggest that Socrates discusses the pleasure of virtue simply because it offers the sort of consideration that his listeners in the dialogue want to hear:[23] that suggestion would at most tell us why Plato muddled his discussion of virtue and happiness, but it would do nothing to make it any less of a muddle.[24] What is more, downplaying the pleasure arguments makes it seem quite odd that Socrates should describe the second pleasure argument as 'the most important and serious fall of the whole competition' between virtue and vice (583b6–7).[25] Indeed, the more we restrict the demonstration that virtue makes its possessor happy to book IV, the more superfluous all the arguments of book IX begin to appear.[26] We cannot avoid the conclusion that the pleasure arguments of book IX are arguments for the thesis that virtue makes its possessor happy, for which Plato had begun to argue in book IV.

So what *is* Plato's argument for the happiness of the virtuous life, and what does the pleasure of that life have to do with its happiness? What we need is a way to understand how Plato could appeal to the pleasures of the virtuous life as

---

[22] N. White (1979: 234) claims that at this point 'Plato sums up the results of his arguments for the superiority of the just life and presents an image of the soul to illustrate those results.' I presume that the result of the pleasure arguments that White is referring to is the fact that no part of the soul gains its own pleasure when anything but reason rules the whole (233, cf. 130).

[23] So suggests, e.g., N. White (1979: 233 f.), who takes Thrasymachus as the target. White's suggestion does have the virtue, however, of offering an explanation why Socrates bothers discussing pleasure in the first place; *con.*, e.g., Kraut (1992: 313 f.).

[24] Notice also that such a shift in Socrates' approach would be a step in entirely the wrong direction at this point in the dialog. For the more seriously we take Plato's arguments that virtue is good in its very nature, the less to the point we shall find arguments that virtue's goodness is dependent on something else. If Socrates has already shown that a virtuous person is a happy person, then he has proven so much of so much importance that his quickly moving on to other, merely 'nice' added bonuses of virtue is anticlimactic at best, and surely must seem so even to Glaucon and Adeimantus. And to say that Plato discusses pleasure for the sake of, say, Thrasymachus is to assume that Plato conceives of the pleasure of virtue as something that Thrasymachus could already recognize as what he is seeking, as if pleasure were commensurable across different kinds of lives, and not peculiar to ways of life. We shall return to this below.

[25] Kraut, (1992: 314) says that it is called the greatest fall because only in this argument is the gap between the virtuous and vicious shown with such emphasis. But this does not explain why the argument is given in the first place, or why the enormous gap in pleasantness of lives is so important that demonstrating its enormity should give us 'the greatest fall'. These are fairly pressing questions, since in 'the greatest fall' Socrates spends a great deal of time and energy trying to show something which he 'was never even asked to show, namely that the just person's life is more *pleasant* than the alternatives' (Annas (1981: 306); cf. Guthrie (1975: 541); Kraut (1992: 313)).

[26] Annas (1981: 348 f.) raises just this objection to Plato's introduction of the (artificial) consequences of virtue in *Republic* X, 612a–614a. This problem is bad enough when it arises after Plato's defense of virtue for its own sake. It would be much worse if it arose *within* that defense.

a way of showing that virtue makes us happy, without making pleasure yet another supreme good alongside virtue. And Plato does just that, on my view, as the pleasure arguments of book IX are parts of a larger argument, begun in book IV, to show that virtue is the health of the soul, and constitutes our well-being. Let us begin again with a closer look at that larger argument.

4.2 Virtue and the Health of the Soul: *Republic* IV

In book IV of the *Republic*, Plato argues famously that the various functions of the soul must belong to three distinct parts of the soul: the rational part; the spirited or passionate part; and the appetitive or desirous part (436a–441c).[27] Plato then shows, first, that in a good soul each of the soul's three parts is in its own particular good condition and performs its function well, as do the parts of the good city:

'So no doubt, Glaucon, we'll also be claiming that human morality is the same in kind as a community's morality.'
'Yes, that's absolutely inevitable, too.'
'We can't have forgotten, however, that a community's morality consists in each of its three constituent classes doing its own job.'
'No, I'm sure we haven't,' he said.
'So we should impress upon our minds the idea that the same goes for human beings as well. Where each of the constituent parts of an individual does its own job, the individual will be moral and do *his* own job.' (441d5–e2)

Having each part doing its own job also keeps each part from its own form of badness, as Plato makes clear in the case of the desirous part: the rational and passionate parts must guide it so as to 'make sure that it doesn't get so saturated with physical pleasures (as they are called) that in its bloated and strengthened state it stops doing its own job, and tries to dominate and rule over things which it is not equipped by its hereditary status to rule over, and so plunges the whole of everyone's life into chaos' (442a7–b3).

Plato then argues, second, that the hierarchical relationship between these three parts of the soul must be of the appropriate kind. Reason must control the whole mind, using passion as its ally to direct and soothe desire:

'Since the rational part is wise and looks out for the whole of the mind, isn't it right for it to rule, and for the passionate part to be its subordinate and its ally?'
'Yes.'
'Now . . . isn't it the combination of culture and exercise which will make them attuned to each other? The two combined provide fine discussions and studies to stretch and educate the rational part, and music and rhythm to relax, calm, and soothe the passionate part'.
'Absolutely.'

---

[27] I discuss this psychological model, and the difficulties it raises, in greater detail in Ch. 7.

'And once these two parts have received this education and have been trained and conditioned in their true work, then they are to be put in charge of the desirous part...' (441e4–442a5)

And third, in such a person, Socrates says, there is health in each part of the soul, and there is health in their integration with one another:

'Now that morality and immorality are in plain view, doesn't that mean that wrongdoing and immoral conduct, and right conduct too, are as well?' I asked.
'Why?'
'Because their role in the mind happens to be identical to that of healthy or unhealthy factors in the body,' I said.
'In what sense?'
'Healthy factors engender health, and unhealthy ones illness.'
'Yes.'
'Well, doesn't moral behaviour engender morality, while immoral behaviour engenders immorality?'
'Inevitably.'
'But you create health by making the components of a body control and be controlled as nature intended, and you create disease by subverting this natural order.'
'Yes.'
'Doesn't it follow,' I said, 'that you create morality by making the components of a mind control and be controlled as nature intended, and immorality by subverting this natural order?'
'Absolutely,' he said.
'Goodness, then, is apparently a state of mental health, bloom, and vitality; badness is a state of mental sickness, deformity, and infirmity.'
'That's right.'   (444c1–e3)

I think that speaking of health and integration[28] here is particularly appropriate. For one thing, this way of thinking of mental or psychic well-being is familiar to us: we commonly think of the good life as one of wholeness and harmony, where a person is not at war within herself but at peace. For another, thinking of virtue as the health of the soul is especially important for Plato. For even if the question 'Which is better for one, virtue or vice?' is not regarded as having an obvious answer, none the less there is an obvious answer to the question, 'Which is better for one, health or degeneration?' Plato's point is to show that the former question is really a special case of the latter question (444c–d), after all, and so if the answer to the one is clear, then so should be the answer to the other (445a–b).[29]

---

[28] See also Annas (1981: 132); Reeve (1988: 156); Irwin (1995: 253).
[29] These features of Plato's argument are especially important in light of the fact that, as C. C. W. Taylor (1998: 66) points out, before Plato's time Heraclitus and Democritus had already located 'doing well' (happiness) in the possession of a certain psychological condition, and so Plato must show not simply that but further what this psychological condition is, in a way that makes its connection to happiness plausible. See also Reeve (1988: 156): 'I think we would all agree that, whatever our goals in life, we would welcome a psyche with a desire structure of this harmonious kind, and that, *ceteris paribus*, we would want to have been brought up in a way that maximized our chance of having such a psyche.' See also Annas (1982: 132, 153, 321).

In short, virtue makes us happy because virtue, by its very nature, is a harmonious and integrated mode of existence.

This is a powerful argument, but at this point we shall probably find it too quick—not surprisingly, since Socrates himself finds it too quick. For the argument shows that to have a virtuous soul is to have a healthy soul, but it is too quick in showing that any other kind of soul is an unhealthy soul (444a–d). It also leaves this issue of the health of the soul a bit sketchy—just what is it, exactly? Just what is the good condition or health of each part? And exactly why is this form of health our greatest good as whole creatures? That is why, I think, Socrates says at the end of book IV that his view needs further clarification (445b). Consequently, Socrates proposes to investigate the alternative, immoral lives in order to see just how they fare worse. This he will do in books VIII and IX.[30]

For now, however, consider two points Socrates has made in book IV about the virtuous soul: each of the parts of this soul is in its good condition, and the appropriate relationship or hierarchy holds among the parts. These points correspond to two desiderata for the soul.

(a) *Each part of the soul must be fulfilled*, where by 'fulfilled' we mean that the part must have its particular good condition, and no part of its nature should be squelched. This point will continue to unfold as Plato goes on to discuss further the psychology of virtue and vice in books VIII and IX.

(b) *Between these parts of the soul there must obtain the appropriate hierarchical relationship*, namely that reason guides the passionate part, and together they control the desirous part.

The important thing to notice is that in book IV these two desiderata are intimately connected, since desideratum (a) is satisfied if and only if (b) is satisfied; that is, (c) *the hierarchy of parts is in order if and only if each part is in its good condition*,[31] in other words, the good condition of the parts and the proper relationship among the parts, stand or fall together. For the nature of each part of the soul contains not only its proper *function* but also its proper *place* in the hierarchy of the mind to which its function suits it (cf. 442a–b).

Reason's function is to plan for the agent as a whole, while the passionate part has affective responses based on our conceptions of ourselves, and the desirous part simply wants what it wants when it wants it. Therefore, since the natural

---

[30] See also Irwin (1995: 256, 281, 283).

[31] For this principle in Plato, see, e.g., Annas (1999: 151): 'when reason rules, then the rational part obtains its own pleasures, and so do the other two parts, the honor-loving and the money-loving; thus all the soul's parts get what is appropriate and the person's life as a whole is pleasant. When, however, reason does not rule, none of the parts gets the pleasure that is appropriate to it, and the whole life goes askew and fails to be pleasant overall.' Similarly, Reeve (1988: 156) claims that 'The three parts of [the virtuous person's] psyche are satisfied or frustrated in unison,' and N. White (1979: 130) that 'The rule of reason is best, [Plato] thinks, because it can be seen to put the soul in the best condition that it can be in, a condition in which there is as little conflict as possible, and in which all of the parts of the soul gain satisfaction in an orderly manner' (referring the reader also to 573c–576b, 588b–590a, which we shall discuss below).

function of reason is to plan for the agent as a whole, its nature is to rule the whole soul. Each part, that is, has a role to play in the order and harmony of the whole soul. The fulfillment of each part, and its integration into the whole, cannot be pulled apart.

Now suppose that we could show that: (d) *the virtuous person alone has the right structure between the parts of the soul and has each of the parts in its good condition.* In that case, it would be the virtuous person alone who has a completely healthy soul, and so clearly virtue would be beneficial and rewarding, considered strictly in its own right. This would give us a powerful demonstration of the happiness of the virtuous life, and so also of how virtue benefits its possessor.

And this is just the form that Socrates' argument is going to take. For the thesis that is expressed by (c) is suggested in book IV, but not fully articulated. Furthermore, in book IV Socrates has not proven (d), since he has not shown conclusively that *only* the virtuous person can have a healthy soul. These, I think, are the main items of unfinished business with which Socrates is concerned at the end of book IV and the beginning of book V. To see how these points develop, let us turn to books VIII and IX where the discussion resumes.

4.3   Virtue, Vice, and the 'Pleasure Arguments'

In books VIII and IX Socrates discusses four kinds of vicious person, in contrast to the virtuous person of book IV. The difference between these vicious types, and between them and the virtuous type, is in the hierarchy of the parts of the soul in each. Socrates first discusses the 'timocratic' or ambitious person (548d–550c), who identifies with his passionate part, and thus seeks power, fame, and prestige above all. Improper education and acculturation have allowed his passionate and desirous parts to become prominent; he thus compromises his rational part by settling for the intermediate between reason and desire, namely passion (see 550a–b).

Notice that this ambitious person arises when his rational aspect is kept from developing properly: his lack of education has the twin consequences of bringing his passionate side to the fore, and of corrupting his attitudes toward goodness (549b). And this happens, Socrates says, because his passion lacks the guidance of reason: ' "Now, as a young man," I continued, "a person of this type will disdain money, but the older he gets, the more he'll welcome it at every opportunity, don't you think? This is because his mercenary side will have come to the fore, and because his attitude towards goodness will be tainted, thanks to his lack of the best guardian" ' (549a9–b4). So he fails to satisfy desideratum (a), since the parts of his soul are hindered and compromised—in particular, his rational grasp of goodness has become 'tainted'. And this is clearly connected to his failure to satisfy desideratum (b) by having the parts of his soul in an improper order. This is one way, then, of illustrating the point that (c) *the hierarchy of parts is in order if and only if each part is in its good condition*; or, rather, it is one way of illustrating *part* of that point, namely:

(c1) *if the hierarchy of parts is out of order, then some part is not in its good condition*;

for (c) is a biconditional that is equivalent to the conjunction of (c1) and:

(c2) *if the hierarchy of parts is in order, then each part is in its good condition.*

Socrates has not yet defended this latter claim. We shall return to it shortly.

Next, the 'oligarchic' or mercenary person (553a–555b), who subjects his reason and passion as slaves to his mercenary desires (553b–d), is led by love of wealth into conflict within his desirous part, as he relies on his mercenary desires to control the unnecessary and expensive ones (554c–e): 'So internal conflict will characterize this sort of person: he isn't single, he's divided into two. His condition is simply that his better desires by and large control his worse ones ... [And] he's afraid of waking up desires which would require him to spend money and of summoning up their assistance in a competitive situation' (554d9–e1, 555a3–4). Again, the corrupted hierarchy in this man's soul is connected to the ill condition of the parts of his soul. For not only are his rational and passionate parts squelched by his desirous part but his desirous part itself is in conflict with itself, as his unguided desires are simply left to duel. And, again, his failure to satisfy desideratum (a) is tied to his failure to satisfy (b), just as thesis (c1) says.

Moreover, the problem is the same in the 'democratic' man (558c–562a), a man of indulgent desires, and in the 'dictatorial' man (571a–576b), a man of lawless and frenzied desires. So in each of these four sketches a vicious person places something besides reason at the top of the hierarchy, with the result that the part of the soul at the top becomes degenerate, and the parts below it are squelched and unfulfilled.[32]

So far, then, Socrates has suggested thesis (c1) in book IV, since the nature of each part of the soul demands that it occupy a particular place in the hierarchy of the parts, and by examining (c1) in his discussion of vicious souls in VIII and IX, Socrates has now given (c1) a fuller statement and firmer footing. But what about (c2)? This point too was suggested in book IV, since the virtuous soul is healthy in both its parts and in its integration of parts. Still, it was *only* suggested; can Socrates enlighten us about what it is like for things to go right in the soul? On my view, this is exactly what Socrates undertakes in his two pleasure arguments in book IX.

4.3.1 The first pleasure argument

As we saw in our thumbnail sketch of the first pleasure argument (580c–583a), Socrates argues that only the philosopher is fully qualified to judge which life is

---

[32] Cf. Irwin (1995: 283), who notes that the injustice of an unjust soul can be traced to the dominance of one of the soul's non-rational parts.

most pleasant, and the philosopher prefers the life of virtue, which is guided by reason, over lives of ambition guided by passion and lives of profit-making guided by desire (580d–581e). Now the philosopher, Socrates says, is the only one of these three types of person who has all the qualifications needed to judge between these kinds of life, namely, experience, intelligence, and rationality (581e–582e). Since these qualities are needed in every choice, it is the philosopher's perspective that counts in this choice between lives. But since the philosopher is the best decision maker, and the philosopher decides that the life of virtue and reason is the most pleasant, it follows that the life of virtue and reason really is the most pleasant (583a).[33]

But does that follow? We may have good reason to be skeptical. Suppose that I have a broad experience of ice cream flavors, and have a very acute intelligence and outstanding critical skills (at least where ice cream is concerned). Suppose, then, that after careful deliberation and much soul-searching, I decide that rocky road ice cream is my favorite. What do my special credentials in choosing ice cream flavors actually imply about my choice of rocky road? Surely they imply that I probably did an outstanding job of deliberating about and settling on my decision, but this does not mean that someone who is partial to (say) chocolate chip instead of rocky road has made any kind of mistake. After all, isn't the best one to speak about the merits of chocolate chip someone who really knows, as I do not, what it is like truly to prefer chocolate chip? Likewise, isn't Socrates' argument just as confused as this? Can there be adjudication of disagreements across such different perspectives?[34]

I do not think that Socrates is making this mistake. Now, if we think of pleasure simply as a feeling, or a sort of thrill—something like the sweet sensation of tasting ice cream—then there may well be no reason to think that there is a privileged perspective regarding which sorts of endeavors are the most thrilling or feel the best, and thus little hope of adjudicating disagreements across *those* kinds of perspectives. However, we have independent evidence that Socrates must not be thinking of pleasure in that sort of way, and the conception of pleasure that Socrates must have, given what he says about pleasure, requires us to start anew and rethink the role that an appeal to pleasure is playing in his argument.

---

[33] This argument is often compared with J. S. Mill's similar argument about the superiority of higher over lower pleasures (see *Utilitarianism*, ch. 2), and the family resemblance between these arguments is strong. The most important similarity is that both arguments hold that some perspectives on pleasure are privileged, and thus are better indicators of what is truly pleasant for humans (see also Aristotle, *Nicomachean Ethics* X.5). But it is also important to note that Mill believes that we prize the activities we find pleasant because we find them pleasant, while Plato seems to believe that things are pleasing to us because we prize them for other reasons. Perhaps the most important difference, however, is that Mill's argument focuses primarily on pleasures of kinds of activities, while Plato's focuses primarily on pleasures of kinds of lives.

[34] This objection is stated by numerous scholars, but most recently by C. C. W. Taylor (1998: 68). *Con.*, e.g., Reeve (1988: 146); Irwin (1995: 291 f.). See Annas (1981: 307–9) (who also talks about preferences of ice cream flavors) and N. White (1979: 228) for good discussions of the problem.

Notice that the things being compared, and thus the things that the pleasures in question are the pleasures of, are *lives* considered as wholes[35] and centered on certain kinds of defining interests—mercenary, ambitious, and philosophical—which belong to the part of the soul with which the person identifies:

'What if we said that what [the desirous part] enjoys, what it cares for, is profit? This would be the best way for us to clarify the issue for ourselves: we could keep our references to this part of the mind concise, and call it mercenary and avaricious. Would that description hit the mark?'

'I think so,' [Glaucon] said.

'And isn't our position that the passionate part always has its sights set wholly on power, success, and fame?'

'Yes.'

'So it would be fair for us to call it competitive and ambitious, wouldn't it?'

'Perfectly fair.'

'And it's patently obvious that our intellectual part is entirely directed at every moment towards knowing the truth of things, and isn't interested in the slightest in money and reputation.'

'Certainly.'

'So we'd be right to call it intellectual and philosophical, wouldn't we?'

'Of course.'　(581a3–b11)

These defining concerns of the different parts of the soul—profit, power, and wisdom—are the things in the scales, as it were (581e–582a), and for Plato they correspond to 'three basic human types' (581c), according as each type of person 'loves' each type of concern.[36] Each concern, that is, represents the kind of person one is and the kind of life one lives. Thus, when the proponents of these different ways of life are asked to comment on the pleasures of their lives they are not asked to comment on the pleasant characteristic episodes of their lives but on their ways of arranging and living their lives as wholes: 'if you were to approach representatives of these three types one by one and ask them which of these ways of life was the most enjoyable, they'd each swear by their own way of life' (581c8–10). And when Socrates comes to the relative ranking of these proponents' preferences, what he ranks is one life (βίος, 583a3, 5, 6) against another; indeed, at one point 'life' and 'pleasure' seem interchangeable: 'Which way of life—which pleasure—comes second, in the assessment?' (Τίνα δὲ δεύτερον, εἶπον, βίον καὶ τίνα δευτέραν ἡδονήν φησιν ὁ κριτὴς εἶναι; 583a6–7)

Notice that while the small episodes of one's life may have a 'feel'—as tasting ice cream has a 'feel'—one's life as a whole does not. Nor does Socrates give any suggestion of a 'sum' of episodic pleasures within a life as a whole. So to think

---

[35] Cf. Annas (1981: 309).

[36] In Greek Plato calls 'the philosophical, the competitive, and the avaricious' φιλόσοφον, φιλόνικον, φιλοκερδές, making each a kind of 'lover' (φίλος) of their respective concerns. See also Plato, trans. Waterfield (1993: 439, note on 581c). As N. White (1979: 226 f.) notes, Plato now shifts from an emphasis on types of persons defined in terms of their civic roles, to an emphasis on types of persons defined in terms of 'temperament' and 'what they predominately seek'.

that Socrates has in mind by 'pleasure' a kind of feeling or sensation is to attribute to him a conception of pleasure on which it cannot be applied to lives, the very things he means to compare for pleasantness.[37] The dispute, then, is not over whether doing ambitious things is more pleasant—more fun, or a better time, or what have you—than doing mercenary things, say, but over whether an ambitious mode of living is more pleasant—more satisfying, more actualizing—than a mercenary one.

Notice also that taking pleasure as a feeling suggests commensurability among pleasures: the person who enjoys rocky road and the person who enjoys chocolate chip are getting the same sort of thing—a pleasant feeling of cool sweetness, say—from different sources. But Socrates makes it clear that the pleasures he has in mind are not like that:[38] they differ in kind as the lives of which they are the pleasures differ in kind, since each part of the soul has its own peculiar pleasure, and the different ways of life are identified by the goals and priorities that are set by the different parts of the soul that lead: 'It seems to me,' says Socrates, 'that each of the three mental categories has its own particular pleasure [ἑνὸς ἑκάστου μία ἰδία], so that there are three kinds of pleasure as well.' (580d7–8)[39] And since each part of the soul is identified with the type of person who identifies with the concerns of that part, the fact that each part has its own peculiar pleasure 'also explains why there are three kinds [τρία εἴδη] of pleasure as well, one for each of the human types' (581c6). Consequently, we need an alternative conception of pleasure—a conception of pleasure that can be applied to a way of living, and is peculiar to the way of living of which it is the pleasure—if we are to understand Socrates' argument. And fortunately there is such a conception available.

As many philosophers have noticed, some pleasures are not feelings or sensations, but kinds of emotional engagement. We can see this, for one thing, in how we take pleasure in many of the activities we enjoy. For instance, a person may teach a class and thoroughly enjoy it, even if she does not experience any particular thrills or nice feelings while she teaches: imagine someone whose full attention is devoted to working students through a difficult idea, who finds the material worth while, who finds it rewarding to spend time doing this kind of thing, who cares about how her students are growing and learning, and so on. For a person with this sort of emotional engagement in teaching, teaching can be a tremendous pleasure, quite apart from any thrills or feelings of elation during the act of teaching, and even if—or, indeed, *especially* if—one is too focused on the task at hand to be bothered with thrills or elation. In fact, that is just the point: it is being focused, putting oneself into it, being engaged in it, sinking one's teeth into it—this is what makes the activity a pleasure. In this way,

---

[37] In fact, as we saw in Ch. 2, it is the deeply mistaken attempt to understand a happy life in terms of certain kinds of episodes that Socrates so harshly criticizes in his refutation of Callicles' hedonism at *Gorgias* 494c–497d.   [38] Cf. Annas (1981: 318).

[39] As Reeve (1988: 153) says, 'Each [of the psychic parts] is a unified source of motivation urging the psyche towards a distinctive kind of pleasure, and representing that pleasure as the content of the good.'

pleasure is thought of not as a feeling that goes along with the activity, but as the way in which one's emotions function with respect to the activity.[40]

We can also see this kind of pleasure, I think, as a kind of pleasure one can take in one's whole *existence*, and in how various parts of one's life fit into one's existence. It is one thing to enjoy what one is doing, and another to enjoy *what one does*. We sometimes hear of people, often famous people, who have had no desire they could not satisfy and no pleasure they could not indulge, only to find themselves deep in despair and hopelessness, to the point of self-destruction. Such poor people, we say, are simply not happy with their lives, and that is a great tragedy. We do not experience our projects and activities in just a piece-meal fashion, but experience them as forming part of a greater whole which, in turn, we find satisfying or unsatisfying as the kind of whole that it is.

In this sense, to talk about the pleasure of a life spent pursuing money, for instance, is not to talk about how money-making feels, but about the value that one's emotions attribute to money-making projects as part of one's whole existence. To be pleased with such a life is to see one's projects as worth spending time on, to see those projects as intimately bound up with an identity that one prizes, and in general to have one's emotions resonate with those projects, seeing them as part of a whole life that one takes to be satisfying and worth living.[41]

I think that this way of understanding pleasure can help us to see just how much sense Socrates' argument can make. Pleasure in this sense tells us a great deal about agents, and in particular about the kind of value they place on their lives, and on events and projects as parts of their lives, considered as wholes. And this is what Socrates' argument is about: it is a debate between proponents of different ways of arranging one's life (581c–d). When each proponent praises the pleasures of a given way of life, then, he is not telling us what makes him feel good, but rather what kind of life he finds worth living, what kind of life is important, what kind of life has real point. What Socrates needs, then, is a

---

[40] For a discussion of this way of understanding pleasure, see Ryle (1949: 107–10). See also Reeve (1988: 145), who claims that the pleasures Plato has in mind are not subjective experiences but activities, which it makes sense to rank as pleasures; cf. Sachs (1963: 146). And, of course, *Nicomachean Ethics* VII.11–14, X.1–5 is the *locus classicus* of the idea that pleasure is a mode of activity; however, it is important to note that in book VII Aristotle defines such pleasure negatively, as the absence of emotional impediment to activity (see also Rudebusch (1999), ch. 6 *et passim*), while in book X he defines it as positive emotional engagement in activity, as I do here.

[41] In an intriguing passage in C. S. Lewis's *Out of the Silent Planet*, two characters—one human, one Martian—discuss the very different meanings their races attach to the pleasures of sex (Lewis (1938: 47 f.)). While the human clearly thinks of this pleasure as a kind of desirable sensation, or perhaps as a kind of satisfying activity, the Martian insists that such pleasures are not fully appreciated unless they are seen as the parts of a larger whole that they are. All kinds of events and projects, he says, outlive their initial occurrence, and have their full significance only as a continuing agent continues to give them meaning, making them part of his inner life—the way that he thinks, what he remembers and how he remembers, and in general how his emotions continue to construe it as part of the meaning of his life. And although it takes someone not human to make the point, I do think that we can recognize what Lewis is so astute to observe: we take pleasure not only in our localized experiences but also in the life as a whole of which we make them a part; in fact, much of a pleasure's significance for us is how we see it fitting into a whole existence that we find to be rewarding and satisfying. I thank Mark LeBar for bringing this passage to my attention.

conception of pleasure that one takes in one's existence as a whole, in order to make a comparison between kinds of lives, in terms of the incommensurable, peculiar pleasures that belong to each one and concern its meaningfulness as a mode of human existence.

Socrates also needs such a conception of pleasure in order to rank such pleasures and adjudicate disputes between their proponents in a rational, principled, and objective way. For the decision whether a life of reason, a life of passion, or a life of desire is the one most worth living is exactly unlike the decision about what feels the best, or which ice cream tastes the best. There *is* a point to bringing experience, intelligence, and rational argumentation to bear on this decision—that is what we do when we do ethics, and what makes philosophical investigation into the nature of happiness and virtue necessary, and possible. There is a point to thinking that not all perspectives are on all fours here, and even that some perspective might be privileged[42]—as Glaucon puts it, '[W]hen a thoughtful person recommends his own way of life, he ought to be taken seriously' (583a4–5). Socrates' argument, then, is the sensible and powerful one that there is an authoritative perspective on the sort of life that is most worth living, and that from that perspective the life of reason and virtue is the clear choice. On Plato's conception of pleasure as a way of viewing one's life as a whole, we do not expect rational adjudication between such pleasures to be easy, but we do find the idea of such adjudication completely intelligible.

The gist of this argument is now clear, and it is instructive. For one thing, this no longer looks very much like an argument that the life of virtue is best on the grounds that it is most pleasant. On the contrary, Plato seems to be arguing that the life of virtue is most worth living on the grounds that from the authoritative perspective one sees that that life is most worth living. The pleasure of this life is not what makes it worth living. The pleasure is not what gives this life its point. Rather, the pleasure of this life is part and parcel of *seeing* its point. The virtuous person's life is not most worth living because it is most pleasant. It is most pleasant because it is most worth living.

This analysis of the first pleasure argument has two especially important results for our purposes. One is that, for Plato, disagreements about the pleasures people take in their ways of living are real disagreements, and disagreements that can in principle be rationally adjudicated. They are disagreements not about tastes but about choices and values, and as such they can be approached intelligently, even methodically. The only person who can enjoy the pleasures of the virtuous life is the one who lives a virtuous life, and likewise for a vicious life and its pleasures; virtuous and vicious people may both take pleasure in their lives, but they no more gain the same thing from their lives than they live each other's lives. A comparison of the pleasures of these lives, therefore, is not a comparison of them from a neutral perspective, but a comparison of the

---

[42] Cf. Annas (1981: 309); Reeve (1988: 145).

judgments of value that these pleasures comprise—judgments which can be rationally and objectively assessed. In fact, Plato's argument serves to underscore the gap between the perspectives of those who find value in ways of life that are very different in moral terms. There is no standpoint from which one can fully assess the merits of a life of virtue (or of vice, for that matter) independent of one's particular values; for Plato, not even considerations of pleasure can afford such a standpoint. For in such cases, disagreements about pleasures *are* disagreements about values. This is not the role that we are used to seeing pleasure play in moral philosophy:[43] we are far more used to treating pleasures as commensurable, and so we tend to expect pleasure to be that in terms of which many choices can be made and disagreements settled. We do not expect pleasure to be the locus of moral disagreement itself.

And second, Plato is not offering a hedonist defense of virtue. The argument does not take the form of claiming that once we see how pleasant the life of virtue is, we shall see that it is the happy life. Rather, it is a demonstration of the rational incorporation by wisdom of one's capacity to find pleasure in a way of living. The wise person does not merely have virtues with respect to pleasure. In the wise person, wisdom takes the form of (among others) an affective life so transformed as to find the greatest degree of satisfaction and actualization in the life according to virtue. Socrates argues that the life one most heartily endorses and finds most absorbing from an authoritative perspective of rationality must be the one most worth living, and the philosopher's pleasure in this way of life is a constituent of that endorsing. So this argument's appeal to pleasure does not replace the unconditional good of virtue with the conditional good of pleasure, as the determinant of happiness. Rather, it further articulates just what kind of good the unconditional good of virtue is for a fully human being. For part of our human nature is our affective life, and if virtue subsumes our good entirely, then it must subsume our affective life by rationally incorporating it into a good, harmonious life as a whole. This idea is developed more fully in the second pleasure argument, to which we now turn.

4.3.2   The second pleasure argument

In the second pleasure argument (583b–588a) Socrates brings the argument back to articulate how virtue can be the health of the soul. Socrates begins by arguing that at the most generic level pleasure is always the meeting of some need we have, but that pleasure properly understood is something more than merely the relief or relieving of pain.[44] This, Socrates claims, is not the kind of satisfaction that is genuine pleasure (583c–585a): for although most people think that

---

[43] For a discussion of the differences between Plato's treatment of pleasure and disagreements about pleasure, and modern treatments of those topics, see Annas (1981: 307 f.).

[44] Gosling and Taylor (1982: 113) argue that Plato conflates 'relief' as a state and 'relieving' as a process. I believe, rather, that Plato deliberately discusses first relief, and then relieving, the shift occurring at 584b.

remission of pain is pleasure, because of the contrast between pain and its remission, 'they're being misled,' Socrates says; 'there's no difference between people who've never experienced [real] pleasure comparing pain with absence of pain, and people who've never experienced white comparing black with grey' (585a2–5). Rather, genuine pleasure is to be found in providing for ourselves what we need most deeply (585a–e). To find out what that is, we need to determine, one, what we are, strictly speaking; and two, what has the greatest power to satisfy us as what we are. This is how Plato means to show how disagreements about pleasures—as ways of attributing value to a way of living—can be rationally adjudicated, by determining what kind of nature humans have, and thus what a meaningful existence for a human must be like.

He begins, much in the fashion of the *Phaedo*, by observing that humans seem to be a union of two different natures. Intelligible things, Socrates argues, are more real than corporeal things (585b–c). Consequently, the mind is more real than the body, and the things of the mind are more real than the things of the body (585d). Socrates now makes the rather (or perhaps, further) bold claim that the more real a thing is and the more real the thing that satisfies it, the more real is the satisfaction (585d–e): 'an object which is satisfied by more real things, and which is itself more real, is more really satisfied than an object which is satisfied by less real things, and is itself less real' (585d7–9). Now 'being satisfied by things which accord with one's nature,' Socrates says, 'is pleasant' (585d11). So, presumably, since the mind is the part of us that is most real (585c–d), and most really what we are, when it is satisfied with what most accords with its nature—namely truth, knowledge, intelligence, and other parts of goodness (585b–c)—this is the most real and true pleasure that is possible for us (585d–e). In short, when the most real part of us—the mind—is satisfied with the most real thing—truth and good-ness—we are the most satisfied. Those who think that they receive true satisfac-tion from other things, then, are mistaken (586a–c), and are acquainted only with 'mere effigies of true pleasure', which are like 'illusory paintings' (586b7–8).

Again, we might think that this is a bizarre argument: why should we think that the reality of a subject and of the object of his or her satisfaction should imply anything about the reality of the pleasure of satisfaction itself?[45] If we think of pleasure as a sort of feeling that comes alongside what we are doing, then this argument will seem unintelligible: surely as long as any two people both feel pleased or satisfied, they both feel pleased or satisfied equally really, no matter

---

[45] This concern arises even if we set aside C. C. W. Taylor's objection (1998: 69) that, in the philosopher's life, the mind will require as much constant filling as the non-philosopher's stomach (say) will, for the philosopher will continue to learn, just as the non-philosopher will continue to eat. There is, I think, an important difference between these two kinds of continued fillings. To use a crude analogy, the philosopher's continued filling is like filling a tank by first placing in it item A, then item B, then item C, and so on for the rest of one's life; the non-philosopher's continued filling is like filling a tank, flushing it, filling it again, flushing it, and so on for the rest of one's life. So by identifying the latter process as ephemeral and less genuinely a filling, Socrates does not thereby place the former process in the same predicament. On the former, it is the things with which one is filled that satisfy, rather than process of filling as on the latter.

what the pleasure or satisfaction is.[46] Again, however, when pleasure is under-stood as a way of valuing one's life as a whole, it does make sense to say that some lives are more really satisfying than others, since lives can be more or less meaningful, and the pleasures that agents take in lives can fail to track the actual worth of those lives. So just how does the life of the virtuous differ from other lives? And how is pleasure more or less real, and how does the difference in level of reality bear on the comparison of the life of virtue with other kinds of lives?

To answer those questions, we need to pay attention to how Plato explains the differences between pleasures taken in lives, through a model of pleasure as the replenishment of some need or the filling of some sort of lack (585a–b). Such a model as this captures the fact that we enjoy getting things we need or want, because we want or need them. We can illustrate this fact with some rather humble observations about more basic pleasures, such as that it is pleasant to eat when one is hungry, but not when one is full. Of course, examples of this sort have very limited power to illustrate the replenishment model; for example, someone suffering from indigestion clearly will not feel better by being filled up with more of anything—certainly such a person has a need, but this need is not plausibly construed as a void to be filled. Furthermore, Socrates points out that some pleasures presuppose no prior awareness of any lack or deficiency, such as the enjoyment of a lovely scent (584b). It is better, then, to understand a more general point here than literal 'filling', namely that human beings are needy creatures, who take pleasure in the satisfaction of their needs, both the needs they perceive and those they do not.

Moreover, when one perceives a need or lack, Socrates says, even the anti-cipation of its satisfaction is a pleasure (584c). Here, then, is another way of advancing over a crude 'filling' model of pleasure as replenishment: for the pleasure of anticipation is a matter not of replenishment itself, but of repres-enting a replenishment to oneself. This is important, as it makes clear that pleasure, in certain crucial cases, is not just a mechanical or physiological process, but involves our ability to 'see' the object of our desire *as* something that will actually satisfy us. Plato, that is, is interested in pleasure primarily as an intentional state, rather than a purely qualitative one.[47]

---

[46] See N. White (1979: 231 f.), who seems to raise this sort of objection, and treats Plato's point as somewhat muddled and awaiting clarification in the *Philebus*.

[47] As is often recognized, pleasure as a kind of anticipation should put us in mind of Plato's discussion of false pleasures of anticipation at *Philebus* 38b–41a. For an excellent discussion, see D. Frede (1985: 158 and n. 15, 165–79); and D. Frede (1993: xlviii). One thing that is clear in that discussion is that Plato again focuses on anticipation in order to isolate the crucial element of intentionality in certain types of pleasure. For example, suppose that I am reflecting today about a dinner in my honor that is to be held tomorrow, and suppose that I am thinking about this dinner in terms of how much I deserve it and what a lovely thing it is going to be for me. Thinking about the dinner in these terms gives the description under which I enjoy the anticipated event. Now Plato's choice of pleasure as an anticipation of something not yet present makes for complications, and these have worried a number of readers of the *Philebus*. Still, we can see his motivation for doing so: if he had talked about my pleasure while I am actually having the dinner, it would be very tempting to think of the pleasure as the way the food tastes or how witty the conversation is, or what have you. Rather, by focusing on my anticipation of the dinner, Plato isolates the intentionality of the pleasure

Pleasure so considered is always to be pleased that such and such is the case. To be pleased in this way is to enjoy something under a description. Plato's view is that the pleased agent construes the object of her pleasure in terms of a need or lack that she takes the object to satisfy. And, Socrates says, it is their ignorance of what really satisfies a person that allows some to pursue less really satisfying things as if they were what one most needed from life (584d–585a, 586a–c). In other words, everyone construes the pursuits they find meaningful in terms of the satisfaction they believe they receive from them,[48] but not everyone really knows what things really will satisfy them. On Plato's model of pleasure, people enjoy their way of life on the basis of seeing it as a way of life that gives them what they believe to be worth while in life. On this basis Socrates argues both that those who are not virtuous experience pleasure, *and* that such people fail to experience the genuine pleasure—the real fulfillment and actualization as a human being—that they think they do.

On this understanding of pleasure, construing oneself as truly satisfied is clearly not sufficient for *being* truly satisfied. Rather, determining whether one is truly satisfied takes intelligence and judgment. To illustrate this point, Socrates first has us imagine three vertically arranged points—a bottom, a middle, and a top (584d). Non-philosophers, Socrates says, begin at the 'bottom' with painful desires, and look 'upward' to see the 'middle' point, the satisfaction of desires. While they are rising to the middle point, they get the appearance of upward motion, and once they have risen to the middle point and look back down, this appearance is confirmed (584d–e). Consequently, such people believe that in satisfying their desires, in attaining the things they think will satisfy them, they have reached the 'top' and are genuinely satisfied (584d–585a):

'You know how things can be high, low, or in between?' I asked.
'Yes.'
'Well, someone moving from the bottom of anything to the middle is bound to get an impression of upward motion, isn't he? And once he's standing at the halfway point and looking down to where he travelled from, then if he hasn't seen the true heights, he's bound to think he's reached the top, isn't he?'
'Yes, I'd certainly have to agree with that,' [Glaucon] said.
'And if he retraced his steps, he'd think—rightly—that he was travelling downwards, wouldn't he?' I asked.
'Of course.'
'And all these experiences of his would be due to his ignorance of the true nature of high, middle, and low, wouldn't they?'
'Obviously.'   (584d3–e6)

I have: enjoying the dinner as a whole is representing it under a satisfying description, as we can see in the case of anticipation, in which there is nothing to the pleasure *but* the representing. We shall return to this feature of anticipatory features, and the nature of pleasure as an intentional state in general, in Ch. 6.

[48] Reeve (1988: 153) correctly notes this feature of the pleasures of the different parts of the soul as a way of representing 'the content of the good'.

The crucial point to notice here is that the non-philosophers' pleasures are not just feelings but ways of construing their replenishments: they see their replenishments *as* bringing them true satisfaction and securing what they really need, *as* bringing them to the 'top', in Socrates' analogy. But such a construal or representation of a replenishment is something that one can be mistaken about. In Socrates' analogy, one can misconstrue the middle as the top, if one has no acquaintance with the real top, simply because one has moved upward to the middle from the bottom:

'So would you think it odd for people who have never experienced truth, and who therefore have unreliable views about a great many subjects, to be in the same position where pleasure, pain, and the intermediate state are concerned? They not only hold the correct opinion that they are feeling pain, and do in fact feel pain, when they move into a state of pain, but they're also certain about the satisfaction and pleasure they feel when they move away from pain and into the intermediate state. But they're being misled: there's no difference between people who've never experienced pleasure comparing pain with absence of pain, and people who've never experienced white comparing black with grey.' (584e7–585a5)

Of course, Socrates nowhere denies that such experiences *are* pleasures,[49] and we can see that on the replenishment model these experiences are sorts of pleasures because they are, after all, satisfactions of desires. However, we can also see that the non-philosophers make a mistake in thinking that they have thereby achieved the top, that is, genuine pleasure and genuine satisfaction. The money-loving man of the first pleasure argument, for instance, desires wealth because he thinks that it is money that is important, that it is money that will truly give him what he needs. As such, the satisfaction of his desire for money is a pleasure, specifically the pleasure of getting money *as* what is worth getting. For, as Socrates takes such pains to show, the person who thinks that getting money is true pleasure pursues money under the description of that which is truly satisfying, for in getting money he believes that he will move from the 'bottom' to the 'top' (584d–585a). And, since his life is centered about activities of satisfying these desires, he thinks that his life is truly rewarding, that is, that his enjoyment of life is complete.

Unfortunately for him, the money-loving man is mistaken about that:

'It turns out, then, that people to whom intelligence and goodness are unfamiliar, whose only interest is self-indulgence and so on, spend their lives moving aimlessly to and fro between the bottom and the halfway point, which is as far as they reach. But they never travel any further towards the true heights: they've never even looked up there, let alone gone there; they aren't really satisfied by anything real; they don't experience steady, pure pleasure. They're no different from cattle: they spend their lives grazing, with their eyes turned down and heads bowed towards the ground and their tables. Food and sex are their

---

[49] See also *Philebus* 37a–b. Socrates does claim that pleasure understood as the state of alleviation of pain is not really a pleasure, because pleasure cannot be static (583c–584a), but he does not make any such claim about pleasure understood as replenishing, which he begins discussing at 585b; *con.* Gosling and Taylor (1982: 113).

only concerns, and their insatiable greed for more and more drives them to kick and butt one another to death with their horns and hoofs of iron, killing one another because they're seeking satisfaction in unreal things for a part of themselves which is also unreal—a leaky vessel they're trying to fill.'   (586a1–b4)

Such a person's life is not truly rewarding, because he has failed to identify what he actually needs. He does, however, get what he thinks he needs, and so has a kind of pleasure in doing so. But his enjoyment of his pleasures is an enjoyment of them as genuine, and herein lies his mistake, because genuine pleasure is to satisfy the most satisfiable part of oneself with what is most satisfying. Since the intellect and the intelligible things with which it is in contact are more real than corporeal things, the satisfaction of the intellect in contacting its objects is a more real satisfaction (585b–d). To live the virtuous life is to identify with reason as representing one's true self, and to satisfy reason with what it most truly needs. For, Socrates says, when the whole soul accepts the leadership of reason, harmoniously and without conflict, then each part of the soul does that job that it is best suited to do within the whole soul, and each part of the soul enjoys the pleasures that are most appropriate and beneficial for it (586c–587b).

Since the philosopher attains the fulfillment of his nature in the genuine provision of what his nature requires, Plato argues, the philosopher's pleasure really is genuine. It is in virtue of attaining this fulfillment of his nature that the philosopher's preference of way of life is the correct one; it is this that the philosopher is right about in the adjudication of disputes between preferred lives. And so here, again, it seems that judgments about pleasure do admit of objective judgment after all. More important, it also seems that what is at stake in these judgments is the goodness of a mode of living, taken on its own terms: the comparison of pleasures turns out to be a comparison between judgments of types of lives as good for their own sake, and as their own reward. It is from this contest that the life of virtue emerges the winner in book IX, just as it had in book IV.

Moreover, this picture of the philosopher has two further implications that we should note here. First, for Plato the philosopher, the person of virtue is not torn but integrated: reason leads, and desire and passion follow in unison with reason.[50] And, thus, while the non-philosopher may endorse his way of life (as we saw in the first pleasure argument as well), he cannot do so in just the way that the philosopher endorses his way of life. For the philosopher's way of life is endorsed by the *whole* soul, by the rational, passionate, and desirous parts. The virtuous life is one of integration and harmony in the soul; reason leads, and the whole soul endorses the leading. But the vicious soul is out of harmony and torn; as we saw in our discussion of book VIII, non-philosophers satisfy the wants of a part of their soul only at the expense of the other parts. By identifying

---

[50] One interesting consequence of this fact is what it shows about how the virtuous person acts: for example, the virtuous person will not merely give to someone in need, but will give charitably, that is, willingly rather than begrudgingly, and with pleasure. In following reason, then, the virtuous person will not merely do good deeds, but will do them in the right spirit. This is important, because the difference between doing good deeds and acting from the virtues is morally important.

with a part of the soul besides reason, the non-philosopher comes to value the wrong things. While he may find a sort of pleasure in attaining those things, and thus believe that his life is truly rewarding, he will never know the true pleasure of harmony and peace.

And second, the difference between the philosopher and the non-philosopher stems from the fact that there are ways that it is good to be passionate, and ways that it is good to be desirous. Reason leads passion and desire into these good ways. That passion and desire find tremendous pleasure in their transformation indicates that their natures are fulfilled by what accords with their natures:

'[The pursuits which people unfamiliar with intelligence and goodness are involved with] impregnate people with an insane lust for the pleasure they offer, and these fools fight over them, as the Trojans in Stesichorus' story, out of ignorance of the truth, fought over the mere apparition of Helen.'
'Yes, something like that's bound to be the case,' [Glaucon] said.
'What about the passionate part of the mind? Won't the situation be more or less the same for anyone who brings its desires to a successful conclusion? He's either ambitious, in which case he's motivated by resentment and seeks satisfaction in status; or he's competitive, in which case he relies on force and seeks satisfaction in success; or he's bad-tempered, in which case he resorts to anger and seeks satisfaction in angry outburst. But none of these involve reason and intelligence.'
'Again, yes, something like that's bound to be the case,' he said.
'All right, then,' I said. 'Shall we confidently state that, where avarice and competitiveness are concerned, any desire which succeeds in attaining its objective will get the truest pleasure available to it when it is guided by truth, which is to say when it follows the leadership of knowledge and reason in its quest for those pleasures to which intelligence directs it? And shall we add that the pleasures it gets will also be the ones which are particularly suitable for it—that is, if suitability and benefit coincide?'
'Well, they do coincide,' he said.
'It follows that when the whole mind accepts the leadership of the philosophical part, and there's no internal conflict, then each part can do its own job and be moral in everything it does, and in particular can enjoy its own pleasures, and thus reap as much benefit and truth from pleasure as is possible for it.'
'Exactly.'
'When one of the other two parts is in control, however, it not only fails to attain its own pleasure, but it also forces the other parts to go after unsuitable, false pleasures.'
'Right,' he agreed.   (586c2–587a6)

Consequently, when passion and desire follow the lead of reason, they find their fulfilled and healthy condition. We know this, because they then find pleasure in all the right things. So, when reason leads the soul, each part of the soul receives what it most truly needs; each part is healthy and in its best condition.[51] And it is

---

[51] See N. White (1979: 232, 233). See also Kelly (1989: 179), who argues that, since truth in this argument is a matter not of correspondence of statement to fact but of approximation to the good, pleasures can in this argument be ranked according to truth, and can be said to be more pleasant the truer they are, since the truer they are the more they satisfy genuine human longing. Cf. Reeve (1988: 149), who claims that 'Truth in pleasure is a matter of having the inanition that is a particular desire

on this basis that Socrates argues that to think vice is beneficial to its possessor is, it turns out, to think that a soul in utter chaos benefits its possessor (588b–592a).[52]

So not only are the pleasures of a virtuous or vicious life peculiar to that life, since they consist in the construal of those lives as worth living—a point we saw in the first pleasure argument—but they also differ in that the soul that enjoys the wrong sort of life cannot enjoy it wholly. So, far from being commensurable, then, the pleasures of lives of virtue and vice are indeed different psychological constitutions, and only one of them is a constitution of integration and health. Of course, to say that each part of the virtuous person's soul is healthy and enjoys its proper pleasures is not to say that each part of the virtuous soul always 'feels good'.[53] For one thing, virtue cannot stop us from being pained at torment and desiring to be rid of it. For another, painful emotions such as regret or anger may sometimes be part of an exercise of virtue.[54] Rather, the philosopher and non-philosopher alike will feel pain at torment, and the philosopher may even experience pains such as regret when the non-philosopher does not. But the reason that we can none the less ascribe genuine pleasure to the philosopher, and the philosopher alone, is that his life is a unified whole: with reason leading, the desires and emotions become transformed so as to be in unison and harmony with the rational direction of the philosopher's life. And it is this that makes it sensible to claim that the philosopher's life as a whole is a pleasure, because it is a life lived to the full, with the whole self in harmony. Indeed, this unique way of enjoying the virtuous life is a reflection of the wholeness and integration of the virtuous soul. Again, then, these pleasures are not the source of the value of the virtuous life, but are a reflection of its value. The pleasure one takes in one's life is a kind of view that one takes on the meaningfulness of one's life and its events and projects, and so that pleasure succeeds only where it follows the direction of practical rationality, which alone encompasses the demands of every part of our nature, and which is the agency by which one can give one's whole nature the sort of direction it needs to flourish.

Plato's second pleasure argument strengthens the psychology underwriting the defense of virtue for its own sake, because that argument is an articulation

---

filled with what always and unalterably instantiates the form that is the natural object of that desire. But only reason knows what will truly satisfy appetite and aspiration, and how to reliably achieve it. It follows that "those desires of even the money-loving and honour-loving parts which follow knowledge and argument, and pursue with their help those pleasures which reason approves, will attain the truest pleasures possible for them because they follow truth, and the ones that are most their own, if indeed what is best for each thing is also most properly its own..." '

[52] And this mistake Plato compares poignantly to Eriphyle's mistake of preferring a necklace to her husband's life (589e–590a, cp. *Laws* V, 727a–728a; Eriphyle forced her husband Amphiaraus into the battle of the *Seven Against Thebes*, having been bribed by Polynices with a magic necklace). This point, then, brings us back to the argument of book IV; for, as Annas (1981: 153) characterizes that argument, 'Once you see the difference between a life that gives all the elements in a person's make-up proper scope, and one that frustrates and misdirects them, you cannot seriously doubt that it is valuable to have the state that ensures the former.'

[53] I thank Scott LaBarge for raising this point.

[54] For this point about regret, see esp. Hursthouse (1999), chs. 2 and 3.

of the health of the virtuous person, which previously had been left rather sketchy. In fact, both of the pleasure arguments are meant to articulate the goodness of the virtuous person, understood as the health of the soul—and it was the health of the soul that Socrates had not explained to his own satisfaction earlier in book IV. For now Socrates has shown just what this goodness or health consists in: it consists in each part of the soul finding completion and fulfillment in the things appropriate to it, and in the whole soul endorsing and engaging in the sort of life that really is best for it. When reason leads the way, every part of the soul becomes fulfilled in its nature. We have evidence for this in the fact that each part of the soul finds its own proper and beneficial pleasures under the leadership of reason (586e–587a).[55] If the pleasures of the virtuous soul are evidence for its fulfillment, integration, and harmony, then we can reasonably conclude that this kind of soul is the good soul—and we shall have shown more fully just what its goodness is like. For each of the parts to find the pleasures appropriate to it is for it to adopt the right sorts of concerns, as the right sorts of concerns.

Consequently, Plato's argument takes the form of showing that the life of wisdom counts as happiness because of the way that wisdom transforms our affections, and not that our affections so transformed are themselves responsible for our happiness. The significance of showing that the virtuous life is also the life of supreme pleasure is not that the life of supreme pleasure is happy. Its significance is that the life of a flourishing human psyche—as observed in its affective health—is the happy life. The life of virtue can be the happy life, because it brings health to the rational and practical aspects of our life, as we see in its possession of the virtues, *and* to the affective parts of our life, and thus is holistic in the right kind of way for happiness.

4.4   The Defense of Virtue, Revisited

The tremendous advantage of articulating the goodness and health of the virtuous soul in this way is that we can read off of this fuller picture that this is the soul that is well off. And by now it should be clear that in these arguments Socrates defends the thesis that

(c2) *if the hierarchy of parts is in order, then each part is in its good condition.*
It is through the discovery of their proper pleasures that we have evidence that each of the parts is in its good condition, and this happens when all of the parts

---

[55] It is thus important to distinguish the view I am attributing to Plato—that the pleasure of virtue is relevant to demonstrating that virtue is itself a kind of psychic health—from the view that one has reason to be virtuous out of a need to avoid psychic pains such as guilt (for a discussion of the latter view see Kavka (1985: 305–7)). As Kavka notes, there may well be other ways of escaping such pains (cf. Schmidtz (1995): 246)). The point for Plato is that it is the condition of the soul itself, and not the pleasure or pain of it, that is to be pursued or avoided.

are in the proper hierarchy (see especially 586a–587a).[56] Since in his examination of various corrupt souls Socrates has shown that

> (c1) *if the hierarchy of parts is out of order, then some part is not in its good condition*

it follows that

> (c) *the hierarchy of parts is in order if and only if each part is in its good condition.*

And since the hierarchy of parts is right in the virtuous soul, and nowhere else, it follows that

> (d) *the virtuous person alone has the right structure between the parts of the soul and has each of the parts in its good condition.*

By defending this thesis, and by articulating the nature of the good condition of the soul and its parts, Plato has provided a powerful argument that it is virtue that makes us well off. So far from being in tension with the argument begun in *Republic* IV, then, the pleasure arguments of book IX *complete* that very argument.

So not only does Plato raise an important question in the *Republic* but he also gives the right answer, or at least the right sort of answer. For it is not an open question whether it is health or sickness that is to be preferred, and in the same way, it turns out, it is not an open question whether it is virtue or vice that is to be preferred. Plato's point is that in the virtuous person, and only in the virtuous person, the soul is in its perfect, healthy, and fulfilled condition, both as a whole and in each of its aspects; and the pleasures of the virtuous soul are evidence for this health. If that is what it is to be virtuous, then to be virtuous just is to live well, on the directive conception of happiness.

For Plato, virtue and vice are different constitutions of soul, and we can evaluate them by determining which of them is identical to a psychologically healthy, integrated, and thriving soul, and which to an unhealthy and twisted one. Pleasure is relevant to this comparison, for one thing, because the ways in which the different aspects of the soul find enjoyment in the world around them is a key factor in the health or sickness of the soul. For another, to take pleasure in one's life as a whole is to judge one's life to be genuinely rewarding and satisfying, to be a truly happy life; and that judgment can be correct or mistaken, and made from within a better or worse perspective. Plato's defense of virtue affords us an exciting avenue along which to reflect on how virtue benefits its possessor, and in which considerations of pleasure figure in new and refreshing ways.

What we have found is that the conception of pleasure and of its role in the happy life that removes the apparent tension between the defense of the virtuous life in *Republic* IV and the defense in *Republic* IX also affords a reading of the *Republic* that keeps the directive conception of happiness intact. As in the *Phaedo*, pleasure is here treated as a conditional good, but the *Republic* also

---

[56] See also Irwin (1995: 294).

shows that pleasure is an especially *important* part of the good life, as it represents the flourishing of a human being as an affective being. This flourishing, however, is not tacked on to wisdom, as if wisdom were not a sufficient form of flourishing. Rather, pleasure in the wise person has been rationally incorporated: the pleasure that a wise person takes in her life is part of the very perspective of wisdom on her life. In a way, this is not surprising, since Plato makes it clear that pleasure is incorporated into *every* type of character and represents its affective outlook on the world and its place in it, an outlook that is one constituent of the character with which it is associated. To be vicious, then, is among other things to have one kind of affective life and outlook; to be wise is to have a very different kind; and remarkably, Plato shows that only the latter is a healthy affective life, taken on its own terms. On Plato's view, then, wisdom determines happiness not only because wisdom is a form of agency with a holistic perspective but also because wisdom turns out to be the *whole* human agent flourishing.

5

The *Philebus*, Part 1: Virtue, Value, and 'Likeness to God'

The directive conception of happiness holds that the unconditional good determines happiness, and that only what directs and organizes one's life in a rational way is unconditionally good. Plato, I have argued, holds the directive conception of happiness, and in particular maintains that happiness is determined not by the 'ingredients' of our lives, but by the wisdom with which we live with respect to those ingredients. This conception of happiness motivates Plato's view that wisdom makes its own success, and indeed all the success one could need for happiness. Although Plato does not seem to have found a way to capture this point about wisdom from within his analogy between wisdom and productive skills, he does motivate this point by a powerful argument that identifies wisdom with the flourishing of rational agency, and thus with the flourishing of a human being as a rational agent. The nature of conditional and unconditional goods, and their respective roles in the good life, Plato discusses in the *Euthydemus*, *Gorgias*, and *Phaedo*, giving special attention to pleasure in the latter two, in which pleasure emerges as a good conditioned on the direction that wisdom gives it. He gives special attention to pleasure again in book IX of the *Republic*, arguing that the lives of people with different sorts of concerns and priorities have correspondingly different sorts of characteristic pleasures, those of the life of wisdom representing genuine psychological health and flourishing, and reflecting realistic attitudes about what matters in human life. This allows Plato to show, on the one hand, that wisdom is neither pallid nor dry but encompasses all of one's personality, by rationally incorporating every part of the personality into an orderly, flourishing whole; and, on the other, what it means for wisdom to lead and direct our behavior, by changing not only our actions but our very attitudes, including affective attitudes like pleasure.

Rational incorporation of pleasure is the transforming of pleasure by wisdom, and so there are two sides to the rational incorporation of pleasure that now demand closer attention: how wisdom is able to transform our attitudes, and how pleasure is the sort of attitude to be so transformed. Plato addresses these two issues in the *Philebus*, and we shall trace the first issue in the present chapter and second in the next. As we have seen, an understanding of the rational incorporation of pleasure is crucial for understanding how pleasure can be part of happiness, so that we might take seriously the notion of happiness as encompassing the whole person, without compromising Plato's claim that wisdom determines happiness. As we saw in the last chapter, the key lies in pleasure's ability to become part of the agent's wisdom itself, by becoming part of the agent's wise perspective on her life, the part of that perspective that is distinctly affective.

What is less clear, however, is whether Plato can, in fact, sustain this account of the rational incorporation of pleasure. One potential source of trouble for this account in Plato's philosophy is his notorious thesis that goodness of character consists in 'likeness to God'. This thesis seems to suggest not the incorporation of such human elements as pleasure by wisdom, but the dissociation of wisdom from them, and thus Plato's embracing of just the sort of asceticism I have argued that Plato rejects. Or perhaps it suggests, if not the dissociation of wisdom from pleasure full stop, the revamping of pleasure into something that looks rather foreign from the human perspective. The gods of the *Phaedrus*, for instance, are said to take great enjoyment ($\epsilon \dot{v} \pi a \theta \epsilon \hat{\iota}$, *Phaedrus* 247d4) in beholding the intelligible realm, which is 'without color and without shape and without solidity, a being that really is what it is, the subject of all true knowledge, visible only to intelligence, the soul's steersman' (247c6–8), and in beholding 'Justice as it is', and 'Self-control', and 'Knowledge' as transcendent, ideal entities (247d6–7). Whatever such delight is, and whatever it is for the gods to experience it, it is surely far removed from the simple pleasures of passing time with friends in conversation that we find Socrates enjoying in the *Phaedo* and elsewhere—and, more important, from the kinds of pleasures that we humans find most intelligible. Nor do I think that this simply represents a lack of imagination on our part. The problem is we are left with a very sterile affective life if our pleasures are to be limited to the sorts of pleasures we find in this rather queer myth. The problem is not that such a change in our affective life is radical. The problem is that it threatens to make our lives something other than human. It is, therefore, a bit startling that Plato should follow his discussion of the richness and pleasantness of the good human life in *Republic* IX with the description of this goodness in *Republic* X as likeness to God (613a8–b3).

I do not believe, however, that Plato's notion of likeness to God does, in fact, commit him to any form of asceticism, or any other form of leaching pleasure out of the account of human happiness. On the contrary, I shall argue in this chapter that the notion of likeness to God affords Plato an interesting and promising direction from which to approach wisdom as something that rationally incorporates the elements of human life into an orderly, thriving whole, and thus as the unique unconditional good that Plato takes wisdom to be.[1] The real ethical work accomplished by the notion of likeness to God is not separation from our

---

[1] Unfortunately, there will remain a very real problem for Plato's account of rational incorporation, which comes from quite another source: his analysis of the psychology of pleasure, or rather the disunity within that analysis. We shall turn to this problem in Ch. 7.

humanity after all, but the moral importance of the practical intelligence with which rational agents bring order and harmony to materials that cannot supply such direction for themselves.

Unraveling likeness to God in Plato requires a fresh approach that makes the greatest sense of it within Plato's larger moral philosophy. And, in fact, we find just such a promising understanding of likeness to God when we take a fresh look at it through the lens of Plato's *Philebus*, where we find the idea that virtue is part of the divine realm right alongside the down-to-earth idea that virtue is rational activity in relation to the world as we find it. We find the same idea, I shall argue, in Stoic ethics as well, in a way that can reveal new options for understanding Plato's conception of virtue as likeness to God. This is not to suppose that the Stoic conception of likeness to God is an interpretation of, or descended from, Plato's conception.[2] It is simply that the Stoics also found it helpful to think of virtue as likeness to God, and it will be enough if the Stoic conception opens up the range of possibilities for understanding such an idea, allowing us to see philosophical alternatives that might take us some distance toward interpreting Plato, and that may have remained otherwise out of view. Such an understanding of the idea that virtue is likeness to God as we find in the Stoics, I argue, offers just this sort of promising and unexplored alternative in Platonism—an alternative that will allow us to see how wisdom can both be a form of likeness to God, and rationally incorporate lives that are thoroughly human.

5.1   Likeness to God: A Troubling Idea

The view that our highest good is to be like God is one we find, in various forms, in the *Phaedrus, Timaeus, Laws, Republic,* and *Theaetetus*, as well as in the *Phaedo* and *Philebus*,[3] and the ancient Platonist Alcinous in his *Handbook of Platonism* tells us that likeness to God (ὁμοίωσις θεῷ) is Plato's 'official' conception of our final end.[4] Until very recently, however, this view has received almost no attention among modern scholars, and indeed many philosophers remain unaware of it, some have simply ignored it or dismissed it as an idle metaphor, and even most of those who have taken it more seriously have also

---

[2] Nor do I suppose that the broader philosophical commitments of the Stoics are of a piece with Plato's; it is, of course, possible to find the treatment of an idea in one system illuminating for understanding the idea in other, quite different philosophical systems (consider, e.g., Philo's appeal in *De opificio mundi* to the pagan account of the *Timaeus* to open up further possibilities for understanding the Hebrew God's creative activities in *Genesis*). What I shall argue is that the consistency of godlikeness with a this-worldly conception of virtue is apparent in Stoic thought, and also that the Stoics and Plato establish such consistency in essentially the same sorts of ways. As for other discontinuities between Stoicism and Platonism, I shall leave them aside for present purposes, and offer the promissory note that the discussion that unfolds will not be jeopardized by my doing so.

[3] See esp. *Phaedrus* 246d, 248a, 249c; *Timaeus* 47c, cf. 89e–90d; *Laws* IV, 716b–d; *Republic* X, 613a–b; *Theaetetus* 176a–c; *Phaedo* 78b–84d (the 'affinity argument', which I discussed in Ch. 3); *Philebus* 28c–30e.

[4] See Alcinous, *Handbook of Platonism* 28 (and his rather odd reference to *Phaedo* 82a–b).

tended to find it too otherworldly to be of much relevance to us. This latter response is due in large measure to viewing likeness to God from the otherworldly perspective of the ancient Neoplatonist Plotinus.[5] But there is certainly no guarantee that Plotinus' perspective on likeness to God gives us an especially accurate reconstruction of Plato's view. In fact, the interpretation of this idea was a matter of considerable debate among Neoplatonists, some of whom offered far less otherworldly interpretations than Plotinus'.[6]

One thing that is quite clear, however, is that Plato means for likeness to God to offer us some insight into the nature of moral virtue. We see this in the *Timaeus*, where Plato offers a model of the three-part soul, in which mastery of the parts is justice (42a–b) and happiness (90b–d), and is what likeness to God comes to (42b–d, 47a–c). Rather curiously, Plato depicts this constitution of soul as a sort of motion which is of the same kind as the motion of the universe itself (90c–d):[7] as the universe consists in orbits which are orderly and reconciled in their motion, so the human soul consists in the different orbits (44d) of reason, passion, and desire, which are out of harmony when we start life, but become more orderly as we mature (43a–44d). Although this is difficult talk, it is clearly meant to depict a self-mastery of the whole soul under the leadership of reason (43a–44d), which is the same as justice, and which consists in the reconciliation of one's inner motions by reason (42b–d).[8] Thus we 'stabilize the straying revolutions within ourselves by imitating[9] the completely unstraying

---

[5] Both Annas (1999), ch. 3 and Sedley (1997) focus on Plotinus (and Sedley on the last half of Aristotle, *Nicomachean Ethics* X as well) in thinking about likeness to God in Plato.

[6] So Plotinus' view does not win by default—on the contrary, it is important to note the broad diversity of interpretations of likeness to God that existed even within Neoplatonism, as Baltzly (2004) shows. In fact, as Baltzly argues, Proclus' interpretation of likeness to God in his commentary *In Timaeum* is rather this-worldly in its explicit rejection of Plotinus' view that we leave behind the standard human virtues when we become like God; and Baltzly seems correct to conclude that Proclus understands likeness to God as an 'ethical' ideal rather than a narrowly 'spiritual' one.

[7] For a discussion of the relation between human and cosmic mind in this passage, see Sedley (1999: 316–19). Philo, too, is attracted to an analogy between man's soul and mind, and the heavens and the outer sphere of heaven, respectively (*Quis rerum divinarum heres sit* 230–6). Elsewhere, Philo compares the human mind as the rational part of the soul to the heavens as the rational part of the universe (*Quaestiones et solutiones in Genesim* 4.215). Of course, given his Jewish cosmology Philo does not think that the cosmos was in any sense a divinity, but he does find the complexity of the cosmos to be illustrative of the complexity of the human psyche. For discussion of this idea, and its analog in the *Timaeus*, see Runia (1986: 213 f.).

[8] But see Sedley (1997: 331), (1999: 322–4), who treats the virtues of the *Timaeus* as narrowly intellectual rather than moral. However, Sedley focuses on 90a–d, which does not mention moral virtue, rather than 42b–d which does (see also 43a–44d), and I think that Plato clearly intends us to connect these two passages, as 89e–90a makes clear when it refers back to the discussion (42a–d, 43a–44d) of reconciling the motions of the three types of soul.

[9] 'Imitating' is the right word, as Plato claims that we develop these orderly motions through philosophic study of the workings of the universe. It is philosophical understanding of the universe that allows us to reconcile the motions within ourselves (47a–c); for, although the universe is literally mundane, a true understanding of the universe is an understanding of the primary principles that guide it, and these principles are purely intelligible (46d). Consequently, it is through empirical observation of the universe that we come to have abstract knowledge of such sciences as mathematics and philosophy in general (47a–b), and it is this scientific, philosophical understanding of the universe—an understanding of its pure, abstract principles—that allows us to culminate our rationality (47b–c).

revolutions of the god' (47c2–4), that is, the god that is the universe itself (see 34a8–b9). For Plato, rationality, self-mastery, happiness, and knowledge all converge as likeness to God (89e–90d).

Moral virtue as a harmonization of the self is, of course, familiar from the *Republic*, and indeed Plato says in *Republic* X that to be virtuous is to liken oneself to God as far as a human can (ἐπιτηδεύων ἀρετὴν εἰς ὅσον ἀνθρώπῳ ὁμοιοῦσθαι θεῷ, 613a8–b1), and that God takes good care of those who are like him (613b2–3). Plato makes the point again in *Laws* IV, 716b–d, as the Athenian claims that 'the moderate man is God's friend, being like him' (ὁ μὲν σώφρων ἡμῶν θεῷ φίλος, ὅμοιος γάρ, 716d1–2), and Plato says in the *Theaetetus* that likeness to God consists in becoming pure and just with understanding (ὁμοίωσις δὲ δίκαιον καὶ ὅσιον μετὰ φρονήσεως γενέσθαι, 176b1–2; more on the *Theaetetus* passage below). Clearly, in thinking of our final end as living a life of likeness to God Plato does not mean this as an *alternative* to living a life of virtue, but takes them to come to the same thing.[10]

But how could likeness to God give us any insight into moral virtue, really? Being like God seems to suggest one's being superior to the world yet displaced and stuck in it, 'among the mire and shit of the world', in Montaigne's colorful phrase.[11] Such a sense of displacement is far more naturally connected to transcending, despising, and perhaps even escaping the world than it is to moral virtue, which consists in how we live *in* the world: how we act with, desire, enjoy, respond to, and treat the parts of the world that we find ourselves in—including other people and their problems—and that we find in ourselves, such as our pleasures, pains, and other passions.[12] If being like God takes us beyond our world, moral virtue—justice, courage, moderation, and so on—brings us right back to it. So how can Plato take becoming like God to *be* moral virtue?

The problem is most palpable in the digression in the *Theaetetus* (172b–177c), where Socrates openly portrays the philosopher as an outsider regarding human life, from which he actually seeks his escape. The philosopher, Socrates says there, grows up not knowing his way to the market-place, or the courthouse, or most other places of public assembly. In fact, 'the philosopher fails to see his next-door neighbor; he not only doesn't notice what he is doing; he scarcely knows whether he is a man or some other kind of creature' (174b1–4). Consequently, the distinctions of kings, the wealthy, and the well-born mean no more to him than the distinctions of farmers whose cows give plenty of milk (174d–175b); worse, he does not even know how to make his bed or cook a tasty meal (175e).

---

[10] Indeed, this is exactly what Alcinous says, *Handbook* 28.1–2. Cf. Annas (1999: 53).

[11] Montaigne (1993: 16). It is worth noting that Montaigne offers this foul depiction of our earthly state—of our being 'bound in the deadest, most stagnant part of the universe, in the lowest storey of the building, the farthest from the vault of heaven'—as an *antidote* to the 'presumption'—the 'original distemper of Man'—that humans are, in virtue of their rational powers, part of the divine or celestial realm.

[12] On Plato's apparent rejection of our worldly, human nature, and the problems with such a view, see Annas (1999: 52 f.); Rue (1993: 86 f.).

Now, instead of being terribly flat-footed,[13] we should naturally take this as hyperbole: *of course* philosophers know their way to the market-places and civic centers, and *of course* they know the species of their next-door neighbors. Socrates says that they do not only to drive home some more serious point, and clearly Socrates' point is that philosophers see past minutiae like money and reputation to matters of deeper significance, such as the nature of justice and happiness (175b–c). Unfortunately, however, we cannot sweep away *all* that strikes us as odd in this passage quite so easily. Socrates does, after all, go out of his way to be shocking in his portrayal of the philosopher as an 'outsider' with respect to 'normal' life. In fact, to illustrate his point he tells of Thales' falling into a well while gazing at the stars, prompting a laugh from a passing servant-girl for knowing what was up in the sky but having no idea what was under his feet (174a).[14] The problem, even granting the hyperbole, is that it is still hard to square all of this philosophical aloofness with thinking of virtue as a way of living in the world, and Plato seems not only to be aware of that fact but also to underscore it for us as well.[15] In fact, Socrates explicitly construes virtue, understood as likeness to God, as a way of *escaping* the world:

[I]t is not possible, Theodorus, that evil should be destroyed—for there must always be something opposed to the good; nor is it possible that it should have its seat in heaven. That is why a man should make all haste to escape (φεύγειν) from earth to heaven; and escape (φυγή) means becoming as like God as possible; and a man becomes like God when he becomes just and pure, with understanding.... In God there is no sort of wrong whatsoever; he is supremely just, and the thing most like him is the man who has become as just as it lies in human nature to be. (176a5–b2, 8–c2)

---

[13] Not, of course, that such flat-footedness would be entirely novel, since some traditions after the time of Plato have looked to passages such as this that can, without too much trouble, be made to fit their otherworldly philosophies. For example as we saw in Ch. 3, the Neoplatonist Damascius claims that one form of education makes the passions moderate, a higher makes one avoid the passions, and the highest form—described in the *Theaetetus*—removes one's very awareness of the passions, as well as removing any awareness of that unawareness (*Lectures on the* Phaedo I.75). Of course, between the fact that a passage can be made to fit a certain world-view and the claim that it *professes* that world-view lies a significant argumentative gap—a far wider one than Damascius, in particular, undertakes to fill.

[14] Jaeger (1948: 426) suggests that the emergence of serious philosophers, who struck laypersons as withdrawn and peculiar, is the main source of anecdotes in the ancient world about philosophers' day-to-day lives, such as Plato's anecdote about Thales at *Theaetetus* 174a. See also Aristotle, *Nicomachean Ethics* VI.7, 1141b3–8: 'This is why we say Anaxagoras, Thales, and men like them have philosophic but not practical wisdom, when we see them ignorant of what is to their own advantage, and why we say that they know things that are remarkable, admirable, difficult, and divine, but useless [ἄχρηστα]; viz. because it is not human goods that they seek.' The contrast between this passage and Aristotle's anecdote about Thales' monopoly of the olive presses at *Politics* I.11, 1259a5–20—a monopoly he acquired precisely in order to demonstrate the practical usefulness of philosophy, Aristotle says—may also suggest that sharp tensions between such anecdotes were met with relatively little discomfort in the ancient world.

[15] This has led a number of scholars to conclude that the philosopher's life that Plato discusses cannot be the one that he himself thinks best, and is noticeably un-Socratic; see Berger, Jr. (1982: 385–407, esp. 386); Waymack (1985: 481–9, esp. 482–7); Rue (1993: esp. 78–82, 86, 87–100); Burnyeat (1990: 35 f.); Annas (1999: 55).

One way to reckon with this passage would be to play down, or cast aside, all of this talk of escape and detachment as merely a wild—and unhelpful—metaphor, but it would be most unfortunate if we could make sense of Plato's fullest discussion of so apparently important a theme only by giving it nothing to say, passing over it in a polite but puzzled silence.[16]

So we seem to face a dilemma. On the one hand, if we take the Theaetetus digression at what seems to be its face value and understand likeness to God as an escapist ideal, then it becomes unpromising and unhelpful as a conception of moral virtue.[17] On the other, if we simply pass over the escapist elements, we risk deflating likeness to God into little more than a vague cliché for 'acting well',[18] whereas Plato and his later tradition do take this idea to do real work. Nor is it immediately clear how we could strike a middle ground between these two approaches, since they fight for 'psychological space and energy', in Julia Annas's phrase.[19]

My point is not to show, heroically, that the Theaetetus passage is not extraordinary after all. That would defeat the purpose: the lengths to which Plato goes in imagery and language in this passage display a clear effort on his part to grab our attention and focus it on a point that must be of particular importance to him.[20] And that makes it all the more important for us to understand just what that point might be, once it is more fully developed than it is here. Looking back on this passage, it is perhaps easy for us to assume that it is no more than a predecessor of certain ascetic and escapist traditions with which we have since become familiar. And perhaps it is no more than that. But, given the importance

[16] Barker (1976: 458–60) also makes the very plausible suggestion that the philosopher is depicted as non-public to underscore Plato's rejection of the Protagorean thesis that justice and right are wholly conventional notions, which have no meaning until a community specifies them for itself. The public man thinks that he knows all about such things because he is an 'insider' with respect to the conventions. But the philosopher comes to know these things as realities that are not dependent on convention: 'The philosopher, the man who seeks the true nature of things, is precisely not the man who thinks that he can find the object of his quest in his immediate environment: he will not seek for the good and the just among the decrees, laws, and customs of his city, nor for the nature of happiness among the successes and failures of his state and his fellow citizens.' Hence, since it is possible for the philosopher to know the nature of justice without even knowing where the local courthouse is, philosophical understanding of things like justice cannot take them to be purely conventional: the philosopher's 'practice implies that there is, as he believes, a "true nature" of things to be discovered, and not merely a set of conventions to be learned.' I think that Barker is certainly right about this; however, he does not discuss the treatment of moral virtue in the digression, and the associated 'escape' imagery, and so it remains difficult to understand likeness to God as a conception of moral virtue, despite the significant illumination of the passage that Barker's view affords.

[17] See Annas (1999), ch. 3; Sedley (1997) and (1999: esp. 322–8).

[18] See Annas (1999: 58 f., cf. 56 f.) for discussion of the problems of such deflationary readings of likeness to God. Sedley (1999: 313 f.) seems to me to be in danger of deflating likeness to God in some such way as this; but see also 315 f.

[19] For this way of characterizing the tension see Annas (1999: 70 f.).

[20] The fact that Plato would put such important ideas in the dialogue's 'digression' does not, we should notice, tell against their seriousness and importance; cf. Annas (1994b: 321 f.). Cp. the 'digressions' and 'interruptions' at Protagoras 341d–348a, where Socrates discusses his own view of virtue and weakness of will—the central topic of the dialog, as it happens—and at Euthydemus 277d–283c, a seminal discussion of what skill one really needs in order to be happy.

and interest the idea seems to have had for Plato, we need more than assumptions to guide us.

Help awaits us along two quite under-explored avenues. First, likeness to God appears also in the *Philebus*—a dialogue seldom consulted in this context—as a way of dealing intelligently with the world as we find it, and there this idea is anything but cliché. Second, in Seneca and other Stoics we find a down-to-earth conception of virtue not only consistent with, but indeed illuminated by, the idea that virtue makes one like God. Plato and Seneca each provide us with a third way of understanding likeness to God, one that affords a new assessment of likeness to God in the *Theaetetus* digression. Our greatest obstacle to understanding likeness to God is the natural assumption that we already know what it means—that it is a spiritual ideal, *rather than* an ethical one. Seneca, and Plato himself in the *Philebus*, show us another way.

5.2   Likeness to God in the *Philebus*

The role of likeness to God in the *Philebus* is primarily that of bringing intelligence, proportion, and order to an otherwise chaotic realm—the inchoate matter, as it were, of one's life. In the *Philebus*, Plato demonstrates this most clearly in reason's activity of giving pleasure the proper place in one's life. Socrates and his interlocutor, Protarchus, agree that the best human life will contain a mixture of pleasure and reason (22a), and in order to determine the respective contributions of pleasure and reason to the best life, Socrates proposes a fourfold classification of being within which to understand the relations between such things as pleasure and reason (23c–27c). First in the classification is the 'unlimited' or 'indeterminate' (τὸ ἄπειρον, 24a–25a, 28a), which includes all things that vary and change but do not have any particular proportion just in virtue of what they are. Plato's discussion of the 'unlimited', and indeed of the whole classification, is rather difficult, but Terence Irwin offers an illustration that I find very helpful.[21] Hot water, for instance, always has some temperature or other, but it can have a wide variety of temperatures and still be hot, or hotter than some other water; but to be the kind of hot water one needs for making tea, say, it must be made a rather specific temperature—it must be not just hot, but hot *in the right way for tea*. When it has been brought into such a condition of being right for making tea, we can say that it now has 'limit', which is the second aspect of being that Plato distinguishes (25a–b, d–26c). The water with this limit, that is the water at the right temperature for making tea, falls into the third

---

[21] Irwin (1995: 324 f.); cf. D. Frede (1993: xxxiv–xxxvi) and (1992: 428). Irwin's account represents a distinct improvement over earlier accounts, as in, e.g., Hackforth (1945: 42). See also Sayre (1987: 51–4, 61 f.), who considers the issue as one of dividing a continuum (sound, heat) into a calibrated scale of values (pitch, degrees of temperature) according to a norm that provides a point of reference for introducing limit (but see 54 f. for the claim that things in the unlimited class 'have no specific properties at all', which Irwin rightly denies).

division of being, which Plato calls the 'mixture' of unlimited and limit (25b–26d, 27d–28a). Finally, Plato says that there must always be a 'cause' (the fourth class) of such mixtures (26e–27c, 28a–31b), that is, something must be the cause of limit being brought to the unlimited to generate a mixture, as when someone boils the water for tea. A mixture is something proportionate and measured, and so it must be the product of an intelligent cause.

Plato classifies reason as the cause of everything,[22] since it causes limit to come about in 'unlimited' things, making them into good, orderly products ('mixtures'). He arrives at this verdict about reason by arguing, first, that the orderliness of the universe must be due to reason, which is king over heaven and earth; and second that the human soul is dependent on, or an offshoot of, the soul of the universe (29a–30b). Finally, since the human soul is wise and is dependent on the soul of the universe, the universe's soul must be responsible for the wisdom of humans; so the soul of the universe must be wise, and this wisdom of the universe's soul manifests itself in the ordering of years, seasons, and months (28c, d–e, 30c–e).

For present purposes we need not bother too much with the cosmology Plato sketches here.[23] But notice that Plato in the *Philebus* focuses on God as an intelligent *producer* of rational order, and so the God we emulate in the *Philebus* is primarily an agent and a cause of order. The point about emulation is an important one: Socrates' discussion is not an idle metaphysical speculation, but is designed to show us something about the activity of God in bringing order to the universe that he says is relevant to his immediate discussion of how rational agents are to bring order to their passions (30d–31b):

You will therefore say that in the nature of Zeus there is the soul of a king, as well as a king's reason, in virtue of this power displayed by the cause, while paying tribute for other fine qualities in the other divinities, in conformity with the names by which they like to be addressed.

Very much so.

Do not think that we have engaged in an idle discussion here, Protarchus, for it comes as a support for the thinkers of old who held the view that reason is forever the ruler over the universe.

It certainly does.

It also has provided an answer to my query, that reason belongs to that kind which is the cause of everything. . . . By now, dear friend, we have arrived at a satisfactory explanation of the class that reason belongs to and what power it has.

Quite so.

And as to pleasure, it became apparent quite a while ago what class it belongs to.

Definitely.

---

[22] Cp. *Phaedo* 97c: 'it is, in fact, intelligence that orders and is the reason for everything . . . intelligence in ordering all things must order them and place each individual thing in the best way possible . . .'.

[23] Although it is worth noting the obvious parallels between this passage and the idea in the *Timaeus* that the movements of heavenly bodies manifest and embody principles of intelligence (see esp. *Timaeus* 46d–47c).

Let us firmly keep it in mind about both of them, that reason is akin to cause and is part of that family, while pleasure itself is unlimited and belongs to the kind that in and by itself neither possesses nor will ever possess a beginning, middle, or end. (30d1–e1, 31a1–10)

Two things about Socrates' discussion of reason as a cause are especially worth noting for our purposes. One, reason and intelligence always belong in the class of cause, both in us and in the universe arranged by God (29b–31a). Reason, then, is what brings unlimited, inchoate matter into proper condition by bringing order about in it. It does so by understanding what proper order, proportion, and limit are, and directing our behavior toward it. And two, the virtuous activity of a human being consists in bringing such order and limit into the inchoate materials of the *self*, such as one's desires, emotions, feelings, and pleasures, which belong to the 'unlimited' class. Thus humans have virtues in so far as they use wisdom and reason to bring order to unlimited matter that is, in the first instance, internal to themselves, such as one's passions and desires; and the virtues *are* this ordering of the aspects of one's self according to wisdom and reason (see 64e).

Plato takes these observations to suggest an important difference between the value of reason, on the one hand, and the value of things like pleasure, on the other. Pleasure left to its own devices, as it were, does not bring about the order and direction that one's life needs, and does not make one place value in the things one should as one should, and may just as well do quite the opposite. In fact, Plato claims that pleasure on its own gives one's life no direction or shape *whatsoever*, such that a life 'directed' by pleasure alone would be like that of a shellfish (21c), aimless, empty, and anything but human.[24] For this reason, pleasure as such has no power to make life good. Here Plato returns to the point that he had made about such goods in the *Euthydemus*, namely that they are 'undifferentiated': on its own, pleasure is neither good nor bad—productive of neither happiness nor misery—because on its own it has no particular direction at all.[25] What does have the power to make life good, rather, is the intelligence or wisdom with which one acts in relation to such things. For this reason, reason and intelligence as cause (26e ff.), and thus moral virtue, are productive of goodness, and therefore are what makes the good life good.[26] Intelligence, then, is both differentiated, having its own direction toward our good, and differentiating, as it brings that direction to other things which, like pleasure, lack a direction of their own. Here, too, Plato returns to the thesis in the *Euthydemus* that only wisdom is genuinely good, other things becoming good only as wisdom leads and directs (or 'uses') them.

Consequently, when Socrates comes at the end of the *Philebus* to a ranking of goods, he argues that the goodness that obtains in the organization of a good life is the chief good, since it is responsible for the goodness of that life, in virtue of

---

[24] I thank an anonymous referee for the *Journal of the History of Philosophy* for pointing out this connection. [25] I discuss this sense of 'undifferentiated' in Ch. 1.
[26] For an excellent discussion of this thesis and its connection to Plato's value schema, see Bobonich (1995: 118–34).

being what its goodness consists in. Next, since all reason is more akin to goodness than pleasure is, Socrates ranks reason as a whole ahead of pleasure, and pleasure is admitted into the good life only in so far as reason as a whole permits (59d ff., 64c ff.). Plato's point is that the contributions that reason and pleasure make to the good life are different in kind, one being what does the work of making a good life a good life; the other being that in relation to which it does it this work.[27] Consequently, they are different kinds of goods, playing radically different roles in the synthesis of a good life.

Notice now that this view of how humans use reason to bring limit to the 'matter' of their souls puts the *Philebus* right in line with the view that our final end is likeness to God. For it is clear in the discussion of intelligence that human reason is continuous with divine reason, that our activity of bringing order to unlimited matter through reason is continuous with divine activity, and that it is with this aspect of ourselves that we are to identify. The concept of likeness to God is especially important in the *Philebus*, since it is also a dialogue in which the good life that is discussed is emphatically and explicitly a *human* life, as opposed to an otherworldly one: it is, after all, for precisely this reason that Plato rejects both the life of pleasure alone—the life of a shellfish—and the life of reason alone as serious candidates for human happiness (see 20c–22e, 60c–61a).[28] On Plato's view, humans seek likeness to God by seeking wisdom, but we seek likeness to God not *as gods*, but *as the humans* that we are,[29] and in the *Philebus* he clearly takes this to mean seeking likeness to God in a way that incorporates human pleasures and passions.[30]

That the good life discussed in the *Philebus* is emphatically human is worth noting for several reasons. For one thing, it is, of course, true that the question whether some way of life is most like the life that the gods actually live is a different question indeed from whether some way of life is the life most like the life that the gods actually live *and is possible for us to live*. It is surely significant that in speaking of likeness to God as a way of understanding the good human life, Socrates regularly adds exactly the latter sort of rider.[31] And, indeed, the subsequent discussion in the dialogue makes it quite clear that Plato has fairly little interest in the most divine life *simpliciter* as a candidate for the most divine

---

[27] Arius Didymus (Stobaeus, *Anthology* II.5b) makes a similar distinction between the 'primary' good, which is virtue, and 'secondary' goods which include (are?) those parts of our affective life that are transformed by virtue. I shall discuss this passage below.

[28] It is worth noting that on Plato's view—and especially his rejection of the life of reason without pleasure as a candidate for happiness—pleasure turns out to be necessary for happiness. We shall return to this issue, and its relation to wisdom's claim to be the unique determinant of happiness, in the next chapter.

[29] Cf. Ficino, *The* Philebus *Commentary* I.30, who in his discussion of the desirability (*expetendum*) of the good refers to the view of Dionysius the Areopagite, that 'all things seek God's likeness [*Dei similitudinem*], each in its own way: . . . those which understand [*intelligunt*] in accordance with the understanding [*secundum intelligentiam*].'

[30] Simply put, if Plato's considered view is that the best human life is one devoid of all pleasure, then the *Philebus* is a most odd dialogue for him to have written.

[31] See, e.g., *Republic* 613b1 ('as much like a god as a human can', (εἰς ὅσον ἀνθρώπῳ ὁμοιοῦσθαι θεῷ), *Theaetetus* 176b1–2 ('as like God as possible', ὁμοίωσις θεῷ κατὰ τὸ δύνατον).

life for us. For this reason, when Plato maintains that the life of reason alone, devoid of any pleasure or pain, may be 'the most godlike' life of all, since the gods experience no pleasure or pain (33b), he none the less gives us no reason to adopt an escapist or ascetic conception of likeness to God, or to think that *we* should therefore seek to experience no pleasure or pain, or as little as possible. From the fact that, as Plato says, a life of no pleasure and no pain is the most godlike life *simpliciter*, it does not follow that such a life is the most godlike life *for us to live*. What does follow, however, is that the life *centered* on pleasure is lived for the sake of something that is excluded from the most godlike life *simpliciter*, so that a human life centered on reason is more godlike than one centered on pleasure.[32] And, in fact, this is all that Socrates says—and all that he needs to say—in taking his observation as a point in favor of the life he recommends and against the life that Protarchus recommends—it is, he says, 'an additional point in favor of reason in the competition' against pleasure for the title of our chief good (33b11–c3).

Moreover, we should make explicit an interesting discontinuity between a human's activity of bringing order to matter and that sort of activity on the part of a god. Pleasure, we have seen, is a paradigmatic sort of 'matter' of the soul in which a human is to bring order, but of course the gods experience no pleasures at all (33b),[33] and this illustrates the more general point that the inchoate matter that a human brings order to is (in the first instance) within himself, whereas the inchoate matter to which the gods bring order must be understood as being always distinct from the gods themselves. This is an important difference to note, but, of course, it is still useful to understand human rationality is to be understood as of a piece with God's creative activity, in so far as they are both cases of transforming matter, which is not capable of transforming itself, into an orderly whole. Plato recommends not that we live the life of a god but that we live the life that is the most godlike of those that are possible for us considered as human beings. We are like God in so far as we follow intelligent principles to bring 'matter'—in our case, our very selves—into an orderly whole.

Likeness to God in the *Philebus*, then, consists in divine reason bringing about order and structure in matter, and likeness to God as a conception of virtue consists in bringing about this order in the matter of our lives and our selves, such as our pleasures, desires, and passions. Moreover, the reason with which we act in relation to matter is, for Plato, good in its very nature—unconditionally and intrinsically good—unlike the matter on which reason acts, and which depends on the leadership of reason for its goodness. This already is a substantive conception of likeness to God as practical rationality, rather than a bland and cliché one. And it is through this conception that we can see how likeness to God can *also* be a kind of transcendence or even 'escape'; that it is possible to weave these two strands together is clear in Seneca's thought about likeness to God.

---

[32] On my way of reading them, then, the *Phaedo* and *Philebus* are in line on this point.
[33] But *con. Phaedrus* 247d. Plato's view on this issue seems to be somewhat fluid from dialogue to dialogue.

5.3   Likeness to God in Seneca

Seneca understands likeness to God primarily as a way of thinking about value, and so we must first take a closer look at the Stoic value theory within which Seneca works. For the Stoics, our good is to live according to Nature, and thus to identify our good we must identify what kind of beings we are and what Nature has set as the primary goal for beings of our kind.[34] Consequently, the Stoics begin by reflecting on what infant humans, as well as animals and even plants, have as the natural goal of their existence; and the Stoics claim that it is self-preservation.[35]

How is the goal of self-preservation supposed to account for what *I*, as an adult human, should take as the primary purpose of all of my activities—what could thinking about bare self-preservation add to my understanding of how my various projects form a rational unity? Here the ingenuity of the Stoic view reveals itself: self-preservation is a goal that is both determinate *and* malleable, able to change and develop as I do.[36] In other words, my goal is always self-preservation, but as the self to be preserved develops, so too changes what it means to preserve that sort of self. We see this notion of a developing self in Seneca, who writes that

There is a different constitution for every age; one for the baby, one for the child, one for the teen-ager, one for the old man. All find the constitution which they are in congenial. A baby lacks teeth; he finds that congenial. For the plant which will turn into mature crop has a different constitution when it is tender and barely poking its nose out of the furrow, another when it gains strength and stands, admittedly with an unripe stalk but one able to support its own weight, and another when it ripens and gets ready for the threshing floor and the ear firms up; it looks to and adapts itself to whatever constitution it achieves. There are different stages of life for a baby, a boy, a teen-ager, and an old man; yet I am, for all that, the same person as the baby and the boy and the teen-ager I used to be. Thus, although each man's constitution changes from one stage to another, the congeniality he feels towards his constitution is the same. For nature does not commend to me a boy or a youth or an old man, but myself. Therefore, a baby finds his own constitution congenial, the one he then has and not the one which he will have as a youth; the fact that he will have something greater to change into some day does not mean that the state in which he is born is not according to nature.   (Seneca, *Letters to Lucilius* 121.15–16)

Seneca makes the interesting observation that while my life is composed of different stages of maturity and development, with correspondingly different concerns, none the less what makes all of these different selves 'me' is their unification within a single goal: the preservation of the self, and thus my congeniality to my self. The same goal and congeniality, then, can be attributed to me, even though what I am, and thus what aiming at that goal amounts to, changes radically over time. Consequently, undertaking the projects of a mature agent just *is* the preservation of the sort of self that a mature agent is.

---

[34] This is, in fact, the common starting-place for otherwise very dissimilar ethical theories in Hellenistic philosophy; see Cicero, *de Finibus* V.17–18.   [35] Diogenes Laertius, *Lives* VII.85.
[36] See also M. Frede (1986: 108 f.).

The most important development of the self in a human is maturing into a being which is completely reflective and capable of self-direction. This is, in other words, the development of reason. Reason does not set humans apart from the natural order; rather, as Zeno and the other Stoics maintain, 'When reason has been given to rational animals as a more perfect governor of life, then for them the life according to reason properly becomes what is natural for them.'[37] Thus the primary goal of purely biological beings—preservation of the self—can be shared with sophisticated rational beings after all: both seek self-preservation, but in a rational being the self that is preserved is the *rational* self.

The significance of this way of understanding our final end, for our purposes, is its power to transform our priorities, and what we take to be the good for the sake of which we act. For as we develop from creatures who pursue the things we need to survive to creatures who seek to do what they do in rational and sensible ways, that rationality itself comes to eclipse the things that we used to think so valuable. The Stoics, Cicero tells us,[38] believe that humans start life by pursuing ordinary things such as food and shelter, at first in messy ways, but as we mature we pursue them in more and more sensible ways. Gradually, then, those who mature come to select things in appropriate ways, and eventually come to select things appropriately in a stable and reliable way. But at that point a maturing person will come to recognize the rationality and stability with which they are coming to select other things, and will recognize that this mode of selecting, rather than the things selected, is what makes him the kind of agent that he is. Consequently, the rationality of his selecting comes to eclipse the selecting itself as what matters in assessing how well he has done as the kind of being that he is.[39]

This transformation Cicero likens to being introduced by a friend to a third person, and then developing a closer relationship with the third person than one has with the original friend.[40] Likewise, he says, 'it is in no way surprising that we are first introduced to wisdom by the starting points established by nature, but that later on wisdom itself becomes dearer to us than the things which brought us to wisdom.' This, he says, illustrates the Stoic claim that, as we develop from creatures who pursue the things we need to survive to creatures who seek to do what they do in rational and sensible ways, that very rationality comes to eclipse the things that we used to think so valuable, until, in a fully mature person, that rationality is seen as 'the only thing which is to be chosen in virtue of its own character and value.'[41] So we start out seeking ordinary things, but we can gradually come to see that the rationality with which we seek them is actually far more important than the things themselves. As we gain reason, we do not come to *stop* caring about those things altogether, but we do come to care about them in a very different way, as our caring for them becomes disencumbered by the false supposition that our happiness or unhappiness somehow

---

[37] See Diogenes Laertius, *Lives* VII.86–7.   [38] Cicero, *de Finibus* III.20–3.
[39] For an excellent discussion of this process in Stoic philosophy, see Engberg-Pederson (1986).
[40] Cicero, *de Finibus* III.22–3.   [41] Cicero, *de Finibus* III.21.

depends on them, as if they had their own power with respect to happiness or unhappiness.

And this marks the difference between practical rationality and everything else: only practical rationality is intrinsically, unconditionally good with respect to happiness, and thus differentiated as a good in its nature—because of its '*own* character and value'—needing nothing else to differentiate it as a good. This is because on the Stoic view virtue is essentially active, and it is because of its unique active power with respect to happiness that it is the only thing good in its nature. The Stoics define goodness not as a property but as a power—the power to benefit and improve—and only virtue is 'such as to benefit', not depending on how it is used but in virtue of what it is itself.[42] This power to benefit is understood as the power to make one's life happy and flourishing, and the Stoics maintain that nothing but virtue has this power:

> The virtues . . . are good; and their opposites . . . are bad; neither good nor bad are those things which neither benefit nor harm . . . For just as heating, not cooling, is a property of the hot, so benefiting, not harming, is a property of the good; but wealth and health do not benefit any more than they harm; therefore, neither wealth nor health is good. . . . To benefit is to change or maintain something in accordance with virtue, while to harm is to change or maintain something in accordance with vice. (Diogenes Laertius, *Lives* VII.102, 103, 104)

Furthermore, it seems that the Stoics also saw this power as involving what we have called rational incorporation. Interestingly, Arius Didymus also allows certain features of the virtuous person—'joy and good spirits and confidence and wish and such things'[43]—to count as good things as well, despite the fact that they are not virtues, but he goes on to point out that only virtue is good in the proper or 'primary' sense, which he identifies as goodness as a source of benefit and that which is 'such as to benefit', while joy and good spirits are good things in the secondary sense of dimensions of the psyche transformed by virtue. This way of understanding the relationship between virtue and the other aspects of our lives is also apparent in Arius Didymus' discussion of 'mixed' and 'unmixed' goods:[44] whereas knowledge is an unmixed good, because it takes nothing in addition to knowledge to make knowledge beneficial, such things as the 'virtuous possession of children' and the 'virtuous use of old age' are mixed goods, since it takes the leadership of knowledge, or virtue, to make one's relation to one's children, one's old age, and even one's death a good thing, that is, to make oneself good where they are concerned:

> Only the virtuous man has good children, though not all have virtuous children since it is necessary for him who has good children to use them as such. Only the virtuous man has a good old age and a good death; for a good old age is conducting oneself virtuously at a

---

[42] See Diogenes Laertius, *Lives* VII.94, 102–4; Stobaeus, *Anthology* II.5d.

[43] Stobaeus, *Anthology* II.5b; see also Diogenes Laertius, *Lives* VII.116–17. I shall return to these 'good affections'—the εὐπάθειαι—below.

[44] Stobaeus, *Anthology* II.5m; see also Diogenes Laertius, *Lives* VII.98.

certain age, and a good death is to make one's end virtuously with a certain kind of death. (Stobaeus, *Anthology* II.11q)

Here the idea is unmistakable: to have a good old age or a good death is not to make the age or the death itself a good thing, but to make one's behavior good with respect to old age or death. Likewise, to have good children is not to have children of a certain sort, but to 'use' them in a virtuous manner—to 'use' them in Plato's sense (*Euthydemus* 281b), which is to make one's behavior virtuous where one's children are concerned.[45] Virtue, then, is what benefits, and things like joy, good spirits, confidence, wish, and the like are things in respect of which virtue is a benefit.

This is, of course, what we mean by rational incorporation: virtue brings about goodness in other things with no goodness of their own, by bringing the right kind of direction and order to one's life where those things are concerned. Consequently, for the Stoics, virtue is a disposition of the soul in agreement with Nature, inasmuch as it is the whole soul is in accordance with right reason, as it is our nature to be.[46] Thus virtue is what brings order and harmony to our lives, allowing us to live well, by acting rationally with respect to all of the concerns of life. Since it is virtue which brings order to our lives, and not the concerns that virtue orders—only virtue, that is, has the power to make a life a good life—it is virtue that is our good. Other things in our life may be worth preferring, but they cannot make us happy just by their very presence; we must incorporate them into our lives in rational ways. Virtue is a special part of our lives because it is that which does the rational incorporating.[47]

Thus for the Stoics only rationality is good, and so while virtue acts in regard to the things we normally regard as good and bad things, it is itself worth living for even if we do not achieve the goals we seek with respect to other things;[48] or, as Plato puts it, wisdom is all the good fortune one will ever really need. This is why the Stoics place all value on acting rationally, whatever one's lot, rather than on what one's lot happens to be. This is a common refrain in Stoicism, and especially in Epictetus:

'Go and salute Mr. So-and-so.' 'All right, I salute him.' 'How?' 'Not in an abject fashion.' 'But you were shut out.' 'That's because I haven't learned how to enter through the window. And when I find the door shut against me, I must either go away or enter through the window.' 'But speak with the man too!' 'I did so.' 'How?' 'Not in an abject fashion.' 'But you did not succeed.'—Now surely that was not your business, but his. So why do you encroach on what concerns someone else? If you always remember what is yours and what concerns someone else, you will never be disturbed. (*Discourses* II.6.6–8)

Epictetus does not think there is anything wrong with trying to win another person's favor, but the important thing to remember, he tells us, is that the

---

[45] This is, I suspect, also the force behind the Stoic idea that among 'external goods' are having a virtuous friend and a virtuous fatherland (Diogenes Laertius, *Lives* VII.95), but I shall not press the point here. [46] See Diogenes Laertius, *Lives* VII.89; Stobaeus, *Anthology* II.5b7.
[47] See Diogenes Laertius, *Lives* VII.102–4. I shall discuss the notion of rational incorporation within Stoicism further in the next chapter. [48] Cicero, *de Finibus* V.20, with V.18.

ultimate goal of this exercise is not to gain a certain outcome but to act in a rational, self-respecting way, whatever the outcome—*that* is the goal of this exercise, as it is *always* the goal of *every* exercise at the end of the day.[49] For this is what valuing one's rationality for its own sake consists in, and that is to live in accordance with Nature, which is happiness.

As if echoing the *Philebus*, then, the Stoics claim that virtue is the rationality with which we act well in relation to all of our various concerns, and that rationality alone is the source of the unifying goodness of our lives. Nothing else has the value of rationality and virtue because nothing else is the source of all goodness. In the terms of the *Philebus*, those things are 'unlimited', the inchoate matter of intelligent action. They have no power of their own, therefore, to make our lives go well. Only virtue has that power, and so only virtue is our good.

The distinction between things good in their nature and things not, is a distinction between what is an active producer and source of goodness in one's life, and what is a passive recipient in need of such a source. Here the Stoics and Plato agree, the Stoics identifying virtue with that which is such as to benefit by bringing the whole self into harmony with our rational nature, and Plato identifying virtue with a kind of reason that brings order to the otherwise undifferentiated matter of the whole self. Perhaps it is not so surprising, then, that the Stoics *also* glossed their conception of virtue, and the culmination of our divine nature as rational beings, as a form of likeness to God: to live according to virtue, they say, is to live in accordance with right reason—that is, to live in accordance with Zeus, which is the same as living rationally and engaging in reasonable behavior.[50] We see this even more clearly in Seneca's *Letters to Lucilius* 92, where he writes:

You and I are at one, I assume, in holding that externals are acquired for the sake of the body, the body is tended out of respect for the soul, and that the agencies of the soul which direct motion and sustenance are given us for the sake of the essential soul. The essential

---

[49] It is this point that is reflected in the Stoic distinction between things we 'choose' (the ultimate goal) and the things we 'select' (proximate goals); see Cicero, *de Finibus* III.22.

[50] See Diogenes Laertius, *Lives* VII.87–8. Cp. the discussion of *Philebus* 33b, above. The same point can be made if we consider two selections from Cleanthes' writings on Zeus. The first is from his so-called 'Hymn to Zeus' (SVF 1.537), in which he says, 'Nor does any deed occur on earth without you, god . . . For thus you have fitted together all good things with the bad, so that there is one eternal rational principle for them all—and it is this which the wicked flee from and neglect . . .' (trans. Inwood and Gerson (1997)). At first blush we might think that there is a simple contradiction here: all things happen 'with' Zeus, and yet some things—the wicked things—happen 'without' Zeus, inasmuch as the wicked flee Zeus. However, Epictetus (*Enchiridion* 53) preserves a fragment of another of Cleanthes' hymns to Zeus that sheds some light on this: 'Lead me, O Zeus, and you O Fate, to whatever place you have assigned me; I shall follow without reluctance, and if I am not willing to, because I have become a bad man, nevertheless I *will* follow' (trans. Inwood and Gerson (1997)). Here we can see that there are two senses in which things are done 'with' (and 'without') Zeus: in one sense, Zeus is the totality of all that happens, or Fate, and in this sense all things that are done are done with Zeus; in another sense, Zeus is right reason, and thus only the rational do things with Zeus in this sense. Consequently, the Stoics distinguish between the leadership of Zeus as a primarily metaphysical notion and as a distinctly ethical one, and understand rationality or virtue as following the leadership of Zeus in the latter sense. (For a discussion of the problems that result from construing our goal as living according to cosmic nature, see Annas (1994*a*), ch. 5.)

soul has an irrational factor and also a rational. The irrational serves the rational and is the one element which is not referred to something else but refers all things to itself.[51] For the divine reason, too, is sovereign over all things, and subordinate to none, and our reasons possesses the same quality because it is derived from the divine.   (92.1)[52]

Notice that rationality has this sovereign value because rationality is divine, and thus is the divinity in human nature. Consequently, to be a fully rational human being is to be like God:

> But where 'virtue and spirit are present in his frame' [*Aeneid* 5.363] a man is equal to the gods [*hic deos aequat*]. He remembers his origin and makes it his goal.[53] It is never wrong to attempt to regain the heights from which you have descended. Why should you not believe that there is an element of the divine in what is part of god? The totality in which we are contained is one, and it is god; and we are his partners [*socii sumus eius*] and his members. Our spirit is capacious, and its direction is toward god, if vices do not press it down. Just as our bodily posture is erect and looks toward heaven, so our soul, which may reach outward at will, was fashioned by Nature to desire equality with the gods [*ut paria dis vellet*]. And if it utilizes its powers and expands outward into its own reaches, it is by no alien path that it makes its way to the heights. A pioneer journey to heaven is a great task; the soul is retracing its path. When it has found its road it marches boldly on, disregarding all distinctions. It casts no backward glance at riches, gold and silver, which are most appropriate to the darkness in which they had been buried, the soul values not by the glitter which overwhelms the eyes of the ignorant, but by the primal muck from which our greed separated them and dug them out.   (92.30–1)

For Seneca, the soul is descended from an originally divine state, retains this divinity in rationality, and is properly directed at regaining this divinity through the pursuit of rationality for its own sake. And since this rationality is the same as virtue, in becoming virtuous one becomes like God. Moreover, in this passage Seneca is at pains to make it clear that in becoming like God one is not becoming some other kind of being than what Nature has made one to be. Rather, one becomes the true fulfillment of what *our* nature is—a rational being.[54]

---

[51] This language seems surprisingly Platonic for a Stoic; but see, e.g., Galen, *On Hippocrates' and Plato's Doctrines* 5.6.34–7 for a similar bifurcation in the soul by Cleanthes, who depicts reason and passion as personified and engaged in debate. *Pace* Galen, however, there seems to be no reason to take this to be in tension with the 'standard' Stoic account—such as Chrysippus'—of a wholly unified soul, and Cleanthes' fictitious conversation seems designed to do little more than show the opposition between the good reasons we entertain at some times and the bad reasons we entertain at other times (see Annas (1992), ch. 5). This is the way to understand Seneca's language here, too.

[52] Translations of letter 92 are from Hadas (1958).

[53] Cp. *Timaeus* 90d, where Timaeus claims that cultivating one's rationality amounts to returning to the original condition of the soul.

[54] It is interesting to note, however, that at least one Stoic seems to have thought that in trying to make choices that are rational one should think not about God but about some wise human. As Epictetus writes, when you are going into association with anyone, especially with a superior, you should 'set before your mind the question, what would Zeno or Socrates have done?'; and similarly, 'If you are not yet Socrates, you still ought to live as one who wishes to be Socrates.' (Epictetus, *Enchiridion* 33, 51, trans. Passmore (1970: 60), who brings out this point well.) But, of course, this does not compete with the Stoic idea that the formal structure of rationality is likeness to God: what

But, we may ask, while Seneca too may understand virtue or rationality as our likeness to God, surely he can mean nothing so radical by this as Plato does? And surely he avoids the sorts of 'escapist' refrains we find in the *Theaetetus*? Quite the contrary:

When the soul has raised itself to this sublimity it regards the necessary burden of the body not as a lover but as a steward, and it does not submit to its ward. No man that serves his body is free. Even if you pass over the other masters that excessive solicitude for the body has contrived, its own lordliness is imperious and touchy. From the body the soul springs forth, now calmly and now with elation, and never thereafter does it ask what is to befall the husk that it has left behind. Just as we are unconcerned about the clippings of beard and hair, so upon its departure from man's mortal frame the divine soul judges that its receptacle's final destiny—whether fire shall consume it, or stone shut it in, or earth cover it, or beasts rend it—is of no more relevance than the afterbirth is to a newborn child.   (92.33–4)

Taking virtue as valuable for its own sake, Seneca says, has radical implications for the sort of priorities that one has. Seneca here shows that the virtuous recognize that their happiness does not depend on the things—wealth, finery, and even physical survival—that most people take to be have some power of their own to make one happy. This finds its most radical expression in the Stoics' confidence in the face of even death itself, which is simply a moving on to what one has been preparing for,[55] just as we do not consider a newborn infant's loss of the afterbirth to be a real loss, but a natural part of maturing to which one must adjust.

Note also that, for Seneca, valuing rationality for its own sake is not in conflict with being a part of the world as one finds it, but rather is the only rational way to be just such a part:

'Well, then,' says the opposition, 'if virtue is not impeded by good health and repose and freedom from pain, will you not seek these things?' Of course I shall, not, however, because they are goods but because they are in accordance with nature and because I shall avail myself of them judiciously. And what good will they involve? Simply this: proper choice. When I put on clothing that is appropriate, when I walk as I should, when I dine as becomes me, it is not the dinner or the walk or the clothing that are good but my own program of observing in every act a measure which conforms to reason. I must add that choice of becoming clothing is a desideratum, for man is by nature a tidy and well-groomed animal. Becoming clothing is therefore not a good per se, but the choice of becoming clothing is; the good lies not in the thing but in the quality of selection. Our modes of action, not the things we do, are honorable.   (92.11–12)

For Seneca, then, likeness to God is not in competition with bringing about goodness and order in our world, but just *is* that. Indeed, even thinking about likeness to God as a way of escaping the world is not, for Seneca, an alternative to being an active part of the world. It is rather his way of understanding what it

being a fully rational being consists in, and what is the best method or heuristic for finding what would be rational in my present situation, are different questions.

[55] Cp. *Phaedo* 64a ff.

is to be an active part of the world in a mature, rational way; for only those who learn to value the rationality with which they act for its own sake are mature as rational beings.

So in Seneca we find the strands that we also find in Plato's conception of likeness to God, and Seneca's weaving them together expands our options for understanding likeness to God. In Seneca, virtue is practical rationality, which is something transcendent and part of our divine nature, but it is also the essence of our humanity, and of good human action *in the world as we find it*. The point for Seneca is not that we should seek to leave our mortal existence in favor of a divine existence. The point is that only a certain set of priorities and values that underlie a person's action with respect to the materials of the world is a mature set, that is, mature for persons understood as rational creatures.

Seneca's discussion of likeness to God not only opens up further possibilities for understanding that idea but also opens up possibilities for understanding what work that idea might be doing in Plato. For one thing, Seneca shows that the idea that virtue consists in likeness to God does not entail that virtue is unworldly and escapist, and thus outrageous.[56] Virtue involves not fleeing from, but bringing order to, one's life, as we see also in the *Philebus* and even the *Timaeus*; and this means having a radically changed set of priorities and values in dealing with the matter of one's life, as we see in the *Theaetetus*. Moreover, these aspects of virtue are united, as Seneca makes clear, in so far as only the person who acts rationally for its own sake with respect to the matter of his life is a fully mature, rational person, and thus like God and prepared to join the company of God.

For another, the idea that virtue is likeness to God does not thereby become bland and cliché. Seneca and other Stoics show that virtue as likeness to God is consistent with the idea that virtue is the rationality one displays in action, without making likeness to God merely a dispensable restatement of that idea. Describing virtue in this way adds to our understanding of virtue. It underscores the value of virtue for its own sake, and thus the radical extent to which the virtuous person's priorities are revised. It allows us to see that virtue is both concerned with, and superior to, the things in relation to which virtue acts, and that only by valuing virtue for its own sake do we really identify with our nature and mature as rational persons.

Moreover, while the Stoics believe that only our practical rationality can make us happy—for it is unique in being that which brings order and harmony to all the aspects of our lives—and therefore that pleasure does not make us happy, needing as it does the direction of reason, they *also* believe that a healthy affective life is a necessary constituent of the happy life, or the life of wisdom, as Plato too insists in the *Philebus*. Our affections are not, in other words, aspects of ourselves that our rationality finds distasteful, even if rationality is understood as likeness to a god without those affections; rather, for us our affections are

---

[56] See also Lovibond (1991: 55), who understands likeness to God to be equivalent to becoming truly human.

potential aspects of our very rationality. We can see this in the Stoic theory of 'good affections'[57] (εὐπάθειαι), and in particular in the good affection of 'joy' (χαρά).[58] The Stoics distinguish good affections from 'emotions' or 'passions' (πάθη), which are unreasonable affective responses that attribute the wrong sorts of values to the things the responses concern.[59] 'Pleasure' (ἡδονή), for the Stoics, is a technical term for an unreasonable response that takes its object to be the sort of good which, in fact, it is not, unlike joy which is a reasonable, realistic affective response. Moreover, for the Stoics joy and pleasure are not simply better and worse forms of the same affective condition, but are, in fact, different *kinds* of affective conditions. For example, on the Stoic view a person who believes that wealth is a key to happiness will have a very different kind of affective or emotional life where wealth is concerned, from that of a person who does not place that kind of value on wealth. As we saw in the previous chapter, the pleasure of a mercenary life is not the same kind of thing as the pleasure of an ambitious life, as if pleasure were some one thing differing only in the sources from which different people obtain it. Rather, each one's pleasure is a complex of various patterns: of emotional response, of desire and satisfaction, of prioritizing and valuing and striving, and thus too of how one's affective nature responds to different kinds of reasons. It is with good reason, then, that the Stoics staunchly deny that pleasures that are unreasonable affective responses, and joys that are reasonable, are simply two versions of what is still just one thing. On the Stoic view, it makes little sense to say that these are two forms of the same affective response,[60] for in that case, a person's affective life would have to be considered in isolation from his character and values, in order to maintain that people of characters different in kind do not so differ in their affective lives; but it seems clear that having a certain affective life is, in fact, part of what it is to have a certain kind of character.[61] For the Stoics, then, joy is not merely the same

---

[57] Unfortunately, there is no completely happy translation of εὐπάθειαι that I know of. The best phrase would be 'good emotions', if 'emotion' were not so common a rendering of the Stoic term of art for irrational affective states (πάθη); 'good feelings' also suggests itself, but 'feelings' is suggestive of non-cognitive states, whereas the Stoics hold the εὐπάθειαι as well as the emotions to be kinds of beliefs (for the distinction in Stoic thought between an emotion and the feeling associated with it, see M. Frede (1986: 102 f.)). I have therefore opted for 'good affections' as merely a less unsatisfactory rendering than most alternatives. For further discussion of the εὐπάθειαι, see Ch. 3.

[58] Diogenes Laertius, *Lives* VII.116–17. For a good overview of the Stoic theory of emotions, see Annas (1992: 113–15).

[59] Diogenes Laertius, *Lives* VII.110–15; Stobaeus, *Anthology* II.10–10e; Galen, *On the Doctrines of Hippocrates and Plato* 4.2.9–18, 4.4.16–18, 24–5, 4.5.21–5.

[60] And indeed this seems to me just the right conclusion to reach. Consider, e.g., the difference in kind between the pleasure one person may derive from playing the piano as a way of connecting with other people, and the pleasure another person derives from playing the piano as a way of withdrawing from people. (I thank Mark Kanaga for the example.) It is good to see, as do the Stoics—and, as I argued in the previous chapter, and shall again in the next, as does Plato—that the most philosophically interesting pleasures always obtain under some description, and that differences in descriptions are differences in the pleasures.

[61] Moreover, the Stoics maintain that all 'impulses' (including πάθη and εὐπαθεῖαι) are forms of belief—assent to appearance—and that πάθη are false beliefs and εὐπαθεῖαι true beliefs; and, of course, a true belief is not a variety of false belief, or a false belief held in the right kind of way.

affective state as pleasure, only 'reigned in',[62] but is a wholly different kind of attitude and way of attributing value to things in the world than pleasure is; for this reason, they say that 'joy and good spirits and the like' are the necessary concomitants of virtue.[63] The Stoic sage is not one who has become sterile, insensitive, and unfeeling,[64] but one who has adopted a new affective life that reflects the mature perspective of practical reason. In other words, joy is an essential component of virtuous character and human rationality.

This fact about the Stoic theory of good affections is instructive for our purposes, for at least a couple of reasons. For one thing, it shows that taking likeness to God seriously as a conception of virtue does not entail any form of asceticism. And the reason that that entailment fails to hold is particularly illuminating of the idea of 'rational incorporation' of pleasure (joy) into the good life: to incorporate pleasure into one's life in a rational way is not to treat one's need for pleasure as an evil, even a necessary one, but to become healthy and fulfilled as an affective, feeling, fully human being. Notice, too, that the Stoic conception of joy as part of good character illuminates how it is possible to maintain, as Plato also does, both that virtue alone is what makes one happy, and that pleasure (or 'joy', in the Stoic vocabulary) is an important part of the happy life: in both Plato and the Stoics, realizing health and order in one's affective life is a crucial part of what it is to be a person of virtue, and thus of what it is to live the life of a person of virtue.[65]

5.4 Likeness to God Revisited

We can now approach the philosopher in the *Theaetetus* digression again from a fresh perspective. There (176a–b, c), as we have seen, Socrates tells Theodorus that evil is an inevitable feature of our world, and so one ought to try to escape

---

[62] In fact, according to the Stoics' psychological theory it is a mistake to suppose that πάθη can be made good by controlling them in reasonable ways, since they deny that reason continues to exert control over the soul while a πάθος is in play, as reason and emotion are 'turnings' of the whole soul in fundamentally different directions, or rather towards fundamentally different perspectives. This feature of Stoic psychology is a fundamental premise in Seneca's *On Anger*, and the basis of his vociferous critique of Aristotle's account of virtues with respect to anger in *Nicomachean Ethics* IV.5, on which irascibility and good temper appear to be two varieties of what is still just one thing, anger.

[63] Diogenes Laertius, *Lives* VII.94–5. M. Frede (1986) rightly points out the importance of the Stoic value theory for the Stoic account of the soul: since nothing in the world, but only the rationality with which one acts on things in the world, has any value of its own, affective states are not *responses* to value in the world around us, but *ascriptions* of value by the agent; the affective states of the virtuous and vicious, then, must be different in kind, since they are wholly different patterns of ascribing value.

[64] That, the Stoics say, would make a person 'hard-hearted and cold', as base people are; Diogenes Laertius, *Lives* VII.117.

[65] If I am correct, then this would also demonstrate the consistency of the thesis that virtue is sufficient for happiness with the thesis that pleasure (or joy) is necessary for happiness, if the necessary pleasure is understood as an aspect of the virtue of character as a whole that suffices for happiness. This would be an interesting result, as the apparent inconsistency of these two theses in Plato's moral philosophy has been a major concern in Platonic scholarship, to say the least. I shall take up this issue in the following chapter.

from earth to heaven where there is no evil; and making such an escape is what it means to become 'as like God as possible'. Now, Socrates certainly does believe that the philosopher's escape is an escape from the world and a flight to heaven, but what exactly does such an escape amount to? From *what* about the world is it an escape? And *to* what about heaven is it a flight? As we have seen, many readers—ancient and modern—have assumed that this escape is an escape from the concerns and affairs of the world, and a flight to a position of complete detachment from the things and people around us. What Socrates says quite clearly, however, is that this escape is an escape from the world's evil, and a flight to justice, purity, and intelligence. Therefore, we should expect an account of becoming like God to be an account of how a person who becomes like God comes to avoid evil by embracing moral virtue in an intelligent way.

And this is exactly what we do find, once we avail ourselves of the Stoic conception of godlikeness as a viable option for our interpretation of likeness to God in Plato. Becoming like God, for Plato as well as the Stoics, is not a matter of refusing to handle the messy stuff of the world, but a matter of handling it with a new set of values and priorities. A person who becomes like God will still acquire and use money, for example, but will place more importance on the rationality with which the money is used than on the money itself. And this must be the case, since rationality, on the one hand, and things like money, on the other, play such radically different roles in one's life, one's attitude toward money being among the undifferentiated matter with respect to which rationality benefits us by leading and directing it intelligently. A godlike person, then, will be thrifty rather than mean or prodigal, and such a person would never seek wealth dishonestly—such a person would never be so foolish as to trade character for money.[66] This person, then, lives and acts in the world, *and* does so in a way that transcends it: this person has made an escape—an escape from evil, from pettiness, envy, meanness, prodigality, thievery, petulance—and a flight to healthy and reasonable priorities where money is concerned. In other words, this person has taken some of the inchoate matter of the world as she finds it and has brought order, reason, and proportion to it. If she can bring about this kind of intelligent order in all areas of her life, she will have become like God.

Perhaps, though, it will be tempting to assume that since the focus is placed first on the state of one's own soul, the sage will be primarily concerned just with himself, and people will not matter to him very much. But that would be a mistake. To say, for instance, that one of the best things in life is to love other people is, of course, consistent with saying that one must first love oneself. And, in general, the fact that ethically the first project is the reconciliation of one's own motivations does not narrow the nature and content of those motivations to purely self-concern. In fact, the Stoics say that while our primary natural

---

[66] Cp. Aristotle's comment about the person of proper pride: 'it would be most unbecoming for a proud man . . . to wrong another [ἀδικεῖν]; for to what end should he do disgraceful things [αἰσχρά], he to whom nothing is great?' (*Nicomachean Ethics* IV.3, 1123b31–2).

impulse is toward self-preservation, none the less the self that a human is made by nature to preserve is a *rational* self—and part of our nature as rational beings is deeply social, since nature has made it that love for others should be part of the nature of humankind.[67] Likewise, in Aristotle's discussion of pride—a virtue concerned primarily with one's attitude toward and treatment of one's self—we learn that the proud person, so far from becoming self-absorbed, realizes that what really is beneath him is having a bad character; as a result, he is considerate of, and gracious toward, other people, because he is beyond having the sorts of motivations that would lead him to act in any other way.[68]

The way in which Aristotle connects a virtue considered as a constitution of one's soul with a virtue considered as a feature of someone with the right sort of involvement in other people's lives is particularly instructive for seeing how Plato connects these ways of thinking about a virtue. In the *Republic*, for instance, after giving an account of the virtues as constitutions of the soul, Plato then tells us that a person with such a soul could never be found stealing, cheating, conniving, breaking his word, committing adultery, or neglecting his parents.[69] And in the *Gorgias*, Socrates argues that a virtuous, disciplined person will therefore always act as he should toward other people, and that this is why we call such a person 'just', and will never seek out what he should not, and that this is why we call such a person 'courageous'.[70] By setting one's own house in order, then, one comes to be truly good to other people, because one is then no longer willing to be anything else.[71]

Becoming truly good to other people, moreover, is more than merely not doing wrong by them. In fact, as the *Theaetetus* digression draws to a close Plato points out the importance of understanding the gap between godlikeness and its opposite: those who pursue cleverness and gain instead of likeness to God do so thinking that they are pursuing happiness, when instead they are guaranteeing the unhappiness of their life. And notice the response that is called for when we see such people: we are not to feel wrath at their injustice and impiety, but to see them for what they are—misguided and ignorant; and instead of dismissing them as hopeless or beyond our understanding them, we see them as intelligible— they are, after all, only seeking happiness, as all people do—and we *reason* with them:

If, therefore, one meets a man who practices injustice and is blasphemous in his talk or in his life, the best thing for him by far is that one should never grant that there is any sort of ability about his unscrupulousness; such men are ready enough to glory in the reproach,

---

[67] See Cicero, *de Finibus* III.16, 20–1, 62–4.
[68] See *Nicomachean Ethics* IV.3, esp. 1123a29–1125a16, 1124b18–23 with 1124a26–b6.
[69] *Republic* IV, 442e–444a, esp. 442e4–443a11.   [70] *Gorgias* 507a7–c3.
[71] Whether or not this is a completely successful or satisfactory account of the linkage between virtue as a state of the soul and virtue as a feature of one who acts well toward others, however, is a different and controversial matter, as Sachs (1963: 141–58) has famously pointed out. For present purposes, I shall leave that issue aside. What matters most at present is that there is no reason to think that Plato, in construing virtue as likeness to God, was therefore indifferent to how a virtuous person actually conducted himself in relation to other people.

and think that it means not that they are mere rubbish, cumbering the ground to no purpose, but that they have the kind of qualities that are necessary for survival in the community. We must therefore tell them the truth—that their very ignorance of their true state fixes them the more firmly therein. For they do not know what is the penalty of injustice, which is the last things of which a man should be ignorant. It is not what they suppose—scourging and death—things which they may entirely evade in spite of their wrongdoing. It is a penalty from which they cannot escape. . . . [namely] the deepest unhappiness. This truth the evildoer does not see; blinded by folly and utter lack of understanding, he fails to perceive that the effect of his unjust practices is to make him grow more and more [unhappy].   (*Theaetetus* 176c–177a2)

Even here, when we imagine a godlike person regarding his opposite, we are to see his response as one of understanding and concern.[72] And this, Plato says, is why we try to engage such a person in philosophy, which can, at least, show this person his ignorance (177a2–b7), which is after all what keeps him from seeing what he needs to see most (176e4–177a2). This is why philosophers must be involved in the lives of other people: all people need to find happiness. Nor is it surprising that Plato should conclude his discussion of likeness to God on this note, since Plato also believes it is in the nature of the gods to care about every detail of human life, as they are completely good and therefore caring.[73] So far from taking us away from other people, likeness to God brings us back to them and enables us to see them with new eyes.

The fresh perspective on Plato that understanding the Stoics can afford us also demands a reassessment of the commonplace depiction of Plato as 'other-worldly'. In fact, even the very 'this-worldly' Aristotle also insists that rationality or wisdom is valuable for its own sake, which is just the view that likeness to God is meant to pick out in Plato's moral philosophy. We can see this in Aristotle's discussion of practical wisdom in *Nicomachean Ethics* VI.12–13, as well as in his discussion of the human function in *Nicomachean Ethics* I.7.

After raising a number of puzzles in VI.12 about what value we can attach to philosophic and practical wisdom, the first point Aristotle makes is this:

Now first let us say that in themselves these states must be worthy of choice because they are the virtues of the two parts of the soul respectively, even if neither of them produces anything.   (VI.12, 1144a1–3)

And he says this again in the next chapter:

. . . with the presence of the one quality, practical wisdom, will be given all the virtues. And it is plain that, even if it were of no practical value, we should have needed it because it is the virtue of the part of us in question.   (VI.13, 1144b36–1145a4)[74]

Nor should it really surprise us that Aristotle makes such claims about the value of practical wisdom, or rationality. For one thing, in *Nicomachean Ethics* I.5 and

---

[72] See Epictetus, *Discourses* I.28 and Seneca, *On Anger* II.6–10 for the Stoic idea that wrongdoers are blinded by their ignorance, and warrant our understanding and compassion rather than our wrath.

[73] *Laws* X, 901c8–903a9.

[74] See also IV.3, 1125a11–12, where Aristotle claims that the possession of good things that are not of value merely for their usefulness (τὰ καλὰ καὶ ἄκαρπα) is characteristic of the self-sufficient person.

I.8 Aristotle insists that happiness consists not in the possession of anything, as if value somehow attached to things themselves, but rather in activity; this is because happiness consists not in what happens to us, or in our circumstances, or in our belongings, or even in our attributes, but in our activity in relation to all those things. For this reason, Aristotle says that it is ultimately virtue that determines our happiness (I.10, 1100a31–b11); for, as Plato also says in the *Philebus*, it is the rational activity of virtue that brings order and harmony to all of the various aspects of our lives. For Aristotle, then, things are not good all by themselves, but our rationally integrating them into a well-proportioned life is good—it is 'the virtue of the part of us in question', namely our capacity for practical rationality.

Furthermore, Aristotle thinks that this rationality is worth choosing for its own sake because that is what our fulfillment as rational beings consists in. We find this idea again in I.7, in the so-called 'function argument':

> Presumably, however, to say that happiness is the chief good seems a platitude, and a clearer account of what it is is still desired. This might perhaps be given, if we could first ascertain the function of man.... [If] we state the function of man to be a certain kind of life, and this to be an activity or actions of the soul implying a rational principle, and the function of a good man to be the good and noble performance of these, and if any action is well performed when it is performed in accordance with the appropriate excellence [ἀρετήν]: if this is the case, the human good turns out to be activity of the soul exhibiting excellence [ἀρετήν], and if there are more than one excellence [ἀρεταί], in accordance with the best and most complete.   (I.7, 1097b22–25, 1098a12–18)

This is a controversial argument, but what seems clear is that Aristotle thinks that for us living well must be understood as living well *as humans*, and thus as beings of theoretical and practical rationality. As Christine Korsgaard puts it:

> This is what the function argument is all about: Aristotle thinks that we cannot have a good life unless our potential for true practical reasoning is actualized. The connection between function and virtue means that this potential cannot be realized without the moral virtues. The moral virtues *are* just those qualities that actualize our potential for rationality: they make us human beings.[75]

Practical wisdom infiltrates and brings order to one's emotions, desires, pleasures, and pains, and as such is the kind of rationality that being fully human amounts to. For Aristotle, the value of being fully human—of being happy as a human being—is not one value among others; it is the value that makes the value of anything else for us possible. The rationality that our humanity so consists in, then, must be good for us, just for its own sake.

This should, of course, remind us of the view we have located in Seneca and, I have argued, in Plato in connection with likeness to God, namely that only by valuing virtue as what determines happiness do we really identify with our nature and mature as rational persons. It should be clear that the thesis that

---

[75] Korsgaard (1986: 278).

rationality is valuable for its own sake is anything but an otherworldly one; it is, in any case, this-worldly enough even for Aristotle.[76]

Plato's embracing likeness to God as a conception of virtue does not entail his holding an otherworldly conception of virtue as his critics have recently complained. Not only does that entailment fail to hold in the case of Seneca's account, but also the reasons that Seneca is able to avoid otherworldliness are reasons that are open to Plato as well—for this is what we find in the *Philebus*, where Plato, like Seneca and the other Stoics, understands virtue as a kind of rationality that brings order to our lives, and is the very special cause of goodness on which all other good things depend. Hence Plato, like Seneca, is able to understand likeness to God as a way of acting rationally in the world as we find it, in a way that makes the rationality with which one acts good for its own sake. On our best evidence, then, this is Plato's understanding of likeness to God.[77]

It should also be clear that we do not have to embrace an ancient cosmology or theology—we need not embrace *any* particular cosmology or theology, for that matter[78]—in order to take seriously the gist of the thesis that virtue is likeness to God. Indeed, even for Seneca the moral force of becoming like God is not so much that doing so is a way of preparing for an afterlife as it is that doing so constitutes the fulfillment of our nature and our full maturity as rational agents. We can thus extract this idea from the cosmology and theology in which it happened to arise, and recognize it as a way of becoming a good human being.

Nor in doing so do we make this idea any less radical. Indeed, I do not pretend that the idea that rationality is valuable for its own sake is an easy one, or that it raises no serious questions. It is a thesis to be reckoned with, to be sure. But that is just the point: it *is* a thesis that we must reckon with, and can take seriously. Unlike some mystical, mysterious, or otherworldly notion that cannot even get on the table for our serious consideration, the thesis that an agent's highest good consists in the rationality with which she acts and lives is a decidedly this-worldly one that is worth our attention.

[76] To be sure, Aristotle takes this view to have different implications than Plato and the Stoics do. In particular, Aristotle famously maintains that excellence as a rational person is not sufficient for happiness, if significant misfortune should befall the person (I.9, 1100a4–9; I.10, 1100b22 ff.). While Aristotle's view is praised today almost universally as more intuitively plausible than the view that virtue is sufficient for happiness, our comparison of Aristotle's account of the causal role and value of rationality in the good life with the account we find in Plato and the Stoics makes it perhaps clearer why among the ancients Aristotle was, in fact, in the minority in denying the sufficiency of virtue for happiness. It may also explain why Aristotle struggles so uncomfortably when he tries to say just how the excellent but unlucky *do* stand with respect to happiness and its opposite (I.10, 1100b22–1101a21). The problem, in short, is that Aristotle is attracted both to the directive conception of happiness, as in the function argument (I.7), *and* to the additive conception, as when he insists that certain projects are necessary for happiness and that events of fortune can enhance or maim happiness (see I.8–10). (And it is for this reason that Antiochus' attempt to unify the Aristotelian position with the Platonist and Stoic positions is doomed to fail, as Cicero argues it is in *de Finibus* V.) These, however, are issues for another time.

[77] And in having to rely on our best overall evidence for Plato's understanding of likeness, all views are on an equal footing.

[78] Nor, for that matter, are the differences in theology between Plato and the Stoics of any particular consequence in this context.

Likeness to God does real work in Plato's ethics, and work that we can find intelligible and serious: for Plato it offers a way of thinking about virtue as rational activity that is valuable for its own sake. The best way to understand the associated talk of 'escape'—in Plato, as in Seneca—is not as withdrawal from the world, but as a radically transformed set of priorities with which one engages the world. That is a thoroughly ethical position, rather than the absence of one. It is also thoroughly humane, an account not of how we throw off what we are, but of how we make what we are the best that it can be. And it is an account of the kind of good that wisdom is, an unconditional good that brings goodness about in other things, by intelligently leading and directing our behavior—including our attitudes, and our affective attitudes—with respect to those things.

Likeness to God gives us an account of rational incorporation and of how wisdom makes the proper 'use' of things in our life, by leading and directing our behavior with respect to them. What is more, it does so in a way that allows us to demonstrate what otherwise may have seemed impossible: that pleasure can be necessary for happiness, even if virtue and virtue alone is what determines happiness. The account of rational incorporation that emerges from Plato's *Philebus*, I argue in the next chapter, shows that the pleasure (or, as in the case of the Stoics, the 'joy') characteristic of the virtuous life is part of a healthy affective life, which is, in turn, part of happy human life as a whole. Such pleasure, then, will be necessary for happiness, because it is part of virtue, and virtue determines happiness. And that is an interesting development indeed.

6

The *Philebus*, Part 2:
Pleasure Transformed, or How the
Necessity of Pleasure for Happiness
is Consistent with the Sufficiency of
Virtue for Happiness

If pleasure is a conditional good, as Plato argues that it is, then it does not determine happiness, it does not increase or complete happiness, and it does not determine its own place as a good in one's life. The distinction between conditional and unconditional goods, after all, is a distinction in terms of the power to benefit. Virtue is an unconditional good because it is 'such as to benefit',[1] and in fact nothing else is such as to benefit, or could be, since only virtue—practical, intelligent agency—gives the direction that being benefited requires. In that case, it seems that there is nothing that pleasure could add to happiness that virtue had not already achieved, and so, evidently, we should conclude that pleasure is not necessary for happiness.

It is therefore striking that Plato should insist unambiguously in the *Philebus* that pleasure *is* necessary for happiness after all. Early in the dialog, Socrates asks his companion Protarchus 'whether any one of us would choose to live in possession of every kind of intelligence, reason, knowledge, and memory of all things, while having no part, neither large nor small, of pleasure or of pain, living in total insensitivity to anything of that kind' (21d9–e2). Not surprisingly, Protarchus recoils from such a life. So too does Socrates, who asserts that the best life must be found in a combination of intelligence and pleasure (21e–22a), since neither the life of pleasure without intelligence *nor* the life of intelligence without pleasure is sufficient or choice-worthy (22b), so that neither can be a happy life (see 20d ff.). Plato's reason for making this claim is sensible: being affectless is inconsistent with human happiness, even if it should turn out to be

---

[1] The phrase is from Arius Didymus, summarizing the similar Stoic position; see Stobaeus, *Anthology* II.5d.

consistent with a god's (22c–d).[2] And Plato never goes back on this claim, but even repeats it toward the dialog's end as one of the defining constraints on Socrates and Protarchus' joint search for the human life that is complete, choice-worthy, and supremely good (60d–61a).[3]

Now *what* Plato concedes is really not striking at all: pleasure is a part of life, and any conception of a good life as a *whole* will have to make it part of the good life. What seems striking is that *Plato* should concede it, if he is, in fact, a proponent of the directive conception of happiness. For, on that conception, happiness is determined by the good direction of the whole of one's life, that is, by the agent's goodness expressed across all dimensions of her life, and not by the goodness of her life's various ingredients, since their goodness, it turns out, is really a matter of the *agent's* goodness where such things are concerned.[4] It seems odd, then, that certain ingredients, and pleasure in particular, should be upgraded as indispensable for a happy life after all, which seems to suggest that pleasure is one of the things that *makes* us happy and our lives good.[5] Once Plato accepts that pleasure is necessary for happiness, it is hard to see how he could deny that it has its own power with respect to happiness, even if that power functions only in a virtuous person.

Notice, however, that this apparent tension rests on the assumption that since pleasure is one of the ingredients or dimensions of one's life, it must therefore be distinct from the agent's goodness where pleasure is concerned, in much the sort of way that an agent's wealth is distinct from the agent's own goodness where her wealth is concerned. But I think the *Philebus* makes clear Plato's view that pleasure is actually part of the agent's own goodness, because her goodness consists in, among other things, the sorts of attitudes she has and perspectives

---

[2] I am thus puzzled by the claim of Hampton (1990: 65), that 'although the divine life of pure intellect is not a viable option for humankind, we should nevertheless strive to approximate this ideal as far as our human nature will allow'. I have no idea what such an 'approximation' would come to, or why we should take Plato to be recommending it.

[3] He repeats it in the *Laws*: 'Human nature involves, above all, pleasures, pains, and desires, and no mortal animal can help being hung up dangling in the air (so to speak) in total dependence on these powerful influences. That is why we should praise the noblest life—not only because it enjoys a fine and glorious reputation, but because (provided one is prepared to try it out instead of recoiling from it as a youth) it excels in providing what we all seek: a predominance of pleasure over pain throughout our lives. That this result is guaranteed, if it is tried out in the correct manner, will be perfectly obvious in an instant. . . . But if we assert that we want anything outside this range [of the preponderance of pleasure over pain], we are talking out of ignorance and inexperience of life as it is really lived' (V, 732e4–733a6, d4–6).

Does this passage suggest not merely the necessity of pleasure for happiness but also some form of psychological hedonism? Annas (1999: 137–45) says that this passage (and II, 662e8–663b6) says only that we all *begin* prizing pleasure, but as reason distinguishes and shapes pleasures reason itself becomes the determining factor in happiness. However, the Athenian nowhere suggests that we stop reasoning in the sort of way that he describes here. Irwin (1995: 344) takes this passage to say only that we do not want the preponderance of pain over pleasure. But it is not clear why the Athenian should need to argue for such an obvious observation. We shall return to this passage in the next chapter.

[4] This point emerges on the account of rational incorporation from the previous chapter. See also Stobaeus, *Anthology* II.11q.

[5] In fact, it is just this sort of view that Irwin (1995: 336) attributes to Plato in the *Philebus*.

she adopts in the various dimensions of her life, and her pleasure is *itself* just such a crucial attitude and perspective. When Plato says that pleasure is necessary for happiness, then, he does not mean that good character could never be enough for happiness without pleasure. Rather, as the dialogue unfolds he reveals that pleasure is actually a part of good character as a whole, the product of reason's transforming all dimensions of the self. Since good character, or virtue, is this sort of whole, pleasure is necessary for happiness, because *virtue* is sufficient for happiness.

So the key to understanding Plato's position, I think, is to be found in his analysis of the nature of pleasure and how it functions in a person's life, since this will tell us in precisely what sense pleasure is 'necessary' for the good life. I shall argue that in Plato's *Philebus* the pleasure of a virtuous character is necessary and important for happiness because it is a necessary and important part *of* that character, which, in turn, is what determines happiness.

6.1   Socrates and Protarchus on the Necessity of Pleasure for Happiness

Plato begins the *Philebus* with a rather garden-variety version of the necessity of pleasure for happiness, expressed by Socrates' interlocutor Protarchus: pleasure is necessary for happiness because it is good by its very nature, and is what makes a person happy. In particular, there are three things about his view to notice. First, pleasure on his view is a simple psychological state—roughly, some sort of gratification—incapable of being right or wrong about anything, or taking a better or worse direction. For while Protarchus is willing to agree that self-controlled people have their own pleasures in their self-control itself, and that fools have their own pleasures, too (12c–d), he none the less insists that this makes no difference about *pleasure*: the *occasions* of pleasure can be opposed, but how on earth could *pleasures* be opposed (12c–13c)?

Second, since Protarchus believes that there is nothing for pleasure to be 'wrong' about, and since he finds pleasant sensations so obviously attractive, it is easy for him to suppose that pleasure is not only necessary for happiness, but also *responsible* for happiness.[6] This is evident in his initial insistence that pleasure could actually be the whole of happiness:

Would you [Protarchus] find it acceptable to live your life in enjoyment of the greatest pleasures?
Why, certainly!
And would you see yourself in need of anything else if you had secured this altogether?
In no way.

---

[6] Cf. D. Frede (1993: xviii–xvix), (1992: 444), (1985: 172); see also Hackforth (1945: 16 n. 1), who unfortunately overlooks the dynamics of the disagreement between Protarchus and Socrates on this point.

But look, might you not have some need of knowledge, intelligence, and calculation, or anything else that is related to them?
How so? If I had pleasure I would have all in all!
And living like that you could enjoy the greatest pleasures throughout your life?
Why should I not?   (21a8–b5)

Socrates does manage to persuade Protarchus that such a life—a life of pleasant sensations *only*—would be too incomplete to be a happy life (21b–d), but now the question is whether it is pleasure or reason that is the '*cause*' (αἴτιον, 22d4) of the goodness of the life that mixes the two, and Protarchus maintains that that cause is pleasure (22d1–4). In fact, Protarchus concedes that the life of pleasure would be incomplete without intellect only on the grounds that intellect enables one to remember past pleasures and to plan for future ones (21c–d); on his view, reason is necessary for happiness only because pleasure is. Consequently, while Protarchus denies that pleasure is always enough to make a life happy, no matter what else is going on in that life, and concedes that certain background conditions must be met, none the less he clearly believes that when they are met it is pleasure that makes the happy life happy.

And third, Protarchus believes that pleasure is such as to benefit *by its very nature*—it need not be differentiated before it can be beneficial. On his view, however disgraceful the source of one's pleasure from may be, this says nothing about the value of the pleasure itself. Pleasure may accompany activities of very different ethical quality, but the value of the pleasure itself never varies. For pleasure, there simply are no better and worse ethical qualities at all:

[You, Protarchus,] say that all pleasant things are good. Now, no one contends that pleasant things are not pleasant. But while most of them are bad but some good, as we hold, you nevertheless call them all good, even though you would admit that they are unlike one another if someone pressed the point. What is the common element in the good and bad pleasures that allows you to call them all good?
What are you saying, Socrates? Do you think anyone will agree to this who begins by laying it down that pleasure is the good? Do you think he will accept when you say that some pleasures are good but others are bad?[7]
But will you grant that they are *unlike* each other and that some are opposites?
Not in so far as they are pleasures.   (13a8–c5)

This claim of Protarchus' is quite revealing. When I enjoy a walk in the country, for instance, we might describe that pleasure either as the pleasure I get *from* my walk in the country, or as the pleasure *of* my walk in the country. On the former, the pleasure is understood as a sort of sensation produced in me by this activity, but which is strictly distinct from my activity, and which in principle may have been produced in me by any of a number of different activities. But on the latter the pleasure consists in how I take in *these* surroundings, how

---

[7] Recall that Callicles' hedonism was abandoned shortly after he conceded that some pleasures are good and others bad, as this is to concede that pleasure is a conditional, extrinsic good. See *Gorgias* 499b ff., discussed in Ch. 2.

they fill my senses, the emotions I have about being *here,* how interested I am in *what I am doing now,* and so on, and therefore such a pleasure is possible for me only by my taking a walk in the country.[8] Here we see the connection between Protarchus' belief that pleasure is a simple sensation, and his belief that pleasure need not be differentiated. Since, on Protarchus' view, pleasure is the same thing regardless of what occasions it, so that the temperate and intemperate are simply getting the same thing from different sources, he must understand pleasure as some kind of sensation or feeling. And since pleasure is simple in that way, there is no more differentiation for it to admit of than there is for a tickle in one's foot, even if in a good human life pleasures must operate according to patterns that require awareness, memory, and planning.

Protarchus' view therefore represents a form of the additive conception of happiness. He recognizes that pleasure gives no direction to one's life—a life of pleasure alone, he admits, would be as directionless as a clam's life (21c–d)—and even concedes that pleasure must be given *some* sort of direction by one's agency (21b–c), but this does nothing to keep pleasure from being the primary determinant of happiness, in his opinion. Happiness, on his view, consists in the ingredients added into one's life—in this case, pleasures (at least if reason is also present)—rather than its direction. And so Protarchus thinks that pleasure is necessary for happiness because pleasure determines happiness, so that virtue could never be enough for happiness.

However, while Socrates agrees that pleasure is necessary for happiness, he must not think that it is necessary in the same way that Protarchus does, because Socrates proposes to show Protarchus that reason, not pleasure, is what is *responsible* for making the happy life happy:

> . . . now I am not arguing that [the life of] reason ought to get first prize over and against the combined life [sc. of reason and pleasure]; we have rather to look and make up our minds about the second prize, how to dispose of it. One of us may want to give credit for the combined life to reason, making it responsible (αἴτιον), the other to pleasure. Thus neither of the two would be the good, but it could be assumed that one or the other of them is its *cause* (αἴτιον). (22c7–d4, emphasis in original)

Plato suggests that, although both reason and pleasure may be necessary for happiness, it is important to understand the complex internal relations[9] that may hold between reason and pleasure within the complete, happy life. Not all of the necessary conditions for happiness are on an equal footing, Plato suggests, because only some of them are also *responsible* for happiness. Socrates and Protarchus agree about that, but disagree over whether it is reason or pleasure that has this responsibility, and this question can be decided only by an investigation into the nature of this notion of responsibility or 'cause', and how reason and pleasure each stand in relation to it. Plato's strategy will be to argue that pleasure is a kind of attitude with complex connections to our underlying

---

[8] Cf. Plato, trans. Waterfield (1994: xxii).   [9] I owe this phrase to Korsgaard (1983: 193).

values, priorities, and conceptions of ourselves, and as such that pleasure has a *role* to play in one's life, so that one must ask whether it is playing the right kind of role in her own life.[10] Consequently, pleasure is good not by its nature, but only when it is an appropriate kind of attitude, and therefore its goodness depends on the direction that reason gives it. And, in that case, it will be reason and not pleasure that is the 'cause' of the goodness of the good life, just as Socrates says it must be (22c–e). Moreover, pleasure will be necessary for happiness inasmuch as it is part of the whole self that reason directs and structures.[11]

6.2   Pleasure and Reason: Internal Relations

Plato now commences his examination of the nature of pleasure by addressing the more fundamental question of what it is for something to take a shape or play a role within a structured whole. This, of course, is Plato's 'fourfold division' of all being (23b–31b), which we touched upon in the previous chapter. The details of this account are difficult and controversial, but the gist of it— and the challenge it presents for Protarchus' position—can be made clear enough. The central idea is that organized wholes are 'mixtures', and for every 'mixture' various factors play different roles in accounting for its being what it is. The factors in these mixtures are not only the mixture's material constituent but also the *structure* of that material constituent, as well as what effects that structure in it.

Consider an ordinary object like a cake. What makes it a cake, as opposed to a meatloaf, say? For one thing, it is made of the stuff of a cake—eggs, milk, flour, and so on. Of course, the stuff of a cake does not a cake make, but must first be measured in the appropriate kinds of quantities and proportions, baked in the appropriate way, and so on. This is so because a cake is not a heap of cake ingredients but a structured whole, and that structure makes the cake what it is in quite a different way than the ingredients do: the structure is not merely what this sort of thing is made of, but in fact determines what sort of thing it *is*. Finally, the agent who brings that structure about in the ingredients—the one who mixes and bakes the cake, in our example—is the one who brings the resulting whole into existence, and makes it what it is.

---

[10] Cf. Gosling and Taylor (1982: 135): 'The importance of [the dissimilarity of pleasures] is as follows:...the problem for someone wishing to live a good life is not how to produce as much as possible of a single product, but rather how to select from and blend into a harmonious whole opposing and dissimilar elements among which are opposing and dissimilar pleasures.'

[11] Hence, while I agree with Carone (2000) that Plato does not mean to demote pleasure to the status of a remedial good (something merely to be dealt with, like an annoying neighbor), I do not agree that pleasure can be an intrinsic good in the *Philebus*, much less that the *Philebus* is consistent with hedonism. It is just this point about the radical differences in roles between pleasure and virtue within the good life that is crucial to their placement in the value schema of the *Philebus*, and I think that Carone overlooks the importance of this difference.

Plato captures these facts about wholes and their structure by dividing all being in four ways. Things like cakes Plato calls 'mixtures' (25b–26d, 27d–28a), a classification that reflects the importance of the internal relations within them: they are 'mixtures' of their constituent matter and the structure that obtains in that matter, and in virtue of which they are what they are. This 'matter' Plato calls the 'unlimited' or 'indeterminate' (24a–25a, 28a), reflecting the fact that they have no direction or structure of their own, with respect to the complete mixture:

> Check first in the case of the hotter and colder[12] whether you can conceive of a limit, or whether the 'more and less' do not rather reside in these kinds, and while they reside in them do not permit the attainment of any end. For once an end has been reached, they will both have been ended as well.
> Very true.
> We are agreed, then, that the hotter and the colder always contain the more and less.
> Quite definitely.
> Our argument forces us to conclude that these things never have an end. And since they are endless they turn out to be entirely unlimited. . . . Wherever [such attributes] apply, they prevent everything from adopting a definite quantity; by imposing on all actions the qualification 'stronger' relative to 'gentler' or the reverse, they procure a 'more and less' while doing away with all definite quantity. (24a7–b8, c3–6)

The structure that must obtain in the unlimited in order for it to constitute a mixture, Plato calls 'limit' (see 25a–b, d–26c):

> But look now at what does not admit of these qualifications but rather their opposites, first of all 'the equal' and 'equality' and, after the equal, things like 'double', and all that is related as number to number or measure to measure: If we subsume all these together under the heading of 'limit', we would seem to do a fair job. Or what do you say?
> A very fair job, Socrates. (25a6–b4)

Having limit is more than just having *some* quantity or proportion or other determinate characteristic, just as 'equality' is not any chance ratio, but the kind of ratio that makes two things equal. More generally, having limit is having the right sorts of characteristics with respect to a determinate standard, namely the being of some mixture: in our example, the eggs always have some quantity or other, and always have some proportion or other relative to the milk, but their having *limit* in this case is their having the quantity and proportion the cake requires of them.[13] Likewise, being unlimited is not to be without any

---

[12] Notice, then, that the 'unlimited' is not only physical stuff but also the properties of stuff. Plato's general point seems to be that anything can be classified as unlimited so long as its being in relation to some standard must be brought about in it by something else. Notice, then, that anything called 'good' in this category must be an *extrinsic*, or *conditional*, good.

[13] As in the previous chapter, I am here indebted to Irwin (1995: 324 f.), who offers the helpful analogy of water being brought to the right temperature for the purpose of making tea.

determinate characteristic or quantity full stop, but to be without the requisite characteristic or quantity with respect to some standard. Consequently, it is only with limit that things—'mixtures'—take on their peculiar mode of being:

We called something hotter and colder just now, didn't we?
Yes.
Now add dryer and wetter to them, and more and less, and faster and slower, taller and shorter, and whatever else we have previously collected together as one kind that has nature of taking on the 'more and less'.
You mean the nature of the unlimited?
Yes. Now take the next step and mix with it the class of the limit.
Which one?
The very one we have so far omitted to collect together, the class that has the character of limit, although we ought to have given unity to it, just as we collected together the unlimited kind. But perhaps it will come to the same thing even now if, through the collection of these two kinds, the unity of the former kind becomes conspicuous too.
What kind do you mean, and how is this supposed to work?
The kind that contains equal and double, and whatever else puts an end to the conflicts there are among opposites, making them commensurate and harmonious by imposing a definite number on them.
I understand. I have the impression that you are saying that, from such mixture in each case, certain generations result?
Your impression is correct.
Then go on with your explanation.
Is it not true that in sickness the right combination of the opposites establishes the state of health?
Certainly....
And there are countless other things I have to pass by in silence. With health there come beauty and strength, and again in our soul there is a host of other excellent qualities.   (25c5–26a1, b5–7)

Notice that since it is in relation to its particular limit that a structured whole has its being, it is also in relation to its limit that it has its characteristic goodness or badness—its health or sickness, its beauty or ugliness, its strength or weakness.

Finally, Plato says that there must always be a 'cause' of such mixtures (26e–27c, 28a–31b), which brings limit to the unlimited to generate a mixture. Moreover, this cause, Plato says, is always some form of intelligent, purposive agency:

But now we have to look at the fourth kind we mentioned earlier, in addition to these three. Let this be our joint investigation. See now whether you think it necessary that everything that comes to be has a cause.
Certainly, as far as I can see. How could anything come to be without one?
And is it not the case that there is no difference between the nature of what *makes* and the *cause* [τῆς αἰτίας], except in name, so that the maker and the cause [τὸ αἴτιον] would rightly be called one?

Right.
But what about what is made and what comes into being, will we not find the same situation, that they also do not differ except in name?
Exactly.
And isn't it the case that what makes is always leading in the order of nature, while the thing made follows since it comes into being through it?
Right. . . .
We therefore declare that the craftsman who produces all these must be the fourth kind, the cause, since it has been demonstrated sufficiently that it differs from the others?
It certainly is different.   (26e1–27a7, b1–3, emphasis in original)

Plato's fourfold division shows not only that there are different dimensions within a thing, but also that they stand in complex relations to one another and contribute to the being of the whole in very different ways. This observation applies even to one's life, Plato says: the best life may be a life of pleasure and reason, but pleasure and reason stand in very different relations to the life—the 'mixture'—of which they are parts. Pleasure is part of the 'unlimited' in this mixture, since it does not by its nature possess any determinate direction or proportion in relation to life as a whole. That 'limit' must be brought about by reason, which is the 'cause' of the mixture, and thus not one ingredient among many but the intelligent agency that makes that life what it is:

Do not think that we have engaged in an idle discussion here, Protarchus, for it comes as a support for the thinkers of old who held the view that reason is forever the ruler over the universe.
It certainly does.
It also has provided an answer to my query, that reason belongs to that kind which is the cause of everything. But that was one of our four kinds. So there you already have the solution to our problem in your hands.
I have indeed, and quite to my satisfaction . . .
By now, dear friend, we have arrived at a satisfactory explanation of the class that reason belongs to and what power it has.
Quite so.
And as to pleasure, it became apparent quite a while ago what class it belongs to.
Definitely.
Let us firmly keep it in mind about both of them, that reason is akin to cause and is part of that family, while pleasure itself is unlimited and belongs to the kind that in and by itself neither possesses nor will ever possess a beginning, middle, or end.   (30d6–e4, 31a1–10)

As Socrates says, a central question of the dialogue has now been answered: reason and pleasure are both necessary conditions for happiness, but they have radically different roles in the good life, and only reason is responsible for—the 'cause' of—the goodness of the good life. Since what it means to bring 'limit' to pleasure in order to make it part of a harmonious whole—as well as what sort of part pleasure will be, and thus in what sense it is necessary for the whole—will depend on what sort of thing pleasure is, Plato turns now to an analysis of pleasure.

6.3   How Pleasure Works

It will be helpful to divide Plato's analysis of pleasure into three parts. One is an inquiry into the 'anatomy' of pleasure, so to speak, in which Plato argues that pleasure arises in an organism when its natural state of being has been disrupted and is restored to order. There is also the pleasure of anticipating such a restoration in beings with sufficient memory to know what will fill their present painful lack (31b–36c). I shall discuss this line of inquiry only as far as it bears on Plato's second line of inquiry, which concerns the more strictly 'psychological' nature of pleasure; and on the third line, concerning the value of pleasure.

One thing that the inquiry into the anatomy of pleasure reveals is Plato's belief that human pleasure is primarily a *cognitive* phenomenon: pleasure— even physical pleasure—is a state of the soul by which one regards the object of one's pleasure in terms of one's estimation of the object's ability to fulfill a perceived need. For example, even a relatively simple desire such as thirst is not merely a brute feeling but a specific type of pain with a determinate shape: it is a desire *for* something, and is experienced only by an agent who knows what it is a desire for:

When we say 'he is thirsty', we always have something in mind?
We do.
Meaning that [the agent] is getting empty?
Certainly.
But thirst is a desire?
Yes, the desire for drink.
For drink or for the filling with drink?
For the filling with drink, I think.[14]
Whoever among us is emptied, it seems, desires the opposite of what he suffers. Being emptied, he desires to be filled.
That is perfectly obvious.
But what about this problem? If someone is emptied for the first time, is there any way he could be in touch with filling, either through sensation or memory, since he has no experience of it, either in the present or ever in the past?
How should he be?
But we do maintain that he who has a desire desires something?
Naturally.
He does, then, not have a desire for what he in fact experiences. For he is thirsty, and this is a process of emptying. His desire is rather of filling.
Yes.
Something in the person who is thirsty must necessarily somehow be in contact with filling.
Necessarily. . . .

---

[14] Cf. the similar point at *Euthydemus* 280c that to desire something is not, in fact, to desire *that thing, simpliciter,* but to desire to engage in some activity with respect to it. Plato's argument at *Gorgias* 466a–468e relies on this point as well. The object of desire, in other words, is not strictly a thing, but an *action.*

Our argument forces us to conclude that desire is not a matter of the body. . . . By pointing out that it is this memory that directs [the living creature] towards the objects of its desires, our argument has established that every impulse, desire, and the rule over the whole animal is the domain of the soul.

Very much so.   (34e9–35b8, 35c6–7, d1–4)

Desire, then, is not bare need, but the *recognition* of need. A very young baby may become parched and experience pain as a result, but without the recognition that that pain is a desire *for drink*, the baby will have the painful need for drink but will not experience the desire of 'thirst', as older children and adults do.[15] Desire is a pain that is *about a lack*, and directed specifically at what (the agent judges) will satisfy it. And so pleasures and pains are, we might say, *concern-laden:*[16] to be pained is to be pained at some state of affairs in so far as one takes it to be unsatisfying, unfulfilling, or inadequate; and to be pleased is to be pleased at fulfillment, to enjoy some state of affairs as satisfying for the agent, given the needs the agent takes himself or herself to have.

6.3.1   False pleasures

This account of desire and satisfaction also suggests that pleasure is a way of 'seeing' or regarding things and attributing value to them in terms of their perceived ability to satisfy. In his inquiry into the psychology of pleasure, Plato develops this idea by exploring a number of ways in which pleasure can be a *mistaken* or *false* way of regarding things. In particular, Plato argues that pleasures can be false in four distinct senses,[17] and in the first sense false pleasure is a kind of epistemic state that is literally false, just as beliefs can be false (36c–41a).

Although the details of this class of false pleasure are difficult and have been the subject of enormous controversy,[18] the basic point seems to be that pleasures are *about* something, and they represent their objects to the agent under such descriptions as 'satisfying', 'worth-while', 'just what I need', and so on,[19] and, as

---

[15] See D. Frede (1993: xliv).

[16] For the notion of affective states as concern-laden, I am greatly indebted to the work of Roberts (2003).

[17] The sense of 'false' in which Plato takes all these pleasures to be false is a matter of great controversy, and not only in recent years (e.g. Damascius tells us of ancient disagreements on this score; *Lectures on the* Philebus, §§ 166–72). Gosling (1975: 212, cf. 213) accuses Plato of 'rank equivocation' on multiple senses of falsity (cp. Plato, trans. Waterfield (1982: 25)), but D. Frede (1993: xlv) is surely right that the equivocation is deliberate and innocuous (see, e.g., 41a); see also (1992: 442 f.).

[18] I am persuaded that D. Frede (1985: 171 ff.), (1993: xlv–liii) presents the best account of this kind of false pleasure; see also Penner (1970); D. Frede (1992: 444–6). To trace this long-standing debate, see esp. Gosling (1959), (1961), (1975: 215–19); Kenny (1960); McLaughlin (1969); Dybikowski (1970); and Hampton (1987), (1990: 54 ff.); see also Tenkku (1956: 193); Plato, trans. Waterfield (1982: 24); and Sayre (1987: 64 f.).

[19] Carone (2000: 275) brings out this point nicely. This is also what we should expect given Plato's thesis that pleasure is a response to something *qua* (perceived as) satisfying. Recall also that, as we saw in our discussion of the *Republic* in Ch. 4, Plato understands certain pleasures as intentional states characteristic of different kinds of persons and their ways of living, depending on what the person thinks is most important in life.

such, they can also misrepresent their objects. We can see this point in the psychological account of pleasure, provisional and compressed though it is, that Socrates offers:

Let us try to achieve more clarity about what we said concerning pleasure and judgment. Is there something we call judging?
Yes.
And is there also taking pleasure?
Yes.
But there is also what the judgment is about?
Certainly.
And also what the pleasure is about?
Very much so.
But what makes a judgment, whether it judges rightly or not, cannot be deprived of really making a judgment.
How should it?
And what takes pleasure, whether it is rightly pleased or not, can obviously never be deprived of really taking pleasure.
Yes, that is also the case.
But what we have to question is how it is that judgment is usually either true or false, while [according to you, Protarchus,] pleasure admits only truth, even though in both cases there is equally real judgment and real pleasure.   (37a1–b8)

Socrates starts by noting that the issue in question in determining whether pleasures can be false in the way that judgments can is not whether such pleasures are not really pleasures. After all, false judgments misrepresent reality, but are still judgments. But before we—and Protarchus—can be convinced that pleasures can misrepresent the world, we need to see more clearly what it means for pleasures to be representational. This task is made somewhat more difficult by the fact that Plato offers the following metaphors in lieu of arguments:

But look, do you share my view on this?
What view?
That our soul in such a situation [of making judgments] is comparable to a book?
How so?
If memory and perception concur with other impressions at a particular occasion, then they seem to me to inscribe words in our soul, as it were. And if what is written is true, then we form a true judgment and a true account of the matter. But if what our scribe writes is false, then the result will be the opposite of the truth.
I quite agree, and I accept this way of putting it.
Do you also accept that there is another craftsman at work in our soul at the same time?
What kind of craftsman?
A painter who follows the scribe and provides illustrations to his words in the soul.
How and when do we say he does this work?
When a person takes his judgments and assertions directly from sight or any other sense-perception and then views the images he has formed inside himself, corresponding to those judgments and assertions. Or is it not something of this sort that is going on in us?
Quite definitely.

And are not the pictures of the true judgments and assertions true, and the pictures of the
false ones false?
Certainly.   (38e9–39c6)

Plato begins by distinguishing pleasure from belief with the vivid metaphors
of the painter and the scribe. The 'scribe' writes down statements which are,
evidently, in the form of sentences in the indicative voice, since they assert, and
thus assert either truly or falsely. They are also the content of belief or assent (as
opposed to speculations one entertains without yet assenting, say), since they are
the result of a concurrence of 'memory and perception' with 'other impressions
at a particular occasion'. The 'painter', on the other hand, puts into images what
the scribe writes down. I think part of the point of portraying the painter as
painting from the sentences that the scribe writes, at second hand, rather than
from the things themselves, is that that these illustrations are, in the first
instance, not about the things that cause or occasion them, but about how one
takes those things to be. They are about things that the mind has already begun
to represent to itself. To return to our earlier example, the pleasure of a walk in
the country is the product not of my surroundings *themselves*, but of the way in
which *I take* my surroundings in, the attitudes *I form* about them, and so on.
These 'pictures', then, illustrate not the country itself, but the country-as-I-take-
it-to-be, given a host of further peculiar facts about me. This also means that we
are not the passive recipients of such pleasures, but the active producers of them,
even if we are rarely aware of the act of producing them. Perhaps the pleasure of
sweet taste is caused in one simply by the candy, say, but the pleasure of a walk
in the country depends ultimately on what attitudes the agent brings to the walk.
     Of course, beliefs are not passively formed, either, but are the work of a
'scribe', and the 'sentences' that form their content are also of the agent's own
making. Why, then, is a painter needed at all—if it is pleasing that such-and-
such is the case, why shouldn't the scribe simply write down that it is? We might
say that the scribe cannot write down the pleasure because a sentence is not a
feeling or a 'glow', as a pleasure is. But this seems to be the wrong reply, since
feelings and glows are not pictures, and do not represent as Plato thinks pictures
can. Moreover, one need not have a *belief* that such and such is the case in order
to have a glow over contemplating it; daydreams and fantasies will do just as
well. But neither should we say that these pictures are really only beliefs of
another sort. To be pleased is to be pleased that something is the case, but being
pleased is not a matter of coming up with yet more sentences about pleasing
things. It is one thing to believe that something satisfies a longing and another to
view it through the lens of satisfaction, as it were. After all, notice that the
painter does much more than report. He produces original works with a significance of their own. This is, I take it, precisely why one should introduce a
painter rather than yet another scribe to bring into vivid relief not merely the
nature but indeed the *significance* of some state of affairs for a viewer. The
paintings do not merely tell us more than the writings do. It is by 'painting'

them within ourselves that we overlay our experience, so to speak, with the vivid shape and color that our concerns lend. Pleasure goes beyond taking things to be such and such, to ascribing to them a value and power that our deeper concerns invest in them.

And so the painter's act is a matter of focusing one's attention and one's emotions on a state of affairs in a concern-laden way. Somewhat less metaphorically,[20] my enjoyment of something is my representing it to myself as something that does—or, for that matter, will—meet my concerns. We can see this way of thinking about the painter's work if we look at Plato's account of anticipatory pleasures. According to Plato, these pictures are not only about the present and past but also about the future (39c–d), and the pictures that we have about those states of affairs that we believe will obtain are pleasures of anticipation (39d–40a):

And is not everyone, as we just said, always full of many hopes?
Certainly.
There are, then, assertions in each of us that we call hopes?
Yes.
But there are also those painted images. And someone often envisages himself in the possession of an enormous amount of gold and of a lot of pleasures as a consequence. And in addition, he also sees, in this inner picture himself, that he is beside himself with delight.   (40a3–12)

Where exactly are we to locate the pleasure of anticipation within this whole act of anticipation? This question has aroused much controversy, and I do not wish to dwell too much on that controversy here.[21] I think it is reasonably clear, however, that the pleasure in question is the representation to oneself of a future state of affairs that one believes will obtain and will be satisfying. On this account, the pleasure of anticipation is the pleasure that something will be the case, placing the state of affairs one anticipates under a description, and thus the enjoyment of the anticipated state of affairs in terms of that description. Such pleasure represents the world, as belief does, but, unlike belief, it represents the world in a more actively concern-laden way.

An example may help to illustrate. Suppose that I set my heart on owning a Jaguar, dreaming of the thrill of speeding along, being the envy of my neighbors and friends, increasing my sex appeal, and so on. But suppose that one day I stop dreaming about Jaguars, and set about acquiring one, perhaps taking a higher-paying job, working harder and longer hours, saving relentlessly, and so on. As this plan begins to come together, I no longer dream about the Jaguar that I *might* have, but anticipate the Jaguar that I now am certain I *shall* have. Now I have articulate beliefs ('Soon I shall own a Jaguar', 'Soon I shall be speeding along', etc.), and the 'scribe' is able to record those beliefs. Of course, I attach

---

[20] Nor is it surprising that metaphor cannot be removed from this account of emotion and pleasure entirely. After all, if we could say in a sentence what more an emotion presents to us than a simple belief does, we should not need anything more than simple beliefs in order for our minds to operate as they do.   [21] For a good discussion see D. Frede (1985: 165–71).

special significance to the content of those beliefs, and thus regard them in a vivid light: not only do I believe that I shall have the Jaguar, but I also 'see' the Jaguar in my future *as* a source of pride and joy for me, as something that *will* do for me all those things I have wanted a Jaguar to do. The thrill of speeding along, the pride of being envied, the excitement of being sexier, and so on, are the images and colors with which the 'painter' inside me depicts my beliefs about having my Jaguar. And that 'painting'—that way of construing what I take to be the facts—is *itself* a pleasure of anticipation.

It is important to distinguish this pleasure from other sorts of pleasures that might be involved in anticipation. For one thing, the pleasure of anticipating the Jaguar is not the pleasure that I anticipate the Jaguar will bring me. The pleasure I think I shall have in the future while I speed along in the Jaguar, for instance— my being 'beside myself with delight' in the future—is, of course, one of the things painted into the picture, but the pleasure that I have *here and now* is the pleasure of anticipating that future. Nor is anticipatory pleasure the feeling or 'glow' derived from the act of anticipating. It may feel good to anticipate that pleasant future—to 'revel' in it—but, again, reveling does not require *belief*, as opposed to fantasy. These pictures are not daydreams about some imaginary or possible future ('Wouldn't it be nice to have a Jaguar!') but ways of viewing or construing a future that we think shall obtain, in terms of some active interest we take in them ('Tomorrow I *shall* have a Jaguar—and *then how satisfied I shall be!*').[22]

Notice now that anticipatory pleasures do especially well at illustrating an important general feature of pleasures, regardless of tense. As Dorothea Frede has noted, focusing on present rather than anticipatory pleasures can conceal the fact that 'what is enjoyed in the present is not the *thing* itself, but the thing *as conceived of* by the person'.[23] In the example above, the cause of my pleasure is not the Jaguar *per se*, but the meaning that I ascribe to the Jaguar. And, although my pleasure is not simply a belief that the Jaguar has such significance, my pleasure of anticipating the Jaguar *does* constitute a way of *asserting* the special significance the Jaguar has for me.[24] My pleasure does not *report* on the Jaguar's significance, but *overlays* the Jaguar with a significance I take it to have, given my concerns regarding it.[25]

---

[22] See D. Frede (1985: 171–3), (1993: xlviii) for discussion and defense of this interpretation; cf. Thalberg (1962: 67 f., 73 f.). *Con.* Gosling (1959: 52), (1961: 44), (1975: 215–19), whose view is criticized in Kenny (1960), both of whom are criticized in McLaughlin (1969).

[23] D. Frede (1993: xlviii), italics in original. See also (1985: 165–79).

[24] Nor is there any particular reason to think that pictures cannot assert, even if they cannot assert discursively. As Wittgenstein pointed out, while images do not represent anything in their own right (a picture of a man on the side of a hill, e.g., could represent either a man ascending or a man descending the hill), still nothing keeps us from *using* such drawn figures to represent and assert, any more than we are kept from using written figures to represent and assert (the black marks on this page, after all, do not assert anything in their own right, either).

[25] It is also worth pointing out that, although these concerns must necessarily be mine, they need not all be *about* me; I can have concerns about my child's welfare, e.g., and thus be pleased at anticipating a prosperous future for my child. There is, at any rate, nothing in Plato's analysis that tells against this.

And here we can see that such a response—such an assertion—can be either true or false: true, when the state of affairs in question does indeed have the significance one attributes to it; and false otherwise.[26] Consequently, Plato argues that such pleasures can be literally *false*. He makes this point in a passage reminiscent of his claim in *Republic* X, 613a–b that the gods benefit good people, as they are dear to them:

> Now do we want to say that in the case of good people these pictures are usually true, because they are dear to the gods, while quite the opposite usually holds in the case of wicked ones, or is this not what we ought to say?
> That is just what we ought to say.
> And wicked people nevertheless have pleasures painted in their minds, even though they are somehow false?
> Right.
> So wicked people as a rule enjoy false pleasures, but the good among mankind true ones?
> Quite true.
> From what has now been said, it follows that there are false pleasures in human souls that are quite ridiculous imitations of the true ones, and also such pains.   (40b2–c6)

Return to the example of the anticipated Jaguar. Suppose that I do acquire my Jaguar, only to find that it is not nearly as satisfying as I thought it would be. Perhaps I find that speeding along is not nearly as exciting as I had thought it would be, or that it doesn't matter to me very much after all that my neighbors envy me, or that I am no more appealing now than I was before. And so, now that I have the Jaguar, I may find that it brings me no satisfaction, and I may even feel more miserable now than before. I had pictured a satisfied future for myself, and I was mistaken—that picture was false. Anticipatory pleasure is a kind of *view* that one takes, and such a view can turn out to be wholly unrealistic. And so Plato believes both that anticipatory pleasures are representational and have content, *and* that they can *misrepresent*. He therefore concludes that Protarchus' initial insistence that, strictly speaking, only the beliefs accompanying pleasures can be false, and not the pleasures themselves (37e–38a), does not withstand the scrutiny of a closer psychological analysis of pleasure.

Notice several things that seem to follow from Plato's analysis of anticipatory pleasure. For one thing, it seems that his account of desire now extends beyond simple animal desires and pleasures to include desires and pleasures that are

---

[26] I offer this gloss with some reservation, as Plato offers no gloss on the notion of falsity here that distinguishes between this case of falsity in which the anticipated thing does not yield the anticipated benefits, and the different case in which the anticipated state of affairs does not come about at all, and the yet further case in which the anticipated state of affairs does obtain, but is not really satisfying for a being like me, even if I happen to find it satisfying (the sort of mistake that Plato depicts in people who get what they think is satisfaction, without ever getting genuine satisfaction; see *Republic* IX, 584c ff., discussed in Ch. 4). However, I shall focus on the first kind of case here, as it is a simpler case than the third (and I think the results of analyzing the first case should apply readily to the third as well), and because it does more than the second case to highlight the concern-ladenness of anticipatory pleasure, which is what we should expect given Plato's analysis of desire.

necessarily connected to an agent's values and self-conception, since the latter also shape an agent's understanding of her needs and what will satisfy them, and especially her beliefs about what is worth while and meaningful. Pleasures of this sort rely not only on memory of what made a pain go away before, as with thirst, but also on estimations of value and priority. For me to think that a life of money-making is going to be satisfying, for instance, is to adopt a whole net-work of beliefs and values about my nature, my personality, what my real needs are, what really matters in life, and so on.[27] Consequently, as we saw in *Republic* IX, to enjoy a money-making life (say) as a life I find worth while and meaningful is to take a certain kind of value-laden attitude toward that life, an attitude that exists only within a network of other value-laden attitudes and beliefs.[28] For another, on Plato's analysis there *is* something for pleasure to be right or wrong about, after all, and there are better and worse directions it can take.[29] For it is all too possible that a person may represent something to herself as satisfying, rewarding, and worth while, when, in fact, it is none of those things.

Plato moves on to a second kind of false pleasure, which is also false in respect of its epistemic status, although in a different way (κατ' ἄλλον τρόπον, 41a7), involving false estimations of less proximate pleasures and pains (41a–42c). Socrates begins by pointing out that pleasure and pain admit of being 'more' and 'less' (41d), and then asks Protarchus,

Do we have any means of making a right decision about these matters?
Where and in what respect?
In the case where we intend to come to a decision about [pleasures and pains] in such circumstances, which one is greater or smaller, or which one is more intensive or stronger: pain compared to pleasure, or pain compared to pain, or pleasure to pleasure.
Yes, these questions do arise, and that is what we want to decide.
Well, then, does it happen only to eyesight that seeing objects from afar or close by distorts the truth and causes false judgments? Or does not the same thing happen also in the case of pleasure and pain?
Much more so, Socrates.
But this is the reverse of the result we reached a little earlier.
What are you referring to?
Earlier it was true and false *judgments* which affected the respective pleasures and pains with their own condition.
Quite right.
But now it applies to pleasures and pains themselves; it is because they are alternately looked at from close up or far away, or simultaneously put side by side, that the pleasures seem greater compared to pain and more intensive, and pains seem, on the contrary, moderate in comparison with pleasures.
It is quite inevitable that such conditions arise under these circumstances.

---

[27] This idea will be familiar from *Republic* IX, 580d ff., discussed in Ch. 4.

[28] This is a most important detail, since Plato is not content to say merely that pleasure is an adverbial attribute of the pleasant activity, but more specifically that it is a particular kind of representation to oneself of the enjoyed activity. I shall say more about this below.

[29] See also D. Frede (1993: xliv f.).

But if you take that portion of them by which they appear greater or smaller than they really are, and cut it off from each of them as a mere appearance and without real being, you will neither admit that this appearance is right or dare to say that anything connected with this portion of pleasure or pain is right and true.
Certainly not.   (41d11–42c4)

This is a breathtakingly quick discussion of these false pleasures, but a few things are fairly clear. For one, the falsity obtains as a result of comparisons of more proximate pleasures and pains with less proximate ones, and somehow is caused by the distortion of 'distance' (41e–42a). Socrates does not expand on the notion of 'distance' in this context, but presumably, whereas in the case of eyesight the distance is distance in space, in the case of pleasures and pains the distance would be distance in time, as for instance when one compares a pleasure today with a pain or pleasure tomorrow. For another, whereas the first type of pleasures were false inasmuch as the 'scribe' wrote falsely (i.e. one made a mistake of fact) and hence the 'painter' painted falsely (one enjoyed as fact something that was only an illusion), here the pleasure is somehow false on its own, and not because of false belief (42a–b). Finally, the estimation of pleasure that Socrates has in mind is not simply how much one enjoys something, but how much one enjoys it *in comparison* with something else, such as some other pleasure, or a concomitant pain, and it is the comparison—the 'how much more'—that makes the pleasure false (42b–c).

It is clear, then, that the falsity involves some exaggerated estimation of pleasures relative to pains and other pleasures, but the details are very sketchy. Many commentators understand Socrates to be speaking of exaggerated estimations of future pleasure, owing to the proximity of one's current situation.[30] To return to our earlier example, I may over-estimate the pleasure I expect from my Jaguar, given the sharpness of my current desire for it. This reading is motivated by Socrates' restatement of his earlier point about the soul's desiring the condition opposite to the actual condition of the body (41b–d), which may suggest that anticipation of a future pleasure is again what he has in mind. Thus, for instance, J. C. B. Gosling argues that this second kind of false pleasure is a special type of the first: it obtains, he says, when one is in distress, anticipates pleasure, and exaggerates that pleasure because of the current distress.[31] Yet on this view these false pleasures are not false 'in a different way' from the previous false pleasures, after all, but are a species of them, being based on false belief. An even greater disadvantage of this kind of approach, however, is that it makes

---

[30] See Gosling (1975: 219 f.); and Mooradian (1995), for different versions of this reading; cf. D. Frede (1993: xlviii f.).

[31] Alternatively, Mooradian (1995) argues that this kind of falsity occurs when a pleasure gives rise to a false opinion, unlike the first kind in a which false opinion gives rise to a false pleasure (cf. 42a); rather, one conceives of a future pleasure, enjoys the act of contemplating it, and tacitly concludes to an exaggerated estimation of that pleasure, owing to a disparity between the future pleasure and the current enjoyment of contemplating it. However, this reading requires us to introduce the pleasure derived from the act of anticipating—the feeling of reveling in the anticipation, say—as having a causal role that seems alien to Plato's analysis thus far.

little sense of Socrates' comparison of this error in pleasure with a purportedly analogous error in visual judgment, in which the relative proximity of observed objects leads to false opinions about their sizes (41e–42c). The analog of exaggerating a future pleasure would be to over-estimate the size of a more distant object in relation to a closer one—an uncommon visual error indeed.[32]

Rather, I think what Socrates has in mind is the sort of mistaken estimation I make when the pleasure I take in tonight's carousing, say, depends on an unrealistically low estimation of tomorrow morning's pains, or of the pleasures I would have had tomorrow if I had moderated myself tonight. This is the often mistaken thought that tonight's pleasures will make bearing tomorrow's pains (or forgoing tomorrow's pleasures) 'worth it'. Jerry Seinfeld makes quite an astute observation about just this kind of mistake:

I never get enough sleep. I stay up late at night, because I'm Night Guy. Night Guy wants to stay up late. What about getting up after five hours' sleep? Oh, that's Morning Guy's problem. 'That's not my problem, I'm Night Guy. I stay up as late as I want.' So you get up in the morning, the alarm, you're exhausted, you're groggy, oh you hate that Night Guy! You see, Night Guy always screws Morning Guy. There's nothing Morning Guy can do. The only thing Morning Guy can do is try and oversleep often enough so that Day Guy loses his job, and Night Guy has no money to go out any more.[33]

Seinfeld reports a disturbingly familiar strategy for reasoning about what to do tonight: let Night Guy have fun without considering the cost—let Morning Guy worry about that.

The possibility of this strategy and of its failure illustrate that pleasure is often not a simple matter of enjoying the present, but a complex matter of enjoying the present *as* having a certain kind of cost for the agent over time. Consider three cases. (1) If I go out for drinks tonight, and in my naiveté I do not know that drinking as much as I am tonight will have a cost tomorrow, I shall drink tonight in blissful ignorance. More than that, the ignorance is *part* of the bliss: I enjoy tonight the way that I do because I have no thoughts about what tonight might cost me tomorrow, and so I enjoy tonight's drinking *as* pain-free. (2) However, if I know that drinking so much tonight will have a cost tomorrow, and I think tonight that the drinking is worth paying for tomorrow, I enjoy tonight's drinking not as cost-free, but as having a cost that I am ready to pay. Whether instances of these two types of pleasure will be 'true' or 'false' depends on whether I am correct or mistaken about the actual cost;[34] consequently, when they are false, they are false in the same basic way as false anticipatory pleasures, being based on a false belief about my future states, and so presumably neither is

---

[32] Gosling (1975: 219), to his credit, recognizes this difficulty.

[33] From *Seinfeld*, 'The Glasses,' Thursday 30 September 1993, 9.00 p.m., NBC. D. Frede (1992: 447) cites the (far more sophisticated) example of Esau, who in the pangs of hunger 'was induced to overrate the worthwhileness of filling himself with a dish of lentils to the point where he thought the pleasure was worth the price of his primogeniture, that is, the future pain of its loss'; and she correctly observes that 'not only does pleasure have its price, we enjoy it as having a price.'

[34] I thank Bill Oberdick for this point.

the sort of case that Plato has in mind here. (3) But suppose that I do know that drinking so much tonight will have a cost tomorrow that I think—correctly—is not worth paying; if I then choose to keep drinking despite the cost, it is no longer available to me to enjoy the drinking *as* having a certain manageable cost, much less as having no cost at all. Perhaps, then, I shall not really enjoy tonight's drinking very much; *or* I might employ the Seinfeld strategy, and simply block the thought of the cost as a cost to *me*, that is, the 'me' that is here and now, in order to enjoy the drinking *as if* cost-free to me, or at least try. Only in that way can I enjoy it '*by that much more*', that is, as if it actually were greater than what will be incurred or forgone tomorrow. This falsity stems not from a false belief about my future states, but from a sort of self-deception embodied in tonight's enjoyment. It is, then, this third kind of case that I think Plato has in mind here.

Notice what all of these cases illustrate: enjoying is typically 'enjoying as', and often what follows the 'as' is a specification of how much one enjoys what one is doing relative to the costs of what one is doing in terms of earned pains or forfeited pleasures.[35] How much I enjoy something often depends on my estimation of the cost of the enjoyment, even if I am not consciously aware of my having made any such estimation (and usually we are not; that is part of why Seinfeld's observation is humorous, since it reveals the absurdity of that estimation once it *is* made conscious). They also illustrate how pleasures differ as estimations do. The blissfully ignorant pleasure is innocent and carefree, requiring no balancing of conflicting emotions about what is happening tonight and what will happen in the morning. The calculating pleasures, by contrast, are more complex, requiring just that sort of balancing to appease the conflicting emotions, and the disassociating pleasures are not only complex but compli-cated, as they block those conflicting emotions.

Since each pleasure represents the enjoyed activities in terms of a certain estimation of their worth for the agent over time, an essential part of the enjoyment is to *represent* the object of the enjoyment *as* having a certain value relative to cost. But, of course, it is possible to misrepresent the enjoyment as having that value relative to that cost, and thus *that* much of the enjoyment—considered in this way as a representational state—can be said to be false, because it misrepresents what one will want over time. And its falsity should worry us if we are concerned to think of ourselves primarily as continuing agents, as 'Night Guy' does not. Bad enough are those pleasures that rest on mistaken estimations, placing the wrong kind of significance on one's anticipated future.

---

[35] It is more likely, then, that Socrates restates the point about the cohabitation of pleasures and pains (41b–d) not to direct the argument once again to anticipation of pleasure but simply to show that the pleasures he has in mind obtain in the context of some pain to which they are connected, for instance, as the pleasure is enjoyed as having a minimal price in future pain, and consequently is seen as having a greater relative proportion to that pain. This view is also taken by Waterfield (Plato, trans. Waterfield 1982: 105 n. 1 *ad* 42b). Cf. D. Frede (1993: xlix), who notes that in this kind of case pleasure is enjoyed '*as* having a certain size and price' (emphasis in original); and D. Frede (1992: 446–8). This interpretation also makes the mistake in judgment analogous to that described at *Protagoras* 356c–d.

Even worse are these pleasures that rest on unrealistic, deluded, and self-deceived estimations, ignoring the relevance of one's future altogether.

Perhaps the greatest advantage of this way of understanding this second class of false pleasures is that it gives Plato an especially strong response to the notion that pleasures determine happiness. Pleasures are intimately bound up with our ability to think of ourselves as continuing agents who can represent their present activities to themselves in terms of their meaning for one's future. Many pleasures, in fact, just *are* such representations of our activities. Consequently, here again we see that pleasure has a *role* to play in one's life. Pleasure is not good by its nature—how could just *any* representation, however unrealistic, of the meaning of one's activity be good by its nature?—but becomes good only if it plays the sort of role that makes sense for it. Notice, then, the connection between this analysis of pleasure and Plato's thesis that reason is the 'cause' of the goodness of the good life: what makes for goodness in one's life is always what gives every dimension of it the right kind of direction and the right kind of role, in this case by grasping a reasonable account of one's real interests are, and thus of what is, in fact, worth what.

The third kind of false pleasure, Plato says, has an even greater falsity than the first two (42c). It is rather disappointing, then, that they are 'false' in the sense that they are not really pleasures at all. These 'pleasures' are what some people confuse with a state without any perceived change or motion (42c–43d), a state of mere absence of pain. Since this state is static and not dynamic,[36] it cannot really be a pleasure, but people only imagine that it is (43e–44a):

It has by now been said repeatedly that it is a destruction of the nature of [animals] through combinations and separations, through processes of filling and emptying, as well as certain kinds of growth and decay, that gives rise to pain and suffering, distress, and whatever else comes to pass that goes under such a name.
Yes, that has often been said.
But when things are restored to their own nature again, this restoration, as we established in our agreement among ourselves, is pleasure.
Correct. . . .
If in fact nothing of that sort took place, I will ask you, what would necessarily be the consequence of this for us? . . .
This much is clear, Socrates, that in such a case there would not be either any pleasure or pain at all. . . .
So we end up with three kinds of life, the life of pleasure, the life of pain, and the neutral life. Or what would you say about these matters?
I would put it in the same way, that there are three kinds of life. . . .
Now, imagine three sorts of things, whichever you may like, and because these are high-sounding names, let us call them gold, silver, and what is neither of the two.
Consider it done.

---

[36] More precisely, we should say that it is static from our perspective, since Socrates concedes to the view that nothing is ever static, but always changing and moving. This does not affect his case, he says, since pleasure obtains only when the changes and motions are perceived by us (42d–43d).

Is there any way conceivable in which this third kind could turn out to be the same as one of our other two sorts, gold or silver?
How could it?
That the middle kind of life could turn out to be either pleasant or painful would be the wrong thing to think, if anyone happened to think so, and it would be the wrong thing to say, if anyone should say so, according to the proper account of the matter?
No doubt.
But we do find people who both think so and say so, my friend.
Certainly.
And do they really believe they experience pleasure when they are not in pain?
They say so, at any rate.
They believe therefore that they are pleased at that time. Otherwise they would not say that they are.
It looks that way.
But they hold a false judgment about pleasure, if in fact freedom from pain and pleasure each have a nature of their own.
But they do have their own.   (42c9–d8, e7–8, 11–12 , 43c13–d3, e1–44a11)

The basic idea here is fairly clear: pleasure is not the same as the absence of pain, and so those who think that the life of absence of pain is a life of pleasure are mistaken. What is much less clear, however, is what *follows* from that basic idea. Surely he means to show what he had suggested earlier, that a person can think that she is experiencing pleasure but be mistaken (36e).[37] Plato's argument shows that, but what is the *importance* of showing that, *here*?

Strangely, Plato does not draw a conclusion from this analysis, but moves immediately to the analysis of the final kind of false pleasure, through a notoriously mysterious transition about unnamed proponents of a false theory of pleasure (44b–d). It would not be wise, then, to press Plato's analysis of the third class of false pleasures too far, for the next kind of false pleasure is clearly more interesting to him. But for all that, we *should* be able to see how thinking about this kind of false pleasure might contribute to the overall evaluation of pleasure in which it appears.

Of course, Plato ought not to think that because some alleged 'pleasures' are actually *non*-pleasures, some *bona fide* pleasures are therefore false. That would be like thinking that because 'false pregnancies' are false, for instance, it follows that some actual pregnancies are false,[38] or that some kinds of knowledge are false, on the grounds that some things that we think we know are not really true after all. Now Plato's argument would be easier if he were to treat this sort of false pleasure as, say, the pleasure of anticipating a state of equilibrium as if it were a kind of pleasure, when, in fact, it is not.[39] This would make the third class merely a special case of the first class, of course, but at least in that case the false anticipatory pleasure would be an *actual* pleasure, whose falsity Plato has prepared us for. But while Plato makes a similar move in *Republic* IX,[40] such a move

---

[37] For a good discussion of these issues, see D. Frede (1992: 448).
[38] For this analogy, see D. Frede (1993: xlix).   [39] This is suggested by Gosling (1975: 220).
[40] See 583c ff., and my discussion of this passage in Ch. 4.

is conspicuously absent from the present passage.[41] What point is Plato making here about actual pleasures?

I think that his point is a modest but important one, namely that we have something to learn from those who treat as supremely valuable a thing or state about which they are fundamentally mistaken. Of course, there is nothing more worrisome, ethically speaking, about thinking that the absence of pain is pleasure, than about most other false beliefs about psychology or anything else. The worry is that people might give this condition pride of place in their lives, on the grounds that it is the greatest pleasure and as such worth pursuing. These people would be pseudo-hedonists, as it were: they do not actually pursue pleasure, but they think that they do—in fact, they seek what they seek *on the grounds that* it is pleasure, and that is their mistake. And so the pseudo-hedonists do not merely have a false belief about psychology, but live their lives as they do on the *basis* of that false belief. And so, at any rate, here again the main point seems to be that goodness is not to be found simply in what one *takes* to be fulfilling and meaningful, but only in what really is. Here again, then, Plato appears to give the direction of one's life—and a realistic perspective on that direction—a central place in understanding the nature of happiness. This is, at any rate, the most I think we can say with any confidence about this class of pleasures. None the less, it is most interesting that we can say even that much.

The fourth and final class of false pleasures[42] that Plato discusses are the 'most intense' ones (44d–45a), which involve a mixture of pleasure and pain. The most intense physical[43] pleasures, Socrates says, are mixed with pain: the greater, and hence more painful, the preceding desire, the more intense the pleasure of satisfying the desire (45b). These kinds of experiences are evidently cases of satisfying-while-lacking, such as satisfying thirst while it is strong, being warmed while one is shivering, satisfying sexual desire while it is highly excited, and scratching while one itches (see 45b–46a). These experiences, Socrates says, are so intensely pleasant *because* they are 'impure', that is, mixed with enough pain to 'spike' them, as it were, but little enough that there is still a preponderance of pleasure (45e–46b).[44]

Plato discusses the nature of this 'mixture' of pleasure and pain in far more detail in his analysis of intense pleasures of the soul (47d–50e). Unfortunately,

---

[41] Perhaps, however, Plato's focus is not on the 'pleasure' that they pursue as a goal—which is not pleasure at all—but on the pleasure taken in the pursuit of that goal. In that case, the false pleasure would be the pleasure of believing that one's mode of life is supremely pleasant, when in fact it is not. This would, of course, bring Plato's analysis of this pleasure right in line with his critique in *Republic* IX of other modes of life that are valued as supremely pleasant, when in fact they are not. But I think that this passage of the *Philebus* is too indeterminate for us to affirm this interpretation of it with much confidence.

[42] I follow D. Frede (1993: l) in considering the mixed pleasures as kinds of false pleasures. See also, Irwin (1995: 329).

[43] Although, strictly speaking, pleasures belong only to the soul, because desires do (35c–d), Plato none the less distinguishes between pleasures that arise primarily through the body, primarily through both the body and the soul, and primarily through the soul (see 31b ff.).

[44] It is a well-established point that these pleasures are more or less equivalent to those prized by Callicles in the *Gorgias*. See Ch. 2 for discussion.

his chosen example is the pleasure of watching theatrical comedy, and it is far from obvious how pain is 'mixed' with such pleasure. Although Plato acknowledges how peculiar this example is (48b), none the less his account of comedic laughter—roughly, that it amounts to laughing at the undeserved misfortunes of others, so that we must bear them some ill-will that is a kind of pain—seems at least as idiosyncratic as the view it is meant to illuminate, and it is unlikely that it will resonate with us.[45] But it still has some light to shed on what it means for pleasure to be mixed with pain.[46]

In order to explain the mixture of pain with the pleasure of our laughter as spectators of theatrical comedy, Socrates returns to an emotion that he and Protarchus had previously agreed was both pleasant and painful (see 47e), namely malice (φθόνος).[47] Malice is a complex emotion. First of all, it is a kind of psychic *pain*, but in virtue of it the malicious person is also *pleased* at the bad lot of the object of his malice (48b). Such delight presupposes ill-will toward another, or a desire (an uncalled for desire, in particular) to see him come to a bad pass, and this is a painful, distressful condition of the soul,[48] which manifests itself in the enjoyment of these misfortunes when they come about. So malicious delight is a 'mixture' of pleasure and pain in that it is an enjoyment of others' misfortunes which presupposes some painful attitude toward those others; the enjoyment of their misfortunes has as a component the ill-will we

---

[45] However, Plato's account of comedy may have resonated at least *somewhat* better with those for whom what we now call Greek Middle Comedy was paradigmatic, since the plots of such comedies rely almost formulaically for climactic comic effect on the reversal of fortune of some ridiculous character (often a procurer, swaggering soldier, cantankerous old man, or the like) who 'gets it in the end' in some hilarious and usually ironic way. This sort of plot, and its frequency, can be seen both in the surviving plays of Greek Middle Comedy, such as those of Menander, and in the later Roman comedies which revived many of the plots of such earlier comedies, especially those of Plautus. Consequently, in Plato's time comic laughter seems to have been primarily a *ridiculing* form of laughter. In fact, being ridiculous and thus worthy of derision is the basic sense of τὸ γελοῖον, which is what Plato is proposing to analyze (48c4). (On τὸ γελοῖον see Stewart (1994). Consider also, e.g., the mocking, ridiculing laughter directed at Thersites, and even Hephaestus, in the *Iliad*.) But I cannot pursue this issue here.

[46] In thinking about this passage I have benefited from discussions with Matt Evans.

[47] I think that it is far preferable to understand φθόνος as malice, and not as envy as some scholars do, esp. Strauss (1966: 5); and Benardete (1993: 201 f.). Our ridiculing laughter at a fraudulent pander who is tricked and humiliated, say—a staple of Greek Middle Comedy—surely does not presuppose that we envy him, as though we regard him as better or better off than we are. Indeed, Strauss (1966: 5) himself recognizes that this is not a generally adequate account of ridicule in comedy contemporary to Plato, but claims that it does capture the *Clouds*: Aristophanes depicts Socrates as ridiculous, Strauss says, because he is 'envious of his wisdom'. See also Benardete (1993: 201 ff.). But even this seems to me a heroic stretch of the imagination at best. Worse, it treats the comic *playwright* as the malicious one, whereas Plato discusses the malice of the comic *spectator*.

[48] See D. Frede (1993: lii), who takes Plato to mean that we would not enjoy watching others' follies committed in ignorance unless we harbor 'a *need* to see them make fools of themselves', a kind of '*Schadenfreude*', where this need 'is a kind of pain'. I prefer Frede's view to that of Hampton (1990: 67) and A. E. Taylor (1972: 74), that for Plato our laughter is based on our identification with, and empathy for, those at whom we are laughing (as Hampton puts it, that our laughter springs from 'some recognition that we also share the delusions of those walking the boards'); *ridiculing* laughter, and the associated ill-will that Plato means to draw our attention to here, is surely in *tension* with such empathy and identification.

bear them,[49] for a crucial part of what we enjoy in their misfortune just is that it happens *to them*. Since comic laughter is unjustified enjoyment of others' misfortunes, and thus is malicious, it presupposes that we bear them some painful ill-will, and so comic laughter is 'mixed' with pain.

At present, we are less concerned with how well or badly this account fares as a psychological analysis of comic laughter than with what this analysis of malicious delight shows about pleasure and pain. Notice that the pain of ill-will does not merely accompany the delight at misfortunes, but makes that delight the sort of delight that it is; such delight is the delight *of* satisfied ill-will. Consequently, these kinds of pleasures are 'false' in the sense that they are metaphysically impure, intimately depending on the presence of their opposite.[50] But what follows from the fact that such pleasures have that sort of metaphysical status?

Again Plato does not say; but we should notice a couple of interesting features of his discussion of these false pleasures. For one thing, this discussion leads once again into thinking about pleasure within the context of a whole life. Plato claims that these most intense, mixed pleasures are praised by many as the most worthy objects to spend one's life pursuing (47b), even though the pain on which these intense, mixed pleasures are based arises from a disturbed psychological or physical condition—indeed, the most intense pleasures would have to be found in a worthless condition of body and soul (45e).[51] That Plato is

---

[49] It is interesting to note how this treatment of φθόνος differs from Aristotle's. Plato treats φθόνος as a pleasant emotion that presupposes a pain, whereas Aristotle treats φθόνος simply as a painful emotion. Φθόνος, Aristotle says, is pain at the good fortune of others like us (*Rhetoric* II.10). This is connected to another difference, namely that Aristotle is concerned with φθόνος in the sense of 'envy', rather than 'malice'. See *Eudemian Ethics* II.3, 1221a–b and *Nicomachean Ethics* II.7, 1108b, in which envy is discussed as a vice of excess of pain (felt at others' deserved prosperity), opposed to the unnamed vice of deficiency of pain (not felt at any prosperity), on the one hand, and to the virtue of indignation as a mean of pain felt at undeserved prosperity, on the other. Plato, however, typically thinks of φθόνος as malice rather than envy; cf., e.g., *Apology* 18d, 28a, *Gorgias* 457d. (See Damascius, *Lectures on the* Philebus § 201, who says in regard to 48b that one who enjoys friends' misfortunes is ἐπιχαιρέκακος, while the one who is annoyed at their prosperity is φθόνερος. Clearly, Damascius took Plato to be discussing malice, and not envy, at 48b, and chose very different vocabulary from Plato's in order to clarify Plato's point.) However, Aristotle does note that envy has a correlative pleasure: if the envious person is pained at the good fortune of equals, then he will also be pleased at their bad fortune (*Rhetoric* II.10). φθόνος can have both of these senses, depending on whether it is a pain, as primarily interests Aristotle, or a pleasure, as interests Plato. This suggests that φθόνος manifests itself either as a pleasure at misfortunes or a pain at good fortunes; what both Plato and Aristotle notice about the emotion of malice is that it always presupposes some single state of soul, namely ill-will toward others, and Plato claims that this state is always a distress. Hence, φθόνος is a 'double' emotion: the painful ill-will itself (as at 48b, 50a), and the manifestation of the ill-will either as pleasure (malice, as at 47e, 49d) or pain (envy). This understanding of malice allows Plato to notice that malice is a pleasure mixed with pain, that is a pleasure of enjoyment which presupposes a pain of ill-will. It also brings malice in line with the other 'mixed' pleasures, which are pleasures one can enjoy only because one also has some kind of pain (e.g. itching or hunger; see 46c–47d).

[50] I think that this fact about Plato's analysis answers the legitimate worry of Gadamer (1983) that φθόνος qua pleasure is separable from φθόνος qua pain, such that the pleasant version of the emotion need not be mixed with the painful version—in which case it would be unclear why, if one side of φθόνος is pleasant, that pleasure must contain pain just because the *other* side of φθόνος is painful.

[51] Cf. D. Frede (1993: li), (1992: 450), who claims that Socrates' point about mixed pleasure is quasi-medical, i.e. that such pleasures rely on disturbed physical conditions. Although Plato makes

denying these pleasures the value they are thought to have is obvious, when one thinks about value in the context of one's life as a whole: how could something have that kind of value, when its presence depends upon the breakdown of one's physical and psychic condition? Indeed, the discussion has ironically come full circle: whereas we began thinking about pleasure as valuable for its 'experience', we now find that when its experience is most intense, its value is most questionable![52]

At this point it is important to return to Protarchus, and ask what sort of impact this analysis of false pleasures has had on him. We find a rather remarkable development. At first, although Socrates had been able to persuade Protarchus that some forms of pleasure can be false, Protarchus was none the less confident that such falsity could have nothing to do with the value of such pleasures, understood as kinds of experience or sensation (41a–b). In fact, in response to Socrates' claim that the falsity of the first class of false pleasures is what their badness consists in (40e), Protarchus had retorted:

What you say is quite the opposite of the truth, Socrates! It is not at all because they are false that we regard pleasures or pains as bad, but because there is some other grave and wide-ranging kind of badness involved.   (41a1–4)

As we have seen, Protarchus originally held that a pleasure could never be bad, however false it is; perhaps some further sort of badness might *attach* to such a pleasure, but *qua* pleasure such a pleasure itself could never be bad. Rather than resolving this issue straightaway, however, Socrates merely recognized Protarchus' objection, and moved on to discuss further sorts of false pleasures (41a–b). Clearly, his discussion of them is meant to expose what is wrong in this sort of objection.[53]

Interestingly, at the end of their discussion of the second class of false pleasures, Protarchus actually agrees with Socrates that the pleasure we over-estimate is false (42c), *without* repeating his familiar refrain that the value of pleasure remains untouched despite its falsity. Why does he make this change? We might think that Protarchus goes along with Socrates simply because the issue of the value of such pleasure is left aside in the discussion of its epistemic status. But

this point during his discussion of specifically physical pleasures, he extends the point to the condition of the body as well as the soul, and so presumably this is meant as a fully general point about all mixed pleasures.

[52] See Plato, trans. Waterfield (1982: 19 f.), who takes Socrates to be offering a *reductio ad absurdum*: the most intense pleasures, which the hedonist should take to be best, require the presence of pain, which the hedonist takes to be bad; the best pleasures according to the hedonist, then, should be excluded from the hedonist's life. Although this is an interesting argument, Socrates himself does not suggest it. My own view is not that Socrates offers such a *reductio*, but that he wants to draw attention to the crucial fact that pleasure cannot be accepted as the good without thinking about what place it is capable of occupying within the good life.

[53] And this is a reasonable way for Socrates to proceed, since what Socrates must do is not offer a tidy refutation, but dig in and change Protarchus' mind. For it is not enough simply to show Protarchus that pleasure can be worthless, but he must also show him *how* that can be the case. I thank George Rudebusch for this way of putting the point.

that cannot be the reason, for Protarchus is the one who raised the point about the value of pleasure in the first place, in response to the point about its epistemic status (37e–38a); so if the point does not get raised here, that is presumably because Protarchus does not feel moved to raise it again. What is more, after their discussion of false pleasures, Protarchus eventually goes on to claim that 'a great absurdity seems to appear, Socrates, if we posit pleasure as a good' (55a9–11)! Clearly, Protarchus no longer thinks of pleasure in the same way. Once we recognize that pleasure is a kind of perspective, and can be an unrealistic perspective on one's projects, we also see that we can think of the value of pleasure as untouchable only by failing to comprehend ourselves fully as continuing agents with lives to construct, in which pleasure can take a better or worse role. The gradual[54] change that Plato depicts in Protarchus, I think, mirrors the change he means to make in us, as we begin to see that our evaluation of pleasure must be connected to our conception of ourselves as continuing agents living a whole life, and this begins slowly to change our evaluation of pleasure itself.[55] Pleasure is not a simple sensation but a complex way of representing its object in terms of an agent's values. As such, the falsity of false pleasures does indeed infect their value (cf. 38a–40e).

I think that Plato's point here is important and insightful. Consider a rather poignant scene from the popular movie *The Green Mile*. The story is set in a prison, and 'the Green Mile' is prison slang for its death row, which has a pale green floor. One of the inmates, Del, is a feeble man but has made several friends among the guards, and when the time for his execution draws near, the guards try to keep him from finding out before necessary by devising a plan to get him off the Green Mile while they do a dry run of the rather complicated execution procedure. Now Del has adopted a mouse he found in his cell and trained it to do simple tricks, and so the guards stage a mock demonstration before certain

---

[54] While Protarchus does undergo a significant change in his attitude toward pleasure, we should not expect his 'conversion' to be much more than partial or preliminary. See D. Frede (1993: lxv); see also (1992: 427 f., 432).

[55] As Annas (1999: 155) notes, there is congruence on this point in the *Gorgias* and the *Philebus*; for in both Plato argues that, 'Pursuit of pleasure unrestrained by the virtues turns out to be a kind of floundering, a pursuit of local satisfaction at the cost of overall coherence.' (See also Ch. 2 and my discussion of *Gorgias* 494c ff.; cf. Irwin (1995: 331).) Irwin (1995: 329, cf. 327 f., 333–5) also sees Plato's strategy as drawing our attention to thinking about lives, not just experiences: 'Plato's task . . . [is] to show that there is something clearly bad about each of these lives [corresponding to the four kinds of false pleasure] and that a hedonist cannot identify what is bad about them.' He also notes astutely that hedonist responses to his discussions of false pleasures—e.g. that the pleasure is distinct in being and value from the mistake associated with them—would be of no help in fending off this strategy: 'The account of false anticipatory pleasures suggests the general form of Plato's objection to the different sorts of false pleasures. In order to have false anticipatory pleasures, we must suffer from some recognizable defect . . . We are justified in preferring to be free of this defect, and so the sort of life that cannot exist without the defect cannot be the best life. . . . If we could have a life that contained pleasure without the cognitive defect involved in false anticipatory pleasure, then we would have reason to prefer that life over the one containing false anticipatory pleasure; but the hedonist requires us to say that the two lives are equally good. This is the basis of a legitimate objection to hedonism' (330). I think that Irwin is correct, but for a dissenting view see Carone (2000: esp. 271 ff.).

'dignitaries'—actually, other prison employees dressed in ill-fitting suits—of the extraordinary talents of Del's mouse. Del believes them, and displays his mouse with excitement and pride. Del believes that his mouse has been 'discovered' and will go on to join a special circus, and this is especially important to Del because the mouse's future is the only future Del can find solace in. But we, the audience, are shown that at the very time that Del is beaming over his mouse, the guards back on the Green Mile are rehearsing his execution.

Del's joy in his mouse's 'discovery' is what Plato would call a false pleasure, and it is instructive in a couple of ways. For one thing, although we are glad that Del has been spared unnecessary pain, and glad that he finally gets to experience what it might be like for a dream to come true, none the less we are not *really* happy for him, since we also find the sight of him crushing: we see, as he does not, that he has nothing to be excited or proud about. Moreover, to feel as if a dream were coming true is not the same as to have a dream come true, and the difference matters. It certainly matters to Del: a guard who hates Del tells him, shortly before his death, that the whole thing was a charade, and Del is utterly crushed. Furthermore, the very fact that this sort of pleasure, this charade, is all that his friends have left to offer him is itself a statement about just how completely badly things really are going for him, at the very time he thinks things are just looking up. The guards orchestrate this charade as a favor, and it is a favor, but only because Del does not have a life left to live, and is, after all, quite feeble.

An illusion may be pleasant, but that is just to say that there are some pleasures from which one cannot build a good life. And this is Plato's point about false pleasures: it matters to us that we not live in a fictional world, but *not* because a fictional world is any less pleasant.[56] I may take the greatest of pleasures in working for a future that will turn out to be cold and lonely, after all; those pleasures are not good despite my mistaken view of that future, since they are *themselves* a mistaken view. I may find the greatest delight in projects and activities, unaware of—or self-deceived about—the damage they are actually doing to me. I can pin my happiness on a goal that it delights me to find myself working toward, even if, in fact, my efforts are not actually working toward that goal, or even if I do not really understand that goal, or even if reaching that goal is not, in fact, what happiness is. I can find the greatest delight in things that satisfy me, even if they do so only because of the painful and ugly desires that lurk below. Like Del's illusion, each of these pleasures, in its own pitiable way, is a pleasure that fails to see one's life and one's world for what it really is. The pleasure of fooling oneself has its place. It is what we want out of a funhouse, an idle flirt, or a daydream. It is not what we want out of life.

---

[56] I am reminded here of Robert Nozick's famous 'experience machine' thought experiment, in which one is given the option of experiencing anything one wishes, for life, but only if one plugs into a machine that generates those experiences while the viewer does nothing (see Nozick (1974: 42–5)). I think that Plato—like the rest of us—would agree with Nozick that the only response is to decline such an offer: it matters that the world in which we live be a real one, however pleasant a fake one may be.

6.3.2   *True pleasures*

Consequently, the initially tempting view that pleasure can make one happy is incompatible with the more realistic view that goodness must be understood in terms of the power that things have for happiness, in the context of the life as a whole of a continuing agent. And since that power is the power of bringing direction to one's life, reason must be what is responsible (αἴτιον) for the goodness of the mixed life, just as Plato says it is.

Furthermore, while Plato's investigation into the psychology of pleasure demonstrates that pleasure has a role to play and a direction to take, and that it is dependent for its role and direction on intelligent agency, it also sheds light on what sort of role and direction pleasure can be capable of. And so Plato now (51b–53c) talks about pleasures which, unlike the false pleasures that are without limit, are 'true', and are among things that 'have measurement' (52d).[57] What Plato finds most interesting about true pleasures is their 'purity', which is not merely the absence of pain from them, but also their *independence* from pain. As we have seen, some pleasures—such as malicious pleasure—can exist only by keeping certain pains alive. I can have the pleasure of enjoying your misfortune, for instance, only so long as I have the pain of wishing to see you come to a bad pass. In general, many pleasures exist only so long as they are underwritten by the pain of needing, which Plato takes to be a sort of disturbance and imbalance. But true pleasures are those that supervene on the filling of lacks that one is not aware of (51b), and thus which presumably do not qualify as desires, as Plato understands them.

These 'true' pleasures are both physical and psychic: they include enjoyment of beautiful shapes, colors, sounds, and (to a lesser degree) scents (51c–e), as well as the enjoyment of learning and exercising the intellect (51e–52b):

But, Socrates, what are the kinds of pleasures that one could rightly regard as true?
Those that are related to so-called pure colors and to shapes and to smells and sounds and in general all those that are based on imperceptible and painless lacks (τὰς ἐνδείας ἀναισθήτους . . . καὶ ἀλύπους), while their fulfillments are perceptible and pleasant.
But really, Socrates, what are you talking about?
What I am saying may not be entirely clear straightaway, but I'll try to clarify it. By the beauty of a shape, I do not mean what the many might presuppose, namely that of a living being or of a picture. What I mean, what the argument demands, is rather something straight or round and what is constructed out of these with a compass, rule, and square, such as plane figures and solids. Those things I take it are not beautiful in a relative sense, as others are, but are by their very nature forever beautiful by themselves. They provide their own specific pleasures that are not at all comparable to those of rubbing! And colors are beautiful in an analogous way and import their own kinds of pleasures. (51b1–d2)

Protarchus surely will not be alone in wondering just what Socrates is on about. In particular, two main issues seem to arise in this part of the dialog, each of

---

[57] See D. Frede (1993: liv) for a good discussion.

which presents its own puzzles. One is the non-relativity of the beauty of beautiful objects of true pleasure, and the other is the purity of true pleasures, understood as their independence from perceived desire.

Socrates gives as an example of 'relative' beauty certain shapes that are beautiful not in their own right but only in so far as they go together to compose a further figure which is itself beautiful. The beauty of those shapes is 'borrowed', as it were, from the beauty of the whole figure they compose. Other shapes, however, are beautiful in their own right. A circle, for instance, is beautiful full stop, and not in virtue of composing into a greater whole that is beautiful (51c–d). Since Plato has in mind things that are forever beautiful in themselves and by their nature, he must not think of beauty as a subjectively perceived quality, such as 'pleasing to the eye', but as some sort of objective, permanent feature of a shape, such as its being proportional or symmetrical, although the precise details here must remain highly conjectural.

We may also wonder how this idea is connected to the second, concerning the 'purity' of the pleasures caused by such objectively beautiful things. This is not helped by the fact that Plato speaks of more than one type of purity in this part of the dialogue. After discussing the purity of the objects of true pleasures, Plato then shifts to the purity of the pleasure taken in these objects, as he says that pleasures of smell and learning are pure because they are not (necessarily) dependent on any sort of prior pain (51e–52b). Apparently, the purity of the object has *something* to do with the purity of the pleasure taken in the object, but what exactly?

The connection will become clearer if we return to the objectivity of beauty. The fact that a pleasure is independent of pain, Plato says, is what makes it pure—unadulterated by its opposite—and therefore true, in the sense of being a *genuine* form of pleasure, in the most proper and strict sense, as the purest shade of white is the most genuine shade of white (52c–53c). So just as true whiteness is found in the purest, rather than the largest, white sample, so too the truest and best pleasure is found in the purest, rather than the most intense, enjoyment (53a–c). Consequently, because naturally beautiful objects—objects with a 'pure' or genuine beauty, a beauty that is their own—depend on no pain of desire in order to bring us pleasure, the pleasure they bring us is therefore pure and genuine as well, being independent of any pain.

Interestingly, pleasure again seems to emerge as a rather special kind of representing, which can work in two directions. On the one hand, it can *project* beauty onto things by taking them to have some sort of power to satisfy the desires it is aware of; for instance, I may take pleasure in acquiring a Jaguar, but only because I desire the Jaguar, and thus attribute to it a value which, absent such desires, it does not have on its own. In this sort of case, the pleasure comes not from the Jaguar *per se*, but from the Jaguar *as I desire it*; its 'beauty'—its power to please and satisfy—is therefore not its own. On the other, pleasure can also *detect* the beauty and value in a naturally beautiful or valuable object itself, independent of any perceived lack in terms of which to construe the object. On

Plato's view, the beauty of a simple, beautiful shape, color, sound, or scent is not projected onto them, but detected in them, since they have a power to please that is not conditioned on a prior desire in terms of which we construe them.[58]

Where does this leave us? Again, Plato could be more helpful, but I do think that two points emerge from this discussion. One is that pleasure gains direction as it becomes more realistic, finding beauty and value in things inasmuch as they really are beautiful and valuable. What we need is not simply to go around attributing beauty and value to anything, but to be in the right kind of contact with what beauty and value there really is. And that is to say that pleasure has a role to play and a direction to take, a direction which must come from reason.

The other, which Plato now discusses, is that giving pleasure a certain kind of pride of place in one's life can actually threaten one's ability to construct the life of a genuine agent, and thus is out of sorts with human nature. He begins his argument for this point as follows:

Have we not been told that pleasure is always a process of *becoming* [γένεσις], and that there is no *being* [οὐσία] at all of pleasure? There are some subtle thinkers who have tried to pass on this doctrine to us, and we ought to be grateful to them.
What does it mean?...
...What is really meant is that all things are either for the sake of something else or they are that for whose sake the other kind comes to be in each case [τὸ μὲν ἕνεκα του τῶν ὄντων ἔστ' ἀεί, τὸ δ' οὗ χάριν ἑκάστοτε τὸ τινὸς ἕνεκα γιγνόμενον ἀεὶ γίγνεται].... Take on the one hand the *generation* [γένεσιν] of all things, on the other their *being* [οὐσίαν].
I accept this pair from you, being and generation.
Excellent. Now, which of the two do you think exists for the other's sake? Shall we say that generation takes place for the sake of being, or does being exist for the sake of generation?...
By heavens, what a question to ask me! You might as well ask: 'Tell me, Protarchus, whether shipbuilding goes on for the sake of ships or whether ships are for the sake of shipbuilding,' or some such thing....
[Very well.] I hold that all ingredients, as well as all tools, and quite generally all materials, are always provided for the sake of some process of generation. I further hold that every process of generation in turn always takes place for the sake of some particular being, and that all generation taken together takes place for the sake of the existence of being as a whole.
Nothing could be clearer.
Now, pleasure, since it turns out to be a kind of generation, comes to be for the sake of some being.
Of course.
But that for whose sake something comes to be ought to be put into the class of the things good in themselves, while that which comes to be for the sake of something else belongs in another class, my friend.
Undeniably.

---

[58] Whether their beauty is thus independent of the existence of agents to perceive this beauty, or whether this beauty is identical to their power to cause perceptions of just these types in agents, is another matter, and one that I shall leave aside for present purposes.

But if pleasure really is a kind of generation, will we be placing it correctly, if we put it in a class different from that of the good?
That too is undeniable.   (53c4–8, e5–7, 54a5–9, b1–4, c1–d3)

This is another puzzling passage. It is tempting to conclude that Plato is arguing that pleasure is an instrumental good, good in so far as it is a *means* to something else; and Protarchus' example of shipbuilding existing for the sake of ships does seem to suggest that. But, of course, it is difficult to see what pleasure could be a means *to*, and in any case I do not think that that captures Plato's real point, which I believe is simply that pleasure is *for* something. Consider working at a job, for example, such as building furniture (or, indeed, ships). The work is for something: it fits into a larger scheme of action that gives it its goal, and if such work did not actually achieve that goal, or if it achieved some pointless goal (e.g. producing unusable, ugly furniture), it would have no purpose. But that is *not* to say that such work is only instrumentally valuable; one can still enjoy and prize the act of building or woodworking for its own sake, that is, as a final good.[59] But it *is* to say that some final goods will be final goods only if they also fulfill some other purpose. Given that furniture serves a purpose, the act of building furniture can be pursued as a final good; if we did not need furniture at all, the act of building it would not have come up as something to spend one's time on, and it would be very odd if we had chosen to contrive some use for it, just so that people could build it.

  Likewise, I think pleasure is both a final good *and* for something, on Plato's account. Pleasure is a matter of finding something satisfying, and to find something satisfying is to find it satisfying of some need. Now, given that humans do have needs, the ability to satisfy them is a good thing, even a final good. But to say that pleasure is a final good, given our neediness, is not to say that we should prefer to be needy in order to be able to have the pleasure of satisfying our needs. Plato does not deny here that, when you are hungry, it is a good thing—even a final good—to enjoy eating a satisfying meal, for instance. On the contrary, I think his point is that what makes it possible for us to value pleasure as a final good is the fact that we do have needs to be satisfied. Rather, Plato's point is that we should not value our neediness itself on account of the pleasures that satisfying our needs can bring. That would make desire—not just satisfying desire, but having desire to satisfy—its own kind of goal. This is not a simple matter of saving one's appetite for a good meal, for instance.[60] For hedonism makes pleasure not merely a final good, but the good around which one's life is to be oriented. Since, on Plato's view, pleasure is not the state of having been satisfied, but the process of becoming satisfied (see 42c–44d), the hedonist life is oriented around neediness and 'becoming'—'a kind of generation' (54c6)—and this threatens one's ability to recognize that ultimately

---

[59] e.g. this is the premise of Roy Underhill's immensely enjoyable PBS show, *The Woodwright's Shop*, in which he demonstrates how to work with wood using only antiquated tools and methods.
[60] For this example, see Gosling and Taylor (1982: 73).

our desires need to be unified under a final end, that is, a goal of *being* a certain kind of person, of being whole.[61] Someone whose goal is the life of pleasure has no goal after all. Unfortunately, Socrates says, it is just this mistake that many people make:

> It is true, then, as I said at the beginning of this argument, that we ought to be grateful to the person who indicated to us that there is always only generation of pleasure and that it has no being whatsoever. And it is obvious that he will just laugh at those who claim that pleasure is good.
> Certainly.
> But this same person will also laugh at those who find their fulfillment in processes of generation.
> How so, and what sort of people are you alluding to?
> I am talking of those who cure their hunger and thirst or anything else that is cured by processes of generation. They take delight in generation as a pleasure and proclaim that they would not want to live if they were not subject to hunger and thirst and if they could not experience all the other things one might want to mention in connection with such conditions.
> That is very like them.
> But would we not all say that destruction is the opposite of generation?
> Necessarily.
> So whoever makes this choice would choose generation and destruction in preference to that third life which consists of neither pleasure nor pain, but is a life of thought in the purest degree possible.[62]
> So a great absurdity seems to appear, Socrates, if we posit pleasure as a good. (54d4–55a11)

The mistake that worries Plato about this way of valuing pleasure is a mistake about self-conception: what matters in life is the way in which one intelligently constructs a life, a future, and a self by one's actions and goals, in a way that will fulfill one's deepest needs as a human, and the view that pleasure makes one's life happy cannot make sense of that. To locate one's good in pleasure rather than in concerns and aims that give one's life direction is to adopt concerns and aims that have no direction—to satisfy this desire, and then that one—and thus to give up on a conception of one's self as an agent who acts for a purpose, who has a life as a whole, and a self, to construct. It is to fail to see that desire needs a direction. Moreover, one can fail to recognize that pleasure also needs a direction in one's life, a direction that it does not give itself. Indeed, this is a failure

---

[61] Cp. the similar objection that Plato makes at *Gorgias* 492d ff. that centering one's existence around pleasure is to give up on the idea of becoming someone in favor of repeating an aimless cycle of need and satisfaction.

[62] This does not mean, however, that a pleasureless life is a preferable life for us, or would be preferable for us if it were possible. *Con.* D. Frede (1993: 66 n. 2 *ad* 55b–c). Now Socrates' mention of the pleasureless life at 55a does refer to the life of the gods, which he mentioned at 22b–c. But I think that Socrates' point is that people who value pleasure as a good would be unable to explain what the goodness of the gods' life could possibly consist in, since on their view generation and destruction is good for its own sake, so that the gods' life must be missing some crucial good.

to recognize that one's whole life needs a direction, which pleasure cannot give. Pleasure as Plato understands it can be adopted as one's ultimate aim in life only at the cost of surrendering the notion of a direction that embraces the whole self. It turns out that the life governed by the pursuit of pleasure really is a clam's life after all.

And this is why Plato turns his attention to 'true', 'pure' pleasures, which exist only as long as one does *not* become agitated about acquiring their objects. To see this, notice that it cannot be just the *object* of a pure pleasure that makes it pure. The simple pleasure of enjoying the sweet fragrance and flavor of good wine can, after all, become anything but simple. When people develop strong cravings for such experiences, what they enjoy is not the beauty of the wine itself, but the more intense pleasure of satisfying their craving for it. In such cases, the craving itself has become integral to the pleasure, and thus to the entire pursuit. Such a pleasure is, therefore, no longer true, on Plato's view, because the same object is now enjoyed not for what it is itself but *qua* object of craving. This illustrates, I think, the key difference between true and false pleasures: false pleasures can elevate neediness itself to the status of a kind of goal, and true pleasures cannot. The difference between them, then, is the place one gives them among one's concerns, and thus in one's life. And so the problem with hedonism is not that it makes some pleasures central in one's life rather than others, but that what it makes central in one's life is something that robs one's life of its direction, by one's very act of making it central.[63]

6.4   Rational Incorporation: Why Pleasure is Necessary for Happiness

Pleasure, then, can be a final good, but it cannot be life's final *end* (τέλος), and that is the fundamental problem with all forms of hedonism. Pleasure is something that looks to a goal, and that explains not only why it cannot be itself a unifying goal for one's life but also how pleasure can be given a direction, for as one's goals take shape, so too do one's pleasures. Here we should recall the idea of 'limit' being brought to the 'unlimited' to form a 'mixture', or structured whole: pleasure is a natural but unstructured part of the human constitution, while reason is a natural part of human constitution that grasps the structure of a happy, flourishing human life and brings it about in the whole of one's nature. Hence, while to do well with wealth is to have good behavior and attitudes where wealth is concerned, to do well with pleasure is for one's pleasure to be itself

---

[63] Consequently, even an alleged 'hedonism of true pleasure' would fare no better on Plato's view. The key to salvaging hedonism, on Plato's view, would not be a matter of identifying the right family of pleasures, since Plato's worry is that hedonism is structurally unfit as a form of eudaimonism, since it embodies a fundamental confusion about the nature of human goals.

a kind of good behavior and good attitude. This is what we mean by rational incorporation in the case of such psychic goods as pleasure.[64]

Plato explores the idea of rational incorporation as he comes at last to consider what sort of mixture the good life is. He begins by examining the types of reason that belong to the good life, arguing that there are many different kinds of knowledge and reasoning, differing in terms of their purity and precision.[65] Of these, the truest and purest is the science of dialectic, which is about what is real in the most absolute sense, and which thus deserves the title of 'intellect' and 'reason' (57e–59d). It is important to see what Socrates thinks knowledge or intelligence is like, in order to understand how and why it plays the role it does in the 'mixing' of the good life. For pleasure is mixed into the good life only after all forms of knowledge and reason, and even then only by their permission (62d–63e), since knowledge and reason have the greatest affinity to goodness (60b). In this mixture, as in all mixtures, the nature of its goodness consists in measure and proportion, as well as beauty, excellence, and truth (64d–65a):

[A]ny kind of mixture that does not in some way or other possess measure or the nature of proportion will necessarily corrupt its ingredients and most of all itself. For there would be no blending in such cases at all but really an unconnected medley, the ruin of whatever happens to be contained in it.
Very true.
But now we notice that the force of the good has taken refuge in an alliance with the nature of the beautiful. For measure and proportion manifest themselves in all areas as beauty and virtue.
Undeniably.
But we did say that truth is also included along with them in our mixture?
Indeed.
Well, then, if we cannot capture the good in one form, we will have to take hold of it in a conjunction of three: beauty, proportion, and truth. Let us affirm that these things should be treated as a unity and be held responsible for what is in the mixture, for its goodness is what makes the mixture itself a good one.
Very well stated.   (64d9–65a6)

What is clear here[66] is that the goodness of the good life consist in the beauty, proportion, and truth that are manifest in all aspects of that life, that is, its order and proportion toward which an intelligent agent organizes the various aspects of a life into a good life. Plato thus ranks reason and pleasure relative to one

---

[64] And we can say the same about *pains*, as well: the capacity to find something grieving and disturbing is as important a part of human existence as the capacity to find something enjoyable. Plato seems to say as much in the *Laws*: 'Pleasure *and pain*, you see, flow like two springs released by nature. If a man draws the right amount from the right one at the right time, he lives a happy life; but if he draws unintelligently at the wrong time, his life will be rather different' (I, 636d7–e3, emphasis added). I shall return to this passage in the next chapter.

[65] Plato first distinguishes two basic branches of knowledge, the 'practical' kinds and the kinds involved in education and learning (55d), the latter being purer than the former. Moreover, within each of these branches are two further groups, which also differ in purity (55d–57a), but with which we need not concern ourselves now.

[66] See Sayre (1987) for a closer (but controversial) discussion.

another, by identifying three aspects of goodness: namely truth, moderation, and beauty, and Protarchus himself now readily claims that on each count reason is more akin to goodness than pleasure is (65b–66a). Furthermore, since the purest forms of reason—being most true and constant—are most akin to goodness, Socrates establishes a serial ordering[67] between reason and pleasure, such that reason is mixed in ahead of pleasure, and pleasure is admitted into the good life only by reason's permission.[68] As we saw in the previous chapter, the contributions that reason and pleasure make to the good life are different in kind: one being what acts to make life good, the other that in relation to which it acts.

When reason is asked about pleasure's admission into the good life, we find that pleasure as a whole cannot be admitted. Great and intense pleasures, reason says, must be left out, as they are disruptive of its work (63d–e);[69] but it does allow true pleasures into the good life, and its reason for doing so is instructive. Reason, colorfully personified,[70] says that the true and pure pleasures are to be considered its own kin, and indeed such pleasures belong to the healthy and self-controlled person, and they accompany virtue as attendants accompany a deity (63e):[71]

> Our discussion [with reason and knowledge] would then continue as follows: 'Will you have any need to associate with the strongest and most intensive pleasures in addition to the true pleasures?' we will ask them. 'Why on earth should we need them, Socrates?' they might reply, 'They are a tremendous impediment to us, since they infect the souls in which they dwell with madness or even prevent our own development altogether. Furthermore, they totally destroy most of our offspring, since neglect leads to forgetfulness. But as to the true and pure pleasures you mentioned, those regard as our kin. And besides, also add the pleasures of health and of temperance and all those that commit themselves to virtue as to their deity and follow it around everywhere.' (63d1–e7)[72]

The key is to see how pleasure is related to virtue, which *is* the constituent of our happiness, since it is as virtue that the unity of beauty, proportion, and truth manifests itself in a human life (64e). Clearly such pleasures, being reason's 'kin', have a close acquaintance with reason, and thus with virtue—they *belong* together. But what does that mean?

---

[67] This is important, because Socrates needs to show more than that the contribution of reason to the good life is merely *different* from that of pleasure; see Gosling (1975: 224 f.); see also Plato, trans. Waterfield (1982: 33), for related concerns; Annas (1999: 152 f.); Irwin (1995: 325); Hackforth (1945: 134, 138). [68] Cf. Gosling (1975: 225f.); Gosling and Taylor (1982: 135).

[69] Cp. the *Phaedo*, in which certain pleasures are to be omitted from the life of virtue because they serve to 'rivet' the soul to the body, frustrating its pure, rational activity. See chapter 3.

[70] Hackforth (1945: 128), notes that the personification of reason and pleasure suggests a harmonious cohabitation within a balanced whole, rather than an imposed *modus vivendi*.

[71] I accept the view that there are five, rather than six, items identified and ranked at 66a–d. For the view that there are five, see D. Frede (1993: lxvi); Gosling (1975: 224). For the view that there are six (the sixth being the necessary pleasures) see Damascius, *Lectures on the* Philebus § 253 (reporting the view of Syrianus); Hackforth (1945: 139, 140 n. 3); Plato, trans. Waterfield (1982: 34).

[72] Cf. the point I made in Ch. 3, that Plato in the *Phaedo* is hostile not toward pleasure *per se*, but toward pleasure inasmuch as one fails to act rationally in relation to it.

It is important to recognize that those pleasures are 'the true and pure pleasures' and 'the pleasures of health and of temperance and all those that commit themselves to virtue'. As we have seen, what makes a pleasure true or false is the place one gives it among one's concerns, and thus in one's life. Notice, first, that Plato thinks that pleasure *can* be given the right kind of place; there are *reasonable* pleasures, and so pleasure is a conditional good. More than that, some pleasures are actually *inseparable* from virtue: the pleasures of temperance, for instance, are clearly not the pleasures in relation to which temperance acts, but the pleasures of being a temperate person, and more generally the pleasures of virtue are the pleasures that are characteristic of a virtuous person. As we have seen, pleasures are value-laden attitudes, and so to be virtuous is to have healthy and realistic values, *and* to enjoy one's life in ways that reflect those healthy and realistic values. This has the important consequence that virtuous people do not merely have a 'handle' on their pleasures, but have been changed and transformed in their pleasures, so that their pleasures are a part of their healthy and reasonable outlook on themselves and their real interests. Pleasure follows goals, and where goals are transformed, so too is pleasure. My reasonable desiring is one aspect of virtue, just as is my treating others reasonably, and the same will be true of my being pleased reasonably—it just is one expression of my wisdom and reason, and thus one *aspect* of my virtuous activity. Enjoying my life in a virtuous way is one kind of being virtuous. It is the product of my reason and wisdom bringing order into my desires and capacities for pleasure.[73] Human virtue consists in reason's informing with order and 'limit' the otherwise unlimited materials of the self as a whole (see 64e), including one's desires, emotions, and pleasures.[74]

Pleasure therefore has a very different role to play in the good life than we—and Protarchus—might have originally thought. And understanding this role will enable us to explain how it is that pleasure is necessary for happiness, despite being only conditionally good: it is necessary not as an indispensable ingredient in addition to reason and virtue, but as a *part* of virtuous character as a whole. This is so because virtue is the perfection not merely of one part or dimension of the self but of the whole self, and pleasure is part of the self—in fact, it is a very

---

[73] Taking the pleasures of the virtuous life as being generated as reason brings order upon the soul also avoids the possible worry that the good life will contain pleasures of *becoming* virtuous, but not of *being* virtuous (see Annas (1999: 156 f.); cp. the similar worries of Gosling and Taylor (1982) regarding *Republic* IX, which I discussed in Ch. 4). For *being* virtuous, on my view, consists in a constant *living* in accordance with reason. The *Philebus*, then, is amenable to the idea that pleasure supervenes on the happy life.

[74] Ficino, *The* Philebus *Commentary* I.34, also argues for the unity of pleasure and wisdom, and says that other Platonists had argued thus as well. Since our happiness, and thus our final end, must be one thing and unified, pleasure and wisdom must therefore be unified. That they are unified is the view, he says, of Porphyry and Plotinus, since the pleasure of understanding can scarcely be distinguished from the act of understanding itself (*quoniam voluptas intelligentiae vix ab ipsa distinguitur*, 425); see also Damascius, *Lectures on the* Philebus §§ 87–8. They become unified as together they seek the good. When the soul grasps the good through the intellect, the result is wisdom; when the soul retains that grasp through the will, the result is pleasure; and this condition in the whole soul is the happiness of the human life. This view suggests that reason structures the soul, and a certain pleasure is itself part of that structure.

special part of the self, in which one's deepest values and concerns find their affective expression. Pleasure is not merely something that we should have the right attitudes about, as for instance wealth is, but actually one of the very attitudes that we take toward other things. It is therefore always a part of one's character, either for better or for worse, and so we cannot give a complete account of virtue unless we take into account the pleasures of the virtuous character that ascribe value to things in rational ways. Pleasure transformed is part of the good life, not because virtue is not enough for the good life, but precisely because virtue *is* enough. Pleasure transformed, like every aspect of the transformed self, is necessary for happiness because that is the kind of whole that virtue is.

One of Plato's central aims in the *Philebus* is to take seriously the thesis that:

(1) *Pleasure is necessary for happiness, because pleasure has a power with respect to happiness that virtue does not have, such that happiness is incomplete without it.*

This thesis, a version of the additive conception of happiness, is embodied in Protarchus' initial position, and in much popular thought. Plato argues against it on the grounds that the power to determine happiness is the power to provide good direction within one's life, in all of its dimensions, and that is a power that pleasure does not have, but which intelligent agency does. This is the point of Plato's claim that pleasure is among the 'unlimited', inchoate material of a good life, while reason is the cause that makes a good life good. Moreover, it is in this sense that pleasure is a conditional good, and intelligent agency an uncondi- tional good.

However, Plato does hold that pleasure is necessary for happiness since pleasure is a part of the self to be transformed and rationally incorporated into the life of virtue. Consequently:

(2) *Pleasure is necessary for happiness, because the pleasure of a virtuous life is necessary for a virtuous life, and a virtuous life determines happiness.*

In fact, the thesis that virtue determines and suffices for happiness actually *requires* the thesis that pleasure is necessary for happiness—so far from being in tension with it—given Plato's understanding of rational incorporation and the holistic nature of virtue.[75]

---

[75] I think that these two ways of thinking of the necessity of pleasure (or rather, 'joy') for happiness are also evident in Arius Didymus' discussion of the εὐπάθειαι. On the one hand, Arius says that while virtue is necessary for happiness, 'joy and good spirits' are not (Stobaeus, *Anthology* II.6d). But, on the other, Arius also classifies joy and good spirits among 'good things' (II.5b, 5c, 5g, 5k), and even claims that being joyful is a morally perfect action (II.11e); this line of thought is clearly related to the Stoic view that joy and good spirits are concomitants of virtue (Diogenes Laertius, *Lives* VII.94, 116–17), in which case being a joyful person is part of what it is to *be* a virtuous person (cf. Seneca, *Letters to Lucilius* 23.3–5). The Stoics never take seriously the idea that the virtuous life could be affectless—in fact, quite the contrary (see Diogenes Laertius, *Lives* VII.117)—and since such a life cannot include unreasonable affections (πάθη), it *must* include reasonable affections, or the εὐπάθειαι. In that case, however, it would seem that joy is necessary for happiness after all. The simplest explanation of this apparent tension, I think, is that what Arius in fact denies is that the εὐπάθειαι are necessary as

Notice too that if rational incorporation rules out thesis (1), it also rules out:

(3) *Pleasure is necessary for happiness, because, lamentably, we cannot do without it.*

On this thesis, pleasure would be rather like an annoying neighbor, to borrow Olympiodorus' example (*Commentary on the* Phaedo 4.3), to whose presence one must simply resign oneself as unavoidable. But Plato does much better than this, by offering a compelling psychological analysis of pleasure which demonstrates not merely that pleasure requires a limit but also what *kind* of limit pleasure is capable of receiving, portraying inchoate pleasure as transformable and capable of coming to adopt limit within itself, given proper guidance, as a child is capable of maturing and coming to accept for himself the sort of direction his parents now seek to instill in him. Thesis (3), by contrast, holds that pleasure can only be managed and contained, as a wild animal can be tamed and taught to act, but only in ways that it never understands, much less accepts for itself. Children can be transformed into mature adults but, with beasts, one must simply gain and keep the upper hand. But to treat pleasures as something for me to get an upper hand over ignores the fact that my pleasures are part of *me*, and as such they are part of the worth of my character, and indeed of my very identity.

Plato's moral psychology is crucial for understanding what place he takes pleasure to have in the good life. I have argued here for a new way of understanding what this place is, that makes sense of both Plato's insistence that pleasure is only conditionally good, and his insistence that pleasure is necessary for the good life. This understanding has allowed us to see a unified and coherent ethical view of pleasure in Plato, avoiding both hedonist and asceticist interpretations, and making sense of the centrality and holism of virtue in Plato's ethics. None the less, while Plato's ethical evaluation of pleasure is quite promising, and while the sort of psychological analysis he provides in the *Philebus* does seem to support it, still it also seems that Plato was attracted to other psychological models as well, which do not. It is to this issue that we now turn in earnest, in the final chapter.

---

producers of happiness, as if they had some power of their own with respect to happiness, without which virtue is insufficient for happiness; I do *not* think that he means to deny that the happy life is a joyful life. Rather, on Arius' view, virtue is such as to benefit, and I think that joy is among those things with respect to which he says virtue brings about benefit. In that case, Arius denies the necessity of joy for happiness in the sense of thesis (1) above, but *not* in the sense of thesis (2).

7

Pleasure, Value, and Moral Psychology in the *Republic, Laws,* and *Timaeus*

In his allegorical novel *The Great Divorce,* C. S. Lewis figuratively depicts the transformation of the various aspects of people's lives by spiritual enlightenment. One character in his story is burdened with a lizard that represents his passion, a depiction intended to illustrate how ugly and deformed this area of his psyche has become. While the man wishes to be rid of the lizard and its tyranny over him, still he cannot bring himself to let it go, which he sees as giving up that part of himself altogether, and he cannot imagine his life without it. Once he does give it up, the lizard passes away, only to be transformed into a beautiful horse, and the man discovers the beauty of which he never knew his passion was capable. He does not get rid of his passion, nor does he merely gain the upper hand over something that remains a lizard. Instead, he becomes free as his passion changes from a tyrannical master over the rest of his psyche to a willing and cooperative partner. This allegory is meant to illustrate that becoming morally mature is not to lose any of the aspects of one's humanity, or to diminish them and subordinate them to some other aspects, but to effect their transformation into new, different, and beautiful things that form a part of one's new life as a whole and integrated being.[1]

Lewis seems to understand the conformity of an integrated person's passions to her practical intelligence as a kind of *agreement*: the passions do not retain their former character, only under tighter rein, but take on a new character altogether; and while in Lewis's allegory that character remains an animal character, its change is clearly intended to depict that the transformed person in the allegory now has an entirely different perspective on his passions, which now work in different, healthier ways. The change from lizard to horse also shows a change from slavery to one's passions—as the lizard forces the man where it wants by sinking its claws into him—to a freedom secured not by forceful control of a naturally unwilling servant, but by a leadership over a willing cohort that, like a good horse, will follow as one directs it. Consequently, Lewis seems to

---

[1] See Lewis (1946: 98–103). I thank Mark LeBar for bringing this work and its relevance to my attention. Compare this sort of transformation to the transformation within the virtuous person from the πάθη to the εὐπάθειαι in Stoic psychology and ethics.

embrace what I shall call the *agreement model* of psychic conformity, and to reject the competing *control model*. On the control model, the passions may conform to reason, but they never change their character so as to cooperate with reason, just as a trained lion conforms to the commands of a tamer whose direction it is never capable of internalizing and cooperating with. If Lewis had adopted this model, he would have depicted the emotional change not as a change within his passion itself, but only in the man's ability to keep the upper hand over something alien that still continues to resist him.

Clearly, the agreement model is a more attractive and hopeful model of the relation between reason and the affective areas of the soul within a mature, virtuous agent. It offers the possibility of real change: of being free at last of harmful and tyrannical desires, wayward emotions, and disturbing impulses, and of taking hold of a new way of living. And it will also account for much of our experience, since we *do* change and grow into new people with new thoughts about who we are and what matters to us. A mature adult, after all, does not merely have greater control over an awkward emotional life that is still essentially what it was in youth. She has a new emotional life that is more complex, and that reflects her more mature way of reasoning and reflecting. However, the control model also seems true to our experience, as, despite these changes, we often find ourselves still struggling with the same desires, emotions, and impulses we have so long wished to be rid of, and unfortunately it can also reinforce the despair and discouragement we sometimes feel as these struggles seem time and again to come to naught. How, then, should we choose between these two very different models of our moral development? Or, if we cannot do without either model, how should we reconcile them into a unified account of moral development?

These are hard questions for philosophical psychology. However, at present I do not wish to argue for one model over the other, but to show that these two models sit side by side in Plato's work on psychology, that Plato does not reconcile them to one another, and why this lack of reconciliation matters for his analysis of pleasure within his ethical framework. It should be clear by now that Plato's ethical analysis of pleasure—resting as it does on the notion of rational incorporation, and on pleasure's capacity to become a part of one's very excellence of character—requires the agreement model of moral maturity and psychic integration, and is in tension with the control model. As we saw in the previous chapter on the *Philebus*, Plato argues that pleasure is a conditional good capable of rational transformation as part of the virtuous perspective, and thus offers a supporting psychological model on which pleasure is a value-laden attitude or perspective, which changes as one's conception of one's self and one's central concerns changes. However, in other dialogs this sort of agreement model of psychic integration will appear alongside the opposing control model, calling into question whether Plato really does have a unified psychology to support the notion of rational incorporation after all.

I shall argue in this chapter that these two models appear together in Plato for the simple reason that each captures, in its own way, aspects of our psychology

Plato finds too important to ignore. As I suggested above, our experience of moral development suggests that pleasures, emotions, and desires are Janus-faced, working now by agreement, now by control, and this Plato was astute enough to see and honest enough to admit. What he did not see—what is, after all, extremely difficult for anyone to see, even after these two and a half millennia—is how to account for the Janus-faced nature of the soul within a single, unified psychological model. Consequently, Plato does not provide for his ethical analysis of pleasure the sort of psychological theory it demands. This does not mean, of course, that we have misunderstood his ethical analysis of pleasure, but only that that analysis has ties to even deeper philosophical issues about which Plato's thought remains incomplete. And there is a payoff for taking a closer look at these issues: not only do we bring into greater relief the connections between an ethical analysis of pleasure and a psychological analysis but we also see more clearly what demands an ethical analysis of pleasure places on philosophical psychology, and what limits our psychology places on our ethical analyses. Consequently, in seeing why and how far short Plato's psychology falls of the ethical ideal of the rational incorporation of pleasure, we shall be better able to see what sort of psychological account *we* shall need to develop, if that ideal should also appeal to us.

7.1 Agreement and Control: Two Models of the Soul in the *Republic*

Let us begin with a closer look at these models of psychic integration. In book IV of the *Republic* Plato famously divides the soul into three parts: the rational part or reason; the spirited or emotional part; and the appetitive or desiring part.[2] Exactly what sort of 'parts' these are is a difficult and controversial issue, but fortunately we need not focus on it here.[3] What is more important at present are Plato's different portrayals of the relationship between reason on the one hand and desire and emotion on the other. Of course, our aim is to examine the relationship between reason and *pleasure*, but it is important to remember that for Plato pleasure cannot be prized apart from desire and emotion. For one thing, we have already seen in the *Philebus* (47d ff.) that Plato treats certain

---

[2] I shall refer throughout to the second part as 'the emotional part' (or simply 'emotion', where this is unlikely to be confused with a particular emotion) since it is evidently that part of us capable of feelings that motivate us and are complex enough to include a sense of shame, of decency, of indignation, of anger, and so on, although Plato does focus primarily on emotions such as anger, which he takes to be aggressive and competitive; see Annas (1981: 127 f.). Whether the third part should be described as desirous or appetitive is actually a deep issue, as we shall see below. For an excellent discussion of the parts of the soul, see Cooper (1999*a*).

[3] See Annas (1981: 124) for a discussion of the indeterminacy of Plato's talk of 'parts' in *Republic* IV (cf. N. White (1979: 125), and 142–6) for a provocative interpretation of the parts as a 'committee of homunculi' (on which *con*. Robinson (1971: 47 f.)). *Con*. Penner (1978), who argues for a strict sense of 'parts', and for a bipartite soul (reason and desire) rather than tripartite. For a discussion of reason and desire as parts, see Robinson (1971) and Stalley (1975).

emotions as kinds of pleasures and pains, and we shall see below that Plato does so in the *Laws* as well; accordingly, the Alcinous tells us that for Plato pleasure and pain are the genera of which the emotions are species.[4] For another, we have also seen in the *Philebus* that desire is connected to pleasure inasmuch as pleasure construes its objects in terms of their perceived ability to fill our lacks. And as we saw in Chapter 4, Plato claims in the *Republic* that the emotional and desiring parts of the soul have their own characteristic pleasures, which also attach to ways of life in which the concerns of those parts of the soul are made one's central concerns in life as a whole. Consequently, if pleasure can be transformed by virtue, then our emotions and desires must be capable of rational transformation as well.[5] Are they?

7.1.1   Reason and emotion

Let us begin with the relation between reason and emotion, and then consider the relation between reason and desire.[6] Plato characterizes the relation between reason and emotion in several different ways at *Republic* IV, 436a–441c and IX, 588b–592b. These characterizations can be seen to fall into roughly three groups.

(1) On the first sort, Plato compares the relation between reason and the emotional part to that between allies in a civil war (IV, 440a–b, e), other allies and friends (IX, 589b), and the rulers of a community and its auxiliary protectors (IV, 440d). Notice that these are relations between *persons*, with a *common* task that they *share*. In some cases, these persons stand as complete equals, as presumably friends and allies do, but even when they do not play equal roles, as rulers and auxiliaries do not, none the less they are still equal as rational beings, as the rulers give directions that the auxiliaries can then understand and adopt for themselves.

(2) Plato also compares the relationship between reason and emotion to that between humans and tame, domesticated animals, saying that the emotional part obeys reason as trained sheepdogs obey a shepherd (IV, 440d). Plato offers this comparison alongside the first, and so he seems to emphasize not the sheepdog's animal nature as such, but rather its intelligence and ability to cooperate with the shepherd as a sort of partner.[7] In each comparison, then, Plato's point is that reason and emotion are meant to work together as some sort of team or other, and this suggests that while the emotional part may depend on reason for rational direction it cannot give itself, none the less it is able to

---

[4] See Alcinous, *Handbook of Platonism* 32.2.

[5] Because of the close connections between pleasure, pain, emotion, and desire, henceforth in this chapter I shall sometimes refer to them *en masse* as 'passions'.

[6] See Gill (1996: 245–60) for an excellent discussion of the agreement and control strands in the psychology of the *Republic*; see also Gill (1985: esp. 21–4). Annas (1981: 116 f.) connects this tension to a similar tension in Plato's account of the relation between classes in the ideal city.

[7] This should remind us of the comparison of reason and emotion to a charioteer and his well-mannered horse at *Phaedrus* 253d–257b, as well as the rider and noble horse of *The Great Divorce*.

incorporate and adopt that direction, and thus be transformed by reason.[8] And, of course, this is what we mean by the *agreement model* of reason and emotion.

(3) However, Plato also compares the emotional part of the soul to a wild, unruly lion set to attack (*Republic* IX, 588e–589d), and reason to a man that must tame it (IX, 588d):

'Make a model, then, of a creature with a single—if varied and many-headed—form, arrayed all around with the heads of both wild and tame animals, and possessing the ability to change over to a different set of heads and to generate all these new bits from its own body.'[9]
'That would take some skilful modelling,' [Glaucon] remarked, 'but since words are a more plastic material than wax and so on, you may consider the model constructed.'
'A lion and a man are the next models to make, then. The first of the models, however, is to be by far the largest, and the second the second largest.'
'That's an easier job,' he said. 'It's done.'
'Now join the three of them together until they become one, as it were.'
'All right,' he said.
'And for the final coat, give them the external appearance of a single entity. Make them look like a person, so that anyone incapable of seeing what's inside, who can see only the external husk, will see a single creature, a human being.'
'It's done,' he said.   (*Republic* IX, 588c7–e2)

Notice the importance of the shift from the sheepdog to the lion: while sheepdogs are capable of working very closely with shepherds, and indeed of working at a rather sophisticated level of self-direction under the shepherd's guidance, lions (and indeed snakes, to which Plato also likens this part of the soul at IX, 590b) are incapable of entering into such genuinely *cooperative* relationships with tamers.[10] A shepherd chooses a certain breed of dog because of its natural cleverness and cooperation, and thus gives it direction by calling upon its tendencies and capacities *as a sheepdog*, but one can direct a lion only by *overpowering* its natural tendencies. Sheepdogs cooperate by learning what they are to do; at best, lions conform by being broken. The characterization of the emotional part as a lion, then, presents the *control model* of reason and emotion.

And so, Plato in one moment suggests that the emotional part of the soul has an inner logic and a capacity for an intelligence of its own, and thus is capable of

---

[8] It is this agreement which Plato invokes in his account of self-discipline at 442c–d. Indeed, in his enthusiasm over this idea he includes the desiring part in this agreement as well, to which it seems ill suited, as we shall see in the next subsection. See also N. White (1979: 129). The relation between reason and emotion is so close that Penner (1978: 108–16) has argued that they should not be treated as separate parts; but *con.* Cooper (1999a: 203–6), who argues that reason and emotion (or 'spirit') can conflict in the *Republic*, as is especially evident in the behavior of Odysseus (*Odyssey* X, ll. 17–18) to which Plato refers at 441b, 390d.
[9] We shall return below to the many-headed monster, which is meant to represent desire.
[10] Indeed, N. White (1979: 235) suggests that in this passage we should not understand 'the spirited and appetitive parts of the soul as actually agreeing, in some quasi-rational way, to taking less than they really want, like a small child who is argued into grumblingly accepting less than a full portion of cake. Rather, Plato believes, desires can be trained (largely by not being overindulged) so that they simply become less insistent.'

being directed as it develops as the kind of psychic impulse it naturally is, and in another that emotion is a naturally brutish force that must be broken and forcibly suppressed. Clearly, these are two very different models of the relation between reason and emotion, and while each model captures some part of our experience, to offer now the one and now the other just is to lack a unified model of the soul.

Perhaps, however, the tension between the agreement and control models in the *Republic* is merely apparent. For instance, we might say that images like that of taming a lion are meant to model only the *process* of educating the emotional part, and not the *relationship* that then holds between reason and the emotional part once the latter has been educated. Alternatively, we might say that the taming images are meant to model the relationship between reason and emotion in *vicious* (or immature) souls, and the alliance images the relationship in the *virtuous* soul.[11] Unfortunately, things are not so easy. For one thing, Plato says that the emotional part as a whole is a lion, but lions once tamed are *still lions*, and not sheepdogs, much less human partners.[12] Consequently, even if these images portray only the process of educating desire and emotion, we are still left wondering how something with a lion's nature could ever arrive at a relationship of agreement with reason at the end of that process. But, more than that, these beastly images are applied to *both* the vicious *and* the virtuous soul, since the comparison of the parts of the soul to a human, a lion, and a monster is introduced to illustrate the inner workings of the virtuous soul *just* as much as those of the vicious soul:

'...[O]ur words and behaviour should be designed to maximize the control the inner man has within us, and should enable him to secure the help of the leonine quality and then tend to the many-headed beast... Now, do you think the reason for the traditional condemnation of licentiousness is the same—because it allows that fiend, that huge and many-faceted creature, greater freedom than it should have?'
'Obviously,' [Glaucon] said.
'And aren't obstinacy and bad temper considered bad because they distend and invigorate our leonine, serpentine side to a disproportionate extent?'
'Yes.'
'Whereas a spoilt, soft way of life is considered bad because it makes this [*sc.* leonine] part of us so slack and loose that it's incapable of facing hardship?'
'Of course.'
'And why are lack of independence and autonomy despised? Isn't it still to do with the passionate part, because we have to subordinate it to the unruly beast and, from our earliest years, get the lion used to being insulted and to becoming a monkey instead of a lion—and all for the sake of money and to satisfy our greed?'
'Yes.'   (IX, 589a6–b2, 590a5–c7)

The difference between virtuous and vicious, then, is a difference in the *hierarchy* between the parts, and not, evidently, in the *nature* of the parts themselves.

---

[11] I thank Ellen Wagner and Eric Brown for suggesting these readings in conversation.
[12] I thank Julia Annas for this way of putting the point.

Notice also that the comparison of reason and emotion to allies (IV, 440a–b, d, e) is offered to explain the dynamics of a soul in which sharp conflict still exists between desire and the other parts, as is the 'sheepdog' analogy (440d). The agreement and control models, then, simply do not correspond to the distinction between mature and immature souls, or to that between virtuous and vicious souls.

Consequently, it is important to recognize that the issue here is not *how* one's emotional capacity is trained, but whether it is, upon training, capable of adopting a rational perspective. Do emotions come to agree with reason, through becoming ways of viewing the world as an extension of reason? Or do emotions come to conform to reason through control or containment? As we mature, do the emotions develop as better ways of viewing the world? Or is maturity a greater ability to control something that remains estranged from us (cf. αἰσχρὰ δὲ τὰ ὑπὸ τῷ ἀγρίῳ τὸ ἥμερον δουλούμενα, 589d2–3)?[13] Curiously, Plato seems to answer 'yes' to all of these questions.[14]

Moreover, it seems unlikely that Plato overlooked the difference between these models. On the contrary, he seems to have relied on that difference, as the agreement and control models appear in different contexts in the *Republic*. First, when Plato models the relation between reason and emotion with respect to the third part of the soul, desire, he depicts them as allied partners. For instance, after recounting the grim story of Leontius, who had become angry with himself for wanting to look at the corpses of executed prisoners, Socrates says:

'. . . what [this story] suggests . . . is that it's possible for anger to be at odds with desires, as if they were different things.'
'Yes, it does,' [Glaucon] agreed.
'And that's far from being an isolated case, isn't it?' I asked. 'It's not at all uncommon to find a person's desires compelling him to go against his reason, and to see him cursing himself and venting his passion on the source of the compulsion within him. It's as if there were two warring factions, with passion fighting on the side of reason. But I'm sure you wouldn't claim that you had ever, in yourself or in anyone else, met a case of passion siding with the desires against the rational mind, when the rational mind prohibits resistance.'
'No, I certainly haven't,' he said.   (IV, 440a5–b8)

---

[13] These questions raise further questions about one's identity: if the parts of my soul can function as allies, then it seems that all of the parts can function rationally together, and that all of them can be 'me'. But if some parts are brutish, incapable of being informed by reason, but must instead be controlled, then they may all conform, but they do not work *together*, and some of them seem less really 'me'. See also Annas (1999), ch. 6.

[14] And that within the same dialogue, so we cannot explain the appearance of these two models as a developmental shift. Nor is their coexistence confined to the *Republic*; as we shall see below, they recur also within the *Laws*, as well as between the psychology of the *Philebus* and that of the *Timaeus*. Consequently, even if we concede that Plato shifts from a model of the soul as unitary to a model of the soul as parsed, as well as from a more 'pedantic' model of moral education in which one's beliefs are changed to a more 'musical' model in which one's desires and emotions are habituated independent of pedantic training of one's reasoning (see Vlastos (1991: 86–8); Penner (1992: 125 f., 128 f.)), still this does nothing to resolve the present tension. Nor is it clear that such a concession would admit the sorts of sea changes in Platonic psychology that developmentalists speak of, but that is a controversy for another time.

There is a conflict, but here it is between desire, on the one hand, and reason and emotion allied, on the other. From the perspective of the desire that opposes reason, then, Plato thinks that reason and emotion appear as a joint force. Plato makes a similar point later, in book IX:

'So the alternative position, that morality is profitable, is equivalent to saying that our words and behaviour should be designed to maximize the control the inner man has within us, and should enable him to secure the help of the leonine quality and then tend to the many-headed beast as a farmer tends to his crops—by nurturing and cultivating its tame aspects, and by stopping the wild ones growing.'   (IX, 589a6–b3)

Here we see not only the opposition of reason and emotion against desire (the 'many-headed beast') but also a hint of the inherent conflict—like that between a man and a lion—between reason and the emotional part considered not from desire's perspective, but within their relation to *each other*. In fact, the relation between reason and emotion themselves seems quite like their joint relation to desire:

'Things are acceptable when they subject the bestial aspects of our nature to the human— or it might be more accurate to say the divine—part of ourselves, but they're objectionable when they cause the oppression of our tame side under the savage side [τὰ μὲν καλὰ τὰ ὑπὸ τῷ ἀνθρώπῳ, μᾶλλον δὲ ἴσως τὰ ὑπὸ τῷ θείῳ τὰ θηριώδη ποιοῦντα τῆς φύσεως, αἰσχρὰ δὲ τὰ ὑπὸ τῷ ἀγρίῳ τὸ ἥμερον δουλούμενα].'   (IX, 589c8–d3)

Evidently, from the point of view of reason, both the emotional and the desirous parts are 'bestial', and both are to be subjugated. So far from being unaware of the difference between these ways of modeling the relations within the soul, then, Plato seems to exploit those differences to capture the nature of those relations as they appear when viewed from different perspectives within the soul. Plato's account of the soul is not unified, and he even seems to find its disunity useful.

Surely Plato offers this Janus-faced account because the emotional part of the soul itself does seem Janus-faced, and Plato captures that fact about it by switching between two different models of reason and emotion.[15] Indeed, this is a fact about emotion that any adequate treatment of emotion must take into account.[16] For instance, Aristotle also attests to the Janus-faced nature of the

---

[15] We should also note that Plato amplifies the Janus-faced nature of the emotions for himself, by committing at the outset to a sharp division between reason and emotion as distinct parts of the soul. Plato therefore struggles because, if emotion is capable of agreeing with reason, then emotion must be able somehow to *share* reason's perspective; but if emotion is not reason, then how can it share reason's perspective—would it not have to *be* a kind of reason to do that? See also N. White (1979: 126), who also comments on a similar problem in relating reason and desire (124). By distinguishing parts of the soul in terms of their conflict with one another, Plato puts himself in a very bad position to account for the agreement he insists often holds between reason and the emotional part of the soul, while keeping them distinct parts.

[16] Nussbaum (1994: 379 f.) captures this fact about emotion especially well: 'We want to give [grief, e.g.] a seat that is specifically human, and discerning enough, complex enough, to house such a complex and evaluatively discriminating response.... But then it will need to be very much like reason: capable of the same acts of selection, evaluation, and vision that are usually taken to be the works of reason.... But ... if it is true that emotion's seat must be capable of many cognitive

emotions, and anger in particular, noting: on the one hand, that anger is based on judgments, is situated within an understanding of such complex matters as social position, manners, and adequate rectification, and tends to arise, terminate, and alter in intelligible ways; but, on the other, that anger can change and even terminate independent of any change in what the anger is about, and in general that anger tends to be 'short-sighted'.[17] Moreover, it is because Plato thinks of the emotions in these two ways that such diverse thinkers as Galen and Chrysippus—the former portraying conflict between reason and emotion as a battle between a rational force and an irrational force, the latter as vacillation between two perspectives on what one has reason to do—could both later claim, with some reason, to be heirs of Plato.[18] But, of course, to say that Plato presents these two models deliberately and even with philosophical motivation is not to say that they constitute a unified theory of emotion (Aristotle does not offer a unified theory of the two faces of emotion, either). Plato depends on the agreement model to underwrite the rational incorporation of emotion and desire, and thus of pleasure; but with such a disjointed psychological account, Plato's hold on the agreement model becomes tenuous.

7.1.2   Reason and desire

Turning to Plato's depiction of the desirous part of the soul in the *Republic*, we should take special note of two things. One is that the part of the soul in which Plato locates desires is actually defined not in terms of desires in the strict sense, but in terms of *appetites*, and the differences matter. For one thing, one needs a reason to desire something, but not to have an appetite; and, for another, desires are frequently terminated without being satisfied, but appetites are not. For example, when I feel the need to drink, I may look at a glass of iced tea and desire to drink it. I have that desire for a reason—in this case, because I feel thirsty, and the iced tea appears cool and satisfying—but I do not feel thirsty for a reason; if I have that appetite then that is all there is to it. Moreover, if the iced tea should turn out to be tepid, say, I may stop desiring it, although I shall be no

operations, there also seems to be an affective side to emotion that we have difficulty housing in the soul's rational part.' Nussbaum goes on to analyze the Stoic theory of emotion as designed to handle this sort of duality. See also Cooper (1999*b*: 461 ff.).

[17] See Aristotle, *Rhetoric* II.1–4, 6, 8.

[18] See esp. Galen, *On Hippocrates' and Plato's Doctrines* 3.3.13–24; for the Stoic view, see esp. Plutarch, *On Moral Virtue* 446f–447a; see also Gill (1983); Annas (2001: 110–18). It is an interesting question whether either of these unified positions can account fully for the Janus-faced nature of the emotions. Unfortunately, Galen seems to have opted for a rather one-sided approach, making emotions work by sheer strength alone (people act as they do depending on the relative strengths of reason and emotion within them, which generally vary, he says, along ethnic lines). Likewise, Alcinous reconstructs a Platonic account of emotion by focusing on only one of the faces of emotion, citing the phenomenon of emotion's behaving in ways that apparently resist our agency (*Handbook* 32.1). By contrast, Posidonius seems to have tapped into the power within the Stoic analysis of emotion to capture its two faces; see Cooper (1999*b*), ch. 21. On issues of conflict, harmony, and partitioning in Platonic psychology, and its possible relations to Chrysippus' psychology, see the recent work of Gill, esp. (1997) and (1998).

less thirsty for it than I was before. Likewise, I can also reason with my desires in a way that I cannot reason with my appetites. I may decide that I prefer, all things considered, to abstain from the iced tea (perhaps my doctor has warned me about caffeine), and so shift my desire to something else, or at least immobilize it, but I cannot do the same with my thirst itself, except by quenching it.

In fact, Plato himself makes just these observations about appetite. Hunger and thirst, for instance, he analyzes as hunger for food and thirst for drink *simpliciter*, as opposed to thirst and hunger for *good* (or hot, or cold) food and drink (437d–439b), in order to capture the familiar and often tragic fact that having nothing good to drink available, or having reasons not to drink, does nothing to stop one's thirst.[19] But where does this leave *desire*? On this account, although appetite is not simply a pain of needing, but a pain that has an intentional object, none the less appetite also seems to have little to do with the sorts of advanced concerns in terms of which agents are able to desire such things as complex plans and even whole ways of life, and enjoy such plans and ways of life *as* meeting their desires.[20] By treating basic physical needs such as raw thirst and hunger as representative of desire in general (ὅλως τὰς ἐπιθυμίας), lumping them together with 'wishing' and 'wanting' (τὸ ἐθέλειν καὶ τὸ βούλεσθαι, 437b8), Plato ends up with an unhappy, heterogeneous amalgam instead of a coherent psychic part.[21]

This analysis presents more problems for Plato than its mere inelegance. It actually conflicts with how Plato thinks desire really works. For example, consider Leontius' morbid curiosity, which seems to work as a desire rather than as an appetite:

'. . . Leontius the son of Aglaeon was coming up from the Piraeus, outside the North Wall but close to it, when he saw some corpses with the public executioner standing near by. On the one hand, he experienced the desire to see them, but at the same time he felt disgust and averted his gaze. For a while, he struggled and kept his hands over his eyes, but finally he was overcome by the desire; he opened his eyes wide, ran up to the corpses, and said, "There you are, you wretches! What a lovely sight! I hope you feel satisfied!" '
'Yes, I've heard that story too,' [Glaucon] said.
'Now, what it suggests,' I said, 'is that it's possible for anger to be at odds with the desires, as if they were different things.'
'Yes, it does,' he agreed.   (IV, 439e7–440a7)

---

[19] Cf. Vlastos (1991: 87).

[20] Notice that although Plato starts with appetites (hunger and thirst, specifically) in his analysis of desire in the *Philebus* (34d ff.), his focus there is on an appetite's necessary orientation toward an object, a point he then extends to more sophisticated desires as well, arguing eventually that desire is always set within a set of concerns and a conception of the self; and so there he seems to avoid either conflating desires with, or reducing them to, appetites. By contrast, in the *Republic* Plato begins with the same similarity between desire and appetite, but develops it in the opposite direction, making desires seem equivalent in scope and sophistication to mere appetites.

[21] Thus, although it might be tempting to treat the desiring part as a purely biological capacity (and who thinks that raw hunger can be directed by reasons?), we must see that it is not *just* that, but an amalgam of biological drives, *and* other, more complex, kinds of desires. Notice also that in books VIII and IX those who follow the desiring part represent not one kind of life, but three very different kinds (more on this below). On this amalgam see Annas (1981: 125, 129–31, 139–42); Cooper (1999a: 195–9).

Now Plato denies that appetites always result in actions aimed at satisfying them, although an appetite can be one reason among many for taking some course of action (see 439a–b). And in principle Leontius might have ceased desiring to look at the corpses without having satisfied that desire, if he had decided that, say, he simply could not spare the time to stop and look, even though such a decision would not cause him to stop feeling curious. So even if we say that Leontius has a curious appetite, still what actually moves him seems to be a curious *desire*, that is, a desire to satisfy his curiosity, all things considered, and so Leontius' action is a case of desire at work, not merely appetite. Of course, we might say that Leontius was angry with himself not only for having a desire to satisfy his curious appetite but also for feeling such curiosity in the first place; but then Leontius must take himself to have no good *reason* for feeling curious, and therefore that he *needs* a reason to feel curious—and in that case even his initial curiosity seems much more like a desire than an appetite, after all.[22] Consequently, Plato seems to offer Leontius as an example not merely of wanting conflicting things, but of deciding badly between conflicting reasons, but that is a point that Plato's analysis of desire as merely a form of appetite cannot support. And that analysis presents an even more serious problem for Plato's discussion of the 'mercenary' life in books VIII and IX, a life spent seeking money in order to satisfy one's desires (580d–581a). Plato clearly believes that the mercenary life has its own distinctive type of plan and conception of the good, and it is difficult in the extreme to see how appetite, as Plato defines it, could ever take that kind of lead.[23] Plato focuses on appetite, when what we really need to understand—and what he really wants to talk about—is desire.

Moreover, while Plato recognizes that the third part of the soul has many diverse 'manifestations', and treats it as one thing only by focusing on its 'most powerful and prevalent aspect . . . because of the intensity of our desires for food, drink, sex, and so on' (580e1, 3–4), still this diversity within the third part threatens Plato's entire tripartite model of the soul. For one thing, it seems that the third part must be split into further parts, since desires are not merely distinct from appetites, but can actually *conflict* with them. In fact, this is apparent in Plato's own example of the thirsty person who desires not to drink (439c–d), as well as from the common experience of being hungry and desiring not to be, or of having a strong sexual appetite when one desires not to (or vice versa). Plato glosses this sort of conflict as a conflict between reason (or, in other cases, emotion) and the third part of the soul, but this only serves to expose a further threat: each part of the soul, on Plato's view, has its own desires and pleasures (see 580d), but it is difficult to see how Plato could then avoid the possibility of conflict among desires within the same part. For instance, Leontius' anger seems to be based on a conception of himself—more precisely, on a *desire* to be a certain kind of person—that he finds out of line with his

---

[22] Notice that one can intelligibly become angry with oneself for having drunk or eaten the wrong thing or in the wrong way, but not for being thirsty or hungry in the first place.
[23] See also Annas (1981: 129 f.).

desire to gawk at the corpses;[24] but, of course, this illustrates that a person may be undecided and uncertain about who he is or wants to be, and may therefore form conflicting desires based on different half-formed conceptions of himself. It would be entirely *ad hoc* to insist that such conflicting desires must be located in separate parts of the soul, since each of these desires seems to be the same basic kind of desire as that on the basis of which Leontius becomes angry with himself, and which seems to characterize the emotional part of the soul generally.[25]

The second thing to notice about Plato's discussion of desire in the *Republic* is his representation of desire not as a kind of animal at all—not even a wild one— but as something hideous and unearthly: while Plato depicts emotion as a lion tamed by reason, he depicts desire as a many-headed monster, a hydra to be conquered by the human with the lion's help (IX, 589a–b).[26] Not only does this depiction seem to rule out any sort of partnership between reason and desire, even a 'partnership' forged and sustained by force, but it is also difficult to miss the point that, on this view, my desires are not really part of who *I* am—after all, Plato thinks we need not merely beastly but *unearthly* images to represent them—and so my desires must be beyond transformation as part of my good character as a whole. In fact, the 'human' in the model of the soul controls desire not even as one would an animal, but as one would a *plant*, by 'pruning' some of the monster's heads and 'cultivating' others (589b). There is a world of difference between training a partner, a dog, or for that matter a lion to do as one wishes, and 'training' a vine to grow where one wishes, which suggests that desire is a completely non-rational force that can be reckoned with only by non-rational means.

This point about desire is especially clear in the case of the 'wild' desires. The differences between the wild desires and between them and the 'tame' ones is evident in Plato's subdivision of the desiring part of the soul, and of the three types of person who identify with the desiring part, in books VIII and IX (see esp. VIII, 547c–IX, 576b). Plato first divides desires into 'necessary' and 'unnecessary' desires (558d–559d; cf. 554a), and then further divides the unnecessary desires into merely unnecessary desires, on the one hand, and wanton and 'lawless' desires on the other (571b). The 'mercenary' or 'oligarchic' person, Plato says, lives for the sake of his necessary desires; these desires either cannot be gotten rid of altogether, such as the desire to eat life-sustaining food, or are beneficial for us to satisfy, such as the desire to eat fortifying food. The 'democratic' person, by contrast, lives for the sake of his unnecessary desires, that is, desires that can be

---

[24] I am persuaded on this point by Annas (1981: 128).

[25] It is perhaps not surprising, then, that the Stoics, who took emotions and desires to be types of perspectives on one's reasons for acting, glossed psychic conflict as a kind of indecision about one's best reasons for acting, all things considered. The importance of this point makes it somewhat alarming, however, that Aristotle should be so blasé about the parts of the soul as he is at *Nicomachean Ethics* I.13, 1102a26–32.

[26] Cp. Plato's likening of the desiring part of the soul to an ignoble, stupid, and reckless horse in the *Phaedrus*.

gotten rid of, at least through training and regimen (such as the desire to eat a large, complex diet), or that do us no good, or even harm us, when we satisfy them; these also tend to be more expensive than the necessary desires, so that the 'democratic' man is typically profligate. Finally, the 'dictatorial' person is ruled by his wanton desires, such as desires for outrageous forms of sex or crime, as are aroused in dreams unless one possess a moral, philosophical mind (571b–572b). Now it seems clear that the 'wild' desires of 589b include the wanton, frenzied desires, and probably at least some of the merely unnecessary desires. And surely the whole point of classifying certain desires as 'wild' is to suggest that there is nothing one can do with them, aside from eradicating them altogether.[27]

But what about the 'tame' desires—are they subject only to control and domination? That is not so clear. Evidently the 'tame' desires include the necessary desires, which Plato calls the 'better' desires in his discussion of the mercenary person (554d–e), and it is important to notice the role of these 'better' desires in controlling the wild, 'lawless' desires:

'... [S]ome of the unnecessary pleasures and desires strike me as lawless. We probably all contain these pleasures and desires, but they can be kept under control by convention and by the cooperation of reason and the better desires (τῶν βελτιόνων ἐπιθυμῶν μετὰ λόγου). Some people, in fact, control them so well that they get rid of them altogether or leave only a few of them in a weakened state, but they remain stronger and more numerous in others.' (IX, 571b4–c1)

Here Plato says that the better desires actually work *alongside* reason (μετὰ λόγου) to control the worse, wild desires. Likewise, although the plant analogy makes desire a non-rational force as much as the hydra analogy does, none the less the plant analogy also brings with it much gentler language, speaking of 'nurturing' and 'cultivating' (τρέφων καὶ τιθασεύων) the tame desires. Moreover, a couple of pages later Plato speaks not of three parts of the soul but of only two (590c ff.), bundling the emotional and desirous parts together, and in some places even seems to speak of a person's 'tame side' as including the better forms of both emotion and desire, along with reason (591b). Consequently, the 'tame' desires seem to be in the same position with respect to reason that emotion is: just as reason and emotion are allies from the perspective of desire as a whole, so too reason and 'tame' desires are allies from the perspective of the 'wild' desires.

However, from the perspective of reason *itself*, the tame desires still look beastly, even more so than the emotions do. Even a monster that has been 'tamed' is still a *monster*, and this way of modeling desires makes it impossible, evidently, for Plato to show that desire allies with reason out of agreement and rational incorporation, instead of merely conforming. For the tame desires conform to reason as the wild desires do not, but this does not tell us whether their conformity is a matter of agreement or of control, and the inherently

---

[27] This is clearly the point of portraying such desires as the savage heads of a hydra, as well, recalling the image of Heracles chopping the heads off the hydra and cauterizing the necks to stop them from growing back.

beastly, monstrous, and even plant-like nature that Plato's model attributes to desire makes its agreement with reason most unlikely.[28] And yet Plato *also* tries to bring desire and reason into agreement and cooperation, suggesting that our desirous part is in its good condition just in case the better desires follow with the leadership of reason.[29] As with reason and emotion, then, Plato offers two distinct models of the relation between reason and desire, and so far from unifying those two models, again leaves it most unclear how they ever could be unified. And again Plato seems to find the disunity of the account helpful for capturing different features of desires as they appear from different angles.

Here, too, it is important to remember that this portrayal of desire is not restricted to the desires of immature or vicious persons, but applies to mature, virtuous persons as well. Plato does not say that worse desires are monsters and better ones are not, but that the desirous part *as a whole* is a monster, having better and worse heads—and even a monster's 'better' head is still a monster's head. Rather, Plato's two models of the soul correspond to two different bodies of psychic phenomena—its potential for intimate harmony and its potential for sharp conflict—both of which Plato seeks to capture, but for which he has no unified psychological theory.[30]

7.1.3   Conclusions from the Republic

Plato offers two models of the relation between reason and the other parts of the soul, and these two models clearly get in each other's way. In those passages in which Plato is describing psychic harmony, his attraction to the agreement model is clear, but he is prevented from developing that psychological model

---

[28] For the indeterminacy in the *Republic* between the agreement or control model of reason and desire, see Gill (1997: 268).

[29] The question remains what is to become of certain merely unnecessary desires, namely the strictly eradicable but harmless ones (e.g. for wine, or for fun). Socrates does not mention these, but there is little reason to exclude them from the 'tame' aspects of the desirous part. In that case, Socrates' division of desires into 'wild' and 'tame' is meant to distinguish necessary and harmless unnecessary desires, on the one hand, from harmful and lawless unnecessary desires, on the other. *Con.* Waterfield (Plato, trans. Waterfield 1993: 444), who, in his note on 589b, simply maps the distinction between 'wild' and 'tame' desires onto the distinction between necessary and unnecessary desires.

[30] Gill (1996: 259 f.) claims that 'it seems clear that the depiction of the appetitive or desiring part of the psyche as "insatiable", capable of "wrecking the lives" of the other parts, and proliferating like a wild, many-headed beast or plant, is a characterization not of desire as such, but of desire as shaped by "unreasonable" beliefs and life-goals. Correspondingly, it seems clear that desire, including the body-based desires especially associated with the *epithumetikon* [desiring] part, can be rendered "reasonable", if shaped by the belief-patterns and life-goals of a (normatively) "reason-ruled" psyche.' I agree that this is one sort of account that Plato wants, but it is unclear to me how the desiring part of the soul is *capable* of that kind of shaping, given Plato's analysis of it; this suggestion is, I think, too tidy for Plato's text. Indeed, as Gill (1985: 11) notes, Plato seems to avoid offering any program for educating the desiring part, apparently thinking that it can be forcibly controlled but not trained, as the image at the end of book IX seems to suggest (22 f., see also 15, 19); and in so far as any education of desire takes place, it does so only in so far as desire is understood not as the desiring part *per se* but as an aspect of the other parts (19–21; for the desires of the different parts see Annas (1981: 142–6); Cooper (1999a: 189 f.)).

more fully because, first, his entire inquiry is shaped at the outset by defining the parts of the soul in terms of the conflicts between them; second, he thus lacks the means to account for the agreement that he none the less thinks naturally obtains between reason and emotion and, it turns out, certain desires as well, despite their beastly and monstrous nature; and third, he focuses his analysis of desire as a whole on basic, unreflective appetites.[31] And so notice also that where Plato's psychological account becomes less able to account for the rational incorporation of emotion and desire, and thus of pleasure, it is also more independently problematic. It seems, then, that in the *Republic* Plato wants and needs most to develop an agreement model of psychic harmony, and has better reasons to do so,[32] but is hindered in doing so by a more problematic control model of the soul which he neither reconciles with the former nor sees his way clear to abandon.

This means that Plato's psychological account in the *Republic* offers only partial support for his account of the transformation and rational incorporation of pleasure within the virtuous soul that has emerged from our reading of Plato. None the less, it is worth noticing that that part of his account that does not offer such support is also the part that presents a score of independent problems for Plato. What works best in Plato's account of the soul, then, is also what gives the most support to his notion of rational incorporation; and so rational incorporation does not rest on a unified line of Platonic thought, but it *does* rest on the independently more promising line of thought within a disjointed account. Moreover, the tension within the psychological account of Plato's *Republic* reveals what sorts of problems we must surmount in order to sustain a promising analysis of the rational incorporation of pleasure, even where it fails to surmount them itself, and for even that much it is an indispensable work in philosophical psychology.[33]

7.2   Development and Intractability: The *Laws*

In the *Republic* Plato makes a number of analogies for moral development and the leadership of practical reason in the soul, and while these analogies are diverse in several important ways, they are, after all, only analogies. Perhaps the disunity

[31]   For this last point cf. Annas (1981: 139–41). It is also worth noticing that his analysis of emotion focuses specifically on a particularly fierce emotion, anger.

[32]   Recall that, as we saw in Ch. 4, Plato's account of virtue as psychic harmony requires the parts of the soul to work in sufficiently sophisticated ways so that they can agree with and endorse the rational direction that reason brings to one's life (see also *Republic* IV, 442c–d). Note also that Plato's assertion in the *Republic* that those who have been properly trained in virtue will stand by their training (see esp. III, 401e–402a, VI, 485d) seems far more tenuous if emotions and desires always retain their inherently unruly character but are contained and controlled, as this relation seems much less stable than a relation of agreement between reason and transformed emotions and desires. Here I have benefited from Brown (2004), who takes the sufficiency of good training for good behavior to be an empirical generalization, but does not suggest any particular model of the soul on which such a generalization would be based.

[33]   It is also, I think, a pioneering work, in so far as it seems to have motivated both later Platonist psychology and Stoic psychology, two main rival theories of the soul in the ancient world.

of Plato's psychology in the *Republic* is due simply to the absence of any more detailed analysis of the actual processes by which humans do, or could, develop into a greater moral maturity and concord between the various motivating forces within the self. Here the *Laws* becomes especially relevant, since it is particularly concerned with the moral development of persons within the civic community. The *Laws* even recommends itself as the primary textbook for understanding the moral basis of their community and its institutions,[34] and explores specific methods and social institutions aimed at the moral development of the population. Perhaps a closer look at the psychology of moral development will hold some promise of a more unified Platonic moral psychology.

Plato introduces one form of adult moral education that he recognizes is unconventional, to say the least: drinking parties for soldiers in training. These parties are necessary not so much as a break from the rigors of training, but as a form of training itself; for, according to the Athenian stranger, soldiers are always trained to resist pain and fear, but they are rarely trained to resist pleasures and confident emotions that take the wrong form (I, 633c–634c). This is unfortunate, he says, because while soldiers need to be fearless in the face of the enemy, they also need to be fearful of disgrace and disrepute in the eyes of their fellows, and thus to be able to resist the pleasant temptations that would lead them to such disgrace (I, 645d–650b). Moreover, the process of training soldiers to resist pleasure is very much like the more familiar process of training them to resist fear: in both cases, soldiers are subjected to stimuli, punished for the wrong response, and rewarded for the proper one. And, whereas in the more familiar training soldiers are treated according to their responses to pain, in drinking-parties soldiers are treated according to their response to the pleasant emotions that wine produces in them, as it breaks down their inhibitions and boosts their confidence (I, 647e–650b). Likewise, the point of both forms of training is to develop the kinds of emotional patterns in soldiers that will conform to their understanding of their orders, their sense of decency, and their sense of what it is their duty to do. Of course, Plato does not suppose that such training will make soldiers into sages, or virtuous persons with fully developed practical intelligence. None the less, this training does illustrate a basic method for shaping the emotions, namely their directed *habituation*.[35]

Habituation, we should notice, is a non-rational process of training. Through habituation one learns to avoid disgraceful behavior not by learning arguments that demonstrate the harmfulness of disgraceful behavior, or what have you, but by coming to despise and feel disgust at disgraceful behavior. But, although habituation is a non-rational training process, this is not to say that it must have a wholly non-rational *outcome*. There is nothing in this account of habituation so far to prevent an emotion from having a perspective which, when properly habituated, is in agreement with reason, even if reason itself must be trained by

---

[34] *Laws* VII, 811c–812a. For a good discussion of this feature of the *Laws*, as well as certain complications involved in it, see Bobonich (1996).

[35] I am only too happy to ignore the question whether such training would actually work.

different methods. The crucial question for our purposes, then, is whether habituation prepares emotions only to be kept in check and under control by reason, or whether habituation can prepare emotions for agreement with reason and for being shaped in their inner structure—that is, whether such habituation prepares our emotions to be 'smarter' as the sorts of emotions that they are, rather than merely under tighter control.

Plato says little about the outcome of the soldier's training, but his description of moral training in children suggests that properly habituated emotions do display their own sort of perspective and understanding. Each of us, Plato says, has within us a pair of affective psychic forces that move us, namely pleasure and pain, and in terms of these we define the further psychic forces of fear and confidence (I, 644c–d). It seems clear, then, that Plato here thinks of pleasure and pain as emotions, and indeed the two basic emotions in terms of which the specific emotions are to be defined.[36] Moreover, Plato says that the proper habituation of pleasure and pain is the beginning of all moral development, since the motivating forces that are forms of pleasure and pain—that is, the emotions—are attitudes by which we approve and disapprove:

I maintain that the earliest sensations that a child feels in infancy are of pleasure and pain, and this is the route by which virtue and vice first enter the soul.[37]. . . I call 'education' (παιδεία) the initial acquisition of virtue by the child, when the feelings of pleasure and affection, pain and hatred, that well up in his soul are channeled in the right courses before he can understand the reason why. Then when he does understand, his reason and his emotions agree in telling him that he has been properly trained by inculcation of appropriate habits. Virtue is the general concord of reason and emotion. But there is one element you could isolate in any account you give, and this is the correction formation of our feelings of pleasure and pain, which makes us hate what we ought to hate from first to last, and love what we ought to love. Call this 'education', and I, at any rate, think you would be giving it its proper name. . . . Education, then, is a matter of correctly disciplined feelings of pleasure and pain. (*Laws* II, 653a5–c4, 7–8)

Here, again, we see that the habituation of the emotions is a distinct process from rational training, and indeed that the former training is a precursor to the latter, and must commence in children who are not yet ready for more rational forms of training.[38] But it is also clear that the outcome of this process— virtue—is a 'concord' (συμφονία) of reason and emotion, in which reason takes the leading role[39] by enabling the agent to understand why the things he has been trained to find pleasing or disgusting really are so.

What exactly is this concord? Clearly it is not the control or domination of emotion by reason, but their agreement. For one thing, what properly trained

---

[36] See also Alcinous, *Handbook* 32.2–3. *Con.* the psychology of the *Republic*, on which emotion apparently belongs to one part of the soul, but pleasure to all three parts.

[37] Cf. Alcinous, *Handbook* 30.3, 24.4.

[38] See Gill (1985) for discussion of this feature of Plato's account, which he argues is connected to an account of the development of the self as essentially social and cultural.

[39] Cf. Stalley (1983: 53, see also 55 f.).

reason adds to the habituated young person is not her first recognition that some things are bad and others good, but rather a distinctly rational grasp on the nature of the goodness and badness that she had *already* been taught to recognize. Reason is introduced not as bringing moral insight anew, but rather as confirming and explaining the insight already present within the emotions.

For another, although moral education is complete only when reason and emotion agree, none the less emotional habituation is its own form of education. In fact, the Athenian goes on to compare emotional habituation to more pedantic training, arguing that where only one form of training is present, emotional habituation yields a better education than pedantic training does:

> Now then, take a man whose opinion about what is good is correct (it really *is* good), and likewise in the case of the bad (it really *is* bad), and follows this judgment in practice. He may be able to represent, by word and gesture,[40] and with invariable success, his intellectual conception of what is good, even though he gets no pleasure from it and feels no hatred for what is bad. Another man may not be very good at keeping on the right lines when he uses his body and his voice to represent the good, or at trying to form some intellectual conception of it; but he may be very much on the right lines in his feelings of pleasure and pain, because he welcomes what is good and loathes what is bad. Which of these two will be the better educated musically, and the more effective member of a chorus?
> As far as education is concerned, sir, the second is infinitely superior.
> So if [we] grasp what 'goodness' is in singing and dancing, we have also a sound criterion for distinguishing the educated man from the uneducated man. If we fail to grasp it, we'll never be able to make up our minds whether a safeguard for education exists, or where we ought to look for it.   (II, 654c3–e1, emphasis in original)

While musical training is intended to teach the difference between good and bad moral character, the student with inferior musical skills and who is inarticulate about goodness and badness none the less has a better understanding of moral character than a more technically skilled and articulate student, so long as the former surpasses the latter in being pleased and pained in the right sorts of ways. Clearly, emotional habituation is a kind of *learning*, and it results not merely in its own form of understanding and insight, but in a form of understanding that is actually a *greater* understanding than the outcome of certain more 'intellectual' forms of training alone.[41] And it is because of this importance of emotional

---

[40] In the surrounding context, the Athenian describes singing and dancing as educational activities by which students portray different types of moral character with either pleasure or pain. The idea that the arts are in large measure concerned with education is, of course, familiar from Plato's dialogs, but it is important to note that it is no innovation on Plato's part, but a feature of Greek culture within which all discussions of art operate. (See also Aristotle, *Politics* VII.17, VIII.3, 5–7.) Indeed, Plato's famous argument in book X of the *Republic* that artistic representation is remote from genuine reality is not (as is sometimes thought) an objection to artistic representation *per se*, but only to the unreflective acceptance of artistic representation as an educational tool in Greek culture, as the argument beginning at 602c makes clear; that artistic representation is regularly employed as an educational tool in Greek culture, Plato takes as given. See also Asmis (1992: esp. 338 f., 352–6); Annas (1981: 336–44); N. White (1979: 247 f., 252).

[41] This is not to say, however, that such emotions are types of belief or judgment. It is extremely unfortunate that Plato does not take up the question of how exactly they are related to belief, as

education that Plato places so much importance in the *Laws* on the role that emotions of pleasure and pain play in one's life:

Pleasure and pain, you see, flow like two springs released by nature. If a man draws the right amount from the right one at the right time, he lives a happy life; but if he draws unintelligently at the wrong time, his life will be rather different.   (I, 636d7-e3)[42]

Moreover, because pleasure embodies a perspective, and when properly habituated embodies some form of understanding and insight, pleasure thus affords a criterion for distinguishing appropriate from inappropriate pleasures—and thus for assessing artistic efforts to habituate the emotions—since we can look to the emotional patterns of people of exceptional character to see what is and is not worth enjoying:[43]

I am, then, in limited agreement with the man in the street. Pleasure is indeed a proper criterion in the arts, but not the pleasure experienced by anybody and everybody. The productions of the Muse are at their finest when they delight men of high caliber and adequate education—but particularly if they succeed in pleasing the single individual whose education and moral standards reach heights attained by no one else. This is the reason why we maintain that judges in these matters need high moral standards: they have to possess not only a discerning taste, but courage too. A judge won't be doing his job properly if he reaches his verdict by listening to the audience and lets himself be thrown off balance by the yelling of the mob and his own lack of training... [This sort of thing is] equally disastrous for the quality of the pleasure felt by the spectators: they ought to come to experience more elevated pleasures from listening to the portrayal of characters invariably better than their own, but in fact just the opposite happens, and they have no one to thank but themselves.   (II, 658e6–659a6, c2–5)

Here again we see that there is no neutral perspective on pleasure, because enjoyment is a function of the value one places on the object of enjoyment and thus is a way of endorsing or approving the object. Since people differ so greatly in their values, they correspondingly differ in what they can appreciate as pleasant. And only when a person's values are correct and his passions have been aligned with those values can a person enjoy the right kinds of things as the right kinds of things.[44]

In his discussion of moral development, then, Plato sees pleasure, pain, and the emotions generally as having a complex inner structure that is first channeled by habituation, and thus prepared to adopt and agree with the direction of the agent's reason so that the agent's motivations and conceptions of goodness

---

answering such a question should shed much light on the choice between the agreement and control models.

[42] Notice also that this passage does not espouse any form of hedonism, because it makes the place of pain in one's life equally important as the place of pleasure, which is as it should be if Plato is here thinking of pleasure and pain as genera of emotion, and not as objects of pursuit and avoidance. See also Stalley (1983: 60 f.).

[43] For further discussion of the Platonic thesis that pleasures are never perspective-neutral, see Annas (1999: 145–9). See also Aristotle, *Nicomachean Ethics* X.5.

[44] See Annas (1999: 146, 151); Stalley (1983: 63 f., 65), who is reservedly pessimistic about this point.

are in harmony. In a mature agent, reason rationally incorporates those attitudes within the agent that have been antecedently prepared for precisely such incorporation; and so reason is the 'cause', as Plato says in the *Philebus*, of the order and harmony in the soul, despite the fact that non-rational processes have prepared the 'unlimited' aspects of the self to receive the sort of 'limit'—to play the sort of role in the agent's life as a whole—that reason brings about for them. This means that reason and emotion form an alliance or partnership, and that they are in *agreement* with one another, reason leading emotion by shaping a structure within emotion that awaits such shaping.

What about psychic conflict? Plato has also mentioned that one's habits or emotional patterns can pull apart from one's intellectual grasp of the moral quality of the objects of one's emotions: one may approve things on an emotional level that one does not approve of on an intellectual level, or be emotionally indifferent about things one does approve of intellectually. And, on the other hand, one's emotions may approve and disapprove in an appropriate and consistent manner, although one lacks a sophisticated grasp of what makes things worthy of this approval and disapproval. Here it seems that one's habits just *are* one's emotional patterns of approval and disapproval. Curiously, however, Plato then goes on to introduce a new source of these patterns besides habit, namely one's 'natural character', and he says that these two groups of patterns can pull apart:

Performances given by choruses are representations of character, and deal with every variety of action and incident. The individual performers enact their roles partly by expressing their own characters, partly by imitating those of others. That is why, when they find that the speaking or singing or any other element in the performance of a chorus appeals to their natural character or acquired habits, or both, they can't help applauding with delight and using the term 'good'. But sometimes they find these performances going against the grain of their natural character or their disposition or habits, in which case they are unable to take any pleasure in them and applaud them, and in this case the word they use is 'shocking'. When a man's natural character is as it should be, but he has acquired bad habits, or conversely when his habits are correct but his natural character is vicious, his pleasure and his approval fail to coincide: he calls the performances 'pleasant, but depraved'. Such performers, in the company of others whose judgment they respect, are ashamed to make this kind of movement with their bodies, and to sing such songs as though they genuinely approved of them. But in their heart of hearts, they enjoy themselves.
You are quite right.   (II, 655d5–656a6)

Notice that one's natural character and one's habits seem to do the same kind of thing: each of them 'applauds with delight and uses the term "good" ' when it finds a representation congenial to itself. But they do not always 'applaud' the same things; the sort of conflict that Plato had earlier glossed as a conflict between intellectual grasp and emotional pattern he now treats as a conflict between different emotional patterns themselves. This is clear from the fact that the cause of one's enjoyment of something one recognizes to be depraved can be either one's natural character or one's habituation; likewise, either can be the source of one's recognition of that depravity. So this is a conflict not between emotional propensity and intellect, but between one emotional propensity and another.

However, not only can these different emotional propensities conflict but one of them also seems relatively immune to the training of the other, since the emotional propensities of one's 'natural character' can remain essentially the same even if one has been successfully trained and habituated to have quite different emotional propensities.[45] The introduction of stubborn natural character raises a number of questions concerning moral development and psychic harmony, but what is most significant for present purposes is that on Plato's view in the *Laws* emotions can remain, at some very basic level, recalcitrant and stubborn, whatever progress one has made elsewhere through emotional training.

Is there anything that can effect significant change in the emotional propensities of one's 'natural character'? Plato seems to be of two minds about this. On the one hand, after noting that one can enjoy something one also finds depraved, he diagnoses this conflict as due to a lack of real conviction within one's disapproval of it:

Now, does a man's enjoyment of bad bodily movements or bad tunes do him any harm? And does it do him any good to take pleasure in the opposite kind?
Probably.
'Probably'? Is that all? Surely there must be a precise analogy with the man who comes into contact with depraved characters and wicked people, and who does not react with disgust, but welcomes them with pleasure, censuring them half-heartedly because he only half-realizes, as in a dream, how perverted such a state is: he just cannot escape taking on the character of what he enjoys, whether good or bad—even if he is ashamed to go so far as to applaud it. In fact we could hardly point to a greater force for good—or evil—than this inevitable assimilation of character.   (II, 656a7–b7)

Apparently, when one's disapproval of a thing—due to either one's habituation or natural character—is insufficient to keep one from enjoying it, this is because one's disapproval is only 'half-hearted', and one merely pays lip-service to the depravity of what one enjoys, rather than taking it completely seriously. While this suggests that one's emotional grasp of depravity can be weak and unstable, it also suggests that it might be strengthened by deepening one's understanding of depravity. Here, perhaps, Plato offers some hope of reforming a wayward natural character through moral education.

Unfortunately, it is not clear that Plato can show how such a reform would come about. It is unlikely that further *emotional* training and habituation would be effective, since Plato has already said that one's natural emotional character can remain recalcitrant despite successful habituation elsewhere in one's emotional

---

[45] In fact, Plato gives no suggestion here that the former type of propensities undergo any type of training at all.

life. It seems, then, that reform would need to come by strengthening one's *intellectual* grasp of the depravity that one's emotions now recognize only half-heartedly. However, the Athenian later claims that reason and even knowledge can fail to put a stop to such psychic conflict:

So when the soul quarrels with knowledge or opinion or reason [ἐπιστήμαις ἢ δόξαις ἢ λόγῳ ἐναντιῶται], its natural ruling principles, you have there what I call 'folly'. This applies both to the state in which people disobey their rulers and laws, and to the individual, when the fine principles in which he really believes prove not only ineffective but actually harmful. It's all these examples of ignorance that I should put down as the worst kind of discord in a state and individual, not the mere professional ignorance of a workman.   (III, 689b2–c3)

It is far from clear how an agent's developed reason[46] is, for Plato, to be so ineffectual a guide to action,[47] how it is to obtain despite the discord within the soul, how it is to be harmful to the agent, and how its presence in the agent might coexist with the worst kind of ignorance. But it is hard to avoid the conclusion that in these passages at least some emotions remain recalcitrant despite the presence of developed reason and emotional propensities.

This is a deep problem within the *Laws*, since such emotional recalcitrance seems to have been built into the very psychological model with which Plato begins his inquiry in the *Laws*. In *Laws* I the Athenian paints a notoriously alarming picture of human agency and motivation: a person, he says, is like a puppet suspended from strings, which are like the various motivating factors of the person's soul. As the Athenian's conversation with Clinias in this passage is as difficult as it is important, I include it in its entirety:

Now a while ago we agreed that those who are able to rule themselves are good, and those who are not are bad.
Yes, that's quite right.
Well, let's consider even more precisely just what we mean by this very point. Perhaps you'll let me clarify this business for you through an illustration, if I should somehow be able.
Go right ahead.
Let's take it that each of us is one, shall we?
Yes.
And he has within himself a pair of contrary and stupid advisors, which we call 'pleasure' and 'pain'?
That's true.
In addition to these two, he also has opinions about the future, which have the general name 'expectation'; but in particular, the expectation of pain is 'fear', and the expectation of its opposite is 'confidence'. And besides these, there is the reasoning that one of them

---

[46] I say merely 'developed reason' because it would be unwise to conclude in this context that by knowledge etc. Plato means full-fledged philosophical understanding, since his discussion concerns the development of the average citizen, not the sage.

[47] See Stalley (1983: 50–2) for a discussion of akrasia in this passage, which he also connects to the *Timaeus* psychology (57).

is sometimes better or worse; and when it becomes the decree of state, it is given the name 'law'.
I am just barely following you, but say what comes next as if I were following.
I [Megillus] am in the same situation, as well.
Let's think about these things in the following way. Let's suppose that each of us living beings is the gods' puppet, put together either as their plaything or for some serious purpose—we don't know which. But this we do know, that these passions in us are like kinds of cords or strings that both oppose us and pull against each other towards contrary actions, for they are themselves contraries; there virtue and vice stand divided. For the argument[48] says that each one [of us] ought to pull against the other cords, by always following one of the pulling forces and never letting go of it—and this one is the golden and holy leadership of reason (which is called in general 'law' of state). The others, however, are stiff and adamant, whereas this one is soft, as it is golden; the others are also like all sorts of things.[49] One ought always to take the side of the finest leadership, i.e. of law: for inasmuch as reason is fine, but mild and not violent, it needs assistants for its leadership, so that the golden kind in us might conquer the other kinds. And so this story of virtue about us being puppets would be complete, and the thought behind 'self-superior' and 'self-inferior' would in some way become clearer . . .   (644b6–645b3, my translation)

This passage is sure to raise more questions than it answers. Notice that on this model the person seems like the patient of all of his motive forces—passion and reason alike—rather than an agent, because the agent is identified not with any of the cords, but with the puppet that is merely suspended from them.[50] But if the person is such a patient, then in virtue of what is she to choose the cord with which she will identify? Plato remarks that the agent must identify and cooperate with the golden cord if it is to be effective,[51] but it is unclear how the person in this model could initiate action in agreement with the golden cord, since puppets do not initiate any action at all; puppets receive the action of their strings, not vice versa. Likewise, it is also unclear how the person so modeled could exert any control over the alloyed cords.

In fact, the possibility of controlling the alloyed cords is problematic even if we set aside the worries about a puppet initiating action independently of its strings. It is far from clear, after all, how the golden cord could exercise any direction over the alloyed cords, since the pliability of the golden cord makes it precisely unsuited to exert control over them, stiff and unyielding as they are. In fact, that seems to be just the point of making the cord pliable: it cannot act as

---

[48] In rendering ὁ λόγος as 'the argument' I follow most translators; but see Annas (1999: 142 and n. 15) for the provocative suggestion that ὁ λόγος is not 'the argument' but 'reason'.

[49] It is difficult to know just what this sentence indicates, but I suggest that it returns to the earlier point in the text that the cords pull in indefinite directions, even against each other. Cp. the image of the desiring part of the soul in *Republic* IX as a many-headed, shape-shifting beast; the idea there as well seems to be that desires and (certain) emotions can run in any direction and take anything as their object (see also the description of the tyrannical soul).

[50] This problem is not often noted; an exception is Stalley (1983: 61). Contrast this model with the depiction at the end of *Republic* IX of a person as the amalgam of a small person, a lion, and a many-headed monster, since in this depiction the agent is identified with the motive force represented by the small person.   [51] On this point, see Annas (1999: 143 f.).

the alloyed cords do, and it cannot exert any force over them.[52] Now we must, of course, be cautious of pressing this analogy too far. All analogies are meant to illuminate just some features of a thing, and not others. What does seem evident, however, is that calculation, which is subtle and persuasive, is not the sort of thing that can control passion, which is fierce and demanding. And this is not merely an artifact of the puppet analogy but also seems to corroborate the recalcitrance of one's 'natural' emotional propensities in the face of emotional training and even some sort of knowledge. Such recalcitrance is precisely what we should expect if the emotions are like stiff iron cords which have neither any unity of direction within themselves, pulling us in all sorts of directions, nor any apparent internal complexity and structure that reason can mold and shape into agreement and partnership, making emotion as unified in direction as reason itself is.[53] The emotions, on this model, seem rough, jerky, and stupid. None the less, Plato *does* say that the golden cord can 'prevail' over them, and so we cannot help but see that Plato portrays reason not as shaping emotion, but as conquering ($\nu\iota\kappa\hat{q}$) and controlling it (see 645a4–b1).

Consequently, while Plato's account of moral development concerns ordinary citizens instead of sages, none the less his model of human psychology leaves it unclear how pleasure and pain could ever develop into agreement with reason at all, since they are portrayed without any internal structure by which reason could shape and direct them. As in the *Republic*, so also in the *Laws* Plato speaks in two ways about the relation between reason and emotion, that is, between reason, on the one hand, and pleasure and pain, on the other, without unifying these two ways of speaking. Plato gives no indication that these two models of the soul are intended to describe different kinds of person. On the contrary, we have seen that he speaks in both kinds of ways for people with the same level of emotional moral development, and indeed he makes a point of highlighting the potential recalcitrance of emotion in the case of persons with successfully developed emotional habits and even developed reason. And as in the *Republic*, I think that Plato's motivation for this Janus-faced analysis in the *Laws* is the same: Plato recognizes, on the one hand, that emotion can be educated as a kind of perspective and insight, and thus must have a complex internal structure, and, on the other, that emotion can remain stubborn and unmanageable, as if it had no such structure but simply pulled one by force. Unfortunately, while the *Laws* does offer a closer look at moral development and its underlying psychology, we do not find in it a more unified moral psychology—much less freedom from puzzling analogies. Plato's frustration in modeling the human soul as capable of both agreement and conflict, then, is both deep and pervasive in his works on philosophical psychology.

---

[52] *Con.* Annas (1999: 143), who suggests that the pliability of the golden cord enables it to deal with emotions in ways that emotions cannot deal with it, namely by managing, leading, and manipulating them.

[53] The unity of reason's direction is suggested by its being a single cord made of a single, pure substance, unlike the emotional cords which are both discordant and alloyed. In fact, the golden cord receives, in addition to 'golden and holy', the further description 'single-formed' ($\mu o \nu o \epsilon \iota \delta \hat{\eta}$) in the Codex Riccardianus, presumably to maintain this symmetry in the text.

To sum up, in the *Laws* Plato offers the agreement model of reason and emotion in order to explain the rational incorporation of pleasure within human moral development. None the less, he also offers the control model, which conflicts with his account of rational incorporation. And so, again, Plato's account of rational incorporation of pleasure in the *Laws* does not rest on a unified moral psychology. Again, however, that account *does* seem to rest on the strand within the moral psychology of the *Laws* that is less problematic for independent reasons, since the control model in the *Laws* is motivated primarily by the introduction of recalcitrant natural character, as well as a bizarre and puzzling analogy for reason and pleasure within the agent, and Plato seems to have given sufficient thought and development to neither of these attempts to capture the recalcitrance of emotion.

7.3 The *Timaeus*

It is clear by now that we cannot explain away the tension between the agreement and the control models as a development from one model to another, since Plato sometimes presents them side by side within the same dialog. Nor can we explain it away as the difference between a model for immature souls and a model for mature ones, or between a model for vicious souls and a model for virtuous ones. In this section I shall consider one final attempt to explain this tension away: these two models, we might say, are parts of different discourses, the one analyzing the parts of the soul as functional parts or 'modules' within a human mental system, and the other analyzing them as psychological phenomena and psychic forces as agents experience them. For the sake of brevity, then, we might say that Plato offers a 'physiological' account of the soul, emphasizing the distinctness of separate psychic forces, as well as a 'psychological' account of the soul on which these forces are experienced as comprising a single agency, within which there can be either conflict or agreement, depending on such factors as habituation, learning, and other forms of upbringing. On this view, the control and agreement models of the soul are not two incompatible models of human psychology, but a model of the soul's construction, on the one hand, and a model of the soul's potential for psychological integration, on the other.

There is something to be said for this sort of explanation of Plato's apparently different ways of speaking of the soul. Plato does speak of the soul on these two levels of discourse, and when speaking on the more physiological level Plato does seem to favor something like the control model, and to favor the agreement model when speaking on the more psychological level. The lion and monster of *Republic* IX, for instance, serve to emphasize the distinctness of emotion and desire as the kinds of motivations they are, as does Plato's focus on appetites in *Republic* IV as impulses immune to reasoning. Here his attention is not on the agent as a whole, but on the agent considered from the bottom up, as it were, taken as a mental system consisting of fundamentally distinct psychic forces. By contrast, the discussion of these parts in *Republic* VIII–IX as each representing a unique kind of perspective on one's life as a whole, around which one's life can be constructed, as well as their ability to cooperate with each other as allies and partners, considers the workings of these parts from the agent's point of view, taken as a whole. Likewise, the puppet model of *Laws* I is a model of the radically different kinds of psychic forces that operate within a human, while the education model of *Laws* II shows how reason and pleasure can actually function as partners within an agent's perspective on his life and values. So perhaps we have not two psychologies, but a psychology and a physiology.

Unfortunately, this explanation is far too neat to be true. As we have seen, Plato moves between the view that reason and emotion are allies and the view that emotion is forced into submission to reason, not because he moves between a psychological and physiological level of discourse but because he looks at their relation now from the perspective of desire facing emotion and reason as a pair, and now from the perspective of emotion and reason themselves—two perspectives, but only one level. Likewise, Plato's pessimism in *Laws* II about those who remain emotionally recalcitrant despite proper emotional habituation comes in a strictly psychological discussion of moral development.

And there are even deeper problems with this explanation. For one thing, the physiological and psychological levels of discourse in Platonic philosophical psychology are far from independent of one another. In fact, Plato's choices at the physiological level are usually based on prior commitments about the nature of the parts of the soul at the psychological level. After all, one reason that Plato distinguishes desire from emotion on the physiological level as he does in the *Republic* is that he is impressed by the conflict between them from the agent's point of view, as in the case of Leontius. And, in any case, it is unlikely that this explanation would be of much help even if it could be made to fit Plato's analysis, since the cruder and more inflexible the physiology the more brutish and recalcitrant the psychology would seem to become. One surely does not motivate an account of psychic agreement and integration with a physiological account of psychic forces that are dumb and incapable of listening to one another in terms that they can share. And so, even if this explanation of Plato's two models were correct, Plato would still be left with a gap between these accounts of the soul, offering nothing to bridge that gap.[54]

These problems are perhaps clearest in Plato's *Timaeus*, which contains Plato's most detailed and sustained physiology of the soul. If the *Laws* leaves it unclear *how* the various parts of the soul are supposed to develop into agreement, then the *Timaeus* leaves it unclear that they ever *could*.[55] But this is not because the physiological account of the soul in the *Timaeus* is detached from a psychological account. On the contrary, that physiology is shaped by Plato's

---

[54] For an excellent discussion of Plato's relating these two levels in the *Timaeus*, and the attraction that it may have held for Chrysippus, see Gill (1997).

[55] For further discussion of the *Laws* and the *Timaeus* with respect to moral psychology, see also Stalley (1983: 47).

commitments about the nature of the soul at the *psychological* level, where he focuses exclusively on the control model of the soul.[56]

Plato's reliance on the control model at the psychological level in developing an account of the soul at the physiological level is evident in the way that he divides and arranges the parts of the soul themselves. In terms that seem to straddle the psychologies of the *Phaedo* and the *Republic*, Timaeus proclaims that the soul is both divine and corporeal, the latter being divisible into two parts, namely the 'ambitious' part and the 'appetitive' part (69c–71e). The divine soul was created by the Demiurge and placed by the created gods within the spherical cranium, and a body was constructed as its vehicle (69c).[57] Within this body itself the mortal, mundane soul was placed, and a concomitant of this mixture of soul with material, fluctuating body is the presence of passions (42a–b), which are among the dreadful, but necessary, disturbances. These passions, or disturbances, are cast in the least favorable light possible:

And within the body [the gods] built another kind of soul as well, the mortal kind, which contains within it those dreadful but necessary disturbances: pleasure, first of all, evil's most powerful lure; then pains, that make us run away from what is good; besides these, boldness also and fear, foolish counselors both; then also the spirit of anger hard to assuage, and expectation easily led astray. These they fused with unreasoning sense perception and all-venturing lust, and so, as was necessary, they constructed the mortal type of soul.   (69c7–d6)

Furthermore, the body was arranged so as best to insulate divine soul from mortal, as mortal soul was placed in the body, separated from the head (the seat of divine soul) by the neck:

In the face of these disturbances they scrupled to stain the divine soul only to the extent that this was absolutely necessary, and so they provided a home for the mortal soul in another place in the body, away from the other, once they had built an isthmus between them to keep them apart. Inside the chest, then, and in what is called the trunk they proceeded to enclose the mortal type of soul. And since one part of the mortal soul was naturally superior to the other, they built the hollow of the trunk in sections, dividing them the way that women's quarters are divided from men's. They situated the midriff between the sections to serve as a partition. Now the part of the mortal soul that exhibits manliness and spirit, the ambitious part, [the gods] settled nearer the head, between the midriff and the neck, so that it might listen to reason and together with it restrain by force the part consisting of appetites, should the latter at any time refuse outright to obey the dictates of reason coming down from the citadel. . . . The part of the soul that has appetites for food and drink and whatever else it feels a need for, given the body's nature, they settled in the area between the midriff and the boundary toward the navel. In the whole of this region they constructed something like a trough for the body's nourishment. Here they tied this part of the soul down like a beast, a wild one, but one they could not avoid

---

[56] Moreover, the account of the soul's physiology in the *Timaeus* had a long after-life; Alcinous presents it as the official Platonist view on the matter (*Handbook* 23); and the psycho-physiology of the *Timaeus* is also the basis of Galen's, in *On Hippocrates' and Plato's Doctrines;* see Hankinson (1991) and (1993); and Gill (1997) for discussion.   [57] Cf. Alcinous, *Handbook* 23.1.

sustaining along with the others if a mortal race were ever to be. They assigned it its position there, to keep it ever feeding at its trough, living as far away as possible from the part that takes counsel, and making as little clamor and noise as possible, thereby letting the supreme part take its counsel in peace about what is beneficial for one and all.   (69d6–70a7, 70d7–71a3)

Notice that Timaeus does not say that the parts of the soul behave as they do because of their location or seat within human anatomy. On the contrary, the parts have the physical seats they do because of the way they behave at the psychological level, luring us toward evil and so forth. It is because of the psychology of the ambitious and appetitive parts and their passions—their propensity away from good and towards evil, their foolishness, the difficulty with which they are guided and the ease with which they are misled, their failure to reflect and discriminate—that they have the physiology they do, seated away from reason and separated from it by the 'isthmus' of the neck. Plato is clearly focusing on a control model of reason and the passions *to which he is antecedently committed* at the *psychological* level, and then building a physiology of the soul around it.

And this is just how later Platonists understood the order of explanation between Plato's psychology and physiology:

That the soul is divided into three parts corresponding to its potencies, and that its parts are distributed rationally into their proper places, we will learn from what follows. First of all, things which are naturally separated are different. Now the affective and the rational parts are naturally separated, seeing as the latter is concerned with intelligible reality, while the former is concerned with what is pleasurable and painful. And furthermore, the affective part is found also in other animals. Then, since the affective and the rational parts are different in nature, it is proper that they occupy different locations; for they are found to conflict with one another. But any single thing cannot be in conflict with itself, nor can things which are in opposition to each other occupy the same place at the same time.   (Alcinous, *Handbook* 24.1–2)

Alcinous argues that since psychological conflict is a reality, there must be distinct parts of the soul which occupy different places within the body. That Alcinous sees conflict on the psychological level as determining the shape of a physiological theory of the soul is also clear in the cases he calls upon as evidence:

One can see in the character of Medea the spirited element in conflict with reason:

> I know what evil I am about to do
> But anger overcomes my resolutions.
> (Euripides, *Med.* 1078–9)

And similarly in the case of Laius, when he abducted Chrysippus, we see desire struggling with reason; for he speaks as follows:

> Alas, alas, for mortals this is an evil sent from God,
> When one sees the good, but makes no use of it.
> (Euripides, *Fr.* 841 N^2)

A further proof of the difference between reason and the affective part of the soul is the fact that the cultivation of the reason is different from that of the affective part; for the former is cultivated through teaching, the latter through the training of one's habitual behaviour. (Alcinous, *Handbook* 24.3–4)

The parts of the soul differ in their nature—and thus must differ in physiology—Alcinous argues, because phenomena at the strictly psychological level demonstrate such a difference: agents' perception of conflict between reason and emotion; agents' conflict between reason and desire; and the different ways in which agents undergo training of their psychic forces.

Not only the relative arrangement of the parts of the soul but also their own inner workings bespeak the crudeness with which Plato believes that the affective parts operate at the psychological level. This is clearest in the case of the appetitive part, as the control exerted by the ambitious and rational parts over the occasionally wayward appetitive part is one of forcible restraint (βίᾳ τὸ τῶν ἐπιθυμιῶν κατέχοι γένος, 70a5–6). The appetitive part, Timaeus says, is located in the belly, furthest away from the head (70d–e), and here are located the appetites for food, drink, and bodily need in general (70e); this part of the soul is depicted as a crude beast feeding at its trough (70e–71a). Plato says that the appetitive part is prone to 'refuse outright to obey the dictates of reason coming down from the citadel' (70a), and a page later that this part of the soul cannot even 'understand the deliverances of reason', but functions instead by dealing with 'images and phantoms' (71a). Plato seems confused here, since presumably one is not capable of choosing to disobey a dictate that one cannot understand or register in the first place. However, rather than charge Plato with contradicting himself within a single page, it is more natural to suppose that the 'reports' coming down from reason in 70a need not speak in reason's own terms, but can be translated into crude images to which the stupid appetitive part can react. In any event, the account of appetite as incapable of understanding reason's dictates is the one that Plato takes forward, and he says that since this part of the soul pays attention only to images, it is through images impressed upon the liver that the appetitive part is either frightened or soothed, depending on the thoughts from the mind that are converted into either frightening or soothing images in the liver (71b–e).[58] The appetites, then, can be forcibly *controlled* only by sending them threatening and soothing images.

The utter lack of rational activity in the appetitive part is further underscored a few pages later, when Timaeus claims that plant life also partakes of this kind of soul, which is totally without opinion, reasoning, or understanding (77a–c).[59] This part of the soul, which partakes of pleasant and painful sensations, as well as desires, is completely passive, being incapable of initiating either its own motion or its reaction to motions from without:

We may call these plants 'living things' on the ground that anything that partakes of life has an incontestable right to be called a 'living thing'. And in fact, what we are talking

---

[58] Cf. Alcinous, *Handbook* 23.2.

[59] This also removes any suspicion that the appetitive soul is capable of being frightened or soothed on the basis of any reflections or norms of its own. If this kind of soul is possessed also by plants, then it must operate entirely on brute reaction to external stimuli. *Con.* Aristotle, who separates the 'vegetative' part of the soul from the appetitive and desirous part (*Nicomachean Ethics* I.13).

about now partakes of the third type of soul, the type that our account has situated between the midriff and the navel. This type is totally devoid of opinion, reasoning or understanding, though it does share in sensation, pleasant and painful, and desires. For throughout its existence it is completely passive, and its formation has not entrusted it with a natural ability to discern and reflect upon any of its own characteristics, by revolving within and about itself, repelling movement from without and exercising its own inherent movement. Hence it is alive, to be sure, and unmistakably a living thing, but it stays put, standing fixed and rooted, since it lacks self-motion.   (77b1–c5)

And in a curious account of transmigration Timaeus later tells us that wild land animals have come from the souls of men who were completely without philosophy, and who abandoned the use of their mind to follow the soul in their chests (91e).[60] Throughout Plato's discussion of the appetitive part, then, it is difficult to avoid the conclusion that Plato has already decided that this part of the soul is incapable of rational incorporation.

However, there may seem to be a greater degree of cooperation between reason and the 'ambitious part', or what we have been calling emotion. The ambitious part of the soul, Timaeus says, is located in the chest, as it is able to listen to reason and to control the appetitive part, should it be disobedient (70a). Perhaps, then, the ambitious part of the soul responds not merely to coercion but indeed to *reasons* offered by the rational part:[61] the ambitious part boils over, Timaeus says, 'at a report from reason [τοῦ λόγου παραγγείλαντος] that some wrongful act involving these [bodily] members is taking place—something being done to them from outside or even something originating from the appetites within' (70b).

If nothing else, we see here the possibility of giving a physiological account based on a prior commitment to the agreement model. But the appearance of agreement between reason and emotion in this passage is seriously complicated, in at least three ways. First, this image of reports coming from reason to the ambitious part is presented alongside an image of such reports coming from reason to the appetitive part as well, and as we have seen the reception of these 'reports' by another part of the soul does not imply that that part is capable of understanding reason in reason's own terms.

Second, the ambitious part is said to listen to reason in only a very limited way: when reason reports some wrongful act (either from without, or within the appetitive part), the spirit boils over, and the heart (seat of ambition) sends exhortations and threats throughout the body (70b). Now, we might say that this is only a physiological account that underlies a psychological account that does operate on reasons.[62] But it is worth noting that, while the ambitious part is susceptible to *arousal* by the rational part, it is apparently not susceptible to *calming* by the rational part. The rational part appears to play no role in the

---

[60] Cf. Alcinous' claim that affective soul—the part of the soul that experiences pleasure and pain, and is contrasted with the rational part—is also found in animals (*Handbook* 24.1). It is also worth comparing this treatment of the desires in the *Timaeus* with the Athenian's description of the stiff and unyielding cords in the puppet analogy in *Laws* I.

[61] See Gill (1997: 268), citing 70b4–5, as well as 70a4–6, b7–c1.   [62] See Gill (1997: 269).

subsidence of strong emotion at all; rather, that subsidence is explained in terms of purely biological processes: the job of calming the ambitious part, Timaeus says, is handled physically by the lungs, acting as radiators to cool ambition in the heart, which is the reason why the heart is situated between the lungs in the first place (70c–d).[63] Even if emotional arousal were to occur in response to reasons, still it appears that the change or subsidence of emotions does not. In fact, now not only the seats of the parts of the soul but even the location of our bodily organs in relation to those seats is determined by a prior conception of how reason and emotion appear to operate at a psychological level—at least so long as one subscribes to the control model of reason and emotion. It thus becomes difficult to see how the ambitious part could operate on norms of its own, as the ambitious part in the *Republic* operates on norms of self-conception.[64] Thus although emotion is said to listen to reason (τοῦ λόγου κατήκοον ὄν, 70a4–5), the agreement of reason and the ambitious part, on the *Timaeus* account, would be most difficult to motivate.

Since Plato's account of the physiology underlying human moral psychology clearly relies on the control model as a prior conception of moral psychology, the control model is operating at the psychological level, and so the tension between it and the agreement model at that level persists. We are thus left with a significant disparity between the agreement model Plato offers in other dialogs and the account of the soul he offers in the *Timaeus*.

But why should Plato's focus in the *Timaeus* be so one-sided? After all, the climax of the *Timaeus* is a discussion of a kind of psychic harmony (90a–d), a topic that usually draws out Plato's interest in the agreement model. Why does it not draw out that interest here? I think that Plato is backed into this one-sided approach to psychology by the general role he assigns to corporeal nature in the *Timaeus*:

So, once the souls were of necessity implanted in bodies, and these bodies had things coming to them and leaving them, the first innate capacity they would of necessity come to have would be sense perception, which arises out of forceful disturbances. This they all would have. The second would be love, mingled with pleasure and pain. And they would come to have fear and spiritedness as well, plus whatever goes with having these emotions, as well as their natural opposites.   (42a3–b1)

Here Timaeus says that pleasure, pain, and the other emotions are a concomitant of mixing soul with material, fluctuating body. Because of this mixture, human soul is impure, contaminated as it is by the corporeal (41d–42b), and the soul's functions that are directly associated with corporeal nature are thus wild, irregular forces to be mastered and subdued:

And if they [*sc*. human males] could master these emotions, their lives would be just, whereas if they were mastered by them, they would be unjust. And if a person lived a good life throughout the due course of his time, he would at the end return to his dwelling place

---

[63] Cf. Alcinous, *Handbook* 23.2.   [64] See Annas (1981: 127 f.); Cooper (1999*a*: 201–6).

in his companion star, to live a life of happiness that agreed with his character. But if he failed in this, he would be born a second time, now as a woman. And if even then he could still not refrain from wickedness, he would be changed once again, this time into some wild animal that resembled the wicked character he had acquired. And he would have no rest from these toilsome transformations until he had dragged that massive accretion of fire-water-air-earth into conformity with the revolution of the Same and uniform within him, and so subdued that turbulent, irrational mass by means of reason. This would return him to his original condition of excellence.   (42b2–d2)

In the *Timaeus*, then, a human's corporeal nature serves primarily as an *obstacle* for reason and intelligence: 'All these disturbances are no doubt the reason why even today and not only at the beginning, whenever a soul is bound within a mortal body, it at first lacks intelligence' (44a–b). Our corporeal nature explains why we are helpless and irrational at birth; why some of us are consigned to prolonged reincarnations as 'lower' living beings; and why our emotions— pleasure that drives us to evil, pain that makes us flee what is good, foolish boldness and fear, stubborn anger, gullible expectation, unreasoning sense perception, all-venturing lust (69d)—present us so much difficulty. When Plato invokes these parts of our nature to explain why our reason is handicapped, intelligent human agency thus goes from being how all the aspects of the self work in harmony, to how a single aspect of the self works in relation to other parts which are strictly patients over which one must gain control.

Notice, then, a fundamental tension between the psychology of the *Timaeus* and that of the *Philebus*. In the *Philebus*, although pleasure is the 'matter' of creative reason in so far as it is not self-directing, and reason is the cause of 'limit' or order within one's pleasure as a dimension of the psyche, none the less that limit comes about as a kind of order *internal* to pleasure itself, as pleasure is rationally altered as the kind of perspective on oneself that it naturally is. On this view, the quality of one's agency is found in the partnership of all of the dimensions of the self. In the *Timaeus*, by contrast, matter not only lacks self-direction but also is essentially incorrigible and inflexible, serving always as a boundary for the potential of reason. Consequently, the quality of one's agency is found not in a partnership between intelligence and these other aspects of the self, since their function by nature is not to serve as partners to intelligence; rather, that quality is found in intelligence alone, in how it copes with material aspects of the person with which the person is not properly identified and which are never rationally incorporated into the whole self. Consequently, in the *Timaeus* psychic harmony obtains not between reason and the other parts, but *within reason* itself, which now turns out to be multi-dimensional:

Now we ought to think of the most sovereign part of our soul as god's gift to us, given to be our guiding spirit. This, of course, is the type of soul that, as we maintain, resides in the top part of our bodies.[65] It raises us up away from the earth and toward what is akin to us in heaven, as though we are plants grown not from the earth but from heaven. In saying

---

[65] See 69c.

this, we speak absolutely correctly. For it is from heaven, the place from which our souls were originally born, that the divine part suspends our head, i.e., our root, and so keeps our whole body erect. . . . [I]f a man has seriously devoted himself to the love of learning and to true wisdom, if he has exercised these aspects of himself above all, then there is absolutely no way that his thoughts can fail to be immortal and divine, should truth come within his grasp. And to the extent that human nature can partake of immortality, he can in no way fail to achieve this: constantly caring for his divine part as he does, keeping well-ordered the guiding spirit that lives within him, he must indeed be supremely happy. Now there is but one way to care for anything, and that is to provide for it the nourishment and the motions that are proper to it. And the motions that have an affinity to the divine part within us are the thoughts and revolutions of the universe. These, surely, are the ones which each of us should follow. We should redirect the revolutions in our heads that were thrown off course at our birth, by coming to learn the harmonies and revolutions of the universe, and so bring into conformity with its objects our faculty of understanding, as it was in its original condition. And when this conformity is complete, we shall have achieved our goal: that most excellent life offered to humankind by the gods, both now and forevermore.   (90a2–b1, b6–d7)

Psychic harmony as an ethical ideal, on this view, is a harmony among movements—the movements originally upset by the soul's introduction to a mortal body (43a–44d)—within reason, which subjugates the other psychic forces, and not a harmony between reason and those other forces.

   Notice this bizarre image of a human agent: a human is identical to a reasoning faculty, housed in a cranium, and below this cranium forms an accretion reaching to the ground. In a manner of speaking, a person does not actually stand on the ground, but is supported in the air by a growth that extends downward from him. A person, then, is a reasoning faculty only, and the body—including, presumably, the psychic functions bound to it—is only an accretion affixed to it, like the barnacles on a whale. There is no missing the point that those parts of my nature that are relegated and bound to this corporeal accretion are not really *me*. Whereas the puppet analogy in *Laws* II dissolves the agent into a collection of distinct psychic forces—a bunch of cords none of which seems to be the agent—the *Timaeus* retains the agent and gives her an identity, but only at the expense of fragmenting that agent and alienating her from some of the psychic forces that we normally think are an important part of making any person the person she is. And, whereas in the *Republic* the agent seems alienated from some of her psychic forces when viewed from some perspectives but not from others, the *Timaeus* simply makes everything but reason foreign to the agent and is done with it.

7.4   Conclusion

In the dialogues we have examined here, Plato faces a serious problem for any philosophical psychology that assigns the various motivations, concerns, and forces within the soul to distinct parts of the soul: once the agent is so fragmented, we lose the agent as a *whole*. If the agent is identical to some of her parts and not others, then what we have is not an agent but only a fraction of one;[66] and if the agent is not identical to any of her parts, then we seem to have no agent at all. Consequently, if the agent is to be a whole consisting of all of these motivations, concerns, and forces, then it seems that the agent must be comprised not of distinct parts, as Plato thinks, but of different modes in which the agent as a whole deliberates and acts. Because Plato assumes that psychic conflict could occur only between distinct parts opposing one another simultaneously, and does not entertain the possibility that psychic conflict could be an agent's vacillation between opposing perspectives, adopting now one perspective for herself as a whole and now another, he does not see any way to avoid dissecting the agent into distinct psychic parts, not all of which can be the agent herself.[67]

Unfortunately, without a psychological model of the agent as a whole, Plato lacks the psychological underpinnings for an account of virtue as the transformation of the agent as a whole, and thus for an account of happiness that is holistic rather than dimensional, consisting not in one's flourishing in some dimension of one's life but in one's flourishing as a harmoniously integrated whole.[68] Consequently, Plato offers a compelling ethical and value-theoretical account of pleasure as a conditional good that is rationally incorporated by practical intelligence, but lacks an adequate unified psychology of the affective and rational activities of the soul to underwrite that ethical and value-theoretical account. Of course, it is not entirely surprising that even so great a thinker as Plato should struggle in constructing a unified psychology that makes sense of the Janus-faced nature of pleasure, emotion, and desire, as this is, after all, one of the deepest problems in all of philosophical psychology. However, understanding the demands that Plato's evaluation of pleasure places on a supporting psychology, as well as the challenges to be faced in constructing such a psychology, will help to point the way for us as beneficiaries of Plato's legacy.

---

[66] It is worth noting that this problem also turns up in Alcinous' discussion of the emotions (*Handbook* 32.1), in which he claims that emotions are irrational motions of the soul. On these grounds, he maintains that the emotions are not really *our* actions (cf. Annas (1999: 135); Stalley (1983: 47)), nor under our control (although he shifts between that stronger claim and the weaker claim that the emotions arise without our wishing). Alcinous does not seem to perceive the tension between his claim that the emotions are entirely irrational motions of the soul on the one hand, and his claim that emotions arise in response to good and bad on the other. Thus, although Alcinous wishes in *Handbook* 30.3 to portray the emotions and desires as able to internalize a cognitive structure supplied by reason (even though they cannot supply such structure for themselves), he also portrays the non-rational parts of the soul as not properly us (32.1). Alcinous, then, like Plato does not in the end present a coherent account of the nature of the passions and their relation to reason. On this tension in Plato, see also Annas (1999), ch. 6 (however, Annas does not present this tension as a phenomenon in Alcinous).

[67] It was not in vain, then, that the Stoics would later identify the agent with a single rational faculty capable of occupying distinct perspectives, each of which represents a 'turning of the whole soul' toward that perspective, and between which the whole soul could vacillate when experiencing psychic conflict (see esp. Plutarch, *On Moral Virtue* 446f–447a; Seneca, *On Anger* I.8.2, 3; Galen, *On the Doctrines of Hippocrates and Plato* 4.4.16–18, 24–5).

[68] The distinction between dimensional and holistic conceptions of happiness will be familiar from the discussion with which we began Ch. 4.

EPILOGUE: PLEASURE AND HAPPINESS IN PLATO'S *PROTAGORAS*

I wish to close with a word about Plato's *Protagoras*, a dialogue that has received enormous attention in discussions concerning Plato on pleasure. It has received this attention because toward the end of the *Protagoras* Socrates discusses a form of hedonism, on the basis of which he then bases his subsequent argument on the nature of virtue and action. Since this hedonism facilitates his argument, it is natural to conclude that Socrates must endorse it. And, of course, this would mean that Plato, at least at some point in his career,[1] was a hedonist.

I think we should be very hesitant about drawing such conclusions, however, for two basic reasons. The first has to do with considerations external to the *Protagoras*. Simply put, if Plato endorses hedonism in the *Protagoras*, then not only does he take a position on the value of pleasure which he may abandon in other dialogs but also he takes a position on the fundamental nature of happiness and value that he certainly does reject elsewhere. As we have seen, hedonism maintains that happiness depends on our flourishing in one of the aspects of our life, not on a life's direction as a whole life, and that the good that determines happiness is a conditional good that needs direction, rather than the unconditional good that brings direction. If Plato was, at some point in his career, a hedonist, then we are faced not merely with a possible change in how Plato thought about pleasure, but, in fact, with a radical sea change in the entire framework of his thought on moral philosophy—a shift from an additive to a directive conception of happiness, and from the view that conditional goods can determine happiness to the view that only the unconditional good can determine happiness. The importance of such a shift has usually gone unseen in the midst of debates over whether the hedonism discussed in the *Protagoras* can survive the critique of Callicles' hedonism in the *Gorgias*, where so much scholarly energy has tended to focus. Unfortunately, what proponents of hedonist readings of the *Protagoras* have not seemed to appreciate is that even if the hedonism of the *Protagoras* should be consistent with the refutations of Callicles' hedonism, none the less hedonism requires a very particular view about the very nature of happiness and of value that is at odds at the most fundamental level with the view that Plato actually develops, in the *Gorgias* and

---

[1] Scholars who believe that Plato espoused hedonism in the *Protagoras* are divided over whether he ever retracted this hedonism in later dialogs, most notably the *Gorgias*. For the view that he did, see, e.g., Irwin (1995: 111–14); cf. (1979: 204). For the view that he did not, see, e.g., Gosling and Taylor (1982); Rudebusch (1999).

elsewhere. This much should be clear from the preceding chapters. Of course, philosophers change their minds, even at the most fundamental levels, and there is no a priori reason to expect Plato to be exempt from such change. The point, however, is that no proponent of a hedonist reading of the *Protagoras* has even appreciated, much less accounted for, such a monumental shift in all of Plato's thought in ethics and value theory that such a reading would entail. Nor is this surprising, as those scholars have simply assumed that Plato must hold one version or other of the additive conception of happiness, not recognizing the possibility of the directive conception or its power to explain Plato's ethics. Once we have recognized that possibility and its power, however, the case for such a controversial reading of what is, on any account, a rather puzzling and complicated dialogue seems very much weaker.

The second major strike against the hedonist reading of the *Protagoras*, in my view, and what will be our main concern here, is that, on the best understanding of the *Protagoras*, we simply do not have to attribute to Plato a commitment to hedonism in the first place. This view has also attracted its proponents, but, of course, it has the burden of showing what Socrates is doing in discussing hedonism if he relies on it to make his argument go through, and yet is not a hedonist. Notice, however, that one's personal investment in the premises of an argument will depend on what one intends for that argument to do: some arguments we give are intended to demonstrate for others our own line of reasoning in support of some thesis, while others are intended to demonstrate for others what seems to follow from *their* own commitments, whether we share them or not. Arguments of the latter sort are often called 'dialectical' arguments, and there is good reason to think that Socrates' argument from hedonism is a dialectical argument intended to show the deficiency of Protagoras' position in Protagoras' own terms.[2] Of course, Protagoras himself is at first reticent to accept hedonism as a theory of the good (see *Protagoras* 351c–e), but to argue in Protagoras' own terms Socrates need not necessarily appeal only to Protagoras' actual beliefs, since it will also be enough for Socrates to portray hedonism as a particularly advantageous position for Protagoras to adopt.[3]

A number of commentators have defended this sort of reading of the *Protagoras*, arguing that hedonism serves as a theory of human motivation and choice that renders virtuous behavior teachable, and thus motivates Protagoras' claim to teach it, and at the same time serves to refute Protagoras' own theory of the nature of the virtues. But how exactly does hedonism serve to refute Protagoras? Some scholars have suggested that hedonism promises the teachability of virtue only to yield an implausible conception of virtues such as courage, say, since the hedonist perspective makes self-sacrifice highly unlikely,[4] or since

---

[2] See especially Zeyl (1989); Weiss (1990b); Hemmenway (1996); and McCoy (1998).

[3] I shall leave aside the view of some scholars that the dialog is an exercise in deliberately fallacious arguments directed by Socrates against Protagoras. For such readings of the *Protagoras* see, e.g., Klosko (1979: esp. 129) (whose reading is endorsed by Zeyl (1989: 13)), and Goldberg (1983: 67, 116–18, *et passim*). [4] See McCoy (1998).

hedonism is neutral with respect to the nobility that Protagoras prizes,[5] or because confidence in an action one estimates to be the most pleasant, and thus the best, is a very odd form of courage.[6]

But I do not think that these sorts of approaches can be quite right. Socrates does not want to show just *any* problem with Protagorean sophistry. He wants to show that Protagorean sophistry is inconsistent with the Protagorean view of the relations between virtues. The main arguments of the *Protagoras*, after all, begin with Protagoras' thesis that the virtues are distinct and separable from one another, rather than grounded in a more fundamental sort of understanding that holds them together as a group, and the question for Protagoras is how the virtues can be teachable without such a basis:

'Now, then, Protagoras, I need one little thing, and I then I'll have it all, if you'll just answer me this. You say that virtue is teachable, and if there's any human being who could persuade me of this, it's you. But there is one thing you said that troubles me, and maybe you can satisfy my soul. You said that Zeus sent justice and a sense of shame to the human race. You also said, at many points in your speech, that justice and temperance and piety and all these things were somehow collectively one thing: virtue. Could you go through this again and be more precise? Is virtue a single thing, with justice and temperance and piety its parts, or are the things I have just listed all names for a single entity? This is what still intrigues me.'
'That is an easy question to answer, Socrates,' he replied. 'Virtue is a single entity, and the things you are asking about are its parts.'
'Parts as in the parts of a face: mouth, nose, eyes, and ears? Or parts as in the parts of gold, where there is no difference, except for size, between parts or between the parts and the whole?'
'In the former sense, I would think, Socrates: as the parts of the face are to the whole face.'
'Then tell me this. Do some people have only one part and some another, or do you necessarily have all the parts if you have any one of them?'
'By no means, since many are courageous but unjust, and many again are just but not wise.'
'Then are these also parts of virtue—wisdom and courage?'
'Absolutely, and wisdom is the greatest part.'
'Is each of them different from the others?'
'Yes.'
'And does each also have its own unique power or function? . . .'
'Yes, it must be the case, Socrates.'
'Then, none of the other parts of virtue is like knowledge, or like justice, or like courage, or like temperance, or like piety?'
'Agreed.' (329b5–330a4, b2–6)

It is the introduction of a sort of 'hedonic calculus' later in the dialogue that renders the virtues teachable, but it does so only because it establishes a shared intellectual basis for the virtues, and this makes a dilemma for Protagoras: either he can continue to claim to teach the virtues, which are teachable on account of

---

[5] See Hemmenway (1996: 21–2).   [6] See Weiss (1990*b*: 30).

their shared intellectual basis; or he can continue to maintain that the virtues are sharply distinct and separable capacities without such a basis[7]—but not both. Since this dilemma arises from—and makes obvious—Protagoras' inattention to the very possibility of teaching what he claims to teach, Socrates thus challenges Protagoras' claim to teach virtue, and gives young men hoping to study with Protagoras the kind of warning that Socrates tried to give the young man Hippocrates in the dialog's opening (311a–314c).[8]

However, in order for Socrates to succeed in posing this dilemma for Protagoras, Protagoras must find hedonism and the conception of virtue that it yields *attractive* and potentially *helpful* for strengthening the appeal of his claim to teach the virtues. If the hedonist interpretation of Protagoras' position makes it patently implausible, then Protagoras need not worry too much—that interpretation was not his idea in the first place, but Socrates'. Unless Socrates' argumentative strategy is confused, his hedonist interpretation of Protagoras' account of virtue should appear to Protagoras as *improving* his account in some important way. The problem for Protagoras, therefore, should not be that hedonism offers a picture of the virtues he is unwilling to accept. If it does, he should simply reject hedonism, as he seemed initially inclined to do anyway, and be done with it.[9] Rather, the problem is that teachable virtues would require an intellectual basis encompassing a more general understanding of good and bad, and yet Protagoras claims to teach virtues with no such general basis. And he will not avoid *this* problem simply by rejecting hedonism, since the hedonic calculus merely serves to illustrate readily what is surely a perfectly general point about *any* intellectual basis for teachable virtues.

So much for a general description of Socrates' aim in the hedonist argument; now for a closer examination of it. In order to understand the hedonist argument itself, we should understand the role that Socrates thinks it has in the larger argument within which it appears (see 353b), concerning the nature of courage. Protagoras maintains that courage is completely different ($\pi\acute{\alpha}\nu\upsilon$ $\pi o\lambda\grave{\upsilon}$ $\delta\iota\alpha\phi\acute{\epsilon}\rho o\nu$, 349d4–5) from all the other virtues, and that an 'exceptionally courageous' person can none the less be 'extremely unjust, impious, intemperate, and

---

[7] It is a matter of some uncertainty and controversy whether Socrates means to attack the denial of the *reciprocity* of the virtues, or the denial of the *unity* of virtue. For present purposes, we can leave this controversy to the side.

[8] We need not worry, then, that Socrates is pointing out a *mere* inconsistency. As Weiss (1990*b*: 29) rightly notes, 'It seems unlikely that Protagoras is upset [at the end] merely about losing the match.' That is, I think, this worry that motivates the other dialectical readings cited above to locate the problem for Protagoras in something more than the inconsistency of his position, and instead in the implausibility of his position once based on hedonism. But if I have described Plato's goal in the dialog correctly, then *this* inconsistency is all he needs to show in order to achieve that goal.

[9] Furthermore, it is sometimes argued that the problem that Socrates raises for Protagoras is an awkward revelation of the true nature of his teaching, which is self-serving and elitist (see esp. Hemmenway (1996), McCoy (1998)). While this probably is accurate of Protagoras' teaching, none the less it is conspicuous that Socrates does very little *explicitly* to draw attention to this. By contrast, Socrates in his discussion of rhetoric throughout the *Gorgias* makes such revelation a central and explicit theme. I suspect, then, that Plato does not ignore this aspect of rhetoric in the *Protagoras*, but none the less has another aspect of it primarily in his sights.

ignorant' (349d6–8). Socrates responds by arguing that knowledge increases well-founded confidence, and that such well-founded confidence is the greatest courage; consequently, it is knowledge that makes one courageous, and since what makes one courageous is courage, courage and knowledge must be the same (349e–350c).[10] Protagoras' response is somewhat convoluted, but the upshot is that he is unwilling to trace courage to skill ($\tau\acute{\epsilon}\chi\nu\eta$) and knowledge ($\grave{\epsilon}\pi\iota\sigma\tau\acute{\eta}\mu\eta$) alone. Rather, he says, it comes from the 'nature and proper nurture' ($\grave{\alpha}\pi\grave{o}$ $\phi\acute{u}\sigma\epsilon\omega\varsigma\ \kappa\alpha\grave{\iota}\ \epsilon\grave{\upsilon}\tau\rho\sigma\phi\acute{\iota}\alpha\varsigma$, 351a3) of the soul, and while he does not expand on this—Socrates instead shifts gears (351b)—it seems clear that Protagoras thinks that courage is not a kind of knowledge, because in some important respect courage is non-epistemic. Thus Protagoras reveals the heart of his disagreement with Socrates: virtues such as courage have certain non-epistemic elements, and so whatever relation knowledge has to virtue, the virtues remain discrete.[11]

Interestingly, however, when Socrates and Protagoras return to courage (359a–360e) after their extended discussion of hedonism, Protagoras no longer makes this sort of objection. Protagoras and Socrates agree that it is impossible for anyone to go toward what he takes to be fearsome, and so they hold that the courageous and cowardly alike go toward what they are confident about. But, since the courageous and the cowardly go toward different things—only the former pursuing warfare, for instance—and since everyone goes for what he takes to be good and pleasant, the courageous must know what the cowardly do not, namely that, all things considered, going to war is honorable, and therefore good, and therefore pleasant, since the pleasant is the good. Notice, then, that the difference between the courageous and the cowardly can only be epistemic: Socrates says that what sets the courageous apart from the cowardly is their honorable and good confidence and fear, while the fear and confidence of the cowardly, foolhardy, and mad are disgraceful because of ignorance and stupidity. Since the cowardly are cowardly through ignorance, cowardice must be ignorance, and since one is courageous by the opposite of cowardice, and the opposite of ignorance is wisdom, one is courageous by wisdom, and so wisdom must be courage. And this, of course, is a dangerous position for Protagoras to find himself in, since the sort of knowledge that courage seems to turn out to be is a general skill of discerning the good and the bad, which would presumably bind together the other virtues as well.

Clearly, then, the intervening discussion of hedonism makes all the difference between these two arguments. So one thing we know is that that discussion is intended to move Protagoras from the view that knowledge or skill is not sufficient for courage to the view that it is; this makes the discussion of hedonism easier to approach, since we already know what work it is supposed to do.[12] How, then, does that discussion move Protagoras to change his mind?

---

[10] My discussion of this argument is, of course, highly compressed. For further discussion see Devereux (1975); Weiss (1985); C. C. W. Taylor (1976), *ad loc.*; Vlastos (1956: xxxiii–xxxv).

[11] Cf. Weiss (1985: 13–14).

[12] This is also the strategy of Weiss (1990*b*: 19 ff.); cf. Zeyl (1989: 13).

Socrates begins by noting that one barrier to teaching virtue that Protagoras recognizes is the possibility of akrasia (352b–353a): that a person could be taught what is good and what bad, but none the less go against his teaching because he is overcome by a desire to seek pleasure and avoid pain. Not surprisingly, then, Protagoras denies that such a thing could occur,[13] but he recognizes that most people do believe it is possible to be overcome by pleasure to go against one's better judgment. Consequently, Protagoras takes himself to have a considerable professional stake in the denial of akrasia, if he means to present his teaching as having an especially effective impact on his students' behavior.

Here Socrates makes the interesting suggestion that Protagoras may be able to meet such popular worries about akrasia after all (353c). Socrates suggests first that ordinary people could be persuaded that so-called bad pleasures are never bad as pleasures, but only for the painful consequences that eventually follow them; in that case, ordinary people would be persuaded that pleasures are always good as such, and that all differences between good and bad really come down to differences between what is pleasant and what is painful (353c–354e). This is so because ordinary people have no other criteria than pleasure and pain by which to call things good or bad (354b), as Socrates notes four times (cf. 354c–355a). They can be persuaded, then, that something is good when it is pleasant on balance, and bad when it is painful on balance (355a–c).

Socrates now uses this popular hedonism to construct an argument to dissuade ordinary people from the popular belief that akrasia is being overcome by pleasure to go against the good. Socrates points out that if people were to hold that it were possible to choose the bad, because one is overcome by something that is pleasant on balance (355c), then they would have to concede the possibility of choosing the bad because one is overcome by the good (355c–e), since we have already supposed they will be persuaded that the pleasant-on-balance is good and the painful-on-balance bad (recall 355a–c). Now, since akrasia is understood as the domination of knowledge by pleasure (see 352b–c), an act will be a genuine case of akrasia only if the agent knows what goodness and badness are—*ex hypothesi*, the pleasant-on-balance and the painful-on-balance, respectively—and how the act in question is a case of such badness. But if the agent knows that such an action is bad—that is, more painful-on-balance—then it is ridiculous, Socrates says, that he should choose it on the grounds of being overcome by its pleasantness.[14]

---

[13] As Kerferd (1981: 138) notes, we have no external evidence that Protagoras held this view, but his agreement is understandable since he holds that education is the key to moral problems. Notice that the sophist Gorgias is also insistent that expertise in matters of right and wrong is inconsistent with wrong behavior (*Gorgias* 458e–461b). See also Stokes (1986: 411–12).

[14] This argument is, of course, more complex than this fairly simple reconstruction might suggest. For one thing, it is difficult to determine whether Socrates argues that it is ridiculous to think that a person who knows an action to be less pleasant (or more painful) than the alternative would, in fact, *do* that action, or that it is ridiculous to think that a person would engage in such an action *because* overwhelmed by its goodness; see esp. Santas (1966); C. C. W. Taylor (1976: 182–6); Gallop (1964); Irwin (1995: 83 f.); Russell (2000a: 322 f.). Second, the argument seems to assume that the many accept psychological hedonism, that is, the thesis that people in fact *do* what they know to be most

Here Socrates is constructing the sort of argument that Socrates supposes Protagoras would need to give to the many, to convince them that one need only learn from Protagoras the skill of measuring ($\mu\epsilon\tau\rho\eta\tau\iota\kappa\grave{\eta}$ $\tau\acute{\epsilon}\chi\nu\eta$) what is pleasant-on-balance and what is painful-on-balance in order to know the difference between good and bad, and to choose accordingly. It is worth noticing that Socrates does not give an argument against akrasia *to the sophists*—their agreement stands (352c–d, 358b–e);[15] rather, the arguments are directed *only* toward the many (354e ff.). Moreover, the problem of convincing the many of the impossibility of akratic action after sophistic training is a problem for Protagoras, not Socrates. It is Protagoras who is committed, after all, to showing before a popular audience that akrasia is eliminated by the training he gives. There is no reason to require Socrates' argument here to be his own, rather than an argument he gives on Protagoras' behalf to Protagoras' imagined audience.[16]

Accordingly, throughout the argument over pleasure Socrates' focus—at every major argumentative juncture—is only on what the many *would or would not be able to say* in conversation with Protagoras. In the discussion of hedonism, Socrates notes that ordinary people would not say that a troublesome pleasure is anything but one which brings bad consequences (353d6–e3); that they have nothing to say but that bad consequences are bad only because they are painful (353e5–354a2); that they have nothing to say but that good pains are so only in virtue of bringing more pleasure as a consequence (354a2–c3); and that they have no other criteria by which to judge good and bad than by pleasure and pain (354b7–c3, 354d1–4, 354d7–e2), and hence would be unable to reject hedonism. Moreover, in the argument against akrasia Socrates says that when one weighs pleasures and pains, the many would have nothing to say but that the greater pleasures are always 'to be chosen' ($\lambda\eta\pi\tau\acute{\epsilon}\alpha$; 356c1–3), and would thus agree that the measuring art must be our salvation (356e2–4).[17] These concessions on behalf of the many are not simply markers of agreement in a debate but call special attention to the limited ability of such an audience to give certain kinds of responses. If Socrates and Protagoras take it that they have convinced the

pleasant (or least painful), and it is difficult to see on what basis Socrates thinks they are committed to that thesis; see esp. Irwin (1995: 82–4); C. C. W. Taylor (1976: 175, 189 f.); Gosling and Taylor (1982: 57 f.); Santas (1966: 18, 20, 22, 29 f.); Russell (2000a: 323–6). And third, the argument also seems to assume that pleasures and pains are to be assessed and compared solely in quantitative terms, which is quite a controversial notion; see Richardson (1990); Rudebusch (1989: 27–40); Russell (2000a: 325 f.); C. C. W. Taylor (1976: 180); Weiss (1990b: 24–6); Stokes (1986: 406); Vlastos (1956: xlii f.); Gallop (1964: 127); Santas (1966: 30 ff.). But at present we can leave these complications aside and focus on the gist of Socrates' argument and what he hopes it will achieve.

[15] See Weiss (1990b: 23, 26). Cf. Socrates' own comment at 345d9–e2: 'I am pretty sure that none of the wise men thinks that any human being willingly makes a mistake or willingly does anything wrong or bad.'

[16] And, of course, this could be the case even though the argument purports to defend a thesis—the impossibility of akrasia—that Socrates himself also maintains, as Aristotle says he does (*Nicomachean Ethics* VII.2, 1145b22 ff.).

[17] See also Santas (1966: 10 f.). The reading offered here, if correct, would address C. C. W. Taylor's worry (1976: 200) that Socrates argues only for the inconsistency of the popular rejection of hedonism given other popular beliefs, and not for hedonism *per se*.

many that akrasia can be explained only as ignorance and that the μετρτικὴ τέχνη would thus preclude akrasia, then they do so thinking simply that it is an argument which the many would be unable to reject.

Socrates' stake in the argument, then, clearly need not go beyond showing Protagoras that he must base the virtues that he teaches on some form of general knowledge of good and bad, if he is ever to present a convincing case to the many for his claim to teach the virtues:

> 'What exactly this art, this knowledge is, we can inquire into later; that it is knowledge of some sort is enough for the demonstration which Protagoras and I have to give in order to answer the question you [*sc.* the many] asked us. You asked it, if you remember, when we were agreeing that nothing was stronger or better than knowledge, which always prevails, whenever it is present, over pleasure and everything else. At that point you said that pleasure often rules even the man who knows; since we disagreed, you went on to ask us this: "Protagoras and Socrates, if this experience is not being overcome by pleasure, what is it then; what do you say it is? Tell us." "If immediately we had said to you 'ignorance', you might have laughed at us, but if you laugh at us now, you will be laughing at yourselves. For you agreed with us that those who make mistakes with regard to the choice of pleasure and pain, in other words, with regard to good and bad, do so because of a lack of knowledge you agreed was measurement. And the mistaken act done without knowledge you must know is one done from ignorance. So this is what 'being overcome by pleasure' is—ignorance in the highest degree, and it is this which Protagoras and Prodicus and Hippias claim to cure. But you, thinking it to be something other than ignorance, do not go to sophists yourselves, nor do you send your children to them for instruction, believing as you do that we are dealing with something unteachable. By worrying about your money and not giving it to them, you all do badly in both private and public life." This is how we would have answered the many. Now, I ask you, Hippias and Prodicus, as well as Protagoras—this is your conversation also—to say whether you think what I say is true or false.' They all thought that what I said was marvelously true.   (357b5–358a5)

We can now see that the argument about hedonism bridges the gap between the two discussions of courage by showing that Protagoras is committed to two things. First, he must say that wrong action is always done in ignorance of the fact that the action is ultimately harmful; it is not done out of akrasia or passion. And second, he must claim to correct people's action by imparting to them the knowledge by which one can successfully judge benefit and harmfulness. Accepting these two claims, Protagoras is therefore committed to the idea that teaching virtue is the teaching of a kind of knowledge: the training he offers comes about by means of teaching students a skill whereby they can assess harmful and beneficial consequences and always act accordingly.

Returning to courage, Socrates and Protagoras now agree that the courageous do not pursue fearsome things, since they know which things are harmful—and thus fearsome—and which not, and no one pursues what he takes to be harmful (359c–d). Moreover, cowards who refuse to go to war—when going to war is, in fact, honorable, good, and pleasant (359e–360a)—must do so out of an expectation of harm, and so out of ignorance. Consequently, confidence and fear must each be of two sorts: knowledgeable confidence and fear, which are honorable; and ignorant confidence and fear, which are disgraceful (360a). So the difference between the courageous and the cowardly is in their understanding or ignorance of what things are and are not to be feared.[18] The courageous, then, are those who are confident because they are able to apprehend the overall benefit or harmfulness of various courses of action. Moreover, one could be a coward only through ignorance, and so since one is a coward through cowardice, cowardice must be ignorance (360c). And since ignorance is contrary to knowledge and wisdom, courage must be a kind of knowledge and wisdom after all (360d).

Notice the pressures that this argument puts on Protagoras. The notion that a knowledge of good and evil in general is the basis of courage is in tension with his position that one could be 'exceptionally courageous' and yet be 'extremely unjust, impious, intemperate, and ignorant' (349d). Instead, the basis of courage would seem to be the basis of all the other virtues as well, suggesting that they are neither separable from one another nor nearly so sharply distinct in their natures, despite Protagoras' initial view.[19] On the contrary, courage does not differ from any other virtue as ears do from eyes, but apparently as the same man in one situation differs from himself in another.[20] Socrates' argument about hedonism, then, contributes directly to his refutation of Protagoras' thesis concerning courage and the other virtues, for that argument prevents Protagoras from introducing non-epistemic elements into courage, and bases courage on knowledge which would seem to form the basis of the other virtues as well.

This, then, is the role of the argument about hedonism in the greater argumentative structure of the examination of courage. The demands of popular appeal require Protagoras to maintain that knowledge is the most powerful force in human affairs. Protagoras finds that this puts pressure on him to show the many that akrasia is really nothing but ignorance of the benefit of virtuous behavior, and that sophistry cures such ignorance. And this means that Protagoras must conceive of the virtues and of moral education as based on knowledge of good and bad generally, but once he has established that conception of the virtues and moral education, he can no longer maintain the sharp separability of the virtues.[21] The argument thus allows Socrates to demonstrate the tension between Protagoras' position on courage, on the one hand, and the demands of his openness in advertising and his professed ability to teach others to be virtuous, on the other. Consequently, naïve young men such as the onlooking Hippocrates have learned to be suspicious of such advertising and

---

[18] Cf. Weiss (1990*b*: 19 f.).

[19] Cf. C. C. W. Taylor (1976: 213 f.). *Con.* Kerferd (1981: 136), who claims that Protagoras could still maintain that the virtues are all qualitatively different kinds of knowledge.

[20] For the analogy see Seneca, *Letters to Lucilius* 113.24.

[21] Notice that it is *not* clear, however, that Protagoras takes these concessions to heart, or that the public commitments which force him to make these concessions represent his own sincere beliefs. It is clear only that Socrates lodges Protagoras between *professions* he makes about teaching and those he makes about the virtues. I thank Scott LaBarge for raising this point.

professions:[22] as Socrates points out, Protagoras' position on whether the virtues can be taught seems to keep shifting, since his view about the nature of the virtues keeps shifting, leaving them all in a muddle which Protagoras says he has not the time to sort out (360e–362a).

Notice that we can understand this strategy of Socrates' in the *Protagoras* without ever appealing to any of Socrates' own beliefs on the nature of hedonism. Consequently, Socrates' endorsement of hedonism, in addition to Protagoras' acceptance of it as a friendly aid in his cause, would be completely otiose. So there are no reasons internal to the dialogue for construing either Socrates or Plato as a hedonist of any kind.

[22] Thus at a very general level I agree with Weiss (1990*b*: 29 ff.), who argues that Socrates places Protagoras in an awkward position by invoking the demands of advertising himself as a teacher.

BIBLIOGRAPHY

ALCINOUS, *The Handbook of Platonism*, trans. with commentary by J. Dillon (Oxford: Oxford University Press, 1993).

ANNAS, J., *An Introduction to Plato's* Republic (Oxford: Oxford University Press, 1981).

—— 'Plato's Myths of Judgment', *Phronesis*, 27 (1982), 119–43.

—— *Hellenistic Philosophy of Mind* (Berkeley: University of California Press, 1992).

—— 'Virtue and the Use of Other Goods', *Apeiron*, 26 (1993), 53–66.

—— *The Morality of Happiness* (Oxford: Oxford University Press, 1994a).

—— 'Plato the Skeptic', in P. A. Vander Waerdt (ed.), *The Socratic Movement* (Ithaca: Cornell University Press, 1994b).

—— *Platonic Ethics, Old and New* (Ithaca: Cornell University Press, 1999).

—— *Voices of Ancient Philosophy* (Oxford: Oxford University Press, 2001).

ARISTOTLE, *The Nicomachean Ethics*, trans. D. Ross, rev. J. L. Ackrill and J. O. Urmson (Oxford: Oxford University Press, 1980).

—— *Eudemian Ethics*, trans. J. Solomon, in J. Barnes (ed.), *The Complete Works of Aristotle, 2* (Princeton: Princeton University Press, 1984).

ASMIS, E., 'Plato on Poetic Creativity', in R. Kraut (ed.), *The Cambridge Companion to Plato* (Cambridge: Cambridge University Press, 1992).

BALTZLY, D., 'The Virtues and "Becoming Like God": Alcinous to Proclus', *Oxford Studies in Ancient Philosophy*, 26 (2004), 297–321.

BARKER, A., 'The Digression in the *"Theaetetus"*', *Journal of the History of Philosophy*, 14 (1976), 457–62.

BENARDETE, S., *The Tragedy and Comedy of Life: Plato's* Philebus (Chicago: University of Chicago Press, 1993).

BERGER, Jr., H., 'Plato's Flying Philosopher', *Philosophical Forum*, 13 (1982), 385–407.

BERMAN, S., 'How Polus was Refuted: Reconsidering Plato's *Gorgias* 474c–475c', *Ancient Philosophy*, 11 (1991a), 265–84.

—— 'Socrates and Callicles on Pleasure', *Phronesis*, 36 (1991b), 117–40.

BLUCK, R. S., *Plato's* Phaedo (London: Routledge & Kegan Paul, 1955).

BOBONICH, C., 'Plato's Theory of Goods in the *Laws* and *Philebus*', *Proceedings of the Boston Area Colloquium in Ancient Philosophy*, 11 (1995), 101–39.

—— 'Reading the *Laws*', in C. Gill and M. M. McCabe (ed.), *Form and Argument in Late Plato* (Oxford: Oxford University Press, 1996).

BOSTOCK, D., *Plato's* Phaedo (Oxford: Oxford University Press, 1986).

BRICKHOUSE, T., and SMITH, N., *Plato's Socrates* (Oxford: Oxford University Press, 1994).

—— *The Philosophy of Socrates* (Boulder: Westview Press, 2000a).

—— 'Making Things Good and Making Good Things in Socratic Philosophy', in T. Robinson and L. Brisson (eds.), *Plato: Euthydemus, Lysis, Charmides* (Sankt Augustin: Academia Verlag, 2000b).

BROWN, E., 'Minding the Gap in Plato's *Republic*', *Philosophical Studies*, 117 (2004), 275–302.

BURNYEAT, M., Introduction to *The* Theaetetus *of Plato*, trans. M. J. Levett (Indianapolis: Hackett Publishing, 1990).

CARONE, G. R., 'Hedonism and the Pleasureless Life in Plato's *Philebus*', *Phronesis*, 45 (2000), 257–83.

CHANCE, T., *Plato's* Euthydemus (Berkeley: University of California Press, 1992).

COOPER, J., 'Plato's Theory of Human Motivation', reprinted in G. Fine (ed.), *Plato 2* (Oxford: Oxford University Press, 1999*a*).

—— *Reason and Emotion* (Princeton: Princeton University Press, 1999*b*).

DAMASCIUS, *Lectures on the* Philebus, *Wrongly Attributed to Olympiodorus*, ed. L. G. Westerink (Amsterdam: North-Holland Publishing, 1959).

—— *Lectures on the* Phaedo, ed. L. G. Westerink, *The Greek Commentaries on Plato's Phaedo*, 2 (Amsterdam: North-Holland Publishing, 1977).

DEVEREUX, D., 'Protagoras on Courage and Knowledge: *Protagoras* 351a–b', *Apeiron*, 9 (1975), 37–9.

DIMAS, P., 'Happiness in the *Euthydemus*', *Phronesis*, 47 (2002), 1–27.

DODDS, E. R., *Plato:* Gorgias (Oxford: Oxford University Press, 1959).

DYBIKOWSKI, J. C., 'False Pleasure and the *Philebus*', *Phronesis*, 25 (1970), 147–65.

ENGBERG-PEDERSON, T., 'Discovering the Good: *oikeiosis* and *kathekonta* in Stoic Ethics', in M. Schofield and G. Striker (eds.), *The Norms of Nature* (Cambridge: Cambridge University Press, 1986).

FICINO, M., *The* Philebus *Commentary*, ed. M. J. B. Allen (Berkeley: University of California, 1975).

FOSTER, M. B., 'A Rejoinder to Mr Mabbott', *Mind*, 47 (1938), 226–32.

FREDE, D., 'Rumpelstiltskin's Pleasures: True and False Pleasures in Plato's *Philebus*', *Phronesis*, 30 (1985), 151–80.

—— 'Disintegration and Restoration: Pleasure and pain in Plato's *Philebus*', in R. Kraut (ed.), *The Cambridge Companion to Plato* (Cambridge: Cambridge University Press, 1992).

—— Translation, Introduction, and Notes, *Philebus* (Indianapolis: Hackett Publishing, 1993).

FREDE, M., 'The Stoic Doctrine of the Affections of the Soul', in M. Schofield and G. Striker (eds.), *The Norms of Nature* (Cambridge: Cambridge University Press, 1986).

GADAMER, H.-G., *Plato's Dialectical Ethics: Phenomenological Interpretations Relating to the* Philebus (New Haven: Yale University Press, 1983).

GALLOP, D., 'The Socratic Paradox in the *Protagoras*', *Phronesis*, 9 (1964), 117–29.

—— translation and commentary, *Plato:* Phaedo (Oxford: Oxford University Press, 1975).

—— translation and notes, *Plato:* Phaedo (Oxford: Oxford University Press, 1993).

GENTZLER, J., 'The Sophistic Cross-Examination of Callicles in the *Gorgias*', *Ancient Philosophy*, 15 (1995), 17–43.

GILL, C., 'Did Chrysippus Understand Medea?', *Phronesis*, 28 (1983), 136–49.

—— 'Plato and the Education of Character', *Archiv für Geschichte der Philosophie*, 67 (1985), 1–26.

—— *Personality in Greek Epic, Tragedy, and Philosophy* (Oxford: Oxford University Press, 1996).

—— 'Galen versus Chrysippus on the Tripartite Psyche in *Timaeus* 69–72', in T. Calvo and L. Brisson (eds.), *Interpreting the* Timaeus-Critias (Sankt Augustin: Academia Verlag, 1997).

—— 'Did Galen Understand Platonic and Stoic Thinking on Emotions?' in T. Engberg-Pedersen and J. Sihvola (eds.), *The Passions in Hellenistic Philosophy* (Dordrecht: Kluwer Academic Publishing, 1998).

GOLDBERG, L., *A Commentary on Plato's* Protagoras (New York: Peter Lang, 1983).

GOOCH, P. W., 'The Relation between Virtue and Wisdom in *Phaedo* 69a–c3', *Journal of the History of Philosophy*, 12 (1974), 153–9.

GOSLING, J. C. B., 'False Pleasures: *Philebus* 35c–41b', *Phronesis*, 4 (1959), 44–54.

—— 'Father Kenny on False Pleasures in Plato's *Philebus*', *Phronesis*, 6 (1961), 41–5.

—— Translation, Notes, and Commentary, *Philebus* (Oxford: Oxford University Press, 1975).

GOSLING, J. C. B., and TAYLOR, C. C. W., *The Greeks on Pleasure* (Oxford: Oxford University Press, 1982).

—— 'The Hedonic Calculus in the *Protagoras* and *Phaedo*: A Reply', *Journal of the History of Philosophy*, 28 (1990), 115–16.

GRUBE, G. M. A., *Plato:* Phaedo (Indianapolis: Hackett Publishing, 1997).

GUTHRIE, W. K. C., *A History of Greek Philosophy*, IV. *Plato, the Man and His Dialogues: Earlier Period* (Cambridge: Cambridge University Press, 1975).

HACKFORTH, R., Translation and Commentary, *Plato's Examination of Pleasure* (Cambridge: Cambridge University Press, 1945).

—— Translation and Commentary, *Phaedo* (Indianapolis: Bobbs-Merrill, orig. 1955).

HADAS, M., Translation and Introduction, *The Stoic Philosophy of Seneca: Essays and Letters* (New York: Doubleday, 1958).

HAMPTON, C., 'Pleasure, Truth and Being in Plato's *Philebus*: A Reply to Professor Frede', *Phronesis*, 32 (1987), 253–62.

—— *Pleasure, Knowledge, and Being* (Albany: State University of New York Press, 1990).

HANKINSON, R. J., 'Galen's Anatomy of the Soul', *Phronesis*, 36 (1991), 197–233.

—— 'Actions and Passions: Affection, Emotion, and Moral Self-Management in Galen's Philosophical Psychology', in J. Brunschwig and M. Nussbaum (ed.), *Passions and Perceptions* (Cambridge: Cambridge University Press, 1993).

HEMMENWAY, S. R., 'Sophistry Exposed: Socrates on the Unity of Virtue in the *Protagoras*', *Ancient Philosophy*, 16 (1996), 1–23.

HURSTHOUSE, R., *On Virtue Ethics* (Oxford: Oxford University Press, 1999).

INWOOD, B., and GERSON, L. P., *Hellenistic Philosophy*, 2nd edn. (Indianapolis: Hackett Publishing, 1997).

IRWIN, T., Translation and Commentary, *Plato's Gorgias* (Oxford: Oxford University Press, 1979).

—— 'Socrates the Epicurean?', in H. Benson (ed.), *Essays on the Philosophy of Socrates* (Oxford: Oxford University Press, 1992).

—— *Plato's Ethics* (Oxford: Oxford University Press, 1995).

JAEGER, W., *Aristotle: Fundamentals of the History of his Development*, trans. R. Robinson, 2nd edn. (Oxford: Oxford University Press, 1948).

JOHNSON, C., 'Socrates' Encounter with Polus in Plato's *Gorgias*', *Phoenix*, 43 (1989), 196–216.

KAHN, C., 'Drama and Dialectic in Plato's *Gorgias*', *Oxford Studies in Ancient Philosophy*, 1 (1983), 75–121.

—— 'Vlastos's Socrates', *Phronesis*, 37 (1992), 233–58.

KANT, I., *Grounding for the Metaphysics of Morals*, trans. J. W. Ellington, 3rd edn. (Indianapolis: Hackett Publishing, 1993).

KAVKA, G., 'The Reconciliation Project', in D. Copp and D. Zimmermann (eds.), *Morality, Reason and Truth* (Totawa, NJ: Rowman and Allanheld, 1985).

KELLY, J., 'Virtue and Inwardness in Plato's *Republic*', *Ancient Philosophy*, 9 (1989), 198–205.

KENNY, A., 'False Pleasures in the *Philebus*: A Reply to Mr. Gosling', *Phronesis*, 5 (1960), 45–52.

KERFERD, G. B., *The Sophistic Movement* (Cambridge: Cambridge University Press, 1981).

KIRWAN, C., 'Glaucon's Challenge', *Phronesis*, 10 (1965), 162–73.

KLOSKO, G., 'Toward a Consistent Interpretation of the *Protagoras*', *Archiv für Geschichte der Philosophie*, 61 (1979), 125–42.

KORSGAARD, C., 'Two Distinctions in Goodness', *Philosophical Review*, 92 (1983), 169–95.

—— 'Aristotle on Function and Virtue', *History of Philosophy Quarterly*, 3 (1986), 259–79.

KRAUT, R., 'The Defense of Justice in Plato's *Republic*', in R. Kraut (ed.), *The Cambridge Companion to Plato* (Cambridge: Cambridge University Press, 1992).

LESSES, G., 'Is Socrates an Instrumentalist?', *Philosophical Topics*, 13 (1985), 165–74.

—— 'Socratic Friendship and Euthydemean Goods', in T. Robinson and L. Brisson (eds.), *Plato: Euthydemus, Lysis, Charmides* (Sankt Augustin: Academia Verlag, 2000).

LEWIS, C. S., *Out of the Silent Planet* (London: Pan Books, orig. 1938).

—— *The Great Divorce* (New York: Macmillan, 1946).

LOVIBOND, S., 'Plato's Theory of Mind', in S. Everson (ed.), *Companions to Ancient Thought 2: Psychology* (Cambridge: Cambridge University Press, 1991).

MABBOTT, J. D., 'Is Plato's *Republic* Utilitarian?', *Mind*, 46 (1937), 468–74.

McCoy, M. B., 'Protagoras on Human Nature, Wisdom, and the Good: The Great Speech and the Hedonism of Plato's *Protagoras*', *Ancient Philosophy*, 18 (1998), 21–39.

McKIM, R., 'Shame and Truth in Plato's *Gorgias*', in C. Griswold (ed.), *Platonic Writings/ Platonic Readings* (New York: Routledge, 1988).

McLAUGHLIN, A., 'A Note on False Pleasures in the *Philebus*', *Philosophical Quarterly*, 19 (1969), 57–61.

de MONTAIGNE, M., *An Apology for Raymond Sebond*, trans. M. A. Screech (Penguin, 1993).

MOORADIAN, N., 'What to Do about False Pleasures of Overestimation? *Philebus* 41a5–42c5', *Apeiron*, 28 (1995), 91–112.

NOZICK, R., *Anarchy, State, and Utopia* (New York: Basic Books, 1974).

NUSSBAUM, M., *The Therapy of Desire* (Princeton: Princeton University Press, 1994).

OLYMPIODORUS, *Commentary on the Phaedo*, in L. G. Westerink (ed.), *The Greek Commentaries on Plato's* Phaedo, 1 (Amsterdam: North-Holland Publishing, 1976).

PASSMORE, J., *The Perfectibility of Man* (London: Duckworth, 1970).

PENNER, T., 'False Anticipatory Pleasures: *Philebus* 36a3–41a6', *Phronesis*, 15 (1970), 166–78.

—— 'Thought and Desire in Plato', in G. Vlastos (ed.), *Plato II* (South Bend: Notre Dame, 1978).

—— 'Desire and Power in Socrates: The Argument of *Gorgias* 466a–468e That Orators and Tyrants Have No Power in the City', *Apeiron*, 24 (1991), 147–202.

—— 'Socrates and the Early Dialogues', in R. Kraut (ed.), *The Cambridge Companion to Plato* (Cambridge: Cambridge University Press, 1992).

PENNER, T., and Rowe, C. J., 'The Desire for the Good: Is the *Meno* Inconsistent with the *Gorgias*?', *Phronesis*, 39 (1994), 1–25.

PLATO, *Platonis Opera*, Vols. 2–4, ed. J. Burnet, (Oxford: Oxford University Press, 1900–7).

—— *Philebus*, trans. R. Waterfield (New York: Penguin Classics, 1982).

—— *Republic*, trans. R. Waterfield (Oxford: Oxford University Press, 1993).

—— *Gorgias*, trans. R. Waterfield (Oxford: Oxford University Press, 1994).

—— *Platonis Opera*, Vol. 1, ed. E. A. Duke, W. F. Hicken, W. S. M. Nicoll, D. B. Robinson, and J. C. G. Strachan (Oxford: Oxford University Press, 1995).

—— *The Complete Works of Plato*, ed. J. Cooper (Indianapolis: Hackett Publishing, 1997).

REEVE, C. D. C., *Philosopher-Kings: The Argument of Plato's* Republic (Princeton: Princeton University Press, 1988).

RESHOTKO, N., 'Virtue as the Only Unconditional—But not Intrinsic—Good: Plato's *Euthydemus* 278e3–281e5', *Ancient Philosophy*, 21 (2001), 325–34.

RICHARDSON, H. S., 'Measurement, Pleasure, and Practical Science in Plato's *Protagoras*', *Journal of the History of Philosophy*, 28 (1990), 7–32.

ROBERTS, R. C., *Emotions: An Essay in Aid of Moral Psychology* (Cambridge: Cambridge University Press, 2003).

ROBINSON, R., 'Plato's Separation of Reason from Desire', *Phronesis*, 16 (1971), 38–48.

ROWE, C. J., *Plato* (New York: St. Martin's Press, 1984).

RUDEBUSCH, G. H., 'Plato, Hedonism, and Ethical Protagoreanism', in J. P. Anton and A. Preus (ed.), *Essays in Greek Philosophy III: Plato* (Albany: State University of New York, 1989).

—— 'Death is One of Two Things', *Ancient Philosophy*, 11 (1991), 35–45.

—— 'Callicles' Hedonism', *Ancient Philosophy*, 12 (1992), 53–71.

—— 'How Socrates Can Make Both Pleasure and Virtue the Chief Good', *Journal of Neoplatonic Studies*, 3 (1994), 163–77.

—— *Socrates, Pleasure, and Value* (Oxford: Oxford University Press, 1999).

RUE, R., 'The Philosopher in Flight: The Digression (172c–177c) in Plato's *Theaetetus*', *Oxford Studies in Ancient Philosophy*, 11 (1993), 71–100.

RUNIA, D., *Philo of Alexandria and the* Timaeus *of Plato* (Leiden: E. J. Brill, 1986).

RUSSELL, D. C., 'Protagoras and Socrates on Courage and Pleasure: *Protagoras* 349d *ad finem*', *Ancient Philosophy*, 20 (2000*a*), 311–38.

—— Review of G. Rudebusch, *Socrates, Pleasure, and Value* (Oxford: Oxford University Press, 1999), *Ancient Philosophy*, 20 (2000*b*), 468–72.

—— 'Misunderstanding the Myth in the *Gorgias*', *Southern Journal of Philosophy*, 39 (2001), 557–73.

—— 'Epicurus on Friends and Goals', in D. Gordon and D. Suits (ed.), *Epicurus: His Continuing Influence and Contemporary Relevance* (Rochester: Rochester Institute of Technology, 2003).

—— 'Virtue as "Likeness to God" in Plato and Seneca', *Journal of the History of Philosophy*, 42 (2004), 241–60.

RYLE, G., *The Concept of Mind* (New York: Barnes and Noble, 1949).

SACHS, D., 'A Fallacy in Plato's *Republic*', *Philosophical Review*, 72 (1963), 141–58.

SANTAS, G. X., 'Plato's *Protagoras* and Explanations of Weakness', *Philosophical Review*, 75 (1966), 3–33.

SAYRE, K., 'The *Philebus* and the Good: The Unity of the Dialogue in which the Good is the Unity', *Proceedings of the Boston Area Colloquium in Ancient Philosophy*, 2 (1987), 45–71.

SCHMIDTZ, D., 'Choosing Ends', *Ethics*, 104 (1994), 226–51.

—— *Rational Choice and Moral Agency* (Princeton: Princeton University Press, 1995).

SCHOFIELD, M., 'Ariston of Chios and the Unity of Virtue', *Ancient Philosophy*, 4 (1984), 83–96.

SEDLEY, D. N., ' "Becoming Like God" in the *Timaeus* and Aristotle', in T. Calvo and L. Brisson (eds.), *Interpreting the Timaeus-Critias* (Sankt Augustin: Academia Verlag, 1997).

——'The Ideal of Godlikeness', in G. Fine (ed.), *Plato 2: Ethics, Politics, Religion, and the Soul* (Oxford: Oxford University Press, 1999).

SENECA, *Epistles 1–65*, trans. R. M. Gummere (Cambridge, Mass.: Harvard, 1996 (orig. 1917)).

SHERMAN, N., *Making a Necessity of Virtue: Aristotle and Kant on Virtue* (Cambridge: Cambridge University Press, 1997).

SPITZER, A., 'Immortality and Virtue in the *Phaedo*: A Non-Ascetic Interpretation', *Personalist*, 57 (1976), 113–25.

STALLEY, R. F., 'Plato's Arguments for the Division of the Reasoning and Appetitive Elements within the Soul', *Phronesis*, 20 (1975), 110–28.

——*An Introduction to Plato's* Laws (Indianapolis: Hackett Publishing, 1983).

STEWART, Z., 'Laughter and the Greek Philosophers', in S. Jäkel and A. Timonen (eds.), *Laughter Down the Centuries* (Turku: Turun Yliopisto, 1994).

STOKES, M., *Plato's Socratic Conversations: Drama and Dialectic in Three Dialogues* (Baltimore: Johns Hopkins University Press, 1986).

STRAUSS, L., *Socrates and Aristophanes* (New York: Basic Books, 1966).

STRAWSON, P. F., *Freedom and Resentment* (London: Methuen & Co., 1974).

STRIKER, G., 'Plato's Socrates and the Stoics', in P. A. Vander Waerdt (ed.), *The Socratic Movement* (Ithaca: Cornell University Press, 1994).

TARRANT, H., 'The *Hippias Major* and Socratic Theories of Pleasure', in P. A. Vander Waerdt (ed.), *The Socratic Movement* (Ithaca: Cornell University Press, 1994).

TAYLOR, A. E., *Plato: Philebus and Epinomis* (New York: Barnes and Noble, 1972).

TAYLOR, C. C. W., Translation and Commentary, *Protagoras* (New York, Oxford: Oxford University Press, 1976).

——'Platonic Ethics', in S. Everson (ed.), *Companions to Ancient Thought 4: Ethics* (Cambridge: Cambridge University Press, 1998).

TENKKU, J., *The Evaluation of Pleasure in Plato's Ethics*, Acta Philosophica Fennica, 11 (Helsinki, 1956).

THALBERG, I., 'False Pleasures', *Journal of Philosophy*, 59 (1962), 65–73.

VLASTOS, G., Introduction to *Plato*: Protagoras, trans. B. Jowett (Indianapolis: Bobbs-Merrill, 1956).

——'Was Polus Refuted?', *American Journal of Philology*, 88 (1967), 454–60.

——*Socrates, Ironist and Moral Philosopher* (Ithaca: Cornell University Press, 1991).

WAYMACK, M. H., 'The *Theaetetus* 172c–177c: A Reading of the Philosopher in Court', *Southern Journal of Philosophy*, 23 (1985), 481–9.

WEISS, R., 'Courage, Confidence, and Wisdom in the *Protagoras*', *Ancient Philosophy*, 5 (1985), 11–24.

——'The Right Exchange: Phaedo 69a6–c3', *Ancient Philosophy*, 7 (1987), 57–66.

——'A Rejoinder to Professors Gosling and Taylor', *Journal of the History of Philosophy*, 28 (1990*a*), 117 f.

——'Hedonism in the *Protagoras* and the Sophist's Guarantee', *Ancient Philosophy*, 10 (1990*b*), 17–40.

——'Killing, Confiscating, and Banishing at *Gorgias* 466–468', *Ancient Philosophy*, 12 (1992), 299–315.

WHITE, F. C., 'The Good in Plato's *Gorgias*', *Phronesis*, 35 (1990), 117–27.

WHITE, N. P., *A Companion to Plato's* Republic (Indianapolis: Hackett Publishing, 1979).

—— 'The Classification of Goods in Plato's *Republic*', *Journal of the History of Philosophy*, 22 (1984), 393–422.

—— 'Rational Prudence in Plato's *Gorgias*', in D. J. O'Meara (ed.), *Platonic Investigations* (Washington, D.C.: Catholic University of America Press, 1985).

—— 'Stoic Values', *Monist*, 73 (1990), 42–58.

ZEYL, D. J., 'Socrates and Hedonism: *Protagoras* 351b–358d', *Phronesis*, 25 (1989), 250–69.

INDEX LOCORUM

GENERAL INDEX

Ackrill, J. L. 15
Adeimantus (*Republic*) 115, 116 n. 24
affective nature of humans, 'passions' 11, 43 f.,
    46, 75, 83, 99 f., 107–9, 127, 134, 137, 138,
    141 f., 146–9, 158 f., 163 f., 167 n. 3, 202,
    206 f., 208 n. 5, 211 n. 14
affectlessness 81, 83, 166 f., 203 n. 75
Affinity Argument (*Phaedo*) 93, 97–101,
    140 n. 3
agreement model of psychic integration 12 f.,
    205–7, 209–13, 217–19, 220–2, 223 n. 41,
    224, 228 f., 230, 234 f.
akrasia, weakness of will 144 n. 20, 226 n. 47,
    244–7
Alcinous 81 n. 8, 103 f., 140, 140 n. 4, 142 n. 10,
    208, 208 n. 4, 213 n. 18, 221 nn. 36, 37,
    231 nn. 56, 57, 232 f., 234 n. 60,
    235 n. 63, 238 n. 66
Amphiaraus 134 n. 52
Anaxagoras 143 n. 14
Annas, J. vii, 14, 18 n. 5, 19 n. 8, 20 n. 10,
    21 n. 14, 24 n. 26, 32 n. 47, 34 n. 55,
    37 n. 64, 38 n. 66, 39 n. 67, 41 n. 76,
    42 n. 78, 49 nn. 1, 2, 67 n. 26, 70 n. 32,
    83 n. 14, 93 n. 33, 113, 113 n. 15,
    114 n. 18, 116 nn. 25, 26, 118 nn. 28,
    29, 119 n. 31, 122 n. 34, 123 n. 35,
    124 n. 38, 126 n. 42, 127 n. 43, 134 n. 52,
    141 n. 5, 142 nn. 10, 12, 143 n. 15, 144, 144
    nn. 17, 18, 19, 20, 155 nn. 51, 52,
    158 n. 59, 167 n. 3, 192 n. 55, 201 n. 67,
    202 n. 73, 207 nn. 2, 3, 208 n. 6,
    210 n. 12, 211 n. 13, 213 n. 18, 214 n. 21,
    215 n. 23, 216 n. 24, 218 n. 30,
    219 n. 31, 222 n. 40, 223 nn. 43, 44,
    227 nn. 48, 51, 228 n. 52, 235 n. 64,
    238 n. 66
Antiochus 41 n. 76, 164 n. 77
Archelaus 53
Archer-Hind, R. 77 n. 2
'argument from opposites' (*Gorgias*) 58–61
Aristophanes 189 n. 47
Aristotle 2 nn. 2, 3, 3 n. 5, 4 n. 7, 17 n. 1,
    26 n. 35, 33 n. 51, 34 n. 52, 37 n. 65,
    41 n. 74, 44 nn. 81, 83, 45 nn. 85, 86,
    65, 65 n. 24, 73 n. 35, 92 n. 30,
    104 n. 52, 107 n. 4, 122 n. 33, 125 n. 40,
    141 n. 5, 143 n. 14, 159 n. 63, 160 n. 67,

161 n. 69, 162, 164, 164 n. 77, 190 n. 49,
    202 f., 213, 213 n. 17, 216 n. 25,
    222 n. 40, 223 nn. 43, 59, 245 n. 16
Arius Didymus, *see* Stobaeus
Armstrong, J. vii
Artz, W. 43 n. 79
asceticism 78–92, 144, 158 f.
    Plato as ascetic 11, 77–92, 101, 139, 149,
    159, 204
Asmis, E. 222 n. 40
Athenaeus 10 n. 16, 71 n. 33

Baltzly, D. 141 n. 6
Barker, A. 144 n. 16
beds, filthy and clean 39
Benardete, S. 189 n. 47
Benson, H. vii
Bentham, J. 6, 6 n. 10, 8 n. 14, 44 n. 82
Berger, H. Jr, 143 n. 15
Berman, S. 9 n. 15, 54 n. 10, 59 n. 17
Bischoff, W. vii
Bluck, R. S. 95 nn. 35, 36
Bobonich, C. 32 n. 47, 33 n. 50, 41 n. 76,
    147 n. 26, 220 n. 34
body, *see* 'mortal' nature
Bostock, D. 77 n. 1, 93 n. 32, 95 n. 37, 96 n. 38,
    99 n. 47
Brickhouse, T. 21 n. 14, 26 n. 34, 28 n. 38,
    29 n. 41, 30 n. 45, 31 n. 46, 32–4,
    32 nn. 48, 49, 33 n. 51, 34 nn. 53, 55, 56,
    35 n. 57, 40 n. 70, 41 n. 76, 42 n. 77,
    54 nn. 6, 7, 70 n. 32, 71 n. 33, 72 n. 34
Brown, E. 210 n. 11, 219 n. 32
Burnet, J. 14
Burnyeat, M. 143 n. 15
Butz, J. vii
Butz, R. vii

Callicles (*Gorgias*) 8, 17 n. 2, 45 n. 84, 52,
    55–66, 72, 188 n. 44
    and hedonism 50 f., 52, 55–66, 72,
    124 n. 37, 169 n. 7, 239 f.
Carneades 17 n. 3, 34 n. 54
Carone, G. 171 n. 11, 176 n. 19, 192 n. 55
Cebes (*Phaedo*) 86, 89, 90
Chance, T. 18 n. 5, 27 n. 37
characteristic of types of lives, *see* lives,
    'types' of